Know Thine Enemy

A History of the Left

Volume I

Mark L. Melcher

and

Stephen R. Soukup

ISBN 978-1-64003-990-2 (Hardcover)
ISBN 978-1-64003-991-9 (Digital)

Covenant Books, Inc.
11661 Hwy 707
Murrells Inlet, SC 29576
www.covenantbooks.com

This book is dedicated to the memory of Russell Kirk,
the "Father of American Conservatism.

It is an undertaking of some degree of delicacy to examine into the cause of public disorders. If a man happens not to succeed in such an enquiry, he will be thought weak and visionary; if he touches the true grievance, there is a danger that he may come near to persons of weight and consequence, who will rather be exasperated at the discovery of their errors, than thankful for the occasion of correcting them. If he should be obliged to blame the favourites of the people, he will be considered as the tool of power; if he censures those in power, he will be looked on as an instrument of faction. But in all exertions of duty something is to be hazarded. In cases of tumult and disorder, our law has invested every man, in some sort, with the authority of a magistrate. When the affairs of the nation are distracted, private people are, by the spirit of that law, justified in stepping a little out of their ordinary sphere. They enjoy a privilege, of somewhat more dignity and effect, than that of idle lamentation over the calamities of their country. They may look into them narrowly; they may reason upon them liberally; and if they should be so fortunate as to discover the true source of the mischief, and to suggest any probable method of removing it, though they may displease the rulers for the day, they are certainly of service to the cause of Government.

—Edmund Burke, "Thoughts on the Cause
of the Present Discontents," 1770

Contents

Part I

Premise and Purpose

The roots of [American] order twist back to the Hebrew perceptions of a purposeful moral existence under God. They extend to the philosophical and political self-awareness of the old Greeks. They are nurtured by the Roman experience of law and social organization. They are entwined with the Christian understanding of human duties and human hopes, of man redeemed. They are quickened by medieval custom, learning, and valor. They grip the religious ferment of the sixteenth century. They come from the ground of English liberty under law, so painfully achieved. They are secured by a century and half of community in colonial America. They benefit from the debates of the eighteenth century. They approach the surface through Declaration and Constitution. They emerge full of life from the ordeal of the Civil War. (Russell Kirk, *The Roots of American Order,* 1992)

The United States is engaged today in a civil war that is testing whether it—or any nation conceived in liberty and dedicated to the proposition that all men are created equal—can endure. Like the Civil War that inspired President Lincoln to write the great Gettysburg Address, from which we paraphrased the above sentence, this war has divided the American people into two distinct camps. It has not yet led to widespread bloodshed, and God willing, it will not. Yet it is tearing the nation apart, and could very likely lead to the destruction that Lincoln feared during those dark days of 1863.

In fact, we would argue that while the stakes involved in Lincoln's Civil War were enormous, they pale in comparison to the potential harm that the current civil war poses to the nation. You see, both sides in the War between the States prayed to the God of Abraham, and neither side sought the destruction of the noble experiment in self-government that Lincoln described as "the last best hope of earth."

In contrast, one side in the current civil war seeks to demolish the entire Judeo-Christian belief system upon which Western Civilization was founded. This system was established when God gave Moses the Decalogue on Mt. Sinai. During the intervening 3,300 years, these ten simple and easily understood admonitions from God were placed in the context of human experience by the seers and prophets as recorded in the Old Testament. They were expanded upon by the divine wisdom of Jesus Christ, and further interpreted and clarified by such scholars as St. Augustine and St. Thomas Aquinas, who integrated Platonic and Aristotelian concepts into its fabric. This system embraces a host of religious holidays, traditions, customs, mores, and societal norms. It is supported by a rich heritage of art, literature, and historic struggles, both religious and secular. The twin concepts of "sin" and "truth" help bind this system together.

Critical to this system is the belief that every human being is a special product of God's love, a unique notion in the history of mankind.

The opposing belief system, which is the subject of this book, is widely known as "the Left." It emerged in the eighteenth century during the so-called Enlightenment period, and was based on the belief that science and reason should replace religion as the foundation of a modern society. The purveyors of his new ideology had trouble agreeing on details of this new belief system, and this resulted in the wide proliferation of leftist prototypes, among the best-known of which are communism, socialism, Marxism, fascism, and, in the United States, progressivism and liberalism. While different from each other in many important ways, all of these models originally shared several important philosophical ideas. These include an aversion to Christianity and religion generally, to capitalism, and to the concept of private property; a belief in the perfectibility of mankind; a belief in the superiority of reason over faith; a claim to an affinity with the working classes; and the promise of a world of peace, equality, and prosperity, free from the evils that religion had foisted on the mankind.

Not surprisingly, the spread of leftist ideology across the globe over the past two-plus centuries has resulted in continuous social and economic chaos and war, as well as the breakdown of traditional societies. Hence, what is widely described today as "post-Christian Europe" is *in extremis*; the United States is a deeply troubled land in which the ancient values and principles upon which its founders constructed its laws are under constant attack by the nation's ruling elite; and well over half of the rest of the world is ruled by totalitarian thugs.

In the United States, traditional standards of morality and ethics have been all but abandoned. Shame has been eliminated as an effective means of controlling behavior. The Constitution has been shredded by damaging amendments, and even that which has been left untouched is widely ignored by members of all three branches of its government. God has been banned from the public square and replaced by nauseating public displays of depravity. The federal government's power has grown to gargantuan proportions, invading virtually all aspects of American life. The bureaucracy has become an uncontrollable beast with an insatiable appetite for money and power. Fiscal responsibility has been replaced by a profligacy that is a prescription for bankruptcy. Corruption within the government and between it and its numerous partners and parasites in the private sector is rampant. "Rights" have been divorced from responsibilities. Upward of one million babies are slaughtered in the womb each year with both the approval and financial help of the federal government.

Of course, these are not novel observations on our part. Hundreds of books and articles have been written over the past half century about the social and economic devastation that leftist ideologues have caused. Our intent in writing this one is to provide conservatives with the single most important weapon in any conflict, namely a comprehensive and intimate understanding of the enemy, his origins, history, goals, words, theories, thoughts, champions, philosophy, manifestos, shortcomings, fears, weaknesses, inconsistencies, and ideological offspring.

In the process, we wish to acquaint you, or reacquaint you as the case may be, with the other most important weapon in the arsenal of the Right, namely a similarly intimate and comprehensive appreciation for the views and efforts of the heroes in this war, whose actions, speeches, writings, and aspirations collectively form the foundation of American conservatism. Our hope and our expectation is that this will strengthen, reinforce, and yes, refine your existing conservative beliefs, and that this will in turn help you and others in the fight against the common foe, because the fate of the nation and, indeed, of Western Civilization itself, depends upon your success in this venture.

Part 1 of this book will explore the historic roots of the evil we face, its birth in France in the eighteenth century, and its march across Europe in the first half of nineteenth.

Let's let the poets in on the fun.

Excerpt from "The Love Song of J. Alfred Prufrock":

> Let us go then, you and I,
> When the evening is spread out against the sky
> Like a patient etherized upon a table;
> Let us go, through certain half-deserted streets,
> The muttering retreats
> Of restless nights in one-night cheap hotels

KNOW THINE ENEMY

And sawdust restaurants with oyster-shells:
Streets that follow like a tedious argument
Of insidious intent
To lead you to an overwhelming question …
Oh, do not ask, "What is it?"
Let us go and make our visit.
T. S. Eliot, 1934

Chapter 1

The Bloody Birth of the Left

Ever since Voltaire found Newton's universe an admirable improvement over Christian polity, writers on man as a political animal have envied science its success in reducing the chaos of sense-experience and the varying fables of common sense to uniformities permitting prediction and therefore control. Ambitious Newtons of politics ... have arisen, but none have quite been accepted in their chosen rôles. Doubtless, this connection between science and political thought has been fruitful enough. The natural order which the eighteenth century borrowed from Newton certainly helped men to a moral if illogical condemnation of the old regime as unnatural and hence encouraged them to action ... Yet a plausible case could be maintained for the statement that the influence of the physical and biological sciences on the study of man in society has been in part evil. (Crane Brinton, *English Political Thought in the Nineteenth Century*, 1949)

The contagion that is known throughout the world today as the "Left" was spawned in eighteenth-century France, the offspring of an unlikely coupling between philosophy and poverty. The gestation period was several decades long. The birth was bloody. Historians disagree over who courted whom in this romance. Some say that the French philosophers seduced the poor with their fancy words and ideas. Others say the philosophers found that their association with the hardships of the poor provided an earthly meaning to their abstract ideas. In any case, there is no disputing that the child of this union was a vicious ideology that subsequently spawned numerous virulent strains of evil, including communism, socialism, fascism, anarchism, American liberalism, and a host of other "smelly little orthodoxies," to borrow a phrase from George Orwell.[1]

We will begin our account of this birth of the Left in 1734. Europe is in the midst of century-and-a-half-long period that would mark the end of the so-called "dark ages" and welcome the emergence of "the modern." Known as the Age of the Enlightenment, it was spearheaded by the genius of Sir Francis Bacon, Rene Descartes, John Locke, and Sir Isaac Newton. Simply stated, in this brave new world, "reason" would replace the medieval reliance on tradition, religion, superstition, and mysticism with an entirely new, "humanistic" perspective on God, mankind, and the norms of society; "individualism" would free the little human animal from the feudal understanding that he or she is the property of the state; and science would replace the received wisdom of the Church.

Central to this "enlightened" era was Newton's scientifically derived proof that the physical universe is governed by rational and universal principles, rather than by an interventionist God. According to the *Stanford Encyclopedia of Philosophy*, this discovery would lead people to question why "we need political or religious authorities to tell us how to live or what to believe, if each of us has the capacity to figure these things out for ourselves?"[2]

Among other things, the "Enlightenment" would lead to capitalism and free markets, which in turn would lead to the industrial revolution, the division of labor, and a growing social and economic gap between the "rich" and the "poor." It would also contain the germ of the mob-based, passion-ridden type of revolutionary fever that would bring down the French monarchy and plague Western Civilization for the next several centuries. Indeed, shortly before the outbreak of the French Revolution, the German philosopher Immanuel Kant would publicly hail the progress that "the sovereignty of reason" had made in the preceding century. To wit:

> Our age is the age of criticism, to which everything must be subjected. The sacredness of religion, and the authority of legislation, are by many regarded as grounds of exemption from the examination of this tribunal. But, if they are exempted they become the subjects of just suspicion, and cannot lay claim to sincere respect, which reason accords only to that which has stood the test of a free and public examination.[3]

Not surprisingly, there was no shortage of individuals who rose to the challenge of subjecting religion and authority to the test of a free and public examination based on reason. Naturally, of course, many took the next seemingly-logical step of attempting to use reason to replace the existing Judeo-Christian society with a new and improved secular one that would be overseen by a set of scientifically-based, allegedly rational and universal principles that would govern human actions in the same way that Newton's laws of physics govern the physical world.

This was, of course, a fool's errand, and if it hadn't led to such a bad end, it would be nothing more than another interesting example of some very smart people doing really dumb things, like the medieval alchemists who spent a great deal of time trying to turn base metals into gold. Many brilliant historians, sociologists, economists, and political scientists have explained the folly involved in this venture. Since we began this chapter with a quote from the renowned historian Crane Brinton, we will cite his thoughtful comment on the topic. To wit:

> Scientists—not all scientists, but certainly the best of them—have always held their laws as at best hypotheses subject to constant modi-

fication. Political theorists, and especially political theorists in action, like Robespierre, have tended to hold their conclusions as dogmas. ... This tendency to dogmatism was accelerated by the fact that the material with which the political thinkers worked was infinitely more complex than the material of the scientists, and by the fact that experimentation, and hence the inductive method, could be but incompletely applied to the study of man ... Moreover, political thought deals with human beings who are at bottom evaluating animals. ... Science ... will sometimes persuade [a man] to choose between apples and beans in accordance with the calories and vitamins they contain. But in the last resort a man will chose to eat apples or eat beams because he prefers one to the other ... Taste, in its widest sense, determines a vast number of the kind of human actions the political thinker must study, and we have as yet no satisfactory calculus of taste.[4]

At this point, our interest turns to one of the most famous of these hapless political theorists. His name is François-Marie Arouet, known to history by the *nom de plume* Voltaire. He is a brilliant and popular intellectual, writer, activist, proponent of reason, and critic of the Church, the clergy, and the French monarchy. In short, he is a leading figure in the ongoing French Enlightenment. He is thirty-nine years old, both famous and quite wealthy, the latter largely due to his having won a sizable state lottery, almost certainly by the skullduggery of friends in high places. He has served time in the Bastille and spent three years in exile in England, largely as the result of his slanderous and satirical attacks on the royal family.

The French authorities had allowed him to return to Paris a few years earlier, but he is once again on the lam, this time for having published a favorable account of the British constitutional monarchy as compared to its French counterpart. He is seeking refuge at the Chateau de Cirey, located in the then-independent duchy of Lorraine.

The Chateau is owned by the Marquis Florent-Claude du Chastellet and his beautiful and talented wife, Gabrielle Émilie le Tonnelier de Breteuil, Marquise du Chastellet, who is known to history as Émilie du Châtelet. Émilie is exceptionally intelligent, well educated, and by all accounts beautiful. She is fluent in Latin, Italian, Greek, and German. She is well versed in mathematics, literature, and science. She fences, rides, and plays the harpsichord.

Aside from being a celebrity of sorts, Voltaire is a priapic fellow. And it just so happens that Émilie, despite her gentile upbringing, or perhaps because of it, has the morals of an alley cat. Indeed, at this particular time, she is in the process of ending a love affair with the famous mathematician and friend of Voltaire's, one Pierre Louis Moreau de Maupertuis, having already had a fling with French Army Marshall Jean-Baptiste Budes, Comte de Guébriant, and Louis François Armand de Vignerot du Plessis, Duc de Richelieu, who is also famous, in his case for having bedded more "titled ladies" of that day than any other contemporary Frenchman.

Émilie is twenty-seven, and has just delivered her third child, this one most probably fathered by Maupertuis. Her husband is a military officer who spends a great deal of time away from home and is largely indifferent to what she does in his absence, in keeping with the "customs" of the upper class at the time, as the explanation goes.

Needless to say, when Voltaire moves in, he and Émilie "fall in love," and for the next fifteen years, they are intimate, both physically for seven or so years and intellectually until she dies in 1749. This was shortly after bearing the child of Jean François de Saint-Lambert, a poet who was then and still is better known for his sexual prowess than his poetry.

On the intellectual front, Voltaire and Émilie share a common interest in the works of Newton. Indeed, three years into their relationship, Voltaire publishes his *Elements of the Philosophy of Newton*, which he notes was written in collaboration with Émilie. During this time, she is working on her translation of and commentary on Newton's greatest work, *Principia Mathematica*, which is still regarded as one of the standard French translations. Naturally, their love of Newton is accompanied by a dedication to the powers of "reason" over "superstition."

Now, Newton's religious views were not always in line with Christian orthodoxy. Yet he avoided trouble with the authorities by making it clear that he believed that his many discoveries about the workings of the physical universe reinforced rather than contradicted the Christian belief in the existence of an almighty God. An example is this famous observation from the *Principia*.

> This most beautiful system of the sun, planets, and comets, could only proceed from the counsel and dominion of an intelligent and powerful Being ... This being governs all things, not as the soul of the world, but as Lord over all; and on account of his dominion he is wont to be called Lord God ... He is not eternity or infinity, but eternal and infinite; He is not duration or space, but he endures and is present. He endures forever, and is everywhere present; and by existing always and everywhere, he constitutes duration and space.[5]

Unlike Newton, Voltaire and Émilie give God no credit whatsoever. Indeed, the centerpiece of their campaign, which they completed in late 1744, is a systematic, textual examination of both books of the Bible, which concludes that Christianity is utter nonsense. More specifically, their antagonism can be seen in the manner and the choice of the words that they use to describe the entire Old Testament (absurd); God Himself ("a strange king who wanted to test the obedience of his subjects on ridiculous things, and who punished them afterward well beyond their crimes"); the story of Jesus's birth (ridiculous, absurd); His Sermon on the Mount (trite, ridiculous, silly); His actions in the Temple (absurd); His miracles (absurd, revolting, injustice, uselessness); His resurrection (fraud, duplicity, comedy); and the entire gospel of St. John (Platonic gibberish, sententious).[6]

Now, everything that Voltaire and Émilie claim or say in their "war against Christianity," to borrow a phrase from the historians Will and Ariel Durant,[7] had already been claimed or said by someone else. Indeed, one could argue that they were simply joining a debate that had begun almost a century earlier between two of France's greatest philosophers, René Descartes and Blaise Pascal, which set the stage for the still ongoing, three-plus-century-long battle between the believers and the skeptics.

Descartes claimed to believe in God and professed to be a Catholic. But he was highly critical of all things that could not be proved by science and reason. His greatness lay in the fact that he identified the essential accord between the laws of mathematics and the laws of nature. As Hanna Arendt put it: "He actually believed that with his kind of thinking, with what [British philosopher Thomas] Hobbes called 'reckoning with consequences' he could deliver certain knowledge about the existence of God, the nature of the soul, and similar matters."[8]

As such, he strongly criticized those men who drew their beliefs from "the ancient books, their histories, and their fables." These were, he said, a "superstitious" lot, who had "weak minds," and consciences agitated by "repentances and remorse." "Revealed truths," he said, "show the way to gain heaven" to which he "aspires as much as any other." But, he said, they are "above our intelligence," and hence are not clear and assured knowledge useful for life. Then, anticipating the efforts of Voltaire, Émilie, and their philosophical compatriots, he argued that a "new method" of establishing a moral scheme must be found that is mathematical, or reason-based, that will "purge the mind of all opinions and beliefs that depend on 'appetites and preceptors.'"[9]

As a sympathizer with Jansenism, Pascal had his own complaints against the Church. Nevertheless, he was a devout Christian who argued that Descartes's mathematics had no place in the study of mankind and morality. He described Descartes as "useless and dubious"[10] and asserted that God had provided man with ample evidence of His existence, and that man's failure to grasp this evidence was due to "the fall." "Not only do we only know God through Jesus Christ," he said, "but we only know ourselves through Jesus Christ; we only know life and death through Jesus Christ. Apart from Jesus Christ, we cannot know the meaning of our life or our death, of God or of ourselves." As for "reason," he argued, "Reason's last step is the recognition that there are an infinite number of things which are beyond it." Then, he famously added, "The heart has its reasons of which reason knows nothing."[11]

Needless to say, Voltaire wholeheartedly incorporated Descartes's argument against the authenticity of faith into his own attacks on the Church. However, unlike Descartes, his interest in the subject was neither philosophical nor academic. It was entirely political. In his eyes, the Church was simply one evil part of a deeply pernicious and corrupt governmental cabal that included the monarchy, the aristocracy, the clergy, and a system of justice that relied heavily on torture and cruelty.

This too was not an original idea. You see, Voltaire was an enthusiast of a testament written by a French Catholic priest named Jean Meslier and discovered after his death in 1729. Simply stated, it declared that religions were "fabrications by ruling elites," and that Christian morality was "indefensible because it encouraged the acceptance of suffering, submission to one's foes, acquiescence in the face of tyranny—just such tyranny as had been practiced by the kings of France, their police censors, and tax gatherers." According to Meslier, "The earliest Christians had been exemplary in sharing their goods, but that ideal had long vanished."

Voltaire's weapon of choice is satire. And he has a perfect target for his biting wit in the person of the great mathematician, philosopher, and polymath Gottfried Wilhelm Leibniz, who, in an essay published in 1714, had attempted to explain the existence of evil by arguing that every single detail in God's universe is absolutely necessary to the proper functioning of the whole, and that because of this the world could not be other than it is; at which time he posited his famous conclusion that the world in which we live is the best of all *possible* worlds.[12]

Of course, Voltaire jumps on this notion like a duck on a June Bug. He begins his critique in 1756 with a poem that directly references and ridicules Leibniz's assertion concerning the best of all worlds, and questions how a loving god could continence the recent earthquake in Lisbon that destroyed almost the entire city and killed thousands.

Three years later, he authors a book entitled *Candide*, which not only expands his ridicule of Leibniz's optimism but is also loaded with satirical smears against monarchy itself. Briefly stated, Candide tells the story of the young lad's many encounters with hardships and evil, which his traveling companion and philosopher friend Professor Pangloss explains to him each time is "necessary" in this "best of all possible worlds." The following exchange is illustrative.

> "Well, my dear Pangloss," said Candide to him, "when you had been hanged, dissected, stunned with blows and made to row in the galleys, did you always think that everything was for the best in this world?"
>
> "I am still of my first opinion," answered Pangloss, "for after all I am a philosopher; and it would be unbecoming for me to recant, since Leibnitz could not be in the wrong and pre-established harmony is the finest thing imaginable, like the plenum and subtle matter."[13]

Once again, this is not new. Indeed, this ground had been famously ploughed almost forty years earlier by François Fénelon, the Archbishop of Cambray, who had been tasked with the chore of preparing the seven-year-old Duke of Burgundy to be King someday. To facilitate his work, Fénelon wrote a book entitled *The Adventures of Telemachus*. First published in 1699, it took the form of a series of lectures on governance to Ulysses's son by an individual named Mentor. According to Fénelon, the book's sole purpose was to "amuse the Duke with a tale of adventure, and to instruct him at the same time ... in all the virtues necessary for a good government, and the faults to which sovereign power is liable."[14]

Fortunately for posterity, it was released to the public by "the treachery of a secretary." And, no surprise here, it was immediately recognized as a biting satire against the absolutist principles of the French monarch Louis XIV and became a runaway best seller, going through many editions and translated into every European language and even Latin verse.

Lord Acton would describe Fénelon as "the Platonic founder of revolutionary thinking," and as the originator of the "season of scorn" that would eventually bring down the monarchy. In fact, he would argue that Louis XVI was not toppled because he abused the power he inherited, but because this power had been discredited and undermined by the likes of Fénelon and his successors.[15]

Naturally, Voltaire maintains that his purpose in attacking the Church is to eliminate corruption and promote justice, which earns him a reputation of being a courageous defender and friend of the poor and oppressed. But of course, the true result of his efforts is to animate the nihilism that will soon destroy the country that he purports to be saving. Indeed, the famous British historian and politician Thomas Babington Macaulay would say this of him: "He could not build—he could only pull down; he was the very Vitruvius of ruin."[16]

In short then, Voltaire's role was not to have created antagonism toward the Church and the monarchy. This had existed and been remarked upon by others for decades. His role was to bring it all together in the person of one of the greatest satirists that the world had ever seen and present it to France's restless and unhappy masses.

And in fact, concomitant with his increasing notoriety, a large and influential gaggle of intellectuals with similar views has gathered in Paris. Some are friendly to him, recognizing him as a brother in the cause of justice. Others are openly hostile, jealous of his fame, and critical of the depth of his intellect. Unlike Voltaire, all have abandoned the hidey-hole of Voltaire's "theism" and are openly atheistic.

This is something new. Europeans had been fighting and killing each other for almost two centuries over such matters as papal infallibility, justification by faith alone, and the seven sacraments. Yet never before had a large contingent of self-described atheists taken to the field in these so-called Wars of Religion. When considering this curious crowd of atheists, it is important to understand that the Edict of Fontainebleau, proffered by Fénelon's nemesis Louis XIV's in 1685, stopped the Reformation in France by ordering the destruction of all Huguenot churches and by giving royal sanction to the brutal persecution of members of that religion. One result was the migration of an estimated two hundred thousand Huguenots to friendlier nations, including the American colonies. Another was that Frenchmen who took issue with the Gallican Church did not have the option of joining a Protestant denomination as they did in England, Germany, Switzerland, Holland, and other European nations. Hence, many chose atheism.

The best known of these individuals is Denis Diderot. He is a brilliant hack who has assumed the messianic role of bringing the truth and details of Enlightenment philosophy and science to the upper ranks of French society, who wish to be regarded as intellectual elites. The great French historian Hippolyte Taine described him as follows:

> "Diderot," says Voltaire, "is too hot an oven, everything that is baked in it getting burnt." Or rather, he is an eruptive volcano which, for forty years, discharges ideas of every order and species, boiling and fused together, precious metals, coarse scoria and fetid mud; the steady stream overflows at will according to the roughness of the ground, but always displaying the ruddy light and acrid fumes of glowing lava. He is not master of his ideas, but his ideas master him … He is a newcomer, a parvenu in standard society; you see in him a plebeian, a powerful reasoner, an indefatigable workman and great artist, introduced, through the customs of the day, at a supper of fashionable livers. He engrosses the conversation, directs the orgy, and in the contagion, or on a

wager, says more filthy things, more "gueullées," than all the guests put together.[17]

To which, years later, the Italian philosopher Georges Sorel added, "If Taine had not been restrained by the respect he declared for the 18th century writers, he would have said that Diderot was patronized in high society like a literary clown."[18]

Diderot admires Voltaire, but maintains some distance from the old man, not wanting to be considered an acolyte. He has a degree in philosophy and is making his living, rather poorly we might add, as a "man of letters." In 1749, at age of thirty-six, he is imprisoned for writing an essay questioning the Catholic view of God. He is released after agreeing to refrain from criticizing the Church, at which point he takes what should be the uncontroversial job of translating the Scottish encyclopaedist Ephraim Chamber's *Universal Dictionary of Arts and Sciences*, which had been published in 1728.

Quickly, however, he turns the project into a vehicle for the promotion of atheism and criticism of the existing order, much to the chagrin of the government. His partner in this effort is the highly opinionated and pugnacious mathematician Jean-Baptiste le Rond d'Alembert. His chief financial backer is Paul Thiry d'Holbach, a wealthy *bon vivant* known as the "master of the Café de l'Europe." The project lasts for eight years and features articles by scores of so-called philosophes, including Voltaire and Diderot's friend at the time, the philosopher Jean Jacques Rousseau. All are honored to contribute to the effort and share their mutual enthusiasm for Enlightenment notions over dinner and drinks at a number of "salons," which are hosted by men such as d'Holback and an impressive number of highly vivacious and, in some cases, sexually voracious women, all known for their wit and their impressive circle of friends and lovers.

Among the most famous of these women are Suzanne Necker, the former fiancée of Edward Gibbon, the wife of Louis XVI's finance minister Jacque Necker, and mother of the soon-to-be more famous than all of them, Madame de *Staël*. Others include Marie-Thérèse de Geoffrin, the "inventor" of the "Enlightenment salons; Claudine Guérin de Tencin, the unwed mother of d'Alembert, who left him on the steps of the Saint-Jean-le-Rond de Paris church a few days after his birth; Jeanne Julie Éléonore de Lespinasse, a close friend of d'Alembert, who lived in her house and promoted her salon; and Marie Anne de Vichy-Chamrond, marquise du Deffand, who famously solved the age-old problem of the unknown by telling Voltaire that "everything that man can know absolutely nothing about is certainly of such a nature that knowledge about it would be of no use to him."[19]

In addition, to hosting the glitterati of the French Enlightenment, these salons also routinely welcome foreigners of similar persuasion into their gatherings, their boudoirs, and their intrigues. The most famous and most popular of these men is the corpulent Scottish philosopher David Hume, who had written his own attack on the belief in God in 1738, oddly enough at the same time that Voltaire and Émilie were collaborating on their critic of Christianity.

Hume's vehicle was his path-breaking and heretical *Treatise on Human Nature*, in which he stated that the notion of "faith" had to be abandoned entirely because it could not be proved by reason. But Hume did not stop there. In subsequent treatises, he carried on his crusade against religion for two decades. It culminated in 1757 with his *Treatise on the Natural History of Religion* in which he challenged the notion of "design" as well as the possibility of miracles. Moreover, he said that concept of a single, all-powerful god "is apt, when joined with superstitious terrors, to sink the human mind into the lowest submission and abasement, and to represent the monkish virtues of mortification, penance, humility, and passive suffering, as the only qualities which are acceptable to him." The *Cambridge Dictionary of Philosophy* describes Hume's idea of morality as "an entirely human affair founded on human nature and circumstances of human life."[20]

Now, these folks are, for the most part, a sorry lot who spend much of their time feeding their gluttonous appetites for food and drink, stabbing each other in the back, and engaging in comically melodramatic romances and sexual trysts. Moreover, most of their literary output is largely lacking in any serious value.

Aside from their role as instigators of social unrest, our interest in them lies in the fact that they are prototypes of all of the leftists of all persuasions that are about to enter onto the world stage. Their atheism has left them with stunted moral values. Their utopianism has rendered them incapable of assessing the secondary and tertiary consequences of their actions. Their lifestyles provide us with the first glimpse into the sickness inherent in the nihilism that would come to be the progeny of their efforts. Finally, their petulance and outsized egos presage the terrible violence that awaits France, as reflected in one of Diderot's most quoted observations.

> If we go back to the beginning we shall find that ignorance and fear created the gods; that fancy, enthusiasm, or deceit adorned or disfigured them; that weakness worships them; that credulity preserves them, and that custom, respect, and tyranny support them in order to make the blindness of man serve its own interests ... *men will never be free till the last king is strangled with the entrails of the last priest.*[21]

Relative to their shortsightedness, Malcolm Muggeridge noted the following in his well-known 1970 essay, "The Great Liberal Death Wish."

> I remember reading in Taine's *Origines de la France Contemporaine* of how, shortly before the Revolution, a party of affluent liberal intellectuals were discussing over their after-dinner cognac all the wonderful things that were going to happen when the Bourbon regime was abolished and freedom à la Voltaire and Jean-Jacques Rousseau reigned supreme. One of the guests, hitherto silent, suddenly spoke up. Yes, he said, the Bourbon regime would indeed be overthrown, and in the process—pointing round—you and you and you will be carried screaming to the guillotine; you and you and you go into penu-

rious exile, and—now pointing in the direction of some of the elegant ladies present—you and you and you will hawk your bodies round from sansculotte to sansculotte. There was a moment of silence while this, as it turned out, all too exact prophecy sank in, and then the previous conversation was resumed.[22]

Relative to the good intentions of these folks, Michal Burleigh says this in *Sacred Causes*.

Like the Christians, they also wanted a happy ending, but could not believe in a transcendental heaven. In the new religion of humanity, heaven would be the perfect future state that a regenerated mankind would create through his own volition. The ultimate arbiter would no longer be a divine judge, but rather future generations of happier mankind vaguely defined as "posterity." Self-fulfillment became a form of atonement, love of humanity a substitute for love of God.[23]

As to their effect on society, Roberto Calasso notes that one of the events of "global importance," which took place in these salons, was the "alliance between snobbery and the Left." He explains it this way:

Suddenly the most imitated and often the most elegant ladies began to discuss customs duties and Virginia tobaccos, spinning mills, and credit, and they even ventured to make a few references to net income ... From that moment on, the higher snobbery, which always needs some discreet disguise, would know what cloak to cover itself with: the worthy Cause. Such causes

were social and musical, humanitarian and progressive, erotic and Asiatic. But the star of the Just
shone on the brow of the ladies as they received
the guests at their dinners, their parties, their lan-
guid picnics.[24]

With that said, we will return to Voltaire and his proposed remedy for the abuses of the Church; that being contained in his famous
and oft-quoted cry "Ecrasez l'infame," or "crush the infamous thing."
This phrase, demanding the death of religion, would become the first
principle and heraldic centerpiece of all variations of leftist thought
from that day on. It began circulating in Paris in or around 1763
when Voltaire was seventy years old and was using his great fame to
defend people whom he believed Church authorities were unjustly
persecuting.

Note that he did not say *reform* the "infamous thing." Or throw
the leaders of the "infamous thing" out on the street and replace
them. He said, "Crush it." Destroy it. Tear it down, which was not
only unique within the context of the long, ongoing attack on the
Church by French intellectuals but within the entire, prior history
of Western Civilization. Moreover, implicit in his famous cry was
the conviction that if the destruction of this pillar of French society
destroys the other pillars upon which it stands and chaos results, then
so be it. "L'infame" will, at least, have been "crushed."

Some historians have argued, on Voltaire's behalf, that when he
advocated "crushing" the Church, he was specifically targeting the
Church hierarchy, not Christianity itself. Yet his direct attacks on
the fundamental beliefs of Christianity are undeniable. He put it this
way in a letter to Frederick the Great in 1767.

[Christianity] is assuredly the most ridiculous, the most absurd and the most bloody religion which has ever infected this world. Your
Majesty will do the human race an eternal service
by extirpating this infamous superstition, I do
not say among the rabble, who are not worthy

of being enlightened and who are apt for every yoke; I say among honest people, among men who think, among those who wish to think. My one regret in dying is that I cannot aid you in this noble enterprise, the finest and most respectable which the human mind can point out.[25]

The above-mentioned Germaine de Staël, the daughter of Louis XVI's finance minister Jacques Necker and a former mistress of Voltaire's, offered a somewhat different if limited apologia for him in her *Considerations on the Principal Events of the French Revolution,* which was published posthumously in 1818. To wit:

> Several writers, above all Voltaire, were highly reprehensible in not respecting Christianity when they attacked superstition; but some allowance is to be made on account of the circumstances under which Voltaire lived. He was born in the latter part of the age of Louis XIV, and the atrocious injustice inflicted on the Protestants [i.e., the above- mentioned Huguenots] had impressed his imagination from his earliest years.[26]

She went on to cite numerous specific instances of malfeasance by the Church, which she said were "puerile in themselves but capable of leading to the effusion of blood," which she said had "naturally impressed Voltaire with the dread of the renewal of religious persecution."[27]

In the final analysis, we have no dog in this fight. Yet we would add two more observations on the subject. The first, on his behalf, is that the Church was indeed corrupt and the abuses of the clergy were contemptible. Moreover, he could well have believed that no matter how much derision he heaped upon the Church and Christianity, the "rabble," as he called them, were so imbued with this particular "superstition" that they would continue to be "believers" no matter what he said or did, and France would thus continue to be fundamentally a Christian nation. The second, not on his behalf, is that he was playing with fire and, as one of the most learned and influential men of the day, should have known that and tempered his attacks accordingly.

Certainly, he knew that while the rise and fall of great nations and entire civilizations had been integral to human history since the beginning of recorded time, no great nation or civilization had ever existed on an entirely secular foundation. Nor had anyone of importance in any of these nations or civilizations suggested that the abolition of public belief in a personal, interventionist god would improve their society.

Salon and Lycurgus had designed new governments for Athens and Sparta respectively. But neither of these great political architects thought to include the destruction of the existing religious foundations as part of their plan. Indeed, even Plato, who favored a highly totalitarian society ruled by omnipotent "philosopher kings," recognized that the absolute authority of these individuals would be enhanced by linking their directives to God and by defining any violations of these directives as a form of "impiety," which in some cases would be punished by death.[28]

Indeed, belief in the gods was so integral to the Greek civilization that Sophocles had the choir raise that wonderful, timeless question in *Oedipus the King* as to why they should dance at the annual festival honoring Dionysus if, as Jocasta had claimed, the gods could be wrong.

> But if any man walks haughtily in deed or word, with no fear of Justice, no reverence for the images of gods, may an evil doom seize him for his ill-starred pride ... Where such things occur, what mortal shall boast any more that he can ward off the arrow of the gods from his life? No. *For if such deeds are held in honor, why should we join in the sacred dance?*[29]

Rome went from a monarchy to a republic to an empire, but in none of these extraordinary transitions did anyone in power, to our knowledge at least, suggest that citizens should be forced or encouraged to abandon their religious beliefs. In fact, according to Edward Gibbon, even during the time of the Empire, when many of the emperors themselves claimed to be gods, the official attitude toward the important relationship between religion and orderly government was as follows:

> They [the emperors] knew and valued the advantages of religion, as it is connected with civil government. They encouraged the public festivals which humanize the manners of the people. They managed the arts of divination as a convenient instrument of policy; and they respected, as the firmest bond of society, the useful persuasion, that, either in this or in a future life, the crime of perjury is most assuredly punished by the avenging gods.[30]

Moreover, they recognized the value of religious tolerance. Gibbon put it this way.

> The various modes of worship, which prevailed in the Roman world, were all considered by the people, as equally true; by the philosopher as equally false; and by the magistrate, as equally useful. And thus toleration produced not only mutual indulgence, but even religious concord.[31]

More recently, England had run their Catholic king James II out of the country and replaced him with the protestant couple William III and his wife, Mary. But the motivation was not to destroy religion but to protect the existing religious order from the king's attempt to change it.

Finally, even Machiavelli, the quintessential religious skeptic and advocate of a strong central government, whose writings were certainly known to Voltaire, had, almost four hundred years earlier, extensively

...cussed the importance of religion to a stable government in his great work *Discourses on the First Decade of Titus Livy*. To wit:

> [Romulus' successor Numa Pompilius] finding the people ferocious and desiring to reduce them to civic obedience by means of the arts of peace, turned to religion as the instrument necessary above all others for the maintenance of a civilized state ... All things considered, therefore, I conclude that the religion introduced by Numa was among the primary causes of Rome's success, for this entailed good institutions; good institutions led to good fortune; and from good fortune arose the happy results of undertakings. And as the observance of the divine worship is the cause of the greatness in republics, so the neglect of it is the cause of their ruin. Because, where the fear of God is wanting, it comes about either that a kingdom is ruined, or that it is kept going by the fear of a prince, which makes up for the lack of religion. And because princes are short-lived, it may well happen that when a kingdom loses its prince, it loses also the virtue of its prince. Hence kingdoms which depend on the virtue of one man do not last long, because they lose their virtue when his life is spent, and it seldom happens that it is revived by his successor. ...
>
> Those princes and those republics which desire to remain free from corruption, should above all else maintain incorrupt the ceremonies of their religion and should hold them always in veneration; for there can be no surer indication of the decline of a country than to see divine worship neglected.[32]

Yet Voltaire is convinced that the Church must be crushed. And he has widespread support for this rash and irresponsible demand. In fact, it appears that the great Irish statesman Edmund Burke is one of the very few men—perhaps the only one—living at the time who fully understands that the destruction of religiosity would lead to a very bad end. He put it this way in his famous, contemporary account of the struggle, known today as *Reflections on the Revolution in France*, which was originally composed in late 1789 as a letter to a "a very young Gentleman at Paris" in reply to a request from that individual for his "thoughts on the late proceedings in France."

> We know, and it is our pride to know, that man is by his constitution a religious animal; that atheism is against not only our reason but our instincts; and that it cannot prevail long. But if, in the moment of riot, and in a drunken delirium from the hot spirit drawn out of the alembick of hell, which in France is now so furiously boiling, we should uncover our nakedness by throwing off that Christian religion which has hitherto been our boast and comfort, and one great source of civilization amongst us, and among many other nations, we are apprehensive (being well aware that the mind will not endure a void) that some uncouth, pernicious, and degrading superstition, might take place of it.[33]

And lo, as was the case with so many of Burke's predictions, an uncouth, pernicious, and degrading superstition did take the place of "the one great source of civilization." In fact, as Burke most certainly knew when he made this forecast, such a thing had been burrowing its way into the consciousness of the French people for almost two decades, planted there by the previously mentioned Jean Jacque Rousseau.

Now Rousseau is brilliant and recognized as such by his fellow philosophes. But his overweening egotism, deep-seated sense of self-pity, constant state of anger, self-developed boorishness, profound paranoia, and myriad other severe personality disorders has cost him his friendship with Diderot. And despite the fact that he presents himself as great friend of humanity and a champion of both truth and virtue, he is a truly despicable human being, having, "with the greatest difficulty in the world," talked his mistress into depositing their firstborn son in a foundling hospital and then had proceeded to do the same with the next four.[34]

Our immediate interest in this strange fellow is a book he wrote entitled *Emile*, which was published in 1763, the same year that Voltaire's famous cry "Ecrasez l'infame" began to echo across France. Oddly enough, given his treatment of his own children, the book took the form of an outline on how one would raise a child in conformance with his beliefs. And it is with these beliefs that we are specifically concerned here. Indeed, very concerned. Because they are based on an idea that would become the second cornerstone of the leftist ideology, which, like Voltaire's demand for the destruction of the church, is entirely new, and, even more than Voltaire's, destructive beyond the imaginations of all but the most gifted seers.

Hyperbole? Well, maybe. But Lord Acton described this idea as "the strongest political theory that had appeared amongst men."[35] In fact, it was so strong an idea that some historians describe Rousseau as "the spiritual father of the French Revolution." Now this is a dubious honor at best, but it actually minimizes his foul impact on the history of the world because he can just as justly be regarded as the father of the bloodiest political ideology in the history of man, namely the Left. Carlyle said this of Rousseau.

> He could be cooped in garrets, laughed at
> as a maniac, left to starve like a wild-beast in his
> cage;—but he could not be hindered from set-
> ting the world on fire.[36]

Karl Löwith noted in his classic *From Hegel to Nietzsche* that Nietzsche too was duly impressed by Rousseau's stamp on history. To wit:

Nietzsche saw in Rousseau's image of man "the greatest revolutionizing force of the modern era," which had also exerted a decisive influence upon the formation of the German spirit through Kant, Fichte, and Schiller. At the same time, he terms him a "monstrous birth at the threshold of the new age," an "idealist and canaille" in one person. His concept of equality set the unequal equal, and brought to power a slave morality. His democratic-humanitarian ideals counterfeit the true nature of man, which is not humanitarian, but rather a "will to power."[37]

So what is this idea that set the world on fire, this extraordinary thought that poured gasoline on the flame that had previously been lit by Voltaire and his fellow philosophes; this exceedingly important principle upon which the Left would build its various evil ideologies? What was the idea that caused this book, *Emile*, ostensibly about education, to be immediately banned in Paris and Geneva and burned in the streets?

Well, it is simple really. It is that the great, foundational, Christian concept of original sin is bogus, that man in his natural state is noble; that vice and error are not natural to mankind but introduced from without, caused mostly by bad institutions. Rousseau had stated it this way in the opening line of *Emile*.

Everything is good as it comes from the hands of the creator; everything degenerates in the hands of man.[38]

The poet W. H. Auden elaborated on the political importance of this concept beautifully in his once well-known 1941 essay, "Criticism in a Mass Society." He put it this way.

The statement, "Man is a fallen creature with a natural bias to do evil," and the statement,

"Men are good by nature and made bad by society," are both presuppositions, but it is not an academic question to which one we give assent. If, as I do, you assent to the first, your art and politics will be very different from what they will be if you assent, like Rousseau or Whitman, to the second."[39]

How different will they be? Well, as Auden said, very different, indeed. Whether one believes in the poetic truth, to borrow a phrase from Auden, or subscribes to the historical accuracy of the story behind original sin, one's expectations of what government can do to make the world a better place are going to be somewhat limited. If, however, one believes that man is naturally good and made bad by his institutions, it becomes not just possible for man to create a utopia on earth, a *saturnia regna*, but imperative that he attempt to do so. Moreover, it fictionalizes the notion of a struggle between good and evil and obviates the need for disciplinary virtues.

The historian Paul Johnson described Rousseau's thought process as follows in his book *Intellectuals*:

> To him [Rousseau], "natural" meant "original" or pre-cultural. All culture brings problems since it is man's association with others which brings out his evil propensities: as he puts it in Emile, "Man's breath is fatal to his fellow men." Thus the culture in which man lived, itself an evolving, artificial construct, dictated man's behaviour, and you could improve, indeed totally transform, his behaviour by changing the culture and the competitive forces, which produced it— that is, by social engineering.[40]

Of course, the notion of social engineering is as old as Plato's *Republic*. But Rousseau laid the groundwork for its modern construct with another unique idea, this one becoming the third principle upon which all leftist ideologies would be built: that being that private property is the source of all crime, and that competition destroys man's inborn communal sense and encourages his most malicious traits, including his desire to exploit others. He put it this way in his 1754 treatise entitled "Discourse on Inequality."

> The first man who, having enclosed a piece of ground, bethought himself of saying *This is mine*, and found people simple enough to believe him, was the real founder of civil society. From how many crimes, wars and murders, from how many horrors and misfortunes might not any one have saved mankind, by pulling up the stakes, or filling up the ditch, and crying to his fellows, "Beware of listening to this impostor; you are undone if you once forget that the fruits of the earth belong to us all, and the earth itself to nobody."[41]

As indicated earlier, all this philosophizing is helping to stir up the already restive French commoners, the so-called "third estate." The Russian prince Peter Kropotkin, one of three great leaders of the nineteenth-century anarchist movement, whom we will discuss in a later chapter, put it this way in his account of the Revolution.

> The eighteenth-century philosophers had long been sapping the foundations of the law-and-order societies of that period, wherein political power, as well as an immense share of the wealth, belonged to the aristocracy and the clergy, whilst the mass of the people were nothing but beasts of burden to the ruling classes. By proclaiming the sovereignty of reason; by preaching trust in human nature—corrupted, they declared, by the institutions that had reduced man to servitude,

but, nevertheless, certain to regain all its qualities when it had reconquered liberty—they had
opened up new vistas to mankind. By proclaiming equality among men, without distinction of
birth; by demanding from every citizen, whether
king or peasant, obedience to the law, supposed
to express the will of the nation when it has been
made by the representatives of the people; finally,
by demanding freedom of contract between free
men, and the abolition of feudal taxes and services—by putting forward all these claims, linked
together with the system and method characteristic of French thought, the philosophers had
undoubtedly prepared, at least in men's minds,
the downfall of the old regime.[42]

Arguably, if the economy had been doing reasonably well, and
the king had made some effort to address the needs of the poor, the
unrest might not have led to revolution. But the economy is bank-
rupt almost beyond repair, caused by heavy expenditures related to
the country's loss of the Seven Years' War to the British, financial
support for the American Revolution, and the financially outlandish
extravagances by both Louis XV and his grandson Louis XVI. Taxes
are extremely high, and the burden is almost entirely on the backs
of the commoners because the nobility had the ways and means of
excluding themselves. Corruption is rampant. Famine stalks the land.
In fact, food riots are a common occurrence from 1774 to 1783.
Ironically, while the king fails to recognize it, the right to philosophize is the only freedom that the people can enjoy. The celebrated
French historian Alexis de Tocqueville put it this way.

[French society] had, however, preserved
one liberty from the destruction of all the others;
we could philosophize almost without restraint
on the origin of societies, on the essential nature
of government, and on the primordial rights of

the human species. All those injured by the daily practice of legislation soon took up this form of literary politics. The taste for it spread even to those whose nature or status most distanced them from abstract speculations ... Every public passion was thus wrapped up in philosophy; political life was violently driven back into literature, and writers—taking in hand the direction of opinion, found themselves for a moment taking the place that party leaders usually hold in free countries ... Above the real society ... there was slowly built an imaginary society in which everything seemed simple and coordinated, uniform, equitable, and in accord with reason. Gradually the imagination of the crowd deserted the former to concentrate on the latter. One lost interest in what was, in order to think about what could be, and one finally lived mentally in that ideal city the writers had built.[43]

And so it comes to pass that on May 5, 1789, the king calls a meeting of the Estates General, an archaic advisory body that had last met in 1614. It is made up of the three "estates" of French society, the first being the clergy, the second the nobility, and the third the commoners. The purpose behind this meeting is to get some sort of public approval for addressing the nation's bankruptcy. The problem is that the Third Estate has changed considerably over years with the emergence of a growing middle class that has become increasingly important to society and unhappy about its lack of influence within the government. The king appears before them on the opening day and acts kingly, which is to say that he antagonizes those from whom he, at least theoretically, is seeking cooperation.

Under the old rules, the Third Estate has as many delegates as the other two combined. A few weeks into the session, some members of nobility join with some the commoners to form a majority, and insist that voting will be by group rather than by numbers. At this point, the commoners walk out, get together at a nearby tennis court along with a few members of both the nobility and the clergy, form a new own organization called the National Assembly, and swear an oath, fashioned after America's Declaration of Independence, declaring that they will stick together until a constitution is written and agreed to by the king.

In the meantime, the king has surrounded this new Assembly with a military contingent and has forced the nobles and others who had stayed behind with the Estates General to join it. On July 9, it is reconstituted as the National Constituent Assembly. The king visits and is greeted with silence. The Assembly then demands that the king remove the troops that they say are threatening them. The king refuses.

Three days later, in the gardens of the Palais Royal, an angry crowd gathers. At three thirty in afternoon, an unsuccessful and destitute lawyer achieves fame when he mounts a table to address the crowd. Thomas Carlyle, arguably the French Revolution's most dramatic chronicler, describes him and his actions as follows in *The French Revolution, A History*, published in 1837.

> But see Camille Desmoulins, from the Cafe de Foy, rushing out, sibylline in face; his hair streaming, in each hand a pistol! He springs to a table: the Police satellites are eyeing him; alive they shall not take him, not they alive him alive. This time he speaks without stammering: —Friends, shall we die like hunted hares? Like sheep hounded into their pinfold; bleating for mercy, where is no mercy, but only a whetted knife? The hour is come; the supreme hour of Frenchman and Man; when Oppressors are to try conclusions with Oppressed; and the word is, swift Death, or Deliverance forever. Let such hour be well-come! Us, meseems, one cry only befits: To Arms! Let universal Paris, universal France, as with the throat of the whirlwind, sound only: To

arms! —"To arms!" yell responsive the innumer-
able voices: like one great voice, as of a Demon
yelling from the air: for all faces wax fire-eyed, all
hearts burn up into madness. In such, or fitter
words, does Camille evoke the Elemental Powers,
in this great moment ... Camille descends from
his table, "stifled with embraces, wetted with
tears;" has a bit of green riband handed him;
sticks it in his hat. And now to Curtius' Image-
shop there; to the Boulevards; to the four winds;
and rest not till France be on fire![44]

At this point, we will turn to Taine's account. (The quotes are
from his contemporary sources.)

The dregs of society at once come to the
surface. During the night between the 12th and
13th of July, "all the barriers, from the Faubourg
Saint-Antoine to the Faubourg Saint-Honoré,
besides those of the Faubourgs Saint-Marcel
and Saint-Jacques, are forced and set on fire." ...
"Ruffians, armed with pikes and sticks, proceed
in several parties to give up to pillage the houses
of those who are regarded as enemies to the public welfare." "They go from door to door crying,
'Arms and bread!' During this fearful night, the
bourgeoisie kept themselves shut up, each trem-
bling at home for himself and those belonging
to him."
During the night between the 13th and
14th of July, the baker's shops and the wine shops
are pillaged; "men of the vilest class, armed with
guns, pikes, and turnspits, make people open
their doors and give them something to eat and
drink, as well as money and arms." Vagrants, rag-
ged men, several of them "almost naked," and

"most of them armed like savages, and of hideous appearance;" they are "such as one does not remember to have seen in broad daylight;" many of them are strangers, come from nobody knows where. It is stated that there were 50,000 of them, and that they had taken possession of the principal guard-houses.[45]

The next day, the mob storms the Bastille, marking the formal beginning of the French Revolution and the end of the Left's long gestation period. The evil thing is born, "hurled headlong flaming from the ethereal sky," to borrow a line from Milton's *Paradise Lost*.[46] They demand that the aging governor of that ancient prison, Bernard René Jourdan, Marquis de Launay, open the gates and allow them access to the fortress's large stock of guns and powder. Carlyle described his fate as follows:

> All morning, since nine, there has been a cry everywhere: To the Bastille! Repeated "deputations of citizens" have been here, passionate for arms ... Towards noon, Elector Thuriot de la Rosiere gains admittance; finds de Launay indisposed for surrender; nay disposed for blowing up the place rather. Thuriot mounts with him to the battlements: heaps of paving-stones, old iron and missiles lie piled; cannon all duly leveled; in every embrasure a cannon—only drawn back a little! But outwards behold, O Thuriot, how the multitude flows on, welling through every street; tocsin furiously pealing, all drums beating the generale: the Suburb Saint-Antoine rolling hitherward wholly, as one man ...
>
> What shall De Launay do? One thing only De Launay could have done: what he said he would do. Fancy him sitting, from the first, with lighted taper, within arm's-length of the Powder-

Magazine; motionless, like old Roman Senator, Bronze Lamp-holder; coldly apprising Thuriot, and all men, by a slight motion of his eye, what his resolution was:—Harmless he sat there, while unharmed; but the King's Fortress, meanwhile, could, might, would, or should in nowise be surrendered, save to the King's Messenger: one old man's life worthless, so it be lost with honour; but think, ye brawling canaille, how will it be when a whole Bastille springs skyward! —In such statuesque, taper-holding attitude, one fancies De Launay might have left Thuriot, the red Clerks of the Basoche, <u>Curé</u> of Saint-Stephen and all the tagrag-and-bobtail of the world, to work their will.

And yet, withal, he could not do it ... De Launay could not do it. Distracted, he hovers between two hopes in the middle of despair; surrenders not his Fortress; declares that he will blow it up, seizes torches to blow it up, and does not blow it. Unhappy old De Launay, it is the death-agony of thy Bastille and thee! Jail, Jailoring and Jailor, all three, such as they may have been, must finish.[47]

He and his garrison of eighty-two French soldiers and thirty-two Swiss guards defend it bravely, killing ninety-eight members of the mob and losing but one of their own. But he runs out of food and supplies and becomes aware that no help is on the way. He offers terms of surrender. When the mob rejects his terms, he considers blowing up the fortress with himself and his men in it. At the behest of his men and to prevent further bloodshed, he does not do it. Instead, he sends the keys out to the mob. Despite his assumption that surrender under a white flag entitles the Bastille's defenders to just treatment, the mob kills seven of his men immediately, then drags him down the street toward the Hôtel de Ville, beating him along the way, arguing among themselves over what to do with him, and finally ripping him to pieces when he defies them.

So de Launay becomes the first casualty of a war that would continue for over two hundred years, take the lives of millions upon millions of innocent people, and give birth to dozens of godless ideologies that together would become a dire threat to the future of Christianity and hence to Western Civilization.

Let's let the poets in on the fun.

> Voltaire at Ferney
> Perfectly happy now, he looked at his estate.
> An exile making watches glanced up as he passed
> And went on working; where a hospital was rising fast,
> A joiner touched his cap; an agent came to tell
> Some of the trees he'd planted were progressing well.
> The white alps glittered. It was summer. He was very great.
> Far off in Paris where his enemies
> Whispered that he was wicked, in an upright chair
> A blind old woman longed for death and letters. He would
>   write,
> "Nothing is better than life." But was it? Yes, the fight
> Against the false and the unfair
> Was always worth it. So was gardening. Civilize.
> Cajoling, scolding, screaming, cleverest of them all,
> He'd had the other children in a holy war
> Against the infamous grown-ups; and, like a child, been sly
> And humble, when there was occasion for
> The two-faced answer or the plain protective lie,
> But, patient like a peasant, waited for their fall.
> And never doubted, like D'Alembert, he would win:
> Only Pascal was a great enemy, the rest
> Were rats already poisoned; there was much, though, to
>   be done,
> And only himself to count upon.
> Dear Diderot was dull but did his best;
> Rousseau, he'd always known, would blubber and give in.

Night fell and made him think of women: Lust
Was one of the great teachers; Pascal was a fool.
How Emilie had loved astronomy and bed;
Pimpette had loved him too, like scandal; he was glad.
He'd done his share of weeping for Jerusalem: As a rule,
It was the pleasure-haters who became unjust.
Yet, like a sentinel, he could not sleep. The night was full
    of wrong,
Earthquakes and executions: soon he would be dead,
And still all over Europe stood the horrible nurses
Itching to boil their children. Only his verses
Perhaps could stop them: He must go on working:
    Overhead,
The uncomplaining stars composed their lucid song.
W. H. Auden, 1939

Chapter 2

The Left's First Mass Murder

The effect of liberty to individuals is, that they may do what they please: We ought to see what it will please them to do, before we risque congratulations, which may be soon turned into complaints. Prudence would dictate this in the case of separate insulated private men; but liberty, when men act in bodies, is power. Considerate people, before they declare themselves, will observe the use which is made of power; and particularly of so trying a thing as new power in new persons, of whose principles, tempers, and dispositions, they had little or no experience, and in situations where those who appear the most stirring in the scene may possibly not be the real movers. (Edmund Burke, *Reflections on the Revolution in France*, 1790)

On the morning of July 15, 1789, the French people awaken to a world in which they are free from the slander on their character imposed by the "myth" of original sin, from the burden of religiously inspired "superstition," and from the pernicious societal influences that Rousseau had said prevented them from living a life at peace with their neighbors.

It is crucial to understand that this circumstance is something quite new to mankind. Of course, coups had brought down many governments. But the standard procedure was for the victorious side to simply install a new leader and make some adjustments in the existing social order. The French revolutionaries have no interest in this. Steeped in the ideas of Voltaire, Rousseau, Diderot, and their like, they seek the complete destruction of the old order and the construction of entirely new one based on reason and science.

Fulfilling the first part of this demand is quick and easy. Needless to say, establishing a new order based on reason and science is not so easy. John Adams pinpointed the difficulties involved in this process when he famously asked, "How is it possible to bring twenty-five Millions of Frenchmen Who have never known or thought of any law but the King's Will to rally round any free constitution at all?"[1]

Naturally, this job falls to the National Assembly, which is still extant. Our interest in the details of the first three years of this effort is limited. Simply stated, the Assembly immediately abolishes feudalism and embraces a declaration of the "Rights of Man" that provides every citizen with a license to react to any perceived infringement on his or her "rights" by any person or any governmental body with force if necessary. Soon thereafter, it seizes the property and takes over the management of the Church and issues a paper currency backed by these confiscated assets, which proves to be worthless and, as such, promotes inflation and civil discord. Finally, on September 3, 1791, it adopts a constitution that retains the monarchy but vests virtually all power in a new Legislative Assembly, which replaces the National Assembly.

In short, it does a very good job of completing the destruction of the old order. But it does little more than to breed widespread corruption and exacerbate the misery and hunger of the masses. As for the new Constitution, by creating a small place within the government for the monarchy, it encourages the royalists to fight for renewal of the power of the monarchy, which, in turn, leads to suspicion of the new government among the masses, who want the monarchy eliminated. Moreover, it leads to a costly war with the monarchies of Austria and Prussia, who wish to free the still-sitting French king from his tormentors.

From the perspective of our history of the Left, the significance of the Assembly is that it takes the revolution out of the streets and the hands of rabble and places it into the hands of the leaders of the various factions, who try to form a peaceful compromise within the Assembly. Of course, given the animosity between and among them, along with the resultant absence of a leader who is widely recognized as such, the Assembly is powerless to achieve this end. The result is chaos. Taine described it this way:

> France ... presents a strange spectacle. Everywhere there is philanthropy in words and symmetry in the laws; everywhere there is violence in acts and disorder in all things. Afar is the reign of philosophy; at hand is chaos ... with the great extension of political rights, the liberty of the individual is in law reduced to nothing, while in practice it is subject to the caprice of sixty thousand constitutional assemblies; that no citizen enjoys any protection against the annoyances of these popular assemblies ... in all sections of the empire, in every branch of the administration, in every report, we detect the confusion of authorities, the uncertainty of obedience, the dissolution of all restraints, the absence of all resources ... without one of the means of real power, and, for their sole support, laws which, in supposing France to be peopled with men without vices or passions, abandon humanity to its primitive state of independence.[2]

With this said, we will resume our narrative three years later, on August 10, 1792, at the headquarters of the Paris Commune. This is the governing body of the city of Paris, which is also the home of the Jacobin Club, the largest and most radical of the many factions within the Assembly. It was originally composed of a handful of anti-Royalist deputies from Brittany, but its membership had grown dramatically during the preceding three years. Taine put it this way:

> In this society, in a state of dissolution, in which the passions of the people are the sole efficient force, that party rules which knows best how to flatter these and turn them to account. Alongside of a legal government, therefore, which can neither repress nor gratify these passions, arises an illegal government, which sanctions, excites, and directs them. While the former totters and falls to pieces, the latter strengthens itself and completes its organization, until, becoming legal in its turn, it takes the other's place.[3]

By this time, the Jacobin Club has seven thousand or so chapters scattered across France and some half million members that cut across class lines. With a few exceptions, its membership does not include the hereditary or landed aristocracy, the highest of the middle class, or the leaders of industrial and commercial enterprises. Nor does it include the small farmers, peasants, and craftsmen, who are too busy to be interested in doctrines and dogmas.

Instead, as Taine points out, its members come from a small minority within the two extremes of the lower stratum of the middle class and the upper stratum of the lower class. These are men whom he describes as innovative, restless, and discontented with their calling or profession, have little or no stake in the existing society, are capable of taking an abstract proposition and deducing its consequences, and who can make a speech, write and editorialize, compose a pamphlet.[4]

While calling itself a "club," it is, in fact, more of a secular, highly puritanical religious cult, complete with elaborate rites, vows of secrecy, the use of "blackballing" as part of a secret procedure for admission, secret codes for recognizing fellow members, and a small and elite minority of leaders, whom Brinton calls the "undisguised oligarchy." Its various chapters have reading rooms filled with pamphlets, books, and newspapers. They print and distribute propaganda circulars and pamphlets, sponsor political discussion groups, and award prizes to schoolchildren for reciting Paine's "Rights of Man." They sponsor communal meals, festivals, civic marriages, civic baptisms, and civic burials. They plant "liberty trees" in town squares and place busts of the apostles of the revolution in public places.[5]

Of course, they have no interest in the British model of "constitutional monarchy," nor of America's democracy. They are devotees of Rousseau's Social Contract, which rests on the idea that the state exists to guarantee the liberty of the individual, and that this liberty can only be expressed and understood within the context of something called the "general will" of the people. Rousseau himself put it this way:

> As long as several men in assembly regard themselves as a single body, they have only a single will which is concerned with their common preservation and general well-being. In this case, all the springs of the State are vigorous and simple and its rules clear and luminous; there are no embroilments or conflicts of interests; the common good is everywhere clearly apparent, and only good sense is needed to perceive it.[6]

This is, of course, a remarkably stupid notion, akin to saying that if we would just all get along, we will all get along. But the Jacobins love it, largely, we suppose, because it gives its blessing to rule by an elite who represent this "general will," and even better, it is accompanied by Rousseau's assertion that *anyone who doesn't abide by the "general will" should be put to death*. To wit:

> There is therefore a purely civil profession of faith of which the Sovereign should fix the articles, not exactly as religious dogmas, but as social sentiments without which a man cannot be

a good citizen or a faithful subject. *While it can compel no one to believe them, it can banish from the State whoever does not believe them*—it can banish him, not for impiety, but as an anti-social being, incapable of truly loving the laws and justice, and of sacrificing, at need, his life to his duty. If anyone, after publicly recognizing these dogmas, behaves as if he does not believe them, *let him be punished by death*: he has committed the worst of all crimes, that of lying before the law. [Emphasis added][7]

Under the banner of this tyrannical creed, the Jacobins announce that they can no longer support the Assembly or the new constitution. Why, they ask, after having overthrown one despotic regime should they tolerate a new one? They storm the Hôtel de Ville, where the king and the queen are housed, seize and imprison them, and, over the next several weeks, dissolve the Assembly, declare the establishment of a Republic, set up something called the National Convention to rule the country on behalf of "the people," and arrest and murder scores of royalty and clergy. The titular leader of the Jacobins at this time is Georges Danton, who is remembered today for having offered the following explanation for the mass murders that would follow:

We will not judge the King, we will kill him … *These priests, these nobles are not guilty, but they must die, because they are out of place, interfere with the movement of things, and will stand in the way of the future.*[8]

True to his word, King Louis XVI is beheaded on January 21, 1793. Three months later, Danton authors the technique of language distortion that would eventually become one of the Left's most effective propaganda tools and which George Orwell would discuss at length in his classic novel *Nineteen Eighty-Four*. He does this by establishing something reassuringly called the Committee of Public Safety, which is charged with protecting the "goals of the revolution" by using whatever measures are necessary, including, it turns out, mass murder.

The immediate problem, however, is that the Jacobins cannot agree among themselves what needs to be done to protect the goals of the revolution. Danton, for all his faults, is the moderate in this quarrel. Now that the king is dead, he wants to restore order. Forgive and forget, so to speak. His rival within the club is Maximilien François Marie Isidore de Robespierre. He accuses Danton of betraying the revolution. Robespierre wins the dispute. Danton and his allies lose their heads, and Robespierre institutes what will become known as the Reign of Terror. He justifies it by declaring the following:

> If, during peace, virtue be the mainspring of a popular government, its mainspring in the time of revolution is both virtue and terror; virtue without terror becomes fatal, terror without virtue is powerless. Subdue, then, the enemies of liberty by terror, and as the founders of the republic, you will act rightly. The government of the revolution is the despotism of liberty against tyranny.[9]

Of course, Robespierre presents himself as a paragon of virtue, a lover of liberty and justice, a great enemy of vice and evil. Like Scrope, the Archbishop of York, in Henry IV, he turns insurrection into religion. He is, in short, the personification of sanctimony, the first in a long line of murderous leaders of the Left for centuries to come. Or more precisely, one of the false prophets of whom Jesus spoke when he told those who would do him harm in Jerusalem, "I am come in my father's name, and ye receive me not: if another shall come in his own name, him you will receive."[10] Tocqueville described the atmosphere of religiosity as follows:

No previous political upheaval, however violent, had aroused such passionate enthusiasm, for the ideal that the French revolution set before it was not merely a change in the French social system but nothing short of a regeneration of the whole human race. It created an atmosphere of missionary fervor and, indeed, assumed all the aspects of a religious revival—much to the consternation of contemporary observers. It would perhaps be truer to say that it developed into a species of religion, if a significantly imperfect one, since it was without a God, without a ritual or promise of a future life. Nevertheless, this strange religion has, like Islam, overrun the whole world with it apostles, militants, and martyrs.[11]

Mignet details the events.

During the four months following the fall of the Danton party, the committees exercised their authority without opposition or restraint. *Death became the only means of governing,* and the republic was given up to daily and systematic executions ... The extermination *en masse **of the enemies of the democratic dictatorship, which had already been effected at Lyons and Toulon by grape-shot, became still more horrible, by the noyades [drownings] of Nantes, and the scaffolds of Arras, Paris, and Orange.***[12]

Thousands are slain in a mad orgy of bloodlust. Estimates of the number of people killed during this campaign range upward to forty thousand, including sixteen thousand, who perished under the blade of the guillotine.[13] Men, women, children, young, old, rich, and poor. Some chroniclers might add "guilty and innocent" to this list, but they would be wrong to do so, because none of the victims are guilty of anything, for there are no recognized laws, secular or moral, to violate. Rule is entirely arbitrary, as is death.

Robespierre is, of course, a devotee of Rousseau whom he describes as "the one man who, through the loftiness of his soul and the grandeur of his character, showed himself worthy of the role of teacher of mankind."[14] When the killing begins, he invokes Rousseau's warning against moderation, as well as his communitarian claim that no single individual has a right against the power of the entirety and that the state shall determine the peoples' will. Robespierre states it this way: "The people is good, patient and generous ... the interest, the desire of the people is that of nature, humanity and the general welfare ... The people is always worth more than individuals ... The people is sublime, but individuals are weak."[15]

Since the dawn of human history, men had slaughtered other men out of wrath, greed, sloth, pride, lust, envy, gluttony, and insanity. They had killed for their god, their country, and their honor. They had killed for the sheer glory of warfare and for the pure joy of killing. However, never before had men slaughtered men under the noble banner of the love of mankind. And, having been done once, it would be done again. Indeed, filled with flowery words of love and compassion, Robespierre's orations would become the prototype for speeches of men like Vladimir Ilyich Ulyanov, a.k.a. Lenin; ioseb Besarionis dze Jughashvili, a.k.a. Stalin; Adolf Hitler; and Mao Tse-Tung, who would murder tens of millions of men, women, and children on behalf of their own evil "religions" of the Left. The following excerpt from Robespierre's speech that began the Terror is illustrative.

> What is the goal toward which we are heading? The peaceful enjoyment of liberty and equality; the reign of that eternal justice whose laws have been inscribed, not in marble and stone, but in the hearts of all men, even in that of the slave who forgets them and in that of the tyrant who denies them.
>
> We seek an order of things in which all the base and cruel passions are enchained, all the

beneficent and generous passions are awakened by the laws; where ambition becomes the desire to merit glory and to serve our country; where distinctions are born only of equality itself; where the citizen is subject to the magistrate, the magistrate to the people, and the people to justice; where our country assures the well-being of each individual, and where each individual proudly enjoys our country's prosperity and glory; where every soul grows greater through the continual flow of republican sentiments, and by the need of deserving the esteem of a great people; where the arts are the adornments of the liberty which ennobles them and commerce the source of public wealth rather than solely the monstrous opulence of a few families.

In our land we want to substitute morality for egotism, integrity for formal codes of honor, principles for customs, a sense of duty for one of mere propriety, the rule of reason for the tyranny of fashion, scorn of vice of scorn of the unlucky, self-respect for insolence, grandeur of soul over vanity, love of glory for the love of money, good people in place of good society. We wish to substitute merit for intrigue, genius for wit, truth for glamour, the charm of happiness for sensuous boredom, the greatness of man for the pettiness of the great, a people who are magnanimous, powerful, and happy, in place of a kindly, frivolous, and miserable people—which is to say all the virtues and all the miracles of the republic in place of all the vices and all the absurdities of the monarchy.

We want, in a word, to fulfill natures's desires, accomplish the destiny of humanity, keep the promises of philosophy, absolve providence from the long reign of crime and tyranny. Let France, formerly illustrious among the enslaved lands, eclipsing the glory of all the free peoples who have existed, become the model for the nations, the terror of oppressors, the consolation of the oppressed the ornament of the world— and let us, in sealing our work with our blood, see at least the early dawn of the universal bliss -that is our ambition, that is our goal.[16]

Of course, as the American economist Herb Stein famously said, if something cannot go on forever, it will stop. And the Reign of Terror is no exception. On July 27, 1794, Robespierre is hoisted on his own petard, as the saying goes, when several members of the National Convention become concerned for their own heads, and think that it might be safer for everyone involved if the next heads to fall are those of Robespierre, his sidekick, the Angel of Death, Louise Antoine de Saint-Just, and scores of their compatriots, bringing to mind Burke's famous warning that "a conscientious man would be cautious how he dealt in blood."[17]

The Directory replaces Robespierre's Committee of Public Safety. It consists of five incredibly inept and corrupt losers, of whom it cannot even be said that they "mean well." The historian Louis Madelin recounts that "when these five men made their first appearance in their gala dress of satin, with à la François Ier, red hats and feathers, laces and scarves and swords, silk stockings and rosetted shoes, the mirth of the public was extreme." Indeed, he notes that one of them, Louis-Marie La Revellière-Lépeaux, had once escaped the guillotine only because an executioner complained of time being wasted on such a "paltry fellow as that."[18]

Of course, the "Directory Era" is a disaster, an eerie portent of the fate of all leftist societies to come. Under its direction, France becomes a playground for corruption, greed, dissolution, and social breakdown. Edmund Wilson, in his masterpiece about that period, *To the Finland Station*, described the resulting situation as follows:

With the Directory the French Revolution had passed into the period of reaction which was to make possible the domination of Bonaparte. The great rising of the bourgeoisie, which, breaking out of the feudal forms of the monarchy, dispossessing the nobility and the clergy, had presented itself to society as a movement of liberation, had ended by depositing the wealth in the hands of a relatively small number of people and creating a new conflict of classes. With the reaction against the Terror, the ideals of the Revolution were allowed to go by the board. The five politicians of the Directory and the merchants and financiers allied with them were speculating in confiscated property, profiteering in army supplies, recklessly inflating the currency and gambling on the falling gold louis. And in the meantime, during the winter of 1795–96, the working people of Paris were dying of hunger and cold in the streets.[19]

Two men of great significance to our narrative emerge from this maelstrom of corruption, murder, and economic chaos, and proceed to change the course of world history. The first of these is the radical and ever-present troublemaker Gracchus (nee François-Noël) Babeuf. He is little known today, but he is important to our narrative because of his justly deserved title as the "first revolutionary communist," given to him by his biographer R. R. Rose.

As noted previously, the French revolutionaries came from all walks of life, and they naturally represented their class preferences in the various factional wars. Babeuf was raised in abject poverty. He was a champion of the *sans-culotte*. In fact, he had adopted the name Gracchus during the revolution in honor of Caius Gracchus, a second-century BC Roman politician who caused a great deal of turmoil by trying to improve the lot of the poor through agrarian reforms and was finally put to death.

He was either present at the storming of the Bastille or arrived in Paris the next day, depending on who is telling the story. He was an active member of the Jacobin Club for several years, but he grew to dislike its elitist and dictatorial nature, which he viewed as an affront to the freedoms that the poor had won in 1789. Naturally then, he supported the overthrow of Robespierre, but fortunately for him, he was in prison during the Terror and kept his head. Later, when he realized that the Directory was nothing more than another, even more corrupt dictatorship, he changed his attitude toward Robespierre and justified his actions as "a safeguard against aristocrats and traitors."[20]

In the fall of 1794, he begins publication of *The Tribune of the People*, and a short time later, he establishes a secret organization called the Conspiracy of Equals, made up largely of former Jacobins. Naturally, their purpose is to bring down the Directory. A friend and compatriot of his, Sylvain Maréchal, writes the organization's "Manifesto of the Equals," which is published a year before Babeuf's death.

> We pretend henceforth to live and die equal, as we were born so. We desire real equality or death; behold what we want. And we shall have this real equality, no matter at what price ... We want that equality not merely written in the "Declaration of the Rights of Man and of the Citizen;" we want it in the midst of us—under the roofs of our houses. ... Perish, if needs be, all the arts, provided real equality abides with us! ... We declare that we can no longer suffer that the great majority of men shall labor and sweat to serve and pamper the extreme minority. Long enough, and too long, have less than a million of individuals disposed of what belongs to more than 20 millions of men like themselves— of men in every respect their equals. Let there be at length an end to this enormous scandal,

which posterity will scarcely credit. Away for ever with the revolting distinctions of rich and poor, of great and little, of masters and servants, of *governors and governed.* Let there be no longer be any other difference in mankind than those of age and sex. Since all have the same wants, and the same faculties, let all have accordingly the same—the same nourishment. They are content with one sun, and the same air for all; why should not the like portion, and the same quality of food, suffice for each according to his wants?[21]

The Tribune was not an ordinary polemical pamphlet. It is the first of many such leftist manifestos to come. The historian James Billington describes it as "an organ of strategy. Not just an outlet for rhetoric."[22] Its first two issues contained 160 pages in which, as Rose noted, Babeuf "declared himself less concerned with purveying news or even comment on immediate events than with the exposition of 'first things' and the promulgation of a 'manifesto of the plebeians.'" Among the many important "first things" was the traditional Rousseauist argument for equality based on natural right. As to its importance, Rose said this:

> *It opened up a new vision for weary revolutionaries of a perfectly attainable world in which their highest moral aspirations could be realized;* a new world of equality and fraternity, freed from the crimes and vices of the old. It would be a world without boundaries, hedges, walls, locks, disputes, litigation, theft, murder, courts, gibbets, punishment, jealousy, pride, fraud or deceit; and, most important of all, without perpetual personal anxiety about the morrow, about old age, and about the future of one's children and grandchildren.[23]

To make a long story short, Babeuf and his friends assault the Directory throughout 1795 and early 1796, taking advantage of the desperate economic times to gain increased support for his movement. Then, in May 1796, he is arrested, tried, and beheaded. He is allowed a trial, which lasts for several days, during which he delivered numerous speeches that provide the first modern blueprint for communism. An excerpt follows:

> It is clear, then, from all that has been said, that everything owned by those who have more than their individual due of society's goods, is theft and usurpation. It is therefore just to take it back from them.
>
> Even someone who could prove that he is capable, by the individual exertion of his own natural strength, of doing the work of four men, and so lay claim to the recompense of four, would be no less a conspirator against society, because he would be upsetting the equilibrium of things by this alone, and would thus be destroying the precious principle of equality.
>
> Wisdom imperiously demands of all the members of the association that they suppress such a man, that they pursue him as a scourge of society, that they at least reduce him to a state whereby he can do the work of only one man, so that he will be able to demand the recompense of only one man. It is only our species that has introduced this murderous folly of making distinctions in merit and value, and it is our species alone that knows misfortune and privation.
>
> There must exist no form of privation but the one that nature imposes upon everyone as a result of some unavoidable accident, in which case these privations must be borne by everyone and divided up equally among them. The prod-

ucts of industry and of genius also become the property of all, the domain of the entire association, from the very moment that the workers and the inventors have created them, because they are simply compensation for earlier discoveries made through genius and industry, from which the new inventors and workers have profited within the framework of social life, and which have helped them to make their discoveries.

Since the knowledge acquired is the domain of everyone, it must therefore be equally distributed among everyone …[24]

The second man of note to emerge during the time of the Directory is Napoleon Bonaparte. He was born in Corsica in 1769. He attended the École Militaire in Paris and graduated as a second lieutenant in the artillery corps. When the revolution began in 1789, he went back to Corsica to join the resistance against the French occupation. He was run out of Corsica and returned to France in June 1793, where he rejoined the French army.

On October 5, 1795, he distinguishes himself in a battle in the streets of Paris against twenty-five thousand royalist forces by killing three hundred of them with what Carlyle would famously describe as a "whiff of grapeshot." At that time, as Carlyle put it, "the thing we specifically call the French Revolution is blown into space by it, and becomes a thing that was."[25]

Elevated to role of a national hero, Napoleon goes on to lead the French forces in their continuing war with Austria, England, Russian, et al. On November 9, 1799, he stages a coup, thus fulfilling Burke's remarkably prescient forecast of the outcome of the French Revolution made nine years earlier. To wit:

In the weakness of one kind of authority, and in the fluctuation of all, the officers of an army will remain for some time mutinous and full of faction, until some popular general, who understands the art of conciliating the soldiery, and who possesses the true spirit of command, shall draw the eyes of all men upon himself. Armies will obey him on his personal account.[26]

His solution to the manifest problems that are slowly but ever so surely destroying France is to launch a war of conquest. It lasts for twelve years, during which time somewhere between three to six million military personnel and civilians lose their lives. When it ends, the fires that had been lit by the ideas of Voltaire and Rousseau are not only still burning but are in the process of lighting vast new blazes that will burn even brighter in years to come and be even more deadly.

Socialism, communism, anarchism, ultranationalism, Bolshevism, National Socialism, Fascism, the Iron Guard, Fabianism, Progressivism, and liberalism would rise from these ashes. God would be declared dead by some of the leading lights of culture. Politics and the great Christian notion concerning the sanctity of man would give way to a variety of symbols, causes, movements, utopian dreams, and political theories. The world would bleed. And contrary to the notions that many conservatives harbor today, this blood would not be shed over great economic or even political disagreements, but over fundamental differences concerning the nature of man, the meaning of human life, and God's role in this drama.

Let's let the poets in on the fun.

Excerpt from "The Hound of Heaven":

> I fled Him, down the nights and down the days;
> I fled Him, down the arches of the years;
> I fled Him, down the labyrinthine ways
> Of my own mind; and in the midst of tears
> I hid from Him, and under running laughter.
> Up vistaed hopes I sped;
> And shot, precipitated,
> Adown Titanic glooms of chasmed fears,
> From those strong Feet that followed, followed after.

But with unhurrying chase,
And unperturbèd pace,
Deliberate speed, majestic instancy,
They beat—and a Voice beat
More instant than the Feet—
"All things betray thee, who betrayest Me."
Francis Thompson, 1893

Chapter 3

Burke: The Birth of the Right

I have observed that the philosophers in order to insinuate their polluted atheism into young minds systematically flatter all their passions natural and unnatural. They explode or render odious or contemptible that class of virtues which restrain the appetite. These are at least nine out of ten of the virtues. In place of all this, they substitute a virtue which they call humanity or benevolence. By this means their morality has no idea in it of restraint, or indeed of a distinct settled principle of any kind. When their disciples are thus left free and guided only by present feeling they are no longer to be depended upon for good or evil. The men who today snatch the worst criminals from justice will murder the most innocent persons tomorrow. (Edmund Burke, Letter to the Chevalier de Rivarol, 1791)

Before there was a Left, there was no Right. Of course, there had been many conflicts during the preceding fifteen or so centuries between the defenders of what was known then as Christendom and a wide variety of its enemies. But it wasn't until Bacon, Descartes, and Newton provided a philosophical, reason-based foundation for a full-scale attack on the principles underlying the Judeo-Christian social order that the assault on the status quo became so serious that a commensurate, secular defense was needed.

To put this in another way, the Right, as we know it today, came into being as a reaction to the emergence of the Left during the French Revolution. Indeed, the first term used by the Jacobins to describe the opposition to their movement was *réactionnaires*. And the term "reactionary" is still used occasionally in the United States today as a pejorative to describe those who are commonly known as conservatives.

The implication is that conservatives are interested solely in conserving the privileges of a corrupt social, economic, and political elite. This charge may have had some validity when applied to such antirevolutionary leaders as Joseph de Maistre and Louis de Bonald. However, we would argue that the one constant among the various forms of the conservatism today is not a desire to protect the ruling elite from change, but to protect society from the kind of ill-advised, politically induced change that wisdom, experience, and knowledge of human nature and history would indicate are likely to do great harm.

Nevertheless, whether conservatives appreciate the term *reactionary* or not, its use within the context of the ongoing political conflict between the Right and the Left is illuminating because it points up the fact that this battle is not a typical contest of the kind that Plato had in mind when he asked his famous question, "Who shall rule?" It is not a matchup between two political factions with differing views as to how to achieve a similar end. It is instead a perpetual revolution, in which one side is ceaselessly attempting to demolish the existing order, which was once called Christendom and is now more commonly referred to as Western Civilization, while the other is constantly fighting to conserve it. All of which explains Lord Acton's famous claim, "Tell me what you think about the French Revolution, and I will tell you what you think about everything else."[1]

In short, then, the Right, or conservatism if you will, is not an ideology. It has no Holy Writ, no manifesto, or as Russell Kirk, who is widely known as the Father of American conservativism, put it, "conservatism is not a fixed and immutable body of dogmata ... conservatives respect the wisdom of their ancestors ... they are dubious of wholesale alteration ... they think society cannot be scrapped and recast as if it were a machine." According to Kirk, conservatives generally share a belief in a transcendent order; the conviction that civilized society requires orders and classes; the understanding that freedom and property are closely linked; a distrust of those who would reconstruct society upon abstract designs; that custom, convention, and old prescription are checks both upon man's anarchist impulse and upon the innovator's lust for power; and that hasty innovation may be a devouring conflagration, rather than a torch of progress.[2]

Naturally, it was not readily apparent to either the participants in or observers of the French Revolution that the principal consequence of this bloody conflict would be the emergence of an entirely new and evil moral system that would sweep the globe and result in the enslavement and murder of millions of individuals over the next two-plus centuries.

As noted in a previous chapter, however, one man did recognize that the practical application of the ideas that were circulating among the French and English radicals posed a dire threat to humanity. His name was Edmund Burke. He was born in Dublin, the son of a Protestant lawyer and a Catholic mother. He was educated at a Quaker boarding school and at Trinity College. He was a committed Anglican all of his life. He came to London at the age of twenty-one to study law, but gave that up and made his living during the next fifteen years or so as a private secretary to several senior Parliamentarians. At the age of thirty-six, he became a Member of Parliament, where he established a reputation as one of the most brilliant men of his age and earned the title that he holds today as the Father of Conservatism.

Samuel Johnson, who is described in the *Oxford Dictionary of National Biography* as "arguably the most distinguished man of letters in English history,"[3] said this of Burke: "You could not stand for five minutes with that man beneath a shed while it rained, but you must be convinced that you had been standing with the greatest man you had ever seen."[4] Adam Smith remarked that Burke was "the only man I ever knew who thinks on economic subjects exactly as I do, without any previous communications having passed between us"[5] The great British statesman William Pitt the Elder said of Burke's maiden speech as a member of the House of Commons that he had "spoken in such a manner as to stop the mouths of all Europe."[6] More recently, Kirk said this of Burke: "If conservatives would know what they defend, Burke is their touchstone; and if radicals wish to test the temper of their opposition, they should turn to Burke."[7]

Thus, we will begin our account of the birth of conservatism in this great man's study at his six hundred–acre estate in Beaconsfield, about twenty-four miles outside of London. It is early February in the year 1790. Burke has just turned sixty-one. He is famous throughout the Western world for his defense of traditional Christian values, morals, mores, and customs, as well as for his continuous concern for the principles of liberty and justice.

He has been a central figure in countless political battles. Fifteen years earlier, he had led the lonely and futile fight against King George's demand to punish the American colonists for their alleged treasonous activities. In fact, on March 22, 1775, six months after the First Continental Congress met in Philadelphia and less than a month before the firing of the first shots in the War of Independence, Burke delivered a speech in the House of Commons in favor of reconciliation. It survives today as one of the most passionate orations in favor of American liberty ever given. To wit:

> In this character of the Americans, a love of freedom is the predominating feature which marks and distinguishes the whole; and as an ardent is always a jealous affection, your Colonies become suspicious, restive, and intractable whenever they see the least attempt to wrest from them by force, or shuffle from them by chicane, what they think the only advantage worth living for. This fierce spirit of liberty is stronger in the English Colonies probably than in any other people of the earth, and this from a great variety of powerful causes; which, to understand the true

temper of their minds and the direction which this spirit takes, it will not be amiss to lay open somewhat more largely.

First, the people of the Colonies are descendants of Englishmen. England, Sir, is a nation which still, I hope, respects, and formerly adored, her freedom. The Colonists emigrated from you when this part of your character was most predominant; and they took this bias and direction the moment they parted from your hands. They are therefore not only devoted to liberty, but to liberty according to English ideas, and on English principles. Abstract liberty, like other mere abstractions, is not to be found. Liberty inheres in some sensible object; and every nation has formed to itself some favorite point, which by way of eminence becomes the criterion of their happiness ...

We thought, Sir, that the utmost which the discontented Colonies could do was to disturb authority; we never dreamt they could of themselves supply it—knowing in general what an operose business it is to establish a government absolutely new. But having, for our purposes in this contention, resolved that none but an obedient Assembly should sit, the humors of the people there, finding all passage through the legal channel stopped, with great violence broke out another way. Some provinces have tried their experiment, as we have tried ours; and theirs has succeeded. They have formed a government sufficient for its purposes, without the bustle of a revolution or the formality of an election. Evident necessity and tacit consent have done the business in an instant. So well they have done it, that Lord Dunmore—the account is among the fragments on your table—tells you that the new institution is infinitely better obeyed than the ancient government ever was in its most fortunate periods. Obedience is what makes government, and not the names by which it is called; not the name of Governor, as formerly, or Committee, as at present. This new government has originated directly from the people, and was not transmitted through any of the ordinary artificial media of a positive constitution. It was not a manufacture ready formed, and transmitted to them in that condition from England. The evil arising from hence is this; that the Colonists having once found the possibility of enjoying the advantages of order in the midst of a struggle for liberty, such struggles will not henceforward seem so terrible to the settled and sober part of mankind as they had appeared before the trial …

All this, I know well enough, will sound wild and chimerical to the profane herd of those vulgar and mechanical politicians who have no place among us; a sort of people who think that nothing exists but what is gross and material, and who, therefore, far from being qualified to be directors of the great movement of empire, are not fit to turn a wheel in the machine. But to men truly initiated and rightly taught, these ruling and master principles which, in the opinion of such men as I have mentioned, have no substantial existence, are in truth everything, and all in all. Magnanimity in politics is not seldom the truest wisdom; and a great empire and little minds go ill together. If we are conscious of our station, and glow with zeal to fill our places as becomes our situation and ourselves, we ought to auspicate all our public proceedings on America with the old warning of the church, Sursum corda! We ought to elevate our minds to the greatness of that trust to which the order of providence has called us. By adverting to the dignity of this high calling our ancestors have turned a savage wilderness into a glorious empire, and have made the most extensive and the only honorable conquests—not by destroying, but by promoting the wealth, the number, the happiness, of the human race. Let us get an American revenue as we have got an American empire. English privileges have made it all that it is; English privileges alone will make it all it can be.

In full confidence of this unalterable truth, I now, *quod felix faustumque sit,* lay the first stone of the Temple of Peace; and I move you—"That the Colonies and Plantations of Great Britain in North America, consisting of fourteen separate governments, and containing two millions and upwards of free inhabitants, have not had the liberty and privilege of electing and sending any Knights and Burgesses, or others, to represent them in the High Court of Parliament."[8]

At this moment, Burke is engaged in the endgame of another losing battle. This one began sixteen years earlier in 1773 when he had come to believe that the East India Company was deeply corrupt and acting in violation of the laws of both India and England, as well as of the principles of justice. Our interest in the controversy is limited. But we offer the famous British historian and politician Thomas Babington Macaulay's description of the speech Burke gave at the opening trial in February 1788 to impeach the former governor-general of India, Warren Hastings, as a means of illustrating the power of Burke's thoughts, rhetoric, and fame at the time.

The box in which the managers stood contained an array of speakers such as perhaps had not appeared together since the great age of Athenian eloquence. There were Fox and Sheridan, the English Demosthenes and the English Hyperides. There was Burke, ignorant, indeed, or negligent of the art of adapting his reasonings and his style to the capacity and taste of his hearers, but in amplitude of comprehension and richness of imagination superior to every orator, ancient or modern. ... The energy and pathos of the great orator extorted expressions of unwonted admiration from the stern and hostile Chancellor, and, for a moment, seemed to pierce even the resolute heart of the defendant. The ladies in the galleries, unaccustomed to such displays of eloquence, excited by the solemnity of the occasion, and perhaps not unwilling to display their taste and sensibility, were in a state of uncontrollable emotion. Handkerchiefs were pulled out; smelling bottles were handed round; hysterical sobs and screams were heard: and Mrs. Sheridan was carried out in a fit. At length the orator concluded. Raising his voice till the old arches of Irish oak resounded, "Therefore," said be, "hath it with all confidence been ordered, by the Commons of Great Britain, that I impeach Warren Hastings of high crimes and misdemeanours. I impeach him in the name of the Commons' House of Parliament, whose trust he has betrayed. I impeach him in the name of the English nation, whose ancient honour he has sullied. I impeach him in the name of the people of India, whose rights he has trodden under foot, and whose country he has turned into a desert. Lastly, in the name of human nature itself, in the

name of both sexes, in the name of every age, in
the name of every rank, I impeach the common
enemy and oppressor of all!"[9]

That was two years earlier, and at the present, the seemingly
interminable legal battle against Hastings is not going well. The
public has lost interest in his alleged transgressions, as have many of
Burke's allies in the fight. Moreover, Burke is tired. In his introduction
to the Penguin Classic edition of *Reflections*, Conor Cruise O'Brien
describes him at this time as a "rather isolated figure, unpopular, frustrated, hard-pressed by exhausting labors, and to some extent already
estranged from his old parliamentary friends and colleagues."[10]

In fact, he will proclaim in his next speech on the floor of the
House of Commons that he is "near the end of his natural, probably
still nearer the end of his political career." That he is "weak and weary,
and wished for rest." That he is "little disposed to controversies."[11]

Yet, Burke being Burke, and despite his protestations of fatigue,
he will once again rise up in defense of the principles in which he
believes and, in doing so, will enter into the greatest political battle
of his life against some of his closest friends and all his many enemies.
He sees no way to escape this. He has been carefully following the
developments in France since the fall of the Bastille and has become
increasingly alarmed, not so much by its terrible impact on the
French nation, but by the renewed enthusiasm that it had brought to
the largely moribund English reform movement.

In retrospect, it is highly unlikely that the English would have
staged a similar revolution. Yet the industrial revolution, which had
begun there in 1760s, had created a large, unhappy urban underclass
of workers with virtually no representation within the workplace, as
well as a growing middle class of factory owners, traders, and bankers
who, as Brinton noted, were "not adequately cared for under existing
conditions."[12] The result had been several nasty riots over a variety
of issues involving food prices and labor management issues. Yet the
conservative hold on the government was overwhelmingly strong.
Indeed, in 1785 Prime Minister William Pitt the Younger had failed

miserably to get Parliament to pass even a paltry few minor reform measures.

Nevertheless, Burke worries about the seemingly overwhelming support the French revolutionaries have within the English establishment. In fact, his best friend and political mentor, the great Whig leader Charles James Fox, has joined the chorus of hurrahs for the revolution, describing it thusly: "How much the greatest event it is that even happened in the world, and how much the best."[13]

One of the leaders of the newly reinvigorated reform movement is a Unitarian minister named Dr. Richard Price. He is a founding member of something called the Revolutionary Society, which had been formed in 1789, ostensibly to celebrate the centennial of the England's Glorious Revolution, but which had become a meeting place for English radicals. Price is on friendly terms with such prominent figures as William Pitt the Elder, David Hume, and Adam Smith. Moreover, his support for the American Revolution had led to visits to his home by such American leaders as Thomas Jefferson, Benjamin Franklin, and John and Abigail Adams.

In November 1789, Price delivers a sermon entitled "A Discourse on the Love of Our Country" in the dissenting chapel in Old Jewry, praising the French revolutionaries and comparing their ongoing bloody revolution to England's bloodless overthrow one hundred years earlier of James II and replacement by William III and his wife, Mary.

This enrages Burke. On February 9, he opens his attack on Price and his fellow radicals during a Parliamentary debate over "Army Estimates," in which he states that "it is with pain inexpressible" that he is "obliged to have even the shadow of a difference with his friend James Fox, whose authority would always be great with him, and with all thinking people."[14] But, of course, he does so, stating his case as follows:

> In the last age, we were in danger of being entangled by the example of France in the net of a relentless despotism. It is not necessary to say anything on the example; it exists no longer.

> Our present danger, from the example of a peo-
> ple whose character knows no medium is, with
> regard to government, a danger of anarchy: a
> danger of being led, through an admiration of
> successful fraud and violence, to an imitation of
> the excesses of an irrational, unprincipled, pro-
> scribing, confiscating, plundering, ferocious,
> bloody, and tyrannical democracy. On the side
> of religion, the danger of their example is no lon-
> ger from intolerance, but from atheism; a foul,
> unnatural vice, foe to all the dignity and conso-
> lation of mankind, which seems in France, for a
> long time, to be embodied into a faction, accred-
> ited and almost avowed.[15]

Four days later, an announcement appears in the press that
Burke will shortly publish a pamphlet on the French revolution and
its British supporters. The "shortly" part turns out to be optimistic, for it is not until November 1 that his previously mentioned
Reflections on the Revolution in France, is published. In accordance
with the title, the book opens with a discussion of the above-mentioned sermon by Dr. Price. To wit:

> For my part, I looked on that sermon as
> the public declaration of a man much connected
> with literary caballeros and intriguing philoso-
> phers, with political theologians and theological
> politicians both at home and abroad. I know they
> set him up as a sort of oracle; because, with the
> best intentions in the world, he naturally philip-
> pizes, and chaunts his prophetic song in exact
> unison with their designs ... Few harangues from
> the pulpit ... have ever breathed less of the spirit
> of moderation than this lecture in the Old Jewry.
> Supposing, however, that something like mod-
> eration were visible in this political sermon; yet

politics and the pulpit are terms that have little agreement. No sound ought to be heard in the church but the healing voice of Christian charity. The cause of civil liberty and civil government gains as little as that of religion by this confusion of duties. Those who quit their proper character, to assume what does not belong to them, are, for the greater part, ignorant both of the character they leave, and of the character they assume. Wholly unacquainted with the world in which they are so fond of meddling and inexperienced in all its affairs, on which they pronounce with so much confidence, they have nothing of politics but the passions they excite. Surely the church is a place where one day's truce ought to be allowed to the dissensions and animosities of mankind.[16]

Burke knows, of course, that with the publication of this book he will be engaging in another major political fight against very serious foes. In fact, he acknowledges this in a letter to his friend and fellow politician Philip Francis, who had warned him of the "mischief" that the book would cause.

I should agree with you about the vileness of the controversy with such miscreants as the "Revolution Society," and the "National Assembly"; and I know very well that they, as well as their allies, the Indian delinquents, will darken the air with their arrows. But I do not yet think they have the advowson of reputation. I shall try that point. My dear sir, you think of nothing but controversies: "I challenge into the field of battle and retire defeated, &c." If their having the last word be a defeat, they most assuredly will defeat me. I intend no controversy with Dr. Price, or Lord Shelburne, or any other of their set. I mean to set in full view the danger from their wicked principles and their black hearts. I intend to state the true principles of our constitution in church and state, upon grounds opposite to theirs. If any one be the better for the example made of them, and for this exposition, well and good. I mean to do my best to expose them to the hatred, ridicule, and contempt of the whole world; as I always shall expose such calumniators, hypocrites, sowers of sedition, and approvers of murder and all its triumphs. When I have done with that, they may have the field to themselves; and I care very little how they triumph over me, since I hope they will not be able to draw me at their heels, and carry my head in triumph on their poles.[17]

To praise this book is to guild the lily. As a political treatise, it has no equal in the modern world. Indeed, we would argue that it, together with Burke's other political writings, are to the Western tradition of political and social commentary what Plato's works are to philosophy, as famously stated by A. N. Whitehead, that being that the European philosophical tradition is nothing more than a series of footnotes to Plato.[18]

That is to say, that on virtually any topic, political, social, or economic, Burke's wisdom trumps that of the brightest of contemporary conservative pundits and politicians. This is not to take anything away from the paladins of conservatism in the United States today. Yet the fact is that anything that any of them say on behalf of the cause was said two hundred years ago, and said better, by Edmund Burke.

He begins this great book with a discussion of liberty, which is the centerpiece of the justification given by the French revolutionaries for their bloody revolt.

I flatter myself that I love a manly, moral, regulated liberty as well as any gentleman of that society, be he who he will; and perhaps I have given as good proofs of my attachment to that cause in the whole course of my public conduct ... But I cannot stand forward and give praise or blame to anything which relates to human actions, and human concerns, on a simple view of the object, as it stands stripped of every relation, in all the nakedness and solitude of metaphysical abstraction ... Abstractedly speaking, government, as well as liberty, is good; yet could I, in common sense, ten years ago, have felicitated France on her enjoyment of a government (for she then had a government) without inquiry what the nature of that government was, or how it was administered? Can I now congratulate the same nation upon its freedom? Is it because liberty in the abstract may be classed amongst the blessings of mankind, that I am seriously to felicitate a madman, who has escaped from the protecting restraint and wholesome darkness of his cell, on his restoration to the enjoyment of light and liberty? Am I to congratulate a highwayman and murderer who has broke prison upon the recovery of his natural rights? This would be to act over again the scene of the criminals condemned to the galleys, and their heroic deliverer, the metaphysic Knight of the Sorrowful Countenance.

When I see the spirit of liberty in action, I see a strong principle at work; and this, for a while, is all I can possibly know of it. The wild gas, the fixed air, is plainly broke loose; but we ought to suspend our judgment until the first effervescence is a little subsided, till the liquor is cleared, and until we see something deeper than the agitation of a troubled and frothy surface. I must be tolerably sure, before I venture publicly to congratulate men upon a blessing, that they have really received one. Flattery corrupts both the receiver and the giver, and adulation is not of more service to the people than to kings. I should, therefore, suspend my congratulations on the new liberty of France until I was informed how it had been combined with government, with public force, with the discipline and obedience of armies, with the collection of an effective and well-distributed revenue, with morality and religion, with the solidity of property, with peace and order, with civil and social manners. All these (in their way) are good things, too, and without them liberty is not a benefit whilst it lasts, and is not likely to continue long.[19]

As noted in the above quote, reverence for the ancient traditions, mores, morals, and social order upon which society rests is a central factor in Burke's polemic. Kirk explained this aspect of Burkian thought as follows in an introduction to Peter J. Stanlis's *Edmund Burke, The Enlightenment and the Revolution.*

Burke's first constitutional principle is that a good constitution grows out of the common experience of a people over a considerable length of time. It is not possible to create an improved constitution out of whole cloth, out of purely rational abstract concepts. As he declared in his "Speech on the Reform of Representation," "I look with filial reverence on the constitution of my country, and never will cut it in pieces and put it into the kettle of any magicians, in order to boil it, with the puddle of their compounds, into youth and vigor. On the contrary, I will drive away such pretenders; I will nurse its venerable age, and with lenient arts extend a parent's breath."[20]

Stanlis characterized Burke's position on this subject as follows:

> Because the moral nature of man was a mixed compound of good and evil passions, of true and false reason, of benevolent and selfish will, Burke believed that prudence and temperance were required to moderate and control the weaknesses and evil instincts in men so that the potential good could prevail. He believed that physical well-being, moral worth, political tranquility, and social happiness, depended largely on the control of desires, appetites, passions, will, imagination, and reason. Prudence restrained or harmonized these human qualities within the normative bounds of moral law and good manners. Even without revolution, the failure to live by the rules of prudence produced great difficulties to individuals and society.[21]

Burke himself put it this way.

> You see, Sir, that in this enlightened age I am bold enough to confess, that we are generally men of untaught feelings; that instead of casting away all our old prejudices, we cherish them to a very considerable degree, and, to take more shame to ourselves, we cherish them because they are prejudices; and the longer they have lasted, and the more generally they have prevailed, the more we cherish them. We are afraid to put men to live and trade each on his own private stock of reason; because we suspect that this stock in each man is small, and that the individuals would

do better to avail themselves of the general bank and capital of nations, and of ages. Many of our men of speculation, instead of exploding general prejudices, employ their sagacity to discover the latent wisdom which prevails in them. If they find what they seek, and they seldom fail, they think it more wise to continue the prejudice, with the reason involved, than to cast away the coat of prejudice, and to leave nothing but the naked reason; because prejudice, with its reason, has a motive to give action to that reason, and an affection which will give it permanence. Prejudice is of ready application in the emergency; it previously engages the mind in a shady course of wisdom and virtue, and does not leave the man hesitating in the moment of decision, skeptical, puzzled, and unresolved. Prejudice renders a man's virtue his habit; and not a series of unconnected acts. Through just prejudice, his duty becomes a part of his nature ...[22]

Men who undertake considerable things, even in a regular way, ought to give us ground to presume ability. But the physician of the state, who, not satisfied with the cure of distempers, undertakes to regenerate constitutions, ought to show uncommon powers. Some very unusual appearance of wisdom ought to display themselves on the face of the designs of those who appeal to no practice and who copy after no model. Has any such been manifested?[23]

Integral to Burke's veneration for the tried and the true, the ancient traditions, and the wisdom of the past was his understanding of the importance of a firm, religiously-based moral code to a just and peaceful society. In a letter to a member of the French National Assembly dated May 1791, he said this:

Men are qualified for civil liberty in exact proportion to their disposition to put moral chains upon their own appetites ... in proportion as they are more disposed to listen to the counsels of the wise and good, in preference to the flattery of knaves. Society cannot exist, unless a controlling power upon will and appetite be placed somewhere; and the less of it there is within, the more there must be without. It is ordained in the eternal constitution of things, that men of intemperate minds cannot be free. Their passions forge their fetters."[24]

Then there is the subject of natural rights, about which Burke said this:

If civil society be made for the advantage of man, all the advantages for which it is made become his right. It is an institution of beneficence; and law itself is only beneficence acting by a rule. Men have a right to live by that rule; they have a right to do justice, as between their fellows, whether their fellows are in public function or in ordinary occupation. They have a right to the fruits of their industry and to the means of making their industry fruitful. They have a right to the acquisitions of their parents, to the nourishment and improvement of their offspring, to instruction in life, and to consolation in death. Whatever each man can separately do, without trespassing upon others, he has a right to do for himself; and he has a right to a fair portion of all which society, with all its combinations of skill and force, can do in his favor. In this partnership all men have equal rights, but not to equal things. He that has but five shillings in the partnership has as good a right to it as he that has five hundred pounds has to his larger proportion. But he has not a right to an equal dividend in the product of the joint stock; and as to the share of power, authority, and direction which each individual ought to have in the management of the state, that I must deny to be amongst the direct original rights of man in civil society; for I have in my contemplation the civil social man, and no other. It is a thing to be settled by convention[25]

Of course, Burke had read the works of Rousseau, and he was under no illusions as to his authorship of the destruction that was going on within France. He put it this way:

Everybody knows that there is a great dispute amongst their leaders, which of them is the best resemblance to Rousseau. In truth, they all resemble him. His blood they transfuse into their minds and into their manners. Him they study; him they meditate; him they turn over in all the time they can spare from the laborious mischief of the day or the debauches of the night. Rousseau is their canon of holy writ; in his life he is their canon of Polycletus; he is their standard figure of perfection. To this man and this writer, as a pattern to authors and to Frenchmen, the foundries of Paris are now running for statues, with the kettles of their poor and the bells of their churches.[26]

Just as Francis had feared, the publication of *Reflections* causes Burke considerable "mischief." More accurately, as he had foreseen, he is pummeled by a powerful group of "miscreants, literary caballeros, and intriguing philosophers." The first to enter the fray is the feminist Mary Wollstonecraft. She teaches school in Newington Green, the vibrant center of London's dissenting community and Dr. Price's home base. Her pamphlet, which is a sound attack on Burke's book from the perspective of a devotee of Dr. Price and Enlightenment ideals, is entitled "A Vindication of the Rights of Men, in a Letter to the Right Honourable Edmund Burke; Occasioned by his *Reflections on the Revolution in France*." It hits the streets of London a few weeks after Burke's work and is followed quickly in March by the publication of Thomas Paine's famous book, *The Rights of Man*, which attacks Burke and defends the French Revolution.

Our interest is focused on two related books, one published a year later and the other a year after that. Both are written by William Godwin, a former dissenting minister who is one of England's leading intellectuals. He is a friend of Dr. Price's. Some years later, he would marry Wollstonecraft, who would die shortly after giving birth to their daughter, Mary, who would one day wed the poet Percy Bysshe Shelley and write the classic gothic novel, *Frankenstein.*

The first of Godwin's books, entitled *Enquiry Concerning Political Justice, and Its Influence on Morals and Happiness*, is published in February 1793. And while it was inspired by Burke *Reflections* and Paine's response, it does not deal with the specifics of the political events of the day as did Wollstonecraft's and Paine's. Nor does it call for reform. Whereas Burke had stressed the importance of faith, tradition, custom, continuity, and the wisdom of one's ancestors, Godwin advocates that the existing government be dismantled and replaced by no government at all. He does not give a name to this construction, but, of course, it comes to be called anarchism.

To say that the book causes quite a stir would be a great understatement. Indeed, the public discussion that it provokes is so intense that Prime Minister Pitt, who has been openly attempting to censor all radical political papers and books, considers prosecuting Godwin for treason. The story goes that he decided against it because of its high price, that is, "a three guinea book could never do much harm among those who had not three shillings to spare."[27] But the more likely explanation is that his government's considerable efforts to control the growing influence of the press had not been greeted well by a population that was not only becoming increasingly literate but had developed a considerable interest in world affairs since the American revolution.

In any case, the *Ninth Edition of the Encyclopedia Britannica* would later describe Godwin's *Enquiry* as "one of the epoch-making books in English thought," and would list it with Milton's *Areopagitica,* John Locke's *Essay on Education,* and Rousseau's *Émile* as "among the unseen levers which have moved the changes of the times."[28] It describes the book's central thesis as follows:

> Believing in the perfectibility of the race, that there are no innate principles, and therefore no original propensity to evil, he considered that "our virtues and our vices may be traced to the incidents which make the history of our lives, and if these incidents could be divested of every improper tendency, vice would be extirpated from the world." All control of man by man was more or less intolerable, and the day would come when each man, doing what seems right in his own eyes, would also be doing what is in fact best for the community, because all will be guided by principles of pure reason.[29]

The aforementioned Prince Peter Kropotkin explained Godwin's philosophy further in the eleventh edition of the *Encyclopedia Britannica* under the term *anarchism.* To wit:

> Laws, he wrote, are not a product of the wisdom of our ancestors: they are the product of their passions, their timidity, their jealousies and their ambition. The remedy they offer is worse than the evils they pretend to cure. If and only if all laws and courts were abolished, and the decisions in the arising contests were left to reasonable men chosen for that purpose, real justice would gradually be evolved. As to the

state, Godwin frankly claimed its abolition. A society, he wrote, can perfectly well exist without any government: only the communities should be small and perfectly autonomous. Speaking of property, he stated that the rights of every one "to every substance capable of contributing to the benefit of a human being" must be regulated by justice alone: the substance must go "to him who most wants it."[30]

Godwin's second book is a three-volume novel entitled *Things As They Are; or, The Adventures of Caleb Williams*, which recounts the trials and tribulations of an impoverished young man's tragic encounters with an unjust world. It too is a political work, specifically designed, as Godwin himself says, to inform "persons whom books of philosophy and science are never likely to reach" that the "spirit and character of the government intrudes itself into ever rank of society."[31]

Suddenly then, the British reformists have more than just a list of complaints and suggested changes that they wish to see implemented. They have a brilliantly written, comprehensive, philosophically derived critique of the current system, along with a detailed proposal for an alternative that borrows heavily from Rousseau, the hero of the French uprising. And with the introduction of the second book, the general public has a romantic, moving, and easily understood presentation of the evils of the system against which the radicals are fighting. In short, Godwin's conflict with Burke emerges as *casus belli* in the war between the Right and Left that will last well into the twenty-first century. Godwin puts his attack on government this way:

> Government ... gives substance and permanence to our errors. It reverses the genuine propensities of mind, and, instead of suffering us to look forward, teaches us to look backward for perfection. It prompts us to seek the public wel-

fare, not in innovation and improvement, but in a timid reverence for the decisions of our ancestors, as if it were the nature of mind always to degenerate, and never to advance[32]

Burke defends the "decisions of our ancestors" and argues "such ancient traditions must, therefore, be examined only with great caution and veneration." He puts it this way:

> An ignorant man, who is not fool enough to meddle with his clock, is however sufficiently confident to think he can safely take to pieces, and put together at his pleasure, a moral machine of another guise, importance, and complexity, composed of far other wheels, and springs, and balances, and counteracting and co-operating powers. Men little think how immorally they act in rashly meddling with what they do not understand. Their delusive good intention is no sort of excuse for the presumption. They who truly mean well must be fearful of acting ill.[33]

The battle is on.
Let's let the poets in on the fun.
Excerpt from "Choruses from the Rock":

> The world turns and the world changes,
> But one thing does not change.
> In all of my years, one thing does not change,
> However you disguise it, this thing does not change:
> The perpetual struggle of Good and Evil.
> Forgetful, you neglect your shrines and churches;
> The men you are in these times deride
> What has been done of good, you find explanations
> To satisfy the rational and enlightened mind.
> Second, you neglect and belittle the desert.

The desert is not remote in southern tropics
The desert is not only around the corner,
The desert is squeezed in the tube-train next to you,
The desert is in the heart of your brother.
The good man is the builder, if he build what is good.
I will show you the things that are not being done,
And some of the things that were long ago done,
That you may take heart, Make perfect your will.
Let me show you the work of the humble. Listen.
T. S. Eliot, 1934

Chapter 4

Communism and Utopian Socialism

Toward the end of the eighteenth century, in a growingly de-Christianized Europe, even while the old isolated island and valley utopias and a newer type of awakened-dreamer utopia continued to be regurgitated, there came into greater prominence the branch of utopian thought that spurned any fictional backdrop, broke with the limitations of specific place, and addressed itself directly to the reformation of the entire species. ... In these rationalist, systematic utopias whose province was the whole world, the means of reaching utopia was transformed from an adventure story or a rite de passage to Elysium into a question of political action. How to change a present misery into a future happiness in this world? The method of reaching utopia and the speed of travel, usually peripheral in the novelistic form, were now central, and the prickly issues of revolution, evolution, the uses of violence, the mechanics of the propagation of a new faith, determinism and free will, the imperatives of blind historical destiny, and the requirement of human freedom became intrinsic to utopian thought. (Frank E. and

Fritzie P. Manuel, *Utopian Thought in the Western World*, 1979)

Napoleon "met his Waterloo" in 1815. Europe was in shambles. Will Durant describes the situation there thusly:

> Millions of strong men had perished; millions of acres of land had been neglected or laid waste; everywhere on the Continent life had to begin again at the bottom, to recover painfully and slowly the civilizing economic surplus that had been swallowed up in war. ... The passage of the Napoleonic and counter-Napoleonic armies had left scars of ravage on the face of every country. Moscow was in ashes. In England, proud victor in the strife, the farmers were ruined by the fall in the price of wheat; and the industrial workers were tasting all the horrors of the nascent and uncontrolled factory system. Demobilization added unemployment.
>
> Yes, the Revolution was dead; and with it the life seemed to have gone out of the soul of Europe. The new heaven, called Utopia, whose glamour had relieved the twilight of the gods, had receded into a dim future where only young eyes could see it ... Only the young can live in the future, and only the old can live in the past; men were most of them forced to live in the present.[1]

The leaders of the victorious nations met, along with France, at the Congress of Vienna to put together a plan that would ensure a lasting peace within the nations of Europe. The first step in this process was to divide the territorial spoils of victory among the principal participants in the war, namely Prussia, Austria, Russia, and England. Not only did these shares have to be proportionate to each nation's contribution to the effort, they had to be designed in such a way as to establish a rough balance of power between them so they would be reluctant to go to war with each other. Then there was the need to weaken France enough to keep it from threatening the peace once again but to keep it strong enough to be an essential factor in the desired balance of power. Finally, there was the age-old, Platonic question, "who shall rule?" Naturally, they chose to place power back in the hands of Europe's old ruling families, whom they charged with using all means to suppress the liberal ideals that the revolutions in America and France had nurtured, and which the aristocrats in Vienna viewed as the cause of all the troubles.

The plan succeeded in ending France's reign as Europe's bully, as was amply demonstrated by Prussia's defeat of France in a relatively brief, ten-month-long dustup a few decades later. More importantly, it succeeded in preventing another widespread European war for a hundred years. However, it did not keep the Left at bay. You see, whether the royalists at the Congress of Vienna liked it or not, the Enlightenment, the industrial revolution, and the French revolution had relegated the age of kings to the dustbin of history.

The result was that secret revolutionary and nationalistic organizations sprung up in France, Italy, Russia, Spain, Portugal, Belgium, Poland, and Switzerland. France had the Society of Avengers, the Friends of the People, the Society of the Rights of Man, the Society of the Families, and the League of the Just. Italy had the Carbonari, which rapidly spread its influence into France, Spain, and Portugal. German revolutionaries united in Paris and formed the League of Outlaws. Revolutions, revolts, uprisings, and insurrections by gangs of radicals and even army officers were a commonplace. Naturally, conservative authorities all across Europe viewed these organizations and events as a clear and present danger and enacted highly repressive laws against all forms of reaction, backed up by aggressive police action, long prison terms, and exile.

Our immediate interest is in France, which was arguably the most unstable nation in this period. As noted earlier, the revolution had destroyed all the foundations upon which French society had existed for centuries. Napoleon had restored order for a short time. However, his humiliating defeat at the hands of the much-hated

English had left the French people with no trusted leader to bind them together as a nation. Yes, there was a new king with the lordly name of Louis XVIII. A pathetic, obese, gouty man, he had been living in exile for twenty-three years and had ingloriously returned to Paris in the entourage of the Duke of Wellington, who had just two weeks earlier defeated Napoleon at Waterloo and was marching toward Paris to begin his tour as commander of the Army of Occupation.

Not surprisingly, the old battles for political influence and a larger piece of the pie between the various factions began anew. This time the Napoleonists joined in the fight between and among the Ultra-Royalists, the Royalists, the Republicans, the petite bourgeois (merchants, shopkeepers, etc.), the financial bourgeois, the industrial bourgeois, the working classes, and the rabble. The result was that Paris became a playground for a new generation of radicals who had been born during the Napoleonic wars and raised on stories about the heroes of a great revolution that the monarchists, rich capitalists, and corrupt politicians had stolen from them.

They raised hell. They were arrested. They went to prison. But they had beaucoup problems. In fact, Billington describes this period as the "nadir of revolutionary hopes."[2] After all, the organizational base of the Jacobins had been destroyed. Its leaders were all either dead or discredited. All the revolutions across Europe since 1789 had failed miserably. The rich still had a stranglehold on power and were keeping it with increasingly heavy police repression. And the poor were as hungry as they were before the Revolution.

Yet it was during this difficult period that the *Left matured from a movement whose primary object was the destruction of the ruling class to a visionary ideology that would change the history of the world*. This process involved two separate and distinct developments. The first of these was the publication of a book that formed the foundation upon which communism would be constructed. The second was the appearance of an odd assortment of nonviolent dreamers who would become known to history as the Utopian Socialists and would lay the foundations for modern-day socialism and American liberalism.

We will begin our account of these events with the book. It was published in 1828, was written by Filippo Giuseppe Maria Lodovico Buonarroti, and was entitled *The History of the Babeuf Conspiracy.* Briefly stated, it was an account of Babeuf's struggles and a manifesto for a new form of government in which everyone would be equal. Marx and his pal Engels said it was through this book that Buonarroti reintroduced the communist idea into France after the Revolution of 1830; that idea being "the *idea **of the** new world system.*"[3]

Billington describes it as having "provided at last both an ancestry and a model for egalitarian revolution by publicizing the all-but-forgotten Babouvists." He says it elevated Buonarroti to the status of "the patriarch of this new generation of militant revolutionaries," "a kind of Plato to Babeuf's Socrates—recording the teachings and martyrdom of the master for posterity." He says it made Buonarroti "the first truly to become a full-time revolutionary in the modern sense of having total dedication to the creation by force of a new secular order." Finally, he quotes the German historian Ernst Barnikol as describing Buonarroti as "the first apostle of modern communism."[4]

Buonarroti was at the time a greatly revered, sixty-seven-year-old revolutionary hero. He had worked for Robespierre in the Committee of Public Safety, been friends with Napoleon in Corsica, had become a friend and devotee of Babeuf in prison, and would have been executed with him had it not been for his friendship with Napoleon. But it was his book that earned him an exalted place in the history of the Left.

Now there is little question that Babeuf sincerely loved and cared for the poor, but he was deeply concerned with their stubborn refusal to recognize just how unhappy was their lot. He ascribed this unfortunate circumstance to the fact that "a people whose opinions have been formed under a regime of inequality and of despotism, is little calculated, at the commencement of a regenerating Revolution, to distinguish wisely (by its suffrages) the men most capable to direct and consummate it with success." His solution to this troubling problem was to create a "temporary dictatorship" of "certain wise and courageous citizens, who, strongly impregnated with love of country, and of humanity, have long before fathomed the sources of public calamity—have disenthralled themselves from the common prejudices and vices of their age—have shot in advance of contemporary intellects, and who, despising money and vulgar greatness, have placed their happiness in rendering themselves immortal by ensuring the triumph of equality."[5]

A less generous Billington described it as providing "a mandate for the continued existence of an elite revolutionary dictatorship, and an implied license for the secret police surveillance of the future."[6] The French historian Georges Lefebvre noted that this little gem of an idea was bequeathed to Lenin by Buonarroti, who "turned it into reality."[7]

Of course, Buonarroti didn't make the book a hit all by himself. That took heroes and, to borrow a phrase from the great John Belushi, "a really futile and stupid gesture be done on somebody's part!"[8] Enter three revolutionaries who, enthralled by Buonarroti's book, established a secret club named the Society of Seasons, and set about planning the first communist revolution. Their names were Louis Blanqui, Armand Barbes, and Martin Bernard.

So it was that on May 12, 1839, these three intrepid but stupid warriors of the Left and an estimated nine hundred members of the Society of Seasons launched a coup against Louis-Phillip. Their venture failed badly, and all three spent the next nine years in prison. However, their bravery, revolutionary personas, and even their failure captured the attention of revolutionaries everywhere. And suddenly, Buonarroti's book became the bible for those who were still in the trenches and those that would soon enter the fray. Recall that Marx was ten years old at the time the book was published.

At this point, we come to Wilhelm Weitling, a Prussian tailor and a member of the League of the Just, which was made up of German leftists who were not welcome in their home country and were living in exile in France, Switzerland, and England. Like the Society of Seasons, they were followers of Babeuf and Buonarroti, but they also subscribed to that which the British historian Tristram Hunt described as "a highly emotional mix of Babouvist communism, chiliastic Christianity and Communism, and millenarian populism," that urged "installing communism by physical force with the help of a 40,000-strong army of ex-convicts."[9]

We have no interest in the details of this ideology. But we are interested in Weitling, who fled Paris to Switzerland in the wake of the Blanqui insurrection and, according to Engels, in doing so *brought communism to Germany*. He put it this way.

> This man, who is to be considered as *the founder of German Communism*, after a few years' stay in Paris, went to Switzerland, and, whilst he was working in some tailor's shop in Geneva, preached his new gospel to his fellow-workmen. He formed Communist Associations in all the towns and cities on the Swiss side of the lake of Geneva, most of the Germans who worked there becoming favourable to his views. Having thus prepared the public mind, he issued a periodical, the Young Generation, for a more extensive agitation of the country. This paper, although written for working men only, and by a working man, has from its beginning been superior to most of the French Communist publications, even to Father Cabet's *Populaire*. It shows that its editor must have worked very hard to obtain that knowledge of history and politics which a public writer cannot do without, and which a neglected education had left him deprived of ...
>
> Having thus established the nucleus of a Communist party in Geneva and its neighbourhood, he went to Zurich, where, as in other towns of Northern Switzerland, some of his friends had already commenced to operate upon the minds of the working men. He now began to organise his party in these towns. Under the name of Singing Clubs, associations were formed for the discussion of Social reorganisation. At the same

time Weitling advertised his intention to publish a book, —*The Gospel of the Poor Sinners*. But here the police interfered with his proceedings.

In June last, Weitling was taken into custody, his papers and his book were seized, before it left the press. The Executive of the Republic appointed a committee to investigate the matter, and to report to the Grand Council, the representatives of the people. This report has been printed a few months since. It appears from it, that a great many Communist associations existed in every part of Switzerland, consisting mostly of German working men; that Weitling was considered as the leader of the party, and received from time to time reports of progress; that he was in correspondence with similar associations of Germans in Paris and London, and that all these societies, being composed of men who very often changed their residence, were so many seminaries of these "dangerous and Utopian doctrines", sending out their elder members to Germany, Hungary, and Italy, and imbuing with their spirit every workman who came within their reach. …

The result of Weitling's trial did very little to satisfy the anticipations of the Zurich government. Although Weitling and his friends were sometimes very incautious in their expressions, yet the charge of high treason and conspiracy against him could not be maintained; the criminal court sentenced him to six months' imprisonment, and eternal banishment from Switzerland; the members of the Zurich associations were expelled from the Canton; the report was communicated to the governments of the other Cantons and to the foreign embassies, but the Communists in other parts of Switzerland were very little interfered with. The prosecution came too late, and was too little assisted by the other Cantons; it did nothing at all for the destruction of Communism, and was even favourable to it, by the great interest it produced in all countries of the German tongue. *Communism was almost unknown in Germany, but became by this an object of general attention.* [Emphasis added.][10]

As mentioned above, two developments formed the intellectual basis for all of today's leftist constructs. The first was the publication of Buonarroti's book. The second was the appearance on the world stage of the so-called Utopian Socialists, who would formally begin the Left's great quest, which continues today, for an earthly utopia.

Of course, countless individuals had used the notion of a perfect society as a literary device to call attention to the errors in the society in which they lived. These include Plato, who originated the exercise in 380 BC with the publication of *The Republic*, Sir Thomas More, whose *Utopia* was published 1516, and Sir Francis Bacon, whose *New Atlantis* came out in 1627.

The French Revolution gave rise to a new group of utopians. They were activists. No fictionalized models for them. They had an actual society in deep distress with which to work. However, too many cooks spoiled the broth, and it turned into a tragic and bloody farce. One of the participants on this adventure who deserves a mention was the justly famous economist, mathematician, and philosopher Marie Jean Atoine Nicholas de Caritat, who is known to history as the Marquis de Condorcet. His most notable contribution was a highly optimistic and learned essay entitled "Outlines of an Historical View of the Progress of the Human Mind," which posited the notion that improvements in science, agriculture, and social organization were signs that mankind was progressing toward a utopian world, and then offered a number of significant social and legal changes that would promote this process.

Unfortunately for him, his wisdom was not appreciated by Robespierre and the Jacobins, who had him imprisoned, where he committed suicide. His essay, however, eventually became widely recognized as one of the major texts of the Enlightenment. It was an inspiration for a new generation of postrevolution leftists, some of whom became known as Utopian Socialists, and others as pioneers in the Romantic movement in literature, which included such notables as William Wordsworth, Samuel Taylor Coleridge, John Keats, Lord Byron, and Percy Bysshe Shelley.

These utopian socialists were not activist revolutionaries. Their intention was to design, implement, and assume the leadership of an ideal society where everything was perfect and everyone was happy. Furthermore, they expected their blueprint to be warmly welcomed and adopted by mankind.

Two of the three most prominent figures in this crowd were the Frenchmen Claude Henri de Rouvroy, Comte de Saint-Simon and Charles Fourier. The third was the Englishman Robert Owen. Of course, each had his own special notion of what a perfect society would look like and how to achieve it. They did, however, share one fundamental characteristic with Plato and with each other; that being the need for a man or group of men who were beyond reproach, morally and intellectually, and whose lives were dedicated exclusively to society's welfare with no regard whatsoever for their own wishes or needs. Plato called these men "philosopher kings" and said this of them.

> Until philosophers are kings, or the kings and princes of this world have the spirit and power of philosophy, and political greatness and wisdom meet in one, and those commoner natures who pursue either to the exclusion of the other are compelled to stand aside, cities will never have rest from their evils—no, nor the human race, as I believe,—and then only will this our State have a possibility of life and behold the light of day.[11]

Therein lay the single most egregious flaw in Plato's dream world and in all subsequent utopian schemes. For, with the exception of Jesus Christ, no such mortal man or group of men has ever existed, and even if by some miracle, one or more were to appear and rule, there is no reason to believe that his or their successor would be similarly gifted. One thinks of Marcus Aurelius, who arguably came as close as any ruler in history to Plato's ideal, and he was followed by his son Commodus, who turned out to be one of Rome's most licentious, demented, and insane emperors.

Whether Plato was aware of this flaw is a matter of speculation. No such mystery surrounds the three heroes of this chapter, for each of them considered himself to be more than qualified to run such a society. Moreover, each sincerely believed that his outline for such a society should and would be adopted throughout the civilized world. Finally, each was convinced that the future of mankind depended upon it.

Of course, these men were nonviolent. But they were revolutionaries nevertheless, inspired by the hardships that they witnessed; Saint-Simon and Fourier as young adults during the bloody French Revolution and the even more bloody Napoleonic Wars, and Owen as a manager of a textile mill in Manchester, England, where he had been shocked by the working conditions, most especially those of the children.

All three were devoted to Rousseau's faith in the goodness of mankind, antagonistic toward Christianity, full-fledged collaborators in Voltaire's quest for a scientifically-based system of laws that would govern society in the same way that Newton's laws govern the physical world, and genuinely convinced that Plato was right about mankind's need for "philosopher kings" to keep things on the straight and narrow.

Moreover, they were extremely fanatical about mankind's need for their own genius. In fact, they were eccentric almost to the point of madness; so out of touch with the way the real world functioned then and had functioned since the dawn of history that they made Marx look as sane as Joe the Plumber. Frank and Fritzi Manuel describe a few of their idiosyncrasies as follows in their comprehensive *Utopian Thought in the Western World*.

Saint-Simon thought that he was the rein-
carnation of Socrates and Charlemagne; Fourier,
though not given to historical learning, demonstrated from Scripture that his appearance had
been foretold; Owen identified himself with
both Jesus and Columbus ... Newton was their
favorite hero and they imagined themselves
achieving for the social universe what he had
for the physical ... their findings were scientific
because they were based on "demonstrable facts"
(Owen), "positive facts" (Saint-Simon), "actual
observations" (Fourier). ... They were the omni-
scient social doctors in the immediate crisis, and
they proffered mankind a universal panacea, an
elixir that was bound to be efficacious because
it was the fruit of the inviolable laws they had
discovered.[12]

The details of the various utopian dreams of these individuals
are not important. We will focus instead on the ideas and beliefs that
drove these men and on the enormous influence they had on the Left
going forward, not only on their immediate successors, such as Marx,
Engels, and even the anarchist Pierre-Joseph Proudhon, but, many
decades later, on the foundational makeup of American's own unique
brand of leftist ideology. Relative to their influence on Marxism, we
will turn to Engels. To wit:

German theoretical Socialism will never
forget that it rests on the shoulders of Saint-
Simon, Fourier, and Owen, the three who, in
spite of their fantastic notions and Utopianism,
belonged to the most significant heads of all time
and whose genius anticipated numerous things
the correctness of which can now be proved in a
scientific way.[13]

We will begin with Saint-Simon, whom Engels likened to the German philosopher Georg Hegel as "the most encylopaedic mind of his age."[14] He was born in 1760, a high-spirited, French aristocrat who is generally credited (if that is the word) with having been the father of French socialism. According to various stories surrounding his life, he was educated by d'Alembert and was so convinced of his own importance that at the age of seventeen, he ordered his valet to wake him up every morning with the exhortation, "Get up, monsieur la comte! Remember you have great things to do!"[15]

In that same year, he joined the military and ended up a few years later fighting with Washington at the battle of Yorktown. Later, the British took him captive following the naval battle between the French and the English at St. Kitts, and after his release, he met the Viceroy of Mexico, at which time he presented him with a plan that he had dreamed up to build an interoceanic canal running through Lake Nicaragua.

He returned to France in the early days of the revolution, and touched by his experiences in America, he abdicated his titles and assumed the peasant surname Bonhomme. He stayed out of the fighting, however, and became involved in investing in the properties of the nobles who had either fled the country or been beheaded. He became quite rich. At one point during the Terror, he ended up in prison. But he kept his head. He was married for a brief period in 1801, apparently for the purpose of hosting a salon where he hoped to expand his knowledge by rubbing elbows with the local intellectuals. According to his own account, these savants "ate much but talked little." He got a divorce and traveled to Switzerland to propose marriage to Madame de Staël, whose husband had just died, saying, according to legend, "Madam, you are the most extraordinary woman on earth and I am the most extraordinary man; together we shall undoubtedly produce a still more extraordinary child."[16] She demurred.

It was during his trip to Geneva that he came up with the idea for the formation of a Council of Newton, which would be made up of three mathematicians, three physicists, three chemists, three physiologists, three littérateurs, three painters, and three musicians.

These men would be elected by the whole of mankind, and presided over by the mathematician who received the largest number of votes. Collectively they would be God's representative on earth, replacing the pope, the cardinals, the bishops, and the priests who had proven themselves incapable of this task by their ignorance of science. Lest you wonder where he came up with this idea, he said he received it directly from God.[17] Not surprisingly, the paper received almost no attention.

Soon after returning to France, he ran into trouble with his partner in the real estate business and lost all his money. It was at then that he began the work for which he is famous, although to say that he had a rough start would be understating matters considerably. Not only was he flat broke but he was neither physically nor mentally well. In fact, at one point he ended up in a private hospital for the insane. The Manuels describe his actions during this period as follows:

> Curious scientific intuitions pour forth in an outburst of disorganized tracts … Cut to the quick [by the fact that no one took him seriously] his letters became a series of wild ravings about genius, his mission, and the persecutions he endured from his enemies. Interspersed among the psychopathic tirades there were moving passages about his passion for glory, written in the grand romantic manner. A family genealogy traced the Saint-Simons back to Charlemagne, and on more than one occasion his great ancestor appeared to him in a vision.[18]

He recovered his health and some of his sanity during the Restoration and gained a modicum of respect by writing political brochures defending the emerging bourgeoisie against those who wished to restore the *ancien régime*. But as the Manuels put it, he "could not long rest content with this limited role as a moderately successful propagandist for the bourgeois."[19]

So he went back to work on a tortured plan to reorder society around a new religion of science. This project underwent so many changes over time that is not unusual to find differing outlines in the literature, each of which is representative of a particular period. Basically, he was fond of dividing people into categories such as scientists, engineers, entrepreneurs, industrialists, artists (poets, writers, painters, musicians), savants, and spiritual advisors and then assigning each a narrow and highly specialized role in society. This arrangement would be highly efficient, but, more importantly, it would end strife. He put it this way:

> Since under this "industrial system" each man would be fulfilling his natural capacity to the utmost, there would be no misfits and no class conflicts. Each "capacity" would labor in its respective branch and would evince no desire to encroach upon the providence of another. Perfect harmony would prevail, the power of the state would disappear, and men would be directed to the exploitation of nature instead of exercising dominion over one another.[20]

His work on this scheme went on for a long time and resulted in numerous pamphlets, papers, and books. He suffered from ill health, poverty, and disappointments, and became deeply discouraged and bungled an attempt to commit suicide by shooting himself *a la tête*, so to speak. He lived for two more years, asking bewilderedly, "Can you explain to me how a man with seven balls of buckshot in his head can go on living and thinking?"[21]

At this point, his writings took on a spiritual element, which resulted in the development of a "New Christianity." This "religion" was founded on three beliefs. The first was that while atheism was fine for the elites, society needed some exoteric religious doctrine to instill order. The second was that Christianity had it all wrong. The third was that God had designated him as a new prophet to set it straight. The great Austrian economists Friedrich Hayek explains the latter two beliefs as follows:

> Since the great schism at the time of the Reformation, he argues, none of the Christian churches represents true Christianity. They have all neglected the fundamental precept that men should behave as brothers towards each other. The main object of true Christianity must be "the speediest improvement of the moral and the physical existence of the poorest class" ... Since the churches have made no use of their opportunity to improve the lot of the poor by the teaching and encouragement of the arts and the organisation of industry, the Lord is now addressing the people and the princes through His new prophet. He undertakes to reconstruct theology, which from time to time needs to be renewed, just as physics, chemistry, and physiology must be periodically rewritten. The new theology will pay more attention to the terrestrial interests of man. All that is required is an organisation of industry that will assure a great amount of work of the kind which will secure the quickest advance of human intelligence. You can create such conditions; now that the extent of our planet is known, let the scholars, the artists, and the industrialists draw up a general plan of the works which must be carried out in order that the terrestrial possessions of the human race be put to the most productive use and made the most agreeable to inhabit in all respects.[22]

Now, if you are wondering if Saint-Simon achieved any sort of fame during his lifetime, the answer is no. For the most part, he was a subject of ridicule. In fact, even the great German poet and social critic, Heinrich Heine, who was an admirer of Saint-Simon, largely because he included scholars and artists in his ruling hierarchy, could not resist a gentle mocking of the man. He once observed that the only possible miracle that Saint-Simon's "newest religion" produced was the cash payment of a tailor's bill by his followers ten years after his death. "Young grocers were taken aback at such evidence of the supernatural," Heine said, adding that, "The tailors immediately began to have faith."[23]

So, why, you might ask, does anyone care about him today? To which we would simply say that as the widely acknowledged "father of French socialism," Saint-Simon was the first person to assemble, codify, and thus provide a justification of sorts for most if not all of the myriad errors and asininities that are central to all leftist ideologies today. Engels put it this way: "In Saint-Simon we find a comprehensive breadth of view, by virtue of which almost all the ideas of later Socialists that are not strictly economic are found in him in embryo."[24]

These include, but are not limited to, the terrible misunderstandings about human nature that stem from the Left's adoption of Rousseau's theory of the noble savage; the overwhelming trust that the Left places on the value of "experts" and "technocrats" to the smooth functioning of society; the leftist belief that too much liberty and freedom of the individual could hamper the good works and fine intentions of these elites; and, finally, the conviction that the leftist enterprise is the natural outcome of historical progress toward a time of permanent peace, prosperity, and happiness, an idea that Marx later mingled with Hegel's similar contention and made the centerpiece of Marxism.

Finally, Saint-Simon was the muse of Auguste Comte, who was the founder of something called Positivism, which the great moral philosopher Alasdair MacIntyre describes as one of "two major attempts in our post-Christian era to create an entirely secular view of the world,"[25] the other one being Marxism. Of course, Positivism didn't catch on as well as Marxism. But it had a significant influence on the formation of numerous other leftists ideologies including

English Fabianism, American Progressivism, and, Charles Maurras's nascent fascism, all of which we will discuss in later chapters.

Next, we turn to François Marie Charles Fourier, who was certainly one of the most eccentric of all the eccentric characters in the entire history of the Left. This from the Manuels:

> Fourier the bachelor lived alone in a garret and ate *table d'hôte* in the poorer Lyons restaurants ... he talked to himself, worked in fits of excitement, could go without sleep for a week, was incapable of concentrating on any one job for long ... his habits were meticulous, his manner frigid. ... He could be a great hater, violently suspicious, and he showed mild symptoms of paranoia ... he was constantly collecting, counting, cataloguing, and analyzing ... he had a mania for measuring things with a yardstick cane ... there were no heroic actions, no grand love affairs, perhaps no amorous relationships at all. Once he perceived that civilization was corroded with vice, [he] retired into his private world and to remain pure held himself aloof from society ... he felt infinite pity for mankind, was acutely sensitive to the suffering of the hungry and to the monotony of their lives.[26]

Relative to this latter point, Beecher and Bienvenu explain in *The Utopian Vision of Charles Fourier* that the philosopher had a special "solicitude for the elderly, the poor, the 'perverts,' for all of those to whom civilization denied sexual gratification." This, they say, "led him to create a variety of 'philanthropic' corporations composed of erotic saints and saintesses, heroes and heroines who would provide erotic gratification for the less appealing members of the community ... Thus everyone would undergo periodic interviews in order to ascertain his libidinal needs of the moment. These interviews would be conducted by ... matrons, fairies, and fakirs. Thus [his utopian society] Harmony would provide employment, prestige, and a rich sexual life for one of the classes most oppressed by civilization—the elderly."[27]

Naturally then, Fourier was very much an original thinker. Indeed, he had nothing but contempt for all previous theories associated with morals and philosophy. The Manuels explained his views thusly: "Libraries of tomes by pompous and sententious thinkers had not brought man one inch closer to happiness."[28] Fourier himself put it this way.

> After the philosophers had demonstrated their incapacity in their experimental venture, in the French Revolution, everyone agreed in regarding their science as an aberration of the human mind; their floods of political and moral enlightenment seemed to be nothing more than floods of illusions. Well! what else can be found in the writings of these savants who, after having perfected their theories for twenty-five centuries, after having accumulated all the wisdom of the ancients and moderns, begin by engendering calamities as numerous as the benefits which they promised, and help push civilised society back toward the state of barbarism? Such was the consequence of the first five years during which the philosophical theories were inflicted on France ... illusions were dissipated, the political and moral sciences were irretrievably blighted and discredited. From that point on people should have understood that there was no happiness to be found in acquired learning, that social welfare had to be sought in some new science, and that new paths had to be opened to political genius. It was evident that neither the philosophers nor their rivals possessed a remedy for the social distresses, and that their dogmas only served to per-

petuate the most disgraceful calamities, among others poverty.[29]

His understanding of mankind and its foibles came from his personal observations as a traveling salesman. Again, we go to the Manuels.

> As a traveling salesman he had observed men in all ranks of society ... these people showed him what men and women really longed for and what they loathed. ... Of the scabrous side of family life he learned in the coaches of the commercial travelers and from his openly promiscuous nieces. Of the cheats of commercial civilization he was amply informed in the business houses where he worked long hours. His understanding of industrial relations came from inside the shops of Lyons, not from treatises on political economy. "I am a child of the market-place, born and brought up in mercantile establishments ... I have witnessed the infamies of commerce with my own eyes, and I shall not describe them from hearsay as our moralists do."[30]

His theory for the creation of a utopia was truly unique. Simply stated, he believed that people should follow their passions. God gave them these desires, and ever since, the philosophers and religious leaders have told men to suppress them. This was unnatural. God would not have given us these passions if they were bad. The trick was to harmonize them.

> People have regarded the passions as enemies of concord and have written thousands of volumes against them. These volumes are going to fall into nothingness. For the passions tend only to concord, to that social unity which we

have thought was so alien to them. But the passions can only be harmonised if they are allowed to develop in an orderly fashion within the progressive series or series of groups. Outside of this mechanism the passions are only unchained tigers, incomprehensible enigmas. For this reason the philosophers have claimed that they must be repressed. Their opinion is doubly absurd since the passions cannot be repressed and since, if they could, civilisation would rapidly disappear and man would rapidly fall back into a nomadic state in which the passions would be even more harmful than they are now. I have no more faith in the virtues of the shepherds than in those of their apologists.[31]

What about murder and robbery? The Manuels explain.

Here again Fourier stuck by his contention that in and of themselves there were no evil passions; there were only corrupted developments of originally salutary passions, for in the perfect harmony of God's creation there were no qualities which did not serve a purpose.

They quote Fourier himself as follows:

Thus ferocity, the spirit of conquest, robbery, concupiscence, and many other unsavory passions are not vicious in the seed; only in growth are they rendered vicious by the civilization that poisons the mainsprings of the passions, which were all considered useful by God, who created none of them without assigning to it a place and purposes in the vast harmonious mechanism. As soon as we wish to suppress a single passion we are engaged in an act of insurrection against God. By that very act we accuse Him of stupidity in having created it.[32]

Simply stated then, Fourier wished to create small utopian communities called Phalanxes in which everyone was happy doing just what he or she wanted to do. He believed that under such a system, everything that needed to be done would get done, naturally and cheerfully. Beecher and Bienvenu provide the following example of how this would work.

> Still enthralled by a work ethic which viewed even creative activity as painful, socialists looked for moral equivalents to capitalism's incentives. Fourier did not make such a search because he believed that most socially necessary work was attractive in itself, unless, of course, it had been perverted and made loathsome by civilization. ...
>
> Fourier's ultimate solution to the problem of thoroughly repugnant work can be found in his description of "The Little Hordes;" that bizarre organization which is perhaps the most widely known of Harmony's institutions. The Little Hordes were designed to put the passions, energy, and inclinations of children to good use. Fourier maintained that fully two-thirds of all sub-adolescent boys between the ages of nine and fifteen were attracted to filth. They loved to wallow in mud and "play with filthy things." Such children were "unruly, peevish, scurrilous and overbearing." Course in speech and noisy, they were willing to brave bad weather and danger "simply for the pleasure of wreaking havoc." In Harmony these hitherto insupportable habits would be put to use by enrolling the children in Little Hordes, which would perform any kind

of work that might degrade a group of workers. Highly honored and given first place among the Phalanx's corporations, the Little Hordes would be allotted "foul functions," such as maintaining the sewers, caring for the dunghill, and cleaning the slaughterhouses.[33]

Fourier published his first book, *Theory of the Four Movements and the General Destinies*, in 1808. He spent the next thirty years repeating the same message, issuing amplifications, abridgments, and summaries. The Manuels note that Fourier was "convinced of the imminent acceptance of his projects for the transformation of mankind. If France could waste blood and treasure on the false systems of the Revolution and the Empire, why should it not invest the paltry funds necessary for the implementation of the true one?"[34]

In pursuit of this conceit, he made it known that he would be home every day at noon to discuss his ideas and projects with anyone who wished to finance them. Each day then, for ten years, he dressed for the occasion and waited. And no one ever appeared.

Again, why do we care? Well, because Fourier had a significant impact on the Left going forward both in Europe and in the United States. No one bought the entire package, of course. However, with a bow to the warning that tracing the roots of ideas is a highly inexact science, we would still note that Fourier's successors heavily mined his observations about the importance of the passions as well as his concept of creating ethical and moral communities.

Marx and Engels were especially interested in Fourier's blanket criticism of Western "civilization" and his contention that it had to be completely changed—not reformed but *changed*. More specifically, Marx welcomed the introduction of the human side of politics and economics into the debate over socialism and communism, which he felt had become mired in arguments over abstractions that were of little or no interest to the working stiff and hardly the source material for political action.

Marx also shared Fourier's view that the division of labor and other changes in the nature of work brought on by industrialization had both diminished the value of labor and made it even more oppressive than in the past. Thus, Fourier's notion of reorganizing "work" in such as a way as to make it attractive and liberating intrigued him. Engels said that Fourier was "at his greatest" when he observed that "civilization moves 'in a vicious circle,' in contradictions which it constantly reproduces without being able to solve them; hence it constantly arrives at the very opposite to that which it wants to attain, or pretends to want to attain, so that, e.g., 'under civilization poverty is born of superabundance itself.'"[35] Engels was also attracted to Fourier's discussion of harmonizing production and consumption as well as his indictment against the middleman, who engaged in schemes to create scarcity and panics in the marketplace.

Fourier's plans to establish Phalanxes was brought to America by Albert Brisbane, a precocious lad from Batavia, New York, whose wealthy parents sent him to Europe at the age of eighteen to study philosophy. He stayed in Berlin for four years, where he became a Saint-Simonian. Eventually, he became disenchanted with the movement and, shortly after he discovered Fourier's work, moved to Paris and spent two years studying Fourierism, partly under the guidance of the master himself. In 1834, he returned to the United States where he quietly promoted Fourierism until 1840 when he went public by publishing a concise exposition of Fourier's system in a book entitled *Social Destiny of Man*. Then things got interesting. The well-known historian of socialism in America, Morris Hillquit, tells the story as follows:

> [Brisbane] engaged Park Benjamin to look over the proof-sheets of *Social Destiny of Man*, he being a practical journalist of wide experience. Talking over the subject together one day, and of the probable effect of the book on the public, he suddenly exclaimed: "There is Horace Greeley, just damned fool enough to believe such nonsense." "Who is Greeley?" I asked. "Oh, he is a young man up-stairs editing the *New Yorker*." "I took my book under my arm and off I went to

Greeley. As I entered his room I said, 'Is this Mr. Greeley?'" "Yes." "I have a book here I would like you to read." "I don't know that I can now," he replied; "I am very busy." "I wish you would," I urged; "if you will, I will leave it." "Well," he said, "I am going to Boston to-night, and I'll take it along; perhaps I'll find time." Greeley took the book with him and read it, and when he came back he was an enthusiastic believer in Industrial Association.

The importance of the new acquisition for the cause of Fourierism in this country soon became manifest. Two years after the episode narrated, when the *Tribune*, founded in the meantime by Greeley, had become a popular and influential metropolitan newspaper, with a daily circulation exceeding 20,000, which was very large for that time, its editor opened the columns of the paper to the teachings of Brisbane.[36]

By 1843, there were thirty Phalanxes scattered across the United States, none of which lasted very long. Yet the socialist seed was planted in American soil. And it was destined to grow.

Finally, we come to Robert Owen, who was unquestionably the big enchilada among the utopian socialists. He was smart, successful, rich, bursting with enthusiasm, energy, and ideas. He was a genuine innovator, a visionary, the first among a new breed of industrialists who came to recognize that human capital is a valuable asset that society could use to produce a better return if it did so justly and with compassion. Engels heaped praise on him.

At this juncture, there came forward as a reformer a manufacturer 29-years-old—a man of almost sublime, childlike simplicity of character, and at the same time one of the few born leaders of men. ... In the industrial revolution most of his class saw only chaos and confusion, and the opportunity of fishing in these troubled waters and making large fortunes quickly. He saw in it the opportunity of putting into practice his favorite theory, and so of bringing order out of chaos. He had already tried it with success, as superintendent of more than 500 men in a Manchester factory. From 1800 to 1829, he directed the great cotton mill at New Lanark, in Scotland, as managing partner, along the same lines, but with greater freedom of action and with a success that made him a European reputation. A population, originally consisting of the most diverse and, for the most part, very demoralized elements, a population that gradually grew to 2,500, he turned into a model colony, in which drunkenness, police, magistrates, lawsuits, poor laws, charity, were unknown. And all this simply by placing the people in conditions worthy of human beings, and especially by carefully bringing up the rising generation. He was the founder of infant schools, and introduced them first at New Lanark. At the age of two, the children came to school, where they enjoyed themselves so much that they could scarcely be got home again. Whilst his competitors worked their people 13 or 14 hours a day, in New Lanark the working-day was only 10 and a half hours. When a crisis in cotton stopped work for four months, his workers received their full wages all the time. And with all this the business more than doubled in value, and to the last yielded large profits to its proprietors.[37]

He was also highly eccentric. Crane Brinton opens his discussion of Owen in the previously mentioned *English Political Thought in the 19th Century* with the following sentence: "Not the least of the

115

puzzles which this world presents to the purely speculative mind is the occasional combination in one person of the successful man of affairs and the crank."[38]

Simply stated, Owen was, like Saint-Simon and Fourier, a dreamer with an extremely poor understanding of the limits of social engineering. He agreed with Rousseau's contention that evil was introduced by the environment in which the person grew up and lived. As such, he felt that men were not morally responsible for their actions. They were, instead, victims of harmful social tenets and religious beliefs. The cure for evil was to change society from the ground up.

His intention was to accomplish this by collectivist means, weighted heavily in favor legislative action. The details of the utopia he envisioned were exceedingly mundane. Society would control everything from wages to levels of production. Production would be limited to only what was essential. There would be no lawyers, soldiers, priests, landlords, or rentiers. The number of merchants would be drastically limited. Then, of course, there was a need for an entirely new religion. The children would be taught this, and would subsequently grow up with no evil tendencies. Owen himself would be the top pooh-bah of the church. He explained it this way.

> To oppose myself to all the most inveterate and hitherto unconquerable prejudices with which the human intellect has been afflicted could not have been a premature and hasty measure on my part. I long knew that to deliver from abject slavery of intellect, from the grossest ignorance, from the vilest passions, from crime, from poverty, and from every species of wretchedness,—I must for a time offend all mankind, and create in many feelings of disgust and horror at this apparent temerity of conduct, which without a new understanding, a new heart, and a new mind, they could never comprehend; but these in due time shall now be given to them. Ere

long there shall be but one action, one language, and one people. Even now the time in near at hand—almost arrived—when swords shall be turned into plowshares, and spears into pruning hooks—when every man shall sit under his own vine and his own fig tree, and none shall make him afraid.

Yes, on this day, the most glorious the world has seen, THE RELIGION OF CHARITY, UNCONNECTED WITH FAITH (caps in original) is established forever. *Mental liberty for man is secured; and hereafter he will become a reasonably and consequently a superior being.* (Italics in original).[39] (Emphasis in original)

Unlike Marx, who would later claim in the "Rules" for the "First International" that the "emancipation of the working classes must be conquered by the working classes themselves," Owen argued that the creation of a utopian society "must and will be accomplished by the rich and powerful." Presaging the "big brother," elitist socialism of future liberal American icons, Franklin Roosevelt and Lyndon Johnson, Owen claimed that it is "a waste of time, talent and pecuniary means" for the poor to attempt this feat. The aim of his socialism, he bluntly noted, is "to govern or treat all society as the most advanced physicians govern and treat their patients in the best arranged lunatic hospitals," with "forbearance and kindness."[40]

Owen's first utopian community was similar to Fourier's Phalanx, but without the Theory of Passionate Attractions. The idea did not catch on. In the early 1820s, he decided to establish a community in Indiana called New Harmony. It was the first and most famous of some sixteen Owenite communities that appeared in the US between 1825 and 1829. None, however, lasted more than a few years as full-fledged socialist communities. New Harmony collapsed when one of Owen's American business partners ran off with all profits. Owen then returned to England, where his attacks on religion, marriage, and traditional society had taken a toll on his celebrity. As for his legacy, Engels had this to say.

> His advance in the direction of Communism was the turning-point in Owen's life. As long as he was simply a philanthropist, he was rewarded with nothing but wealth, applause, honor, and glory. He was the most popular man in Europe. Not only men of his own class, but statesmen and princes listened to him approvingly. But when he came out with his Communist theories that was quite another thing. ...
>
> He knew what confronted him if he attacked these—outlawry, excommunication from official society, the loss of his whole social position. But nothing of this prevented him from attacking them without fear of consequences, and what he had foreseen happened. Banished from official society, with a conspiracy of silence against him in the press, ruined by his unsuccessful Communist experiments in America, in which he sacrificed all his fortune, he turned directly to the working-class and continued working in their midst for 30 years. Every social movement, every real advance in England on behalf of the workers links itself on to the name of Robert Owen. He forced through in 1819, after five years' fighting, the first law limiting the hours of labor of women and children in factories. He was president of the first Congress at which all the Trade Unions of England united in a single great trade association. He introduced as transition measures to the complete communistic organization of society, on the one hand, cooperative societies for retail trade and production. These have since that time, at

least, given practical proof that the merchant and
the manufacturer are socially quite unnecessary.[41]

At this point, we need to note that the Utopian Socialists were
closely allied with the Romantic Movement in literature that swept
through Europe in the opening days of the nineteenth century. Our
interest in the individuals involved in this movement is limited, but
no history of the Left can overlook the great poet Shelley, whose rantings against religion, capitalism, family values, and marriage, resulted
in his expulsion from Oxford and arguably had a greater impact on
English society than that of his father-in-law and mentor, William
Godwin. Indeed, Shelley and his contemporary poet Lord Byron
became early poster boys for a long line of tedious, sanctimonious,
sybaritic, atheistic children of privilege who have since become one
of the most familiar features on the leftist landscape, reflective not so
much of the time in which they live, but the spiritual rot that their
Godlessness inflicts upon them.

They and others in the Romantic Movement created a humanistic, leftist alternative for those who couldn't take the deeply atheistic
and nihilistic versions of leftist ideology undiluted. Brinton described
this movement as "modern socialism," and said this about it.

> All the elements of the old eighteenth-cen-
> tury creed are thus to be found in these modern
> exponents of Shelley—the natural goodness of
> man, his corruption by civilization ("culture"),
> the domination of man's affective instincts
> ("love") over reason in all its forms, social and
> individual, the leadership of the divinely inspired
> poet-legislator, who is a leader precisely because
> the expansive energies of his emotions are not
> checked by fear of social consequences.
>
> Modern socialism, like any great movement
> for reform, rests on a gospel, which can command
> the hearts as well as the head of its followers. It
> must contain an element of mysticism; that is,

it must provide itself with a superhuman justification, with a common something from which each individual believer can draw strength. There can be no doubt that socialism, for most of the faithful, at least, rests at bottom on the dogma of the natural goodness of man ... But what is most natural is also most divine, and therefore the struggling proletarian finds in his own craving the high justification of faith. Socialism has a hold on men precisely because through it self-interest is made socially operative in the only way possible—as a mystic attachment to a corporate reality which has a sanctity not conferred upon it by the mere fact of association, but by the nature of things, by divinity. ...

He [Shelley] took over from Godwin the anarchical principles that must logically follow the assumption that all men are potentially capable of guiding their actions in accordance with a perfect, rational justice. Into these principles he breathed an emotion which transformed them from a speculation into a faith. ...

He shared to the full the acquisitive spirit of the "[French] Revolution. "The vital truth Shelley everywhere enforced," wrote [the English philosopher] George Henry Lewes in 1841, "although treated as a chimaera by most of his contemporaries, and indulged as a dream by some others, has become the dominant Idea—the philosophy and faith of this age, throughout Europe. It is progression, humanity, perfectibility, civilization, democracy—call it what you will, this is the truth uttered unceasingly by Shelley, and universally received by us." ...

Stanley, of African fame, once told a member of the Shelley Society ... "You are a funny people, you Shelleyites: You are playing—at a safe distance yourselves may be—with fire. In spreading Shelley you are indirectly helping to stir up the great Socialist question—the great question of the needs and wants and wishes of unhappy men, the one question which bids fair to swamp you all for a bit." ... For he is one of the accredited poets of Socialism. ...

Shelley ... is one of the poets of the men who are seeking to carry out the humanitarian principles of the democratic revolution to their logical conclusion, and achieve a proletarian revolution. His faith in the natural goodness of man has persisted as a social faith through all the trials of science and experience; his belief in the coming miracle of a bloodless revolution, divinely guided by that divinity which is in common men, has been strengthened by the influence of writers like Marx. ...

Marx said: "The real difference between Byron and Shelley is this: those who understand them and love them rejoice that Byron died at thirty-six, because if he had lived he would have become a reactionary bourgeois; they grieve that Shelley died at twenty- nine, because he was essentially a revolutionist and he would always have been one of the advanced guard of socialism."[42]

And so, in keeping with Godwin's intellectual guidance, Shelley used his great gift to attack the accumulation of capital, the economic benefits of specialization in the production process, the importance and stability of the family, the concept of free will, and the institution of marriage, all in the name of his own overweening "compassion" and moral certainty. The following drivel from his "Notes" to his utopian allegory Queen Mab could be mistaken today, two centuries after they were written, for an excerpt from a keynote address at a Democratic national convention.[6]

> There is no real wealth but the labour of man. Were the mountains of gold and the valleys of silver, the world would not be one grain of corn the richer; no one comfort would be added to the human race ... wealth is a power usurped by the few, to compel the many to labour for their benefit. The laws which support this system derive their force from the ignorance and credulity of its victims: they are the result of a conspiracy of the few against the many, who are themselves obliged to purchase this pre-eminence by the loss of all real comfort ... Love is free: to promise for ever to love the same woman is not less absurd than to promise to believe the same creed ... It is a calculation of this admirable author [Godwin], that all the conveniences of civilized life might be produced, if society would divide the labour equally among its members, by each individual being employed in labour two hours during the day ... A husband and wife ought to continue so long united as they love each other: any law which should bind them to cohabitation for one moment after the decay of their affection would be a most intolerable tyranny. ... Every human being is irresistibly impelled to act as he does act: in the eternity which preceded his birth a chain of causes was generated, which, operating under the name of motives, make it impossible that any thought of his mind, or any action of his life, should be otherwise than it is.[43]

Finally, as with all of today's leftists, Shelley blamed both society's ills and his own shortcomings on religion. "I brought my daughter RELIGION, on earth, She smother'd Reason's babes in their birth."[44]

In the final analysis, while the utopian ideas of these men and the communities that sprung up in their name disappeared into the mists of history, their muddled dreams lived on and formed the premise upon which American liberalism would build its temple to a false god and await the coming of the secular rapture.

On a lighter note, they and their ilk can most probably be credited with being the inspiration behind one of the great novelist Anatole France's finest and wisest observations. To wit: "When you wish to make men good and wise, free, temperate, and generous, you are of necessity led to the desire to kill them all. Robespierre believed in virtue, he produced the Reign of Terror: Marat believed in justice, he demanded two hundred thousand heads."[45]

Let's let the poets in on the fun.

Excerpts from "Queen Mab":

> How sweet a scene will earth become!
> Of purest spirits, a pure dwelling-place,
> Symphonious with the planetary spheres,
> When man, with changeless nature coalescing,
> Will undertake regeneration's work,
> When its ungenial poles no longer point …
> But hoary-headed selfishness has felt
> Its death-blow, and is tottering to the grave :
> A brighter morn awaits the human day,
> When every transfer of earth's natural gifts
> Shall be a commerce of good words and works
> When poverty and wealth, the thirst of fame,
> The fear of infamy, disease, and woe,
> War with its million horrors, and fierce hell
> Shall live but in the memory of Time,
> Who, like a penitent libertine, shall start,
> Look back, and shudder at his younger years.
> Percy Bysshe Shelley, 1813

Chapter 5

Kant, Hegel, Marx, Marxism

> *In my opinion it is quite impossible that this dialectical hocus-pocus constituted the ground and source of Marx's own convictions. It would have been impossible for a thinker such as he was (and I look upon him as an intellectual force of the very highest order) to have followed such tortuous and unnatural methods had he been engaged, with a free and open mind, in really investigating the actual connections of things, and in forming his own conclusions with regard to them; it would have been impossible for him to fall successively by mere accident into all the errors of thought and method which I have described, and to arrive at the conclusion that labor is the sole source of value as the natural outgrowth, not the desired and predetermined result, of such a mode of inquiry.*
>
> *I think the case was really different. That Marx was truly and honestly convinced of the truth of his thesis I do not doubt. But the grounds of his conviction are not those which he gives in his system. They were in reality opinions rather than thought out conclusions.*[48] (Eugene Bohm-Bawerk, *Karl Marx and the Close of His System*, 1896)

W e will begin the discussion of the birth of Marxism in 1770 in a small house on a quiet street in Königsberg, Prussia, where there lives a forty-six-year-old professor of philosophy named Immanuel Kant. He is a short, frail, quiet, lifelong bachelor of Scottish descent. He has been teaching for twenty years at the local university, where he had also done his undergraduate study. He is a popular professor and author of numerous well-received books.

As a philosopher, he considers himself to be a *selbstdenker*, an independent thinker rather than an adherent to any particular school of thought. Two years earlier in a letter to his former student Johann Herder, he had expressed his ideological impartiality by describing himself as being "not attached to anything" and as having a "deep indifference" to either his own opinion or any others on the matters of truth.[1]

On this particular day, he is contemplating the Scottish philosopher David Hume's claim that reason cannot be used to conclude that a specific action will result in a specific cause. Now to a mind not trained in the arcana of philosophy, this "suggestion," as Kant calls it, might not seem that electrifying. Yet it was the foundation upon which Hume had built his famous *Treatise on Human Nature* in which, as we mentioned in a previous chapter, he had challenged the existence of God. Kant would describe it later as having "first interrupted my dogmatic slumber, and gave my investigations in the field of speculative philosophy quite a new direction."[2]

This new direction takes the form of an eleven-year-long period of self-imposed, partial isolation during which Kant writes his own famous book entitled *Critique of Pure Reason*, which earns him the distinction of being recognized as one of the most important European philosophers of all time. From our narrow perspective here, it also earns him the dubious honor of being the father of the nihilism that would sweep across Europe in the nineteenth century, leaving in its wake a plethora of new philosophical theories, including those of Hegel, which will become the basis on which Karl Marx would construct Marxism.

Our interest in the details of Kant's *Critique* is limited to his views on God and religion. Briefly stated, he agrees with Hume's claim that "reason" cannot prove the existence of God. However, he disagrees with Hume's claim that experience is the sole basis on which one can make judgments. Kant famously claims that man has an *a priori*, transcendental knowledge that is independent of sense experience, and this, he says, creates a "moral sense." He famously describes this as a "categorical imperative" that requires men to "act as if the maximum of our action were to become by our will a universal law of nature."

The bottom line is that Kant does not give up on the idea of God. He gives up on the validity of all ontological proofs of His existence and proposes an alternative, practical reason for belief in God. This is based on his contention that the "highest good is capable of being realized in the world only if there exists a supreme cause of nature whose causality is in harmony with the moral character of the agent." With this in mind, he *postulates* the existence of God as follows:

> There is therefore *implied*, in the idea of the highest good, a being who is the supreme cause of nature; and who is the cause or author of nature through his intelligence and will, that is God. If, therefore, we are entitled to *postulate* the highest derivative good, or the best world, we must also *postulate* the actual existence of the highest original good, that is, the existence of God. Now, it is our duty to promote the highest good, and hence it is not only allowable but it is necessarily bound up with the very idea of duty that we should *presuppose* the possibility of this highest good. And as this possibility can be established only under condition that God exists, the presupposition of the highest good is inseparably connected with duty, or, in other words, it is *morally necessary* to hold the existence of God." [Emphasis added][3]

This is pure naval gazing, of course. In an essay written in 1833, when the dire consequences of Kant's attack on God were becoming evident, Heine would describe Kant's strange, backhanded support for the existence of God this way:

> Up to this point Immanuel Kant presents the picture of the relentless philosopher; he stormed heaven, put the whole garrison to the sword, the sovereign of the world swam unproven in his own blood, there was now no all-merciful-ness, no paternal kindness, no reward in the other world for renunciation in this, the immortality of the soul lay in its last throes—you could hear its groans and death rattle; and old Lampe [Kant's manservant] stood there, a mournful spectator, his umbrella under his arm, cold sweat and tears pouring from his face.
>
> Then Immanuel Kant relented and showed that he was not simply a great philosopher but also a good man, and he deliberated and said, half good naturedly and half ironically, "old Lampe must have a God otherwise the poor fellow can never be happy. But, man ought to be happy in this world—practical reason says so—that's certainly all right with me then let practical reason also guarantee the existence of God."[4]

At this point, Heine would ask rhetorically whether Kant "undertook this resurrection, not simply for old Lampe's sake, but also because of the police?"[5] After which he contrasted Kant unfavorably to none other than Robespierre, charging that the former had far surpassed the latter "in terrorism," since Kant's book was the "sword with which deism was executed in Germany," while all Robespierre did was "kill a king."[6]

Now we have no opinion on this comparison. Either way, Kant's feeble defense of God satisfies neither the censors nor the members of the religious community who quickly come to despise him. Indeed, it is said that priests had begun naming their dogs Kant.[7] What we do know is that by opening up this new path of inquiry into the unknown and unknowable, Kant starts a firestorm within the philosophical and religious communities. In fact, the reaction from the government to Kant's work is particularly intense. In early October 1794, Prussian king Frederick William II presents Kant with an Order in Council saying this:

> Our most high person has for a long time observed with great displease how you misuse your philosophy to undermine and debase many of the most important and fundamental doctrines of the Holy Scriptures and Christianity ... We demand of you immediately a most conscientious answer and expect that in the future, towards the avoidance of our highest disfavor, you shall give no such cause for offense, but rather in accordance with your duty, employ your talents and authority so that our Paternal Purpose may be more and more attained. If you continue to resist you may certainly expect unpleasant consequences to yourself.[8]

This order is too little too late. Kant's place in history is already firmly established. Heine noted that any future proof of God's existence is now impossible, that Kant's book should carry Dante's warning above the gates to hell: "Leave hope behind."[9] Kant complies with the order, but as Heine notes, "Germany had been drawn onto the path of philosophy and philosophy became a national cause. A sizable troop of great thinkers suddenly emerge from German soil as if conjured up by magic."[10] The most important of these are Johann Gottlieb Fichte and Hegel.

A comprehensive account of Fichte's contribution to Kantianism is far beyond the interests of our narrative. Suffice it to say, he takes Kant's measured skepticism a step further in a 1798 essay entitled

"On the Basis of Our Belief in a Divine Governance of the World."
Among other things, he raises the specter of pantheism, which differs
from deism in that it envisions a god who inhabits the world of men
as did the ancient German Gods of the Forest rather than existing
in a remote and unknowable place like the God of the deists. This
results in his expulsion from his professorship at Jena, on grounds
that he is an atheist. In defense of his work, he notes that he has never
denied God's existence, but has simply portrayed Him differently
from the orthodox understanding of God. He puts it this way.

> *The moral world itself is God*, and we require
> no other *God*. Indeed, *they* and *I* and *all of us* are
> members who constitute this moral world, and
> our relationship to one another (for the moment,
> anyway, it may remain undecided whether this
> relationship is present without our having to
> do anything, or whether it has to be produced
> through our morality) is the *order* of this world.
> We ourselves, therefore, either are or daily make
> God, and nothing similar to a God remains any-
> where—nothing except we ourselves." [Emphasis
> in original][11]

In any case, Heine claims that just as the French Revolution and
the chaos caused by the Napoleon wars eliminated God in France,
Kant and Fichte accomplish this same purpose in Germany. Indeed,
Heine would compare Kant to the French Revolution and Fichte to
Napoleon, the first causing the "terrorist work of destruction" and
the second representing the "great inexorable Ego in which thought
and action are one."[12]

When considering Kant's skepticism and Fichte's pantheism, it
is important to understand that by undermining the Christian belief
in a loving, omnipresent, and omnibenevolent god, they are not simply engaging in an innocent debate over the nature of the creator.
They are threatening the entire social order of Prussia: its laws, which
are based unapologetically on the Decalogue as given directly by God

to Moses on Mount Sinai; its government, which is headed by a King who rules by divine right; its moral system, which is based on the principles outlined in the New and Old Testaments; and virtually all of the shared traditions, customs, mores, and myths that make a nation a nation rather than simply a group of people who share a piece of ground.

Moreover, they are making this threat at a time when the largest and most powerful country in Europe is in the midst of a bloody revolution against the Church, the monarchy, and the aristocracy, which has already resulted in the beheading of that nation's king and queen and the execution of hundreds of priests and members of the aristocracy. Indeed, Frederick William II's Order in Council is delivered to Kant almost exactly one year to the day after Marie Antoinette had been beheaded. A few years later, at the time of Fichte's dismissal, France is in social and financial chaos under the control of the deeply corrupt and inept Directory.

Of course, at this point, God still has numerous defenders, one of whom is the highly influential cultural Christian apologist and critic of the Enlightenment Friedrich Heinrich Jacobi, who writes a famous open letter to Fichte charging that by reducing God to nothing more than a creation of the human imagination, he was committing the "most horrible or horrors." Then he uses the then little-known term "nihilism" (some say he coined the word) to describe the end point of Fichte's muddled view of God. "Truly, my dear Fichte, it should not grieve me, if you, or whoever it might be, want to call chimerism what I oppose to idealism, which I reproach as nihilism." Finally, then, he put forth his own view of God. To wit:

> Man has this choice and this alone: nothing or God. Choosing nothing he makes himself God; that means he makes God an apparition, for it is impossible, if there is no God, for man and all that is around him to be more than an apparition. I repeat: God is and is outside of me, a living essence that subsists for itself, *or I*

am God. There is no third possibility.[13] [Emphasis added]

Little does he know. Enter Hegel, a thirty-one-year-old divinity student who joins the faculty at Jena in 1801, shortly after Fichte gets the boot. He is a friend and former roommate of Friedrich Schelling, who is the professor of philosophy at Jena. Schelling is a noted Kantian but is of no particular interest to our narrative. Hegel, on the other hand, is very much of interest.

Now when reading what follows, keep in mind that this is our understanding of Hegel, taken from sources that we consider reliable. Yet we would note that it is not only perfectly all right if your views or those of anyone else is different from ours because Hegel is so obtuse that no one can say for certain what he meant by what he wrote. Indeed, the great philosopher Arthur Schopenhauer, a contemporary of Hegel's, who always presented his thoughts and ideas concisely and unambiguously, said this about him.

> Hegel, installed from above, by the powers that be, as the certified Great Philosopher, was a flat-headed, insipid, nauseating, illiterate charlatan, who reached the pinnacle of audacity in scribbling together and dishing up the craziest mystifying nonsense. This nonsense has been noisily proclaimed as immortal wisdom by mercenary followers and readily accepted as such by all fools, who thus joined into as perfect a chorus of admiration as had ever been heard before. The extensive field of spiritual influence with which Hegel was furnished by those in power has enabled him to achieve the intellectual corruption of a whole generation. ...
>
> But the height of audacity in serving up pure nonsense, in stringing together senseless and extravagant mazes of words, such as had previously been known only in madhouses, was

131

finally reached in Hegel, and became the instrument of the most bare-faced general mystification that has ever taken place, with a result which will appear fabulous to posterity, and will remain as a monument to German stupidity.[14]

Years later, the *Cambridge Dictionary of Philosophy* described Hegel this way. "His language and approach were so heterodox that he has inspired as much controversy about the meaning of his position as about its adequacy."[15] *The Oxford Companion to Philosophy* said this: "His style is anything but 'user-friendly'; at first glance most readers will find his sentences simply incomprehensible. This had led some to denounce him as a charlatan, hiding an emptiness of thought behind a deliberate obscurity of expression in order to give an air of profundity."[16]

Maybe so. But the fact is that Hegel changed the world. The philosopher Karl Popper said it best in the second volume of his classic *The Open Society and Its Enemies* when he explained that not only did Hegel lay the foundations for Marx's Marxism and for Mussolini's and Hitler's fascism, but that "nearly all the more important ideas of modern totalitarianism are directly inherited from Hegel." He listed them thusly:

> (a) Nationalism, in the form of the historicist idea that the state is the incarnation of the spirit (or now, of the Blood) of the state-creating nation (or race); one chosen nation (now, the chosen race) is destined for world domination. (b) The state as the natural enemy of all other states must assert its existence in war. (c) The state is exempt from any kind of moral obligation; history, that is, historical success, is the sole judge; collective utility is the sole principle of personal conduct; propagandist lying and distortion of the truth is permissible. (d) The "ethical" idea of war (total and collectivist), particularly of

young nations against older ones; war, fate and fame as most desirable good. (e) The creative role of the Great Man, the world historical personality, the man of deep knowledge and great passion (now, the principle of leadership. (f) The ideal of the heroic life ("live dangerously") and of the "heroic man" as opposed to the petty bourgeois and his life of shallow mediocrity.[17]

From the perspective of our history of the Left, it is useful to view Hegel as a latter-day version of the previously mentioned utopian socialists, St. Simon, Fourier, and Owen. For his world was every bit as much of a fantasy as theirs. Secondly, it is important to understand that his contribution to the history of the Left occurred in two separate but related fields. The first had to do the influence that his theological theories had on the further spread of nihilism that was then rampaging across the European landscape. The second involved the influence that his theories of history had on Marxism. MacIntyre explained this duality as follows: "Hegel's concern from the outset is with history, not with theology, but he approaches history with categories drawn from a religion background."[18]

Regarding his contribution to nihilism, Hegel was off-put by Kant's contention that God's existence could not be proven by *reason*. After all, philosophy is all about the search for truth, and this guy Kant, who claimed to be a philosopher, had said some truths were beyond the reach of philosophy. So naturally, Hegel set about correcting this error, which he "accomplished" by—you guessed it—redefining reason. The Canadian American philosopher Stephen Hicks explains the loopy way he did it.

The antinomies of reason are a problem only if one thinks that logical contradictions are a problem. That was Kant's mistake—he was too trapped in the old Aristotelian logic of non-contradiction. What Kant's antinomies show is not that reason is limited but rather than we need a new and better kind of reason, one that embraces contradictions and sees the whole of reality as evolving out of contradictory forces. ... Hegel's reason operates by dialectical and contradictory means, and not in accordance with the Aristotelian principle of non-contradiction ... Enlightenment theology had been to alter religion by eliminating its contradictory thesis in order to make it comparable with reason. Hegel's strategy was to accept that Judeo-Christian cosmology is rife with contradiction, but to alter reason in order to make it compatible with contradiction ... Since reality involves contradictorily, *truth is relative to time and place.*[19]

It stood to "reason" then, that if "reason" is filled with contradictions, then truth itself must be relative. And so, just as Kant had killed God, Hegel killed both reason and truth. Needless to say, this was a very big deal. As noted earlier, the Enlightenment had set reason against religion. Now reason itself had been debunked.

But Hegel had more to say. For example, there was his theory alienation, which became central to the Marx's thoughts and to those of other Leftist philosophers and gadflies. MacIntyre explains it as follows:

Man does not obey the moral law that he makes for himself. He has a bad conscience as a result of this failure. He sees the moral law—the product of his own mind and will—set over against him, external to him. Man is at odds with the society of which he is a member, which indeed would not exist but for his participation. Because man does not live up to the standards of society that he has made, he has a bad conscience with regard to it also ... Thus within the Christian world there is an inheritance of estrangement and

alienation which manifests itself in the conflicts
of Church and society. ... Man in origin and in
essence is a free being. In his estrangement, he
loses that freedom ... So that in understanding
his estrangement so as to overcome it, man passes
from art and religion to philosophy ... Hence it
is philosophy which finally exhibits the truth of
spirit in his historical form of the free society.[20]

From this starting point, there came Hegel's assertion that
world history is the progress of the "consciousness of Freedom." This
process, he said, began with the Oriental kingdoms of China, India,
and Persian, which were ruled by tyrants, continued with the Greek
and Roman Empires in which some citizens were free but others were
slaves, and first "attained the consciousness that man, as man, is free"
"under the influence of Christianity."[21] Finally, the Reformation put
the frosting on the cake by liberating the Germans from the authority of the pope.

Hegel was vague about the details of the end point of all of this.
Simply stated, he compared history to the mythical phoenix that
eternally prepares its own funeral pyre, is consumed by it, and then
rises from its ashes in a new life. But then he noted that while history
is self-consuming like the phoenix, "it does not merely return to the
same form but comes forth 'exalted, glorified,' with each successive
phase becoming, in turn, a material on which the spiritual history of
man proceeds to a new level of fulfillment. Thus the conception of
mere change gives place to one of spiritual perfection."[22]

An important aspect of this historical progression was the presence of those whom Hegel described as "world historic characters,"
or *Volksgeisters*. They were the embodiments of the *Geist*, whose role
was to bring forth the fundamental idea of the particular stage of
history in which they lived. These individuals did not know that they
are fulfilling some important purpose in the history of mankind, but
were, instead, simply tools of what Hegel described as "the cunning
of reason," which he said works behind the scenes to accomplish the
goal of history.

Napoleon was Hegel's prototype. Hegel had been in Jena on October 13, 1806, the day before Napoleon's army defeated Frederick William III's Prussian forces, and he was deeply impressed by the little Corsican general, not simply as a character in history but as a spiritual force in the progress of mankind's struggle. He put it this way in a letter to his friend, the theologian Friedrich Niethammer: "I saw the Emperor—this soul of the world—go out from the city to survey his reign; it is a truly wonderful sensation to see such an individual, who, concentrating on one point while seated on a horse, stretches over the world and dominates it."[23]

Of course, the truth was that this "soul of the world" was a nasty creature who pursued his bloody *Geist* for nine more years before getting his butt kicked by the English general Wellington, and leaving Europe in severe economic distress and largely Godless.

Not surprisingly, Marx loved Hegel's contention that history progresses via a dialectic system of thesis and antithesis toward an eschatological fulfillment at the end of time. He particularly liked the fact that Hegel was optimistic about the eventual outcome of history but not specific about the details because this allowed him to create his own fairy-tale eschaton that would appeal to his beloved proletariat. It is worth noting here that the source of Hegel's overt optimism, and thus Marx's, is somewhat puzzling given the course of history up to that time. MacIntyre attributes it to the influence of Adam Smith's invisible hand theory, which "suggested to Hegel that self-interest and other evils are overcome in the historical process."[24] So it was that Hegel's optimistic historicism became *the fourth principle in all leftist models*, without which Marx would have been left with a simple polemic on the evils of Christianity and capitalism rather than a "scientific" theory of the history of mankind, delightfully ending in a "workers' paradise."

Of course, there was a minor problem involving his acceptance of Hegel's contention that history is inevitably moving toward a certain predetermined end and Marx's determination to take control of the direction and pace of this movement. However, as with so many such inconsistencies and errors in Marxism, Marx found a phony explanation in time for the publication of his masterwork *Das Kapital*. To wit:

> And even when a society has got upon the right track for the discovery of the natural laws of its movement—and it is the ultimate aim of this work, to lay bare the economic law of motion of modern society—it can neither clear by bold leaps, nor remove by legal enactments, the obstacles offered by the successive phases of its normal development. *But it can shorten and lessen the birth-pangs.*[25]

Yes, indeed, there were to be *birth pangs*. And this brings us to a gaggle of young, energetic, brilliant, fascinating, quarrelsome, scruffy, and petulant German students who gathered in the late 1830s in a small cafe in Berlin called Hippel's Weinstube at 94 Friedrichstrasse. They are drinking heavily, laughing, arguing loudly, and sometimes angrily, over politics, religion, the meaning of history, and most importantly, the philosophy of Hegel.

They are the spawn of the miasmic era mentioned above, having all been born during or shortly after the Napoleonic Wars. They are atheists. They are deeply antagonistic to the oppressive and corrupt governments that the Congress of Vienna gifted to Europe. They are fascinated by Buonarroti's account of Babeuf's life and philosophy, by the efforts of the utopian socialists to come up with a better form of government, and by the mystical mishmash of Hegel, who is, because of his position at the University of Berlin, a rock star of the profession.

When taken together, they would form an all-important bridge between Hegel's *worldself* god and Nietzsche's dead one. When reading of them, one thinks of Satan and his Stygian council of fallen angels after their ejection from heaven, that is, "on the beach of that inflamed sea he stood and called his legions ... who lay entranced, thick as autumnal leaves ... Princes, Potentates, Warriors, the Flower of Heaven ... by falsities and lies the greatest part of mankind they corrupted to forsake God their Creator."[26]

A reach? Well, Marx's friend and compatriot Friedrich Engels would not have thought so. While he had not yet met Marx, he had heard about him and the "Free Ones" from his fellow leftist Hegelians in England and had been so impressed that he had written a lengthy poem in 1839 entitled "A Christian Epic in Four Cantos" in which he described this crowd as follows, clearly channeling Milton's great description of "the fall."

> What do I see? A frenzied host so glittering bright
>
> With Blasphemy, the very sun has lost its light?
>
> Who are they? See them, how they all come surging forth,
>
> Foregathering from East, and South, and West, and North.
>
> The scum of Germany, they meet in convocation
>
> To whip their spirits up for still more evil action.
>
> Already they have felt the Lord's hand moving o'er them,
>
> Already they have guessed how Satan's clutch could claw them
>
> Down to a dreadful doom. Knowing despair full well,
>
> They've felt like letting Atheism go to Hell.
>
> Then *Arnold* [Ruge] summons all those of the Free persuasion
>
> To meet at *Bockenheim* in Hellish congregation.
>
> "Arise, you Free ones all! How can you sit so tight,
>
> When the Romantics plunge the whole world into night?

> Or when Reaction stirs and, cunning as of old,
> Almost has Science in its deadly stranglehold?[27]

As noted in the poem, they refer to themselves as *Die Freien* (the Free Ones). They call their gathering the Doktorklub, but they will become known to history as the Young Hegelians. Of course, the modifier "young" implies that there are some "old" Hegelians around. There are, but the differences between the two groups are manifold. Roughly speaking, the latter are interested in mining Hegel's wisdom, whereas these younger disciples are determined to correct the master's shortcomings, which Engels would later describe as follows:

> Notwithstanding his enormous learning and his deep thought, [Hegel] was so much occupied with abstract questions, that he neglected to free himself from the prejudices of his age—an age of restoration for old systems of government and religion. But his disciples had very different views on these subjects.[28]

Needless to say, then, these young Hegelians begin their critique of Hegel by rejecting out of hand all notions of God, including Hegel's. Not surprisingly, they are particularly antagonistic toward Christianity, which they believe to be the origin of society's many problems and the principal stumbling block to the formation of a new order. For this reason, conservatives will remember Hippel's Weinstube as the modern-day equivalent of Pandora's jar from which evils untold and uncounted emerged. Had Marx been asked for a mythological antecedent to this gathering, he would have chosen Prometheus's rebellion against God. As Edmund Wilson notes, this myth was such a favorite of Marx that he used the speech of Aeschylus' Prometheus to Hermes as a prefix to his doctor's dissertation. To wit:

> Know well that I would never be willing
> to exchange my misfortune for that bondage of
> yours. For better do I deem it to be bound to this
> rock than to spend my life as Father Zeus' favor-
> ite messenger.[29]

Besides their interest in Hegel, another commonality is their social distance from the proletariat, the maltreatment of whom supposedly fuels their revolutionary anger. Wilson discusses the nature of this hypocrisy as follows:

> We must realize how radical and how diffi-
> cult a step for German intellectuals of the forties
> was this getting into relations with the working
> class. [Alexander] Herzen [a Russian intellectual
> and leftist] says of Heine and his circle that they
> never "knew the people ... to understand the
> moan of humanity lost in the bogs of today, they
> had to translate it into Latin and to arrive at their
> ideas through the Gracchi and the proletariat of
> Rome"; that on the occasions when they emerged
> from their "sublimated world," like Faust in
> Auerbach's cellar, they were hindered like him
> by "a spirit of scholastic scepticism from simply
> looking and seeing"; and "would immediately
> hasten back from living sources to the sources of
> history; there they felt more at home."

Wilson then quotes Heine telling of the poet's embarrassment on once meeting Weitling:

> What particularly offended my pride was
> the fellow's utter lack of respect while he con-
> versed with me. He did not remove his cap and,
> while I was standing before him, he remained sit-
> ting, with his right knee raised by the aid of his

right hand to his very chin and steadily rubbing the raised leg with his left hand just above the ankle. At first, I assumed that this disrespectful attitude was the result of a habit he had acquired while working at the tailoring trade, but I was soon convinced of my error. When I asked him why he was always rubbing his leg in this way, Weitling replied in a nonchalant manner, as if it were the most ordinary occurrence, that he had been compelled to wear chains in the various German prisons in which he had been confined and that as the iron ring which held his knee had frequently been too small, he had developed a chronic irritation of the skin, which was the cause for his perpetual scratching of his leg. I confess that I recoiled when the tailor Weitling told me about these chains. I, who had once in Munster kissed with burning lips the relics of the tailor John of Leyden—the chains he had worn, the pincers with which he had been tortured and which are preserved in the Munster City Hall—I who had made an exalted cult of the dead tailor, now felt an insurmountable aversion for this living tailor, William Weitling, though both were apostles and martyrs in the same cause."[30]

In regard to this distance from and seeming distaste for the working class, the historian Paul Johnson notes in *Intellectuals* that throughout Marx's entire lifetime, "the only member of the working class that he ever knew at all well, his one real contact with the 'proletariat,' was his household maid, Helene Demuth." Lenchen, as she was called, was a peasant girl who had worked for Marx's mother-in-law, the Baroness Caroline von Westphalen, since she was a child. According to Johnson, the Baroness "felt sorrow and anxiety for her married daughter" Jenny, and gave Lenchen to her "to ease her lot." True to his concern for the proletariat, Marx treated Lenchen with as much respect as he did his well-born wife. In fact, in 1850 he knocked her up. Paul Johnson described the happy event as follows:

> Eventually, Jenny found out or had to be told and, on top of her other miseries at this time, it probably marked the end of her love for Marx. She called it 'an event which I shall not dwell upon further, though it brought about a great increase in our private and public sorrows … Marx was terrified that Freddy's paternity would be discovered and that this would do him fatal damages as a revolutionary leader and seer … He eventually persuaded Engels to acknowledge Freddy privately, as a cover-story for family consumption … Marx never knew him. They met only once.[31]

But back to the Doktorklub. Although Marx is the youngest member, he is widely recognized as the group's leader, and according to his biographer, Francis Wheen, he is "already a legend" among Europe's leftist intellectuals. Engels's description of Marx in the above-mentioned poem is as follows:

> Who runs up next with wild impetuosity?
> A swarthy chap of Trier, a marked monstrosity.
> He neither hops nor skips, but moves in leaps and bounds,
> Raving aloud. As if to seize and then pull down
> To earth the spacious tent of Heaven up on high,
> He opens wide his arms and reaches for the sky.
> He shakes his wicked fist, raves with a frantic air,

As if ten thousand devils had him by the hair.[32]

While in Berlin, Marx is in the process of writing the above-mentioned doctoral thesis; a comparative study of Epicurus and Democritus, which would argue, in the words of Wheen, that "theology must yield to the superior wisdom of philosophy, and that skepticism must triumph over dogma." Marx outlines this thought as follows on the first page of the thesis.

As long as a single drop of blood pulses in her world-conquering and totally free heart, philosophy will continually shout at her opponents the cry of Epicurus: "Impiety does not consist in destroying the gods of the crowd but rather in ascribing to the gods the ideas of the crowd." Philosophy makes no secret of it. The proclamation of Prometheus— "In one word, I hate all gods"—is her own profession, or one slogan against all gods in heaven and earth who do not recognize man's self-consciousness as the highest divinity. There shall be none other beside it.[33]

The most accomplished member of the group at the time is Marx's then friend and mentor Bruno Bauer. He already holds a professorship in theology at Berlin University but is about to lose it because of his recent noisy conversion to the glories of atheism. He is working on a study of the *New Testament* that will conclude that Jesus never existed and that the gospels are forgeries.

Another member is the soon-to-be-famous Ludwig von Feuerbach. He is hard at work upon his greatest contribution to philosophy; a book entitled *The Essence of Christianity*, which, very simply stated, will attempt to humanize, or secularize, Christianity, to free it from its mythological underpinnings. MacIntyre explains his view of the Christian god as "a vision of humanity," and "God is love." Feuerbach himself put it this way: "The source of man's error is wrong thinking, the corrective is right thinking." And this: "If you want to better the people give them better food instead of exhortations against sin. Man is what he eats."[34]

Then there is Arnold Ruge, another figure in Engels's poem. He is the oldest member of the crowd and the most experienced in revolutionary affairs. He had been involved in the left-wing student organizations known as the *Burschenschaft* movement, which sprung up in the wake of the Napoleonic Wars and was banned in 1819. This led to the so-called Demagogue Hunt for student radicals, which landed Ruge in jail for six years. In 1838, he cofounded a publication entitled *Hallische Jahrbücher*, to which the Young Hegelians contributed.

Finally, we come to Max Stirner, a pen name for one Johann Kaspar Schmidt. From our perspective, he is the second most important man in the room. Indeed, Marx himself will eventually come to this realization and make Stirner the subject of the lengthiest and most vitriolic of the many polemics he will launch against his former colleagues. In fact, Marx's attack on Stirner, which will take the form of a line-by-line critique in *The German Ideology*, will be longer than the book that Stirner wrote that generated Marx's ire.

So, who is this fellow shown in a sketch by Engels at one of these nightly meetings sitting on the sidelines quietly smoking a cigarette while the others are shouting and gesticulating? What has he done that will make Marx come to hate and fear him so? And why is he so important?

Well, he is a schoolteacher in a gymnasium for young girls owned by a Madame Gropius. Like many of the other "doctors" in the room, he is working on a book. It will be entitled *Der Einzige und sein Eigentum*, which will translate into English as *The Ego and His Own*, and will be described for decades after its publication in 1845 as the most dangerous book ever written. In his classic 1909 volume, *Egoists*, James Huneker summarizes Stirner's beliefs as follows:

> His ego and not the family is the unit of his
> social life. In antique times when men were really
> the young, not the ancient, it was a world of real-

ity. Men enjoyed the material. With Christianity came the rule of the spirit; ideas were become sacred, with the concepts of God, Goodness, Sin, Salvation. After Rousseau and the French Revolution humanity was enthroned, and the state became our oppressor.

Our first enemies are our parents, our educators. It follows, then, that the only criterion of life is my Ego. Without my Ego I could not apprehend existence. Altruism is a pretty disguise for egotism. No one is or can be disinterested. He gives up one thing for another because the other seems better, nobler to him. Egotism! ... The one sure thing of life is the Ego. Therefore, "I am not you, but I'll use you if you are agreeable to me." Not to God, not to man, must be given the glory. "I'll keep the glory myself." What is Humanity but an abstraction? I am Humanity. Therefore the State is a monster that devours its children. It must not dictate to me ... Socialism is but a further screwing up of the State machine to limit the individual. Socialism is a new god, a new abstraction to tyrannize over the Ego ... "crimes spring from fixed ideas." The Church, State, the Family, Morals, are fixed ideas. "Atheists are pious people." They reject one fiction only to cling to many old ones. Liberty for the people is not my liberty. Socrates was a fool in that he conceded to the Athenians the right to condemn him ... Your Ego is not free if you allow your vices or virtues to enslave it.[35]

In short, he is the original nihilist, *the augury of both Nietzsche's dead God and the Left's coming adaptation of post-modernism.* He is the only man among the members of that Stygian Council who truly knows and understands the nature of the exlizer they are brewing up. He alone senses that the result will not be a "new breed of men" living in a "workers' paradise," but tortured souls living in a world in the midst of a spiritual crisis, populated by egotistical killers, void of all traditional constraints, marked by nihilism, barbed wire, and death trains. And he seems to relish the thought. Engels describes him as follows in his poem.

> See Stirner too, the thoughtful moderation-hater;
> Though still on beer, he'll soon be drinking blood like water.
> And if the others shout a wild: "down with Kings"
> Stirner is sure to add: "down with the law as well." ...
> Then Stirner, dignified: "Who binds his will around?
> Who would impose a law by shouting people down?
> You tie his will and have the nerve to say you're free;
> A lot you've done to break away from slavery!
> Down with all rules and laws, say I!" ...
> There's Stirner, see him flinging bales of books entire,
> While hordes of Pious warriors melt beneath his fire.[36]

Marx's hatred for Stirner will stem from his fear that if the proletariat ever adopts Stirner's extreme egoism and cynicism, they will find that the dream of a "worker's paradise"—a secular eschaton—is as unappealing as the Christian version. Löwith put it this way:

> Stirner no longer "dreams" of freedom and emancipation, but "decides" for individuality. As

an individual "I" he lives neither in the bourgeois state nor in the communistic society—neither the heavy cords of blood nor the light threads of humanity bind him—but in the "association" of egoists. Only they, precisely because of their superiority, are his equals ... The "I" enjoys life, unconcerned with the *idée fixe* of God and mankind.[37]

The dust cover of the first English edition, published in 1963 by the Libertarian Book Club, New York, reads as follows:

> As Herbert Read [the British anarchist/ existentialist poet] observed [in 1945] in an essay commemorating the centennial of Stirner's [book] ... "the giants whom Marx thought he had slain show signs of coming to life again," and Stirner is one of them. The fact that Stirner was the real antithesis of Marx (and incidentally, of Hegel) has long been ignored, blurred, or suppressed, though [Sidney] Hook, in his durable *From Hegel to Marx*, emphasized that in their controversy, Marx and Stirner were discussing "the fundamental problems of any possible system of ethics or public morality." How a number of lesser figures have been posed as Marx's prime antagonists over the years is a tribute to the determination to escape the far more uncomfortable and demanding Stirnerite alternative.[38]

The following discussion of the root of Stirner's quarrel with Marx and his other colleagues in the Doktorklub is an excerpt from the above-mentioned book by the philosopher Sidney Hook first published in 1936.

> What is a moral idea? Stirner asks. Something which dominates or controls conduct. Whose

conduct? My conduct. What is a political or religious fetish? Something which dominates my
conduct until I have realized why and how it has
been constructed. What is the difference, then,
between a religious fetish and an ethical ideal?
None, answers Stirner, except that we are usually
more conscious of the fetishistic character of the
first than of the second. Consider all the ideals
which the Young-Hegelians have discarded as
empty abstractions—God, the state, the nation,
the church, respectability. Why, asks Stirner,
should they be rejected, refuted and denounced?
Because instead of serving man's interests they
have been used to serve the interests of the ruling group which has propagated these ideals
most widely: because they correspond to nothing which *I* can objectively experience; because,
upon analysis, they turn out to be meaningless
abstractions: and finally, because they stand in
the way of the free assertion of my unique personality, imposing rules or claims which are irrelevant to my own best interests in any particular
situation.

But now, Stirner goes on, let us look at
what our Young-Hegelian friends offer us in their
stead. Humanity, justice, truth, love, communism, etc. They are admirable and enthusiastic
slogans. But what do they mean? Why should I
die for humanity or communism any more than
for God and Country? After all, what is humanity? It does not seem to be particularly concerned
about me.[39]

Given these observations, it would be not just appropriate but
necessary to let Stirner speak for himself, hence the following short
excerpt from *The Ego and His Own*.

Crimes spring from *fixed* ideas. The sacredness of marriage is a fixed idea. From the sacredness it follows that infidelity is a *crime*, and therefore a certain marriage law imposes upon it a shorter or longer *penalty*. But by those who proclaim "freedom as sacred" this penalty must be regarded as a crime against freedom, and only in this sense has public opinion in fact branded the marriage law.

Society would have *every* one come to his right indeed, but yet only that which is sanctioned by society, to the society-right, not really to *his* right. But I give or take to myself the right out of my own plenitude of power, and against every superior power I am the most impenitent criminal. Owner and creator of my right, I recognize no other source of right than—me, neither God nor the State nor nature nor even man himself with his 'eternal rights of man,' neither divine nor human right." (Emphasis in original)[40]

The Doktorklub breaks up 1843, and Engels outlines its accomplishments and its importance to the goal of spreading leftist ideology across Germany in that same year.

The political revolution of France was accompanied by a philosophical revolution in Germany. Kant began it by overthrowing the old system of Leibnitzian metaphysics, which at the end of last century was introduced in all Universities of the Continent. Fichte and Schelling commenced rebuilding, and Hegel completed the new system. There has never been, ever since man began to think, a system of philosophy as comprehensive as that of Hegel. Logic, metaphysics, natural philosophy, the philosophy of mind, the philosophy of law, of religion, of history, all are united in one system, reduced to one fundamental principle. The system appeared quite unassailable from without, and so it was; it has been overthrown from within only, by those who were Hegelians themselves. ...

We had friends in almost every considerable town of Germany; we provided all the liberal papers with the necessary matter, and by this means made them our organs; we inundated the country with pamphlets, and soon governed public opinion upon every question. A temporary relaxation of the censorship of the press added a great deal to the energy of this movement, quite novel to a considerable part of the German public. Papers, published under the authorisation of a government censor, contained things which, even in France, would have been punished as high treason, and other things which could not have been pronounced in England, without a trial for blasphemy being the consequence of it.

The movement was so sudden, so rapid, so energetically pursued, that the government as well as the public were dragged along with it for some time. But this violent character of the agitation proved that it was not founded upon a strong party among the public, and that its power was produced by the surprise, and consternation only of its opponents. The governments, recovering their senses, put a stop to it by a most despotic oppression of the liberty of speech. Pamphlets, newspapers, periodicals, scientific works were suppressed by dozens, and the agitated state of the country soon subsided. It is a matter of course that such a tyrannical interference will not check the progress of public opinion, nor quench the principles defended by the agitators; the entire persecution has been of no use whatever to the ruling powers; because, if they had not put down the movement, it would have been checked by the apathy of the public at large, a public as little prepared for radical changes as that of every other country; and, if even this had not been the case, the republican agitation would have been abandoned by the agitators themselves, who now, by developing farther and farther the consequences of their philosophy, became Communists. *The princes and rulers of Germany, at the very moment when they believed to have put down republicanism forever, saw the rise of Communism from the ashes of political agitation; and this new doctrine appears to them even more dangerous and formidable than that in whose apparent destruction they rejoiced.* [Emphasis added.][41]

Marx left Berlin for Cologne in the spring of 1842 to begin work as a journalist on a radical newspaper, *Neue Rheinische Zeitung*. It is here, writing about the problems of the poor, that Marx the philosopher turns into Marx the radical, communist, political activist. It is also here that he meets Moses Hess, Engels, and Heine, whose poetry he had revered since childhood. Hess, like Weitling, had become a communist while spending time in Paris among the revolutionaries there. According to the author/journalist Michael Goldfarb, "he was more thoroughly versed in modern theories of socialism" than Marx. Yet he was in awe of Marx's intelligence. In a letter of introduction to a friend, he described Marx as follows:

He is a phenomenon who made the deepest impression on me. Be prepared to the meet the greatest, perhaps the only real philosopher living now. Dr. Marx—this is the name of my idol—is still a very young man, hardly 24 years

old but he will give the final blow to all medieval
religion and politics. Can you imagine Rousseau,
Voltaire, Holbach, Lessing, Heine and Hegel
combined into one person? If you can, you have
Dr. Marx[42]

Hess had converted Engels to communism and will have a significant impact on Marx's transition to communism. In 1843, he
and Marx and Heine philosophize and write. In 1840, Heine had
written, "Welcome be a religion that pours into the bitter chalice of
the suffering human species some sweet soporific drops of spiritual
opium, some drops of love, hope and faith." Hess borrowed this idea
in an 1843 essay, putting it this way: "Religion can make bearable
the unhappy consciousness of serfdom in the same way that opium
is help in painful disease." The next year, Marx famously wrote in
his Critique of Hegel's Philosophy of Right, "*Religious* suffering is,
at one and the same time, the *expression* of real suffering and a *protest* against real suffering. Religion is the sigh of the oppressed creature, the heart of a heartless world, and the soul of soulless conditions. It is the *opium* of the people."[43]

In March of 1843, the authorities close down the newspaper. In
June, Marx marries the aristocratic but obviously dim-witted Jenny,
and for the next seven years or so, they and their growing family kick
around Europe, often with Engels in tow, driven from place to place
by censors and police authorities. During this time, Marx begins for-
mulating the ideas and theories that will later be compiled into his
classic work *Das Kapital.*

It is at this time that he develops his penchant for launching
venomous assaults on anyone who is pursuing the same goal as he,
that is, attempting to develop and implement a new moral system to
replace Christianity and the private ownership of property.

Marx loves the proletariat as an abstraction. He loves the French
revolutionaries who confronted the authorities at the barricades and
went to prison for it, again as an abstraction. Yet he viciously attacks
the first proletarian revolutionary that he ever meets in person, the
little tailor Weitling at what was supposed to have been a friendly

dinner of colleagues. Wheen tells us that Weitling was dressed nattily and happy to be among those whom he considered both friends and admirers of his work, "expecting nothing more than an evening of liberal commonplaces." Marx, however, was "spoiling for a fight."

> "Tell us, Weitling," he interrupted, glaring across the table, "you who have made such a noise in Germany with your preaching: on what grounds do you justify your activity and what do you intend to base it on in the future?" … Marx moved in for the kill. To rouse the workers without offering any scientific ideas or constructive doctrine, he said, was "equivalent to vain dishonest play at preaching which assumes an inspired prophet on the one side and on the other only the gaping asses."
>
> Weitling's cheeks coloured. In trembling voice, he protested that a man who had rallied hundreds of people under the same banner in the name of justice and solidarity could not be treated like this … This attempt to play the proletariat card was more than Marx could bear. Leaping from his seat, and thumping the table so hard that the lamp on it shook and rang, he yelled, "Ignorance never yet helped anybody!"[44]

However, the Weitling incident is not unique. Earlier, Marx had publicly savaged both the ideas and the character of his two closest friends and colleagues from the Doktorklub, Bauer and Feuerbach, and he would continue to do this to his "friends" throughout his lifetime. In fact, anyone who spends any time at all studying Marx, the man, quickly learns that he hated everything and everybody. He hated the bourgeoisie, the aristocracy, the capitalists, all governmental agencies, and all religious organizations. He hated the fact that he was expected to work for a living. He hated landlords, bankers, and store owners who expected to be paid for their goods. Relative to the latter, this "groundbreaking economist" once wrote a letter to Engels complaining bitterly about the "*Schweinhund*" grocer who had canceled his credit because he had not paid his bills.[45]

The following anecdote related by Paul Johnson captures the extent of the unreasonableness of his hatred. According to Johnson, Marx led a particularly unhealthy life, drinking heavily, smoking, eating highly spiced foods, and getting virtually no exercise. In addition, he rarely took baths or even washed. This combination, Johnson maintains, could explain the fact that he suffered for twenty-five years from a "virtually plague of boils," that "varied in numbers, size, and intensity but at one time or another appeared on all parts of his body," including his cheeks, the bridge of his nose, and his private parts. He said the following about this medical problem in a letter he wrote to Engels in which he said the following: "I hope the bourgeoisie as long as they exist will have cause to remember my carbuncles."[46]

In short, Marx, who claimed to feel deeply about the plight of the proletariat, had never really met one much less associated with any of them. In fact, with two exceptions, it seems he never met a man whom he did not come to hate. One of these exceptions was Engels, whose father's factory in England was the teat upon which Marx and family most often fed. The other was Heine, who was likely the only man whom Marx could stand to be around who disagreed with his worldview. Eleanor Marx explained their relationship this way: "He loved the poet as much as his works and looked as generously as possible on his political weaknesses. Poets, he explained, were queer fish and must be allowed to go their own ways. They should not be assessed by the measure or ordinary or even extraordinary men."[47]

Now one would think that, given the enormous and unquestionable importance of Marx's "scientific communism" to the history of the entire world for the next century and a half, it would be necessary here to intensely explore and analyze it. Oddly enough, that is not the case, for, in the final analysis, Marxism is social and economic nonsense. It does not reflect the slightest understanding of the world as it was when Marx developed it, or as it had ever been, or was ever to become.

If Marx were alive today, he would, of course, argue that all the many political leaders who tried to put his theories into practice did it wrong or were not persistent enough. However, that would be rubbish. Indeed, one would be hard-pressed to find the views of any secular visionary in the entire history of mankind whose theories have been more aggressively pursued and trusted by more people over a longer time than those of Karl Marx.

In fact, the leaders of two of the largest nations in the world, along with those in numerous smaller ones, such as North Korea, North Vietnam, Cuba, Cambodia, Nicaragua, Venezuela, have murdered, tortured, imprisoned, and destroyed the lives and families of tens of millions of their citizens and wasted unfathomable resources in pathetically futile attempts to make Marxism produce the happy and prosperous world that he promised.

Simply stated, the best way to describe the philosophy upon which Marx built Marxism is with the phrase, "turning Hegel on his head." You see, Hegel begins with the understanding that ideas such as truth, justice, and religion are the roots of social order; that the state promotes and encourages these ideas; that this process moves along through a dialectic system of thesis and antithesis, always progressing, or improving if you will, sometimes slowly through accretion and sometimes via violent upheavals, but always toward the eschatological fulfillment when mankind would reach the final form of society.

In contrast, Marx argued that ideas such as truth, justice, and religion are not the starting points but the end points; that they are not absolute concepts but are defined by the social order in which they develop, which is in turn determined by the way in which society is divided into classes, which in turn is decided by the method by which society produces its goods.

Marx agreed with Hegel's theory that history represents a progress toward an eschatological fulfillment, but he maintains, as Francis Fukuyama stated in his classic *The End of History and the Last Man*, that Hegel's state "did not represent the universalization of freedom, but only the victory of freedom for a certain class, the bourgeoisie." In such a society, Fukuyama continues, Marx argued that "man remains alienated from himself because capital, a human creation, has turned into man's lord and master and controls him. ... The Marxist end of history would come only with victory of the true 'universal class,' the proletariat, and the subsequent achievement of a global communist utopia that would end class struggle once and for all."[48]

Now it is normal for utopians to fashion their illusionary best of all possible worlds around their own particular or peculiar idea of a good time. The great philosopher Eric Voegelin once noted, for example, that the perfect world envisioned by the aforementioned Marquis de Condorcet was one in which everyone was a French intellectual.[49]

Marx certainly considered himself to be an intellectual. Yet his own best of all possible worlds was in keeping with his almost pathological aversion to work, the resultant poverty, and the anger he focused on folks like the "schweinhund" grocer. Thus, it is no surprise that this "great economist" cherished the expectation of a world where "each" was provided for "according to his needs," and no one would need to work at any one particular job in order to feed his family. He described this Huckleberry Finn dream world as follows in *The German Ideology*, a notion, by the way, that he picked up from Fourier.

> In communist society, where nobody has one exclusive sphere of activity but each can become accomplished in any branch he wishes, society regulates the general production and thus makes it possible for me to do one thing today and another tomorrow, to hunt in the morning, fish in the afternoon, rear cattle in the evening, criticize after dinner, just as I have a mind, without ever becoming hunter, fisherman, herdsman or critic.[50]

Of course, few people pay any attention today to the world that Marx believed would follow his much-anticipated revolution. However, it is still important because it is a prime example of the extent to which leftist ideologies can distort the common sense of those who buy into their follies. With that said, here are a few lines from the political philosopher Joseph Cropsey's description of the childish, fairy-tale-like, secular eschaton of which Marx dreamed.

> Upon the dissolution of classes will necessarily ensue the end of the class struggle and the beginning of strictly human history. When that has occurred, the relations among men will have caught up with the latest great development in the mode of production; the conditions of oppression disappearing, the need for coercion will disappear as well, and the state will wither away to be replaced by the universal brotherhood of man ... When this new breed of man is generated by the common ownership of the means of production, all the old (natural) categories of right will fall before the logic of history, and subphilosophic men will live in uncoerced and myth-free (i.e., perfectly rational) society, as only the rarest of men were thought to be able to do, but even more emancipatedly than the rarest, who never had the benefit of the perfect environment.[51]

It is important to understand when considering this that while Marx assumed that the transition to this fanciful world would necessarily involve a violent revolution, he did not view violence as the driving force behind it. Instead, he insisted that "the contradictions inherent in the old society brought about by its end"; that is, that the "emergence of a new society was preceded, but not caused, by violent outbreaks."[52]

He put this way in an article in *Neue Rheinische Zeitung* in November 1848 while revolutions swept across Europe. "There is only one way in which the murderous death agonies of the old society and the bloody birth throes of the new society can be shortened, simplified and concentrated, and that way is revolutionary terror."[53]

This insistence on the inevitability of a revolution was the foundation for Marx's complaint against his intellectual "competitors," who he said failed to translate their philosophical beliefs into action. He referred to this aspect of his philosophy as "praxis," which Hess once explained as follows: "The time has come for the philosophy of spirit to become a philosophy of action."[54] Löwith put it this way: "In Hegel, the world was given philosophical form; in Marx, philosophy must become completely worldly."[55] *A Dictionary of Marxist Thought* said this:

> In Marx, the concept of praxis became the central concept of a new philosophy which does not want to remain philosophy, but to transcend itself both in a new meta-philosophical thinking and in the revolutionary transformation of the world.[56]

Finally, in that section of *The German Ideology* in which Marx attacks his former chum Feuerbach, he said this:

> The question whether objective truth can be attributed to human thinking is not a question of theory but is a practical question. Man must prove the truth, i.e. the reality and power, the this-worldliness of his thinking in practice. The dispute over the reality or non-reality of thinking that is isolated from practice is a purely scholastic question.[57]

Reflecting this call to action, Marx and Engels published their famous *Communist Manifesto* in February 1848, which opens chapter 1 with this bogus claim:

> The history of all hitherto existing society is the history of class struggles. Freeman and slave,

patrician and plebeian, lord and serf, guild-master and journeyman, in a word, oppressor and oppressed, stood in constant opposition to one another, carried on an uninterrupted, now hidden, now open fight, a fight that each time ended, either in a revolutionary reconstitution of society at large, or in the common ruin of the contending classes.

It ends with the following two paragraphs, which must have filled the demented outcast and his *fidus Achates* with pleasurable expectations when they wrote it. However, it was, in fact, nothing more than the dream of two queer fellows, to paraphrase a title from a short story by Dostoevsky, whose forte was probing the depths of delusional nihilists.

Hitherto, every form of society has been based, as we have already seen, on the antagonism of oppressing and oppressed classes. But in order to oppress a class, certain conditions must be assured to it under which it can, at least, continue its slavish existence. The serf, in the period of serfdom, raised himself to membership in the commune, just as the petty bourgeois, under the yoke of the feudal absolutism, managed to develop into a bourgeois. The modern labourer, on the contrary, instead of rising with the process of industry, sinks deeper and deeper below the conditions of existence of his own class. He becomes a pauper, and pauperism develops more rapidly than population and wealth. And here it becomes evident, that the bourgeoisie is unfit any longer to be the ruling class in society, and to impose its conditions of existence upon society as an over-riding law. It is unfit to rule because it is incompetent to assure an existence to its slave within his slavery, because it cannot help letting him sink into such a state, that it has to feed him, instead of being fed by him. Society can no longer live under this bourgeoisie, in other words, its existence is no longer compatible with society.

The essential conditions for the existence and for the sway of the bourgeois class is the formation and augmentation of capital; the condition for capital is wage-labour. Wage-labour rests exclusively on competition between the labourers. The advance of industry, whose involuntary promoter is the bourgeoisie, replaces the isolation of the labourers, due to competition, by the revolutionary combination, due to association. The development of Modern Industry, therefore, cuts from under its feet the very foundation on which the bourgeoisie produces and appropriates products. What the bourgeoisie therefore produces, above all, are its own grave-diggers. Its fall and the victory of the proletariat are equally inevitable.[58]

With the publication of the *Manifesto*, Marx is kicked out of Belgium, moves to Paris, then to Germany, then back to Paris, and finally in August 1949, he is deported to London, where he begins work in the library of the British Museum on *Das Kapital*, which is published in 1867. One of the ironies of history is that this book was responsible for untold misery, and yet, as Bohm-Bawerk noted, it was pure hocus-pocus. Edmund Wilson described it thusly:

It contains a treatise on economics, a history of industrial development and an inspired tract for the times; and the morality, which is part of the time suspended in the interests of scientific objectivity, is no more self-consistent than the economics is consistently scientific or the history undistracted by the exaltation of apocalyptic vision. And outside the whole immense structure, dark and strong like the old Trier basilica, built by the Romans with brick walls and granite columns, swim the mists and the septentrional lights of German metaphysics and mysticism, always ready to leak in through the crevices.[59]

It should be noted that by the time Marx wrote *Das Kapital*, he had expanded his grudge against God to a battle against all earthly idols of the modern capitalist society. One of the worst of these, in his opinion, was the so-called "fetish nature" of commodities, which he said turns the product of the laborer into a commodity that then takes on an idolatrous nature and dominates his maker's life. Marx put it this way.

A commodity is therefore a mysterious thing, simply because in it the social character of men's labour appears to them as an objective character stamped upon the product of that labour; because the relation of the producers to the sum total of their own labour is presented to them as a social relation existing not between themselves, but between the products of their labour. This is the reason the products of labour become commodities, social things whose qualities are at the same time perceptible and imperceptible by the senses ... In order, therefore, to find an analogy, we must have recourse to the mist-enveloped regions of the religious world. In that world the productions of the human brain appear as independent beings endowed with life, and entering into relation both with one another and the human race. So it is in the world of commodities with the products of men's hands. This I call the Fetishism which attaches itself to the

KANT, HEGEL, MARX, MARXISM

products of labour, so soon as they are produced
as commodities, and which is therefore inseparable from the production of commodities.[60]

A few years later, in a letter to a confidant, Ludwig Kugelmann,
he claimed that new equally pernicious myths related to property,
money, and other capitalistic forms were replacing the myth of religion. He put it this way: "Up to now, it was supposed that the growth
of the Christian myth under the Roman Empire was possible only
because printing had not yet been invented. Just the reverse is true.
The daily newspaper and telegraph, which disperses its inventions
in a moment over the entire surface of the earth, fabricate more
myths ... in one day than formerly could be constructed in a year."[61]
The irony in all of this is, of course, that Marx's "scientifically based"
ideology was, in essence, nothing more than the secularization of the
Christian belief in the inevitable and final redemption of mankind
during the "end times." British sociologist Bryan Turner describes
this correlation as follows:

> In Marxism, "history" is located in the long
> interval between the loss of communal innocence
> in primitive communism and its restoration in
> the final transition to communism. The vale
> of tears in the Marxist historical framework is
> occupied by the creation of private property, the
> division of labour, the organization of a market
> by exchange values, and the brutalization of the
> working class by capitalists.[62]

Voegelin would famously describe this notion as the "imma-
nentization of the Christian eschaton," and assert that the attempt
to construct a secular "*eidos* of history" to compete with the beatific
Christian belief in the "end times" was patently fallacious and anyone
contemplating it should have been realized this. He attributed this
obtuseness not to ignorance but to the overwhelming need among

these men who had lost their faith in God to achieve some certainty about history and their place in it. He put it this way:

> A man cannot fall back on himself in an absolute sense, because, if he tried, he would find very soon that he has fallen into the abyss of his despair and nothingness ... The fall could be caught only by experiential alternatives, sufficiently close to the experience of faith that only a discerning eye would see the difference, but receding far enough from it to remedy the uncertainly of faith in the strict sense ... The attempt at immanentizing the meaning of existence is fundamentally an attempt at bringing our knowledge of transcendence into a firmer grip than the *cognitio fidei*, the cognition of faith, will afford. ... This expansion will engage the various human faculties; and, hence, it is possible to distinguish a range of Gnostic varieties according to the faculty which predominates in the operation of getting this grip on God.
>
> Gnosis may be primarily intellectual and assume the form of speculative penetration of the mystery of creation and existence, as, for instance, in the contemplative gnosis of Hegel or Schelling. Or it may be primarily emotional and assume the form of an indwelling of divine substance in the human soul, as, for instance, in paracletic sectarian leaders. Or it may be primarily volitional and assume the form of activist redemption of man and society, as in the instance of revolutionary activists like Comte, Marx, or Hitler. These Gnostic experiences, in the amplitude of their variety, are the core of the redivinization of society, for the men who fall into these experiences divinize themselves by substituting more massive

163

modes of participation in divinity for faith in the Christian sense.[63]

Marx lived for sixteen years after the publication of *Das Kapital*, during which time he did nothing of note. While his historical forecasts, his economic model, and his understanding of human nature all proved to be rubbish, he is widely regarded today as one of the modern world's most influential intellectuals, largely, but not exclusively, because three of the world's most notorious mass murderers—Lenin, Stalin, and Moa Tse-tung—built their regimes on his principles. This alone would qualify him as a *Volksgeister*, or a "great man," as famously defined by Carlyle, who accorded this status to those individuals who shaped history on the strength of some combination of intelligence, wisdom, charm, political acumen, courage, and determination.[64]

Yet, when considering this, it is important to keep in mind the philosopher Herbert Spencer's critical response to Carlyle's thesis, that is, "If it be a fact that the great man may modify his nation in its structure and actions, it is also a fact there must have been those antecedent modifications constitution national progress before he could be evolved. Before he can remake his society, his society must make him."[65] This was certainly the case for Marx. The genesis of his greatness was, as we said in the beginning of this chapter, the nihilism that rolled across Europe in the wake of the Enlightenment and the French revolution. Without these, he and his "scientific ideas" would have gone down in history with those of the medieval sorcerers.

Of course, his relentless attack on Christianity contributed substantially to the continued growth of this nihilism, which reached a historic crescendo in 1883, the year before Marx died, when Nietzsche's "Madman" announced in *The Gay Science* that the God of Abraham, who had served as the foundation of Western society for almost two thousand years, was dead. To wit:

> "Where is God gone?" he called out. "I mean to tell you! We have killed him, you and I! We are all his murderers! But how have we

done it? How were we able to drink up the sea? Who gave us the sponge to wipe away the whole horizon? What did we do when we loosened this earth from its sun? Whither does it now move? Whither do we move? Away from all suns? Do we not dash on unceasingly? Backwards, sideways, forwards, in all directions? Is there still an above and below? Do we not stray, as through infinite nothingness? Does not empty space breathe upon us? Has it not become colder? Does not night come on continually, darker and darker? Shall we not have to light lanterns in the morning? Do we not hear the noise of the grave-diggers who are burying God? Do we not smell the divine putre-faction? —for even Gods putrefy! God is dead! God remains dead! And we have killed him! How shall we console ourselves, the most murderous of all murderers? The holiest and the mightiest that the world has hitherto possessed, has bled to death under our knife—who will wipe away the blood from us? With what water could we cleanse ourselves? What lustrums, what sacred games shall we have to devise? Is not the mag-nitude of this deed too great for us? Shall we not ourselves have to become Gods, merely to seem worthy of it? There never was a greater event— and on account of it, all who are born after us belong to a higher history than any history hith-erto!" —Here the madman was silent and looked again at his hearers; they also were silent and looked at him in surprise. At last he threw his lantern on the ground, so that it broke in pieces and was extinguished. "I come too early," he then said, "I am not yet at the right time. This prodi-gious event is still on its way, and is travelling— it has not yet reached men's ears. Lightning and thunder need time, the light of the stars needs time, deeds need time, even after they are done, to be seen and heard. This deed is as yet further from them than the furthest star—and yet they have done it!"[66]

Let's let the poets in on the fun.

> On the Death of a Metaphysician
> Unhappy dreamer, who outwinged in flight
> The pleasant region of the things I love,
> And soared beyond the sunshine, and above
> The golden cornfields and the dear and bright
> Warmth of the hearth, —blasphemer of delight,
> Was your proud bosom not at peace with Jove,
> That you sought, thankless for his guarded grove,
> The empty horror of abysmal night?
> Ah, the thin air is cold above the moon!
> I stood and saw you fall, befooled in death,
> As, in your numbed spirit's fatal swoon,
> You cried you were a god, or were to be;
> I heard with feeble moan your boastful breath
> Bubble from depths of the Icarian sea.
> George Santayana, 1894

Chapter 6

Anarchy and the First Whiff of Fascism

Anarchism: The name given to a principle or theory of life and conduct under which society is conceived without government—harmony in such a society being obtained, not by submission to law, or by obedience to any authority, but by free agreements between the various groups, territorial and professional, freely constituted for the sake of production and consumption as also for the satisfaction of the infinite variety of needs and aspirations of a civilised being. In a society developed on these lines, the voluntary associations which already now begin to cover all the fields of human activity would take a still greater extension so as to substitute themselves for the state in all its functions. They would represent an interwoven network, composed of an infinite variety of groups and federations of all sizes and degrees, local, regional, national and international temporary or more or less permanent—for all possible purposes: production, consumption and exchange, communications, sanitary arrangements, education, mutual protection, defence of the territory, and so on; and, on the other side, for the satisfaction of an ever-increasing number of scientific, artistic, literary and sociable needs. Moreover, such a society would represent nothing immutable. On the contrary—as is seen in organic life at large—harmony would (it is contended) result from an ever-changing adjustment and readjustment of equilibrium between the multitudes of forces and influences, and this adjustment would be the easier to obtain as none of the forces would enjoy a special protection from the state. (Prince Peter Kropotkin, 11th Edition of the *Encyclopedia Britannica*, 1911)

Marxism, as outlined in the Communist Manifesto and later in *Das Kapital*, had several contemporary competitors that were quite different in their approach to collectivism and their ultimate goals. However, all of them all traced their origins to some combination of the thoughts of Rousseau, the events of the French revolution, and the efforts of the Babeufian revolutionaries and the Utopian Socialists to create a new world order in the immediate aftermath of the post–Napoleonic Wars.

The most important of these was Godwin's anarchism, as revised and promoted many years later by three extraordinary individuals: Pierre-Joseph Proudhon, the philosopher; Michael Bakunin, the hammer; and Prince Peter Kropotkin, the propagandist.

We will begin our discussion of this virulent form of leftist thought by noting that there are almost as many types of anarchism as there are anarchists, which stands to reason given their distrust of authority. However, most anarchists are not advocates of political chaos, or no government whatsoever, as the name implies. They are, instead, against hierarchies.

Simply stated, then, they advocate government by a committee of the whole with no chairperson. This is, of course, an amazingly stupid idea, as any child with even limited playground experience can attest because, like it or not, leaders emerge naturally in human societies. Man is a competitive animal. Power is an aphrodisiac. As a practical matter, however, this flaw in anarchism is not that important, since anarchists have historically been more interested in attacking existing hierarchies than with the task of creating leaderless societies. Like recreational sailing, anarchy is more about the voyage than the destination.

All of this is not to imply that anarchists are stupid. In fact, anarchism's pedigree is arguably more prestigious than that of Marxism, and its intellectual foundation, while deeply flawed, is more honest and straightforward than the "scientific" hogwash contained in the *Das Kapital*. While no nation ever adopted it as a government model, many individual anarchists profoundly altered the course of history by both deed and philosophy. In fact, while Proudhon regarded all forms of government as enemies of freedom, his theories on the subject provided philosophical succor to the founders of Italian Fascism and German National Socialism.

As noted previously, Godwin first formulated anarchism in 1793, which was twenty-five years before Marx was born and a half century before he and his radical friends began meeting in a Berlin tavern. Of course, the form of anarchism that would challenge Marxism in the mid-nineteenth century was somewhat different from that outlined by Godwin, but it was based on the same arguments and contained many of the same elements that made Godwin's formulation both exceedingly popular and dangerous.

Proudhon is often cited as the "father of anarchism," and while this may not exactly true, he was the first to notable person to describe himself one. He was born in 1809, the son of a barrel maker. He was a brilliant child, and his mother taught him to read. At the age of eighteen, he went to work as a printer and then as a proofreader in a shop that concentrated on ecclesiastical books. In the course of his work, he became interested in theology, taught himself to read Latin, Greek, and Hebrew, and by 1838 he had earned a small, three-year monetary award from the Academy of Besançon for being a young man of promise.

At that point, he moved to Paris, where he lived an ascetic life and began writing socialist tracts, including one of the first, great revolutionary tomes of the period entitled "What Is Property?", in which he answered his own question with the declaration, "Property is theft." He put this in the first paragraph of the book, which was published in 1840, about the time that Marx and his fellow young Hegelians were meeting in a Berlin tavern. To wit:

> If I were asked to answer the following question: What is slavery? and I should answer in one word, It is murder, my meaning would be understood at once. No extended argument would be required to show that the power to take from a man his thought, his will, his personality, is a power of life and death; and that to enslave a man is to kill him. Why, then, to this other question: What is property! may I not likewise answer, It is robbery, without the certainty of being misunderstood; the second proposition being no other than a transformation of the first?[1]

The young Marx was impressed, and in 1845, shortly after Hess had converted him to communism, he wrote Proudhon a letter asking him to contribute to an organized correspondence, designed to keep communists in different countries in touch with each other. In his reply, Proudhon agreed to cooperate with the project, but then, taking a swipe at the authoritarian nature of Marx, warned against becoming "leaders of a new intolerance ... apostles of a new religion." To add salt to the wound, he stated that he was no longer in favor of a violent revolution as a means of achieving a better world, which, of course, would become the sine qua non of Marxism.[2]

Marx quickly realized that Proudhon presented least as great a threat to his vision of the future as Stirner. So he and Engels wrote a pamphlet entitled "The Poverty of Philosophy." Published in 1847, it viciously attacked Proudhon and his ideas and accused him, among other things, of being nothing more than a "petty bourgeois." Shortly after, Proudhon published a pamphlet entitled "The Philosophy of Poverty," in which he added God to his list of evils. To wit:

For God is stupidity and cowardice; God is hypocrisy and falsehood; God is tyranny and misery; God is evil. As long as humanity shall bend before an altar, humanity, the slave of kings and priests, will be condemned; as long as one man, in the name of God, shall receive the oath of another man, society will be founded on perjury; peace and love will be banished from among mortals. God, take yourself away! for, from this day forth, cured of your fear and become wise, I swear, with hand extended to heaven, that you are only the tormentor of my reason, the spectre of my conscience.

I deny, therefore, the supremacy of God over humanity; I reject his providential government, the non-existence of which is sufficiently established by the metaphysical and economical hallucinations of humanity, —in a word, by the martyrdom of our race; I decline the jurisdiction of the Supreme Being over man; I take away his titles of father, king, judge, good, merciful, pitiful, helpful, rewarding, and avenging. All these attributes, of which the idea of Providence is made up, are but a caricature of humanity, irreconcilable with the autonomy of civilization, and contradicted, moreover, by the history of its aberrations and catastrophes. Does it follow, because God can no longer be conceived as Providence, because we take from him that attribute so important to man that he has not hesitated to make it the synonym of God, that God does not exist, and that the theological dogma from this moment is shown to be false in its content?[3]

In 1851, he stated his case against all governments in a book entitled *General Idea of the Revolution in the Nineteenth Century.*

To be GOVERNED is to be kept in sight, inspected, spied upon, directed, law-driven, numbered, numbered, enrolled, indoctrinated, preached at, controlled, estimated, valued, censured, commanded, by creatures who have neither the right nor the wisdom nor the virtue to do so. To be GOVERNED is to be at every operation, at every transaction noted, registered, enrolled, taxed, stamped, measured, numbered, assessed, licensed, authorized, admonished, forbidden, reformed, corrected, punished. It is, under pretext of public utility, and in the name of the general interest, to be place[d] under contribution, trained, ransomed, exploited, monopolized, extorted, squeezed, mystified, robbed; then, at the slightest resistance, the first word of complaint, to be repressed, fined, despised, harassed, tracked, abused, clubbed, disarmed, choked, imprisoned, judged, condemned, shot, deported, sacrificed, sold, betrayed; and to crown all, mocked, ridiculed, outraged, dishonored. That is government; that is its justice; that is its morality.[4]

Here we come to Proudhon's—not anarchism's but Proudhon's—odd relationship to fascism. You see, as Marx correctly noted, Proudhon was indeed a champion of the "*class moyenne.*" Yes, he was a bona fide revolutionary who hated capitalism, but he also hated socialism. His heart was with the small shopkeepers, the artisans, the worker-owners. After all, he was the son of a cooper and had managed his own printing operation. These folks were not only threatened by capitalists, with their machines and their Jewish bankers, whom Proudhon detested, but also by socialism and Marxism, which regarded them as the enemy whose business needed to be nationalized.

In short, as the historian J. Salwyn Schapiro explained it, Proudhon chose anarchism because it was "an antidote to socialism."

His problem then was "How to preserve property rights and, at the same time, abolish capitalism? How to safeguard the small property owner against his economic enemies: big business and revolutionary socialism?" The first part of his answer to this conundrum was to eliminate the ownership of property by *rentiers*, while leaving the ownership of the "possessions of production" to those who actually used them. Here's Schapiro:

> According to Proudhon, property was, in essence, a privilege to obtain rent, profit, and interest without any labor whatsoever. It reaped without sowing, consumed without producing, and enjoyed without exertion. It was the "worst usurer as well as the worst master and worst debtor." There could be no justification for property on any ground natural right, law, or occupation because, according to Proudhon, it creates and maintains social inequality, the prime source of all human woe. All efforts to abolish it had been in vain. The greatest of all changes in history, the French Revolution, did not abolish the rule of propertied classes; all that it did was to substitute the rule of bourgeois for that of aristocratic property owners. Therefore, the revolution must go on until property is abolished altogether. Then, and only then, will mankind enjoy equality.[5]

The second part of this solution to the problem was to take the monopoly on money away from the capitalists and extend credit to everyone.

> This revolution, the greatest in history, was to be accomplished by the establishment of free credit, *credit gratuit*. A People's Bank (Banque du Peuple) was to be organized to take the place

of the Bank of France. Unlike the latter, the former was to have no subscribed capital, no stock-
holders, no gold reserve. It was neither to pay
nor to charge interest, except a nominal charge
to cover overhead. All business transactions in
the nation were to be centralized in the People's
Bank, which was to be a bank of exchange and a
market for all the products of the nation. It was
to issue notes; based neither on specie nor on
land but on actual business values. The producer
or seller would consign his product to the bank
and receive in return not money but exchange
notes, the amount of which would be based on
the value of the goods consigned, as determined
by the amount of labor that produced them. The
seller would use these notes to purchase whatever
he needed. The goods would then be sold by the
bank to buyers, who would give to the bank the
same amount, in notes, as that paid to the sell-
ers. No profit would result from either transaction. The chief function of the bank would be
to universalize the bill of exchange by facilitating
the exchange of goods between producers and
consumers through exchange notes instead of
money. ...

With free credit a new economic order
would arise, more free, more enterprising, more
productive than capitalism. ... Private enterprise
would remain, and competition, the vital force
that animated all society, would continue to regulate market prices ... This greatest of all revolutions in history would be put through "without
confiscation, without bankruptcy, without an
agrarian law, without common ownership, without state intervention, and without the abolition
of inheritance."[6]

Of course, this idea went nowhere, even within the anarchist movement itself. Yet, *Proudhon's idea of a revolution waged on behalf of the middle class against the capitalists, their Jewish bankers, and the communists would find a comfortable home in Italy and Germany during the interregnum.*

We will discuss this unfortunate happenstance in a later chapter. In the meantime, Michael Bakunin, one of nineteenth-century Europe's most colorful characters, would carry Proudhon's anarchism to barricades. He was a Russian aristocrat, a giant of a man who weighed over 250 pounds, sported a huge black beard, had a booming voice, and a seemingly bottomless supply of courage and energy. He was the inspiration for Turgenev's character Rudin in his novelette by that name.[7] According to George Bernard Shaw, he was used by Richard Wagner as the model for Siegfried in the opera by that name.[8] He coined the phrase "the passion for destruction is also a creative passion."[9] He coauthored Nechayev's "Catechism of a Revolutionist," which Max Nomad described in his classic 1939 book *Apostles of Revolution* as describing a "system of complete disregard for any tenets of simple decency and fairness in [the revolutionaries] attitude towards other human beings."[10]

After serving in the Russian military, he studied philosophy and became a fan of Fichte, which led him to Hegel, which led him to Berlin, and then to Dresden where he made a name for himself within the radical community by writing for Ruge. When Ruge ran into trouble with the authorities, Bakunin left for Switzerland where he was associated for a while with Weitling. In 1847, he wound up in Paris, where he finally met Proudhon. Bakunin earned his spurs in 1849 during an uprising in Dresden. Bakunin's friend and comrade in arms, the anarchist James Guillaume, described Bakunin's adventures in Dresden as follows.

> For five days the rebels controlled the city. Bakunin, who had left Leipzig for Dresden in the middle of April, became one of the leaders of the rebellion and inspired the highest measure of heroism in the men defending the barricades

against the Prussian troops. A gigantic figure of a man, already renowned as a revolutionary, Bakunin became the focus of all eyes. An aura of legend soon enveloped him. To him alone were attributed the fires set by the rebels; about him it was written that he was "the very soul of the Revolution," that he initiated widespread terrorism, that to stop the Prussians from shooting into the barricades he advised the defenders to take the art treasures from the museums and galleries and display them from the barricades—the stories were endless.

On May 9, the rebels—greatly outnumbered and outgunned—retreated to Freiberg. There Bakunin pleaded in vain with Stephen Born (organizer of the *Arbeiter Verbruderung*, the first organization of German workers) to take his remaining troops to Bohemia and spark a new uprising. Born refused, and disbanded his forces. Seeing that there was nothing more to be done, Bakunin, the composer Richard Wagner, and [the noted physician Otto] Heubner—a democrat, very loyal to Bakunin—went to Chemnitz. There, during the night, armed bourgeois arrested Heubner and Bakunin and turned them over to the Prussians. Wagner hid in his sister's house and escaped.[11]

Bakunin was arrested and sentenced to death. His sentence was commuted to life, and he spent two years chained to a wall in an Austrian prison and then was sent back to Russia where he served six more years under brutal conditions in the infamous Fortress of Peter and Paul. He was eventually exiled to Siberia, where he escaped via Japan, San Francisco, the Panama Canal, New York, Boston, Liverpool, and finally to London where we walked in on his old friend, writer and Russian revolutionary Alexander Herzen while he was having dinner and declared that "I shall continue to be an impossible person so long as those who are now possible remain possible."[12]

After his return, he traveled all over Europe, founding secret conspiratorial societies and participating in every uprising he could find.

> It was during this period that he conceived the plan of forming a secret organization of revolutionaries to carry on propaganda work and prepare for direct action at a suitable time. From 1864 onward he steadily recruited Italians, Frenchmen, Scandinavians, and Slavs into a secret society known as the International Brotherhood, also called the Alliance of Revolutionary Socialists. He and his friends also combated the devoutly religious followers of the republican [Giuseppe] Mazzini, whose watchword was "God and Country." In Naples, Bakunin established the journal *Libertà e Giustizia* ("Liberty and Justice"), in which he developed his revolutionary program.
>
> In July 1866, he informed his friends Herzen and [Herzen's friend and fellow exile Nikolay] Ogarev about the secret society and its program, on which he had been concentrating all his efforts for two years. According to Bakunin, the society then had members in Sweden, Norway, Denmark, Belgium, England, France, Spain, and Italy, as well as Polish and Russian members.[13]

Needless to say, Marx despised Bakunin not only for his beliefs but for his immense popularity and legendary magnetism. Historian Paul Thomas described this characteristic as follows:

> To Marx, Bakunin represented some old, pre-given *bête noire*—Proudhonism in Russian

clothing, or Russia itself. Yet in fact Bakunin represented much more than Marx's old bugbears. The extraordinary thing is that he could personify emancipation, revolt, revolution, that he could be *l'homme* révolté even to the distinctly non-revolutionary bourgeois ... An eyewitness account of Bakunin's appearance at the Geneva Congress of the League [for Peace and Freedom] makes this clear:

As with heavy, awkward gait he mounted the steps leading to the platform where the bureau sat, dressed as carelessly as ever in a sort of gray blouse, beneath which was visible not a shirt but a flannel vest, the cry passed from mouth to mouth: "Bakunin!" Garibaldi, who was in the chair, stood up, advanced a few steps, and embraced him. This solemn meeting of two old and tired warriors of revolution produced an astonishing impression ... Everyone rose, and there was prolonged and enthusiastic applause.[14]

Of course, Bakunin was no fan of Marx's either. He expounded on his feelings toward Marx and Marxism in numerous essays written in and around 1870. Here are two such.

Marx as a thinker is on the right path. He has established the principle that juridical evolution in history is not the cause but the effect of economic development, and this is a great and fruitful concept. Though he did not originate it—it was to a greater or lesser extent formulated before him by many others—to Marx belongs the credit for solidly establishing it as the basis for an economic system. On the other hand, Proudhon understood and felt liberty much better than he. Proudhon, when not obsessed with metaphysi-

178

cal doctrine, was a revolutionary by instinct; he adored Satan and proclaimed Anarchy. Quite possibly Marx could construct a still more rational system of liberty, but he lacks the instinct of liberty—*he remains from head to foot an authoritarian.* [Emphasis added][15]

But in the People's State of Marx there will be, we are told, no privileged class at all. All will be equal, not only from the juridical and political point of view but also from the economic point of view. At least this is what is promised, though I very much doubt whether that promise could ever be kept. There will therefore no longer be any privileged class, but there will be a government and, note this well, an extremely complex government. This government will not content itself with administering and governing the masses politically, as all governments do today. It will also administer the masses economically, concentrating in the hands of the State the production and division of wealth, the cultivation of land, the establishment and development of factories, the organization and direction of commerce, and finally the application of capital to production by the only banker—the State. All that will demand an immense knowledge and many heads "overflowing with brains" in this government. It will be the reign of *scientific intelligence,* the most aristocratic, despotic, arrogant, and elitist of all regimes. There will be a new class, a new hierarchy of real and counterfeit scientists and scholars, and the world will be divided into a minority ruling in the name of knowledge, and an immense ignorant majority. And then, woe unto the mass of ignorant ones!

Such a regime will not fail to arouse very considerable discontent in the masses of the people, and in order to keep them in check, the "enlightened" and "liberating" government of Mr. Marx will have need of a not less considerable armed force. For the government must be strong, says Engels, to maintain order among these millions of illiterates whose mighty uprising would be capable of destroying and overthrowing everything, even a government "overflowing with brains."[16]

At one point, Marx became so concerned about the rising influence of the Bakuninists that he called for a meeting of the International in The Hague, which Bakunin could not attend because he would have had to pass through Germany, where he would have been arrested. The plan succeeded in keeping Bakunin away, but to cement his victory, Marx moved the headquarters of the International from London to New York City.

In any case, when the dust finally settled on the battleground early in the twentieth century, it was clear that Marx had won. The prototype for the new, tacitly united leftist ideology turned out to be, much as Bakunin had forecast, that is, a highly centralized, governmental behemoth managed by an elite crowd of officials and agencies and offices and bureaus and thought police who were collectively even more powerful, entrenched, and oppressive than the one that the revolutionaries had toppled, and bore no resemblance whatsoever to the "worker's paradise" that theoretically had been the goal of the entire exercise.

Indeed, if any of early founders of the Left had lived to see the result of their efforts, none would have been pleased. Not the revolutionaries who manned the barricades, spent time in prison, and sacrificed their lives on the altar of "reason," nor the intellectuals who had devoted their time, energy, intellect, and reputations to the discovery of an alternative moral and economic system to replace the old Judeo-Christian one.

The third remarkable figure in the early history of anarchism was the above-mentioned [Prince] Peter Kropotkin. His father was a wealthy prince of the Rurik dynasty. It was one of Europe's oldest royal families having ruled Russia before the Romanovs. He had once been a page at the court of the Tsar, had served in the Russian military, and was a highly respected geographer who did extensive work in Siberia. Over the years, however, he dropped the title of prince, became enthralled by Herzen's fight for the emancipation of the serfs, took an interest in the workers' movement in Europe, and was particularly taken by reports of the Paris Commune that ruled France for a brief period following the Franco-Prussian War. He went to Switzerland where he encountered Bakunin's close friend James Guillaume and became a committed anarchist.

In 1874, he returned to Russia and became engaged in revolutionary activities. He was arrested and imprisoned in the Fortress of Peter and Paul. In his *Memories*, he describes the horrible conditions there and notes that he kept his faith by thinking of Bakunin, who had survived six years there and had emerged "fresher and fuller of vigor than his comrades who had remained at liberty."[17] After two years, he escaped with the help of friends. He stayed in London for a while. Then he went back to France where he was arrested for engaging in revolutionary activities and imprisoned for four years, from 1882 to 1886. He then moved back to London, where he spent the next thirty-five years writing anarchist books and pamphlets inciting workingmen around the world to violence against the established order.

Richard Suskind, in his classic book on the subject of anarchism, *By Bullet, Bomb and Dagger* (a phrase taken from a Kropotkin pamphlet), describes Kropotkin as the "one of the most dangerous men who ever lived, for he had an apocalyptic vision of the revolution that was rivaled only by that of Bakunin himself." Then he notes that George Bernard Shaw described Kropotkin as "amiable to the point of saintliness, and with his full beard and loveable expression might have been a shepherd from the Delectable Mountains," and that Oscar Wilde spoke of him as a "man with a soul of that beautiful white Christ that seems to be coming out of Russia." This paradox, Suskind notes "would have both saddened and delighted Proudhon, this gentle soul rather than Bakunin, the 'complete rebel,' who raised anarchism to its final apotheosis of violence and who gave it the semi-mystical and religious connotation it has had ever since." For him, talk was not enough. He put it this way: "To hurl mankind out of its ruts into new roads, revolution becomes a peremptory necessity."[18]

And lo, his clarion call to the "propaganda of the deed," a phrase minted by the Italian anarchist Carlo Pisacane, set the stage for the future anarchists who, in the late nineteenth and early twentieth century, murdered thousands of innocent people all over Europe and the United States.

One of these innocents was US President William McKinley, which led to the presidency of "His Accidency" Vice President Teddy Roosevelt, the first "Progressive" to occupy the Oval Office and thereby the father of the political Left's attack on the US Constitution. Another victim of the anarchists was the Austrian Archduke Franz Ferdinand, whose murder started the largest and ghastliest war in human history up to that point and led the "Progressive" Woodrow Wilson's pledge to "make the world safe for Democracy."

Let's let the poets in on the fun.

> Gare du Midi
> A nondescript express in from the South,
> Crowds round the ticket barrier, a face
> To Welcome which the major has not contrived
> Bugles or braid: something about the mouth
> Distracts the stray look with alarm and pity.
> Snow is falling. Clutching a little case,
> He walks out briskly to infect a city
> Whose terrible future may have just arrived.
> W. H. Auden, 1938

Part II

The Early Years in Europe

> *Those who wanted to destroy social inequalities and exploitation found themselves facing three questions. Were they going to use revolutionary or legal means? Should a mass-movement of peasants or workers remain entirely separate from the middle class, or should it collaborate with bourgeois radicals who shared some of the same goals? Lastly, should the aim be to seize political power in order to further social reform, or should political power itself be destroyed as exploitative and evil in itself?*
> (Robert Gildea, in *Barricades and Borders, Europe 1800–1914*)

By the mid-nineteenth century, leftist radicals had become a significant factor in the politics of every European nation. However, in none had they achieved real political power. Myriad barriers stood in their way. These included the lingering religious convictions of much of the public; the rise of European imperialism; a steady increase in the size and influence of the bourgeoisie; a resultant improvement in living standards of the proletariat; and the relentless march of new technology, including electricity and steam power. All of which spurred revolutionary changes in the size and structures of industries and created what Harvard historian Alfred Chandler would later describe as a Second Industrial Revolution, which he noted required much larger commitments of capital than the first one.[1]

Perhaps the most formidable obstacle to the left's acquisition of political power was the incessant, internecine struggle between the various factions within the movement over how to achieve victory. On one side, there were the Marxists and anarchists, who believed that violent revolution was the only choice. On the other side, there those who became known as socialists, who recognized that Marx's dream of vast proletariat revolution was not going be realized and that the more realistic pathway to success was to work within the existing political system.

Part 2 will focus on the leading combatants in this internecine conflict, whose ideas and actions changed the history of both the Left and the world.

Let's let the poets in on the fun.

> Hem and Haw
> Hem and Haw were the sons of sin,
> Created to shally and shirk;
> Hem lay 'round and Haw looked on
> While God did all the work.
> Hem was a fogey, and Haw was a prig,
> For both had the dull, dull mind;
> And whenever they found a thing to do,
> They yammered and went it blind.
> Hem was the father of bigots and bores;
> As the sands of the sea were they.
> And Haw was the father of all the tribe
> Who criticize to-day.
> But God was an artist from the first,
> And knew what he was about;
> While over his shoulder sneered these two,

And advised him to rub it out.
They prophesied ruin ere man was made:
'Such folly must surely fail!'
And when he was done, 'Do you think, my Lord,
He's better without a tail?'
And still in the honest working world,
With posture and hint and smirk,
These sons of the devil are standing by
While Man does all the work.
They balk endeavour and baffle reform
In the sacred name of the law;
And over the quavering voice of Hem
Is the droning voice of Haw.
Bliss Carman, 1924

Chapter 7

Germany: Bismarck, Lassalle, and Schmoller

At that time Bismarck had no rival in Europe for intelligence. The kings and the emperors could not think or could not act. Francis Joseph lacked experience; Napoleon was worn out; Alexander was too dense; William, Victoria, and Victor Emmanuel were mediocrities, incompetent to carry out polices of their own; neither 'Gladstone nor Disraeli had yet attained the summit of power; Gorchakoff was too vain; Cavour, notable after his fashion, died just at the time when Bismarck came to the front. Only in Prussia was there yet another political genius. His name was Ferdinand Lassalle. Though he had no considerable party to back him up, though he was a revolutionist, though he could not allure his great opponent either by kinship of ideas or by power, Lassalle speedily won recognition from Bismarck. It was the magnetism of genius, nothing else, that drew Bismarck and Lassalle together ... both were ani-mated by the same impulse. The Jewish socialist and the Pomeranian Junker were alike spurred to action by pride, courage, and hatred; in both of them, these motives engendered the will-to-power; neither knew the meaning of fear, neither could put up with a superior, neither really loved. Just as Bismarck hated powerful Austria more strongly than he loved the less powerful Prussia, so was Lassalle less inspired by sympathy with the fourth estate than dislike of the third. (Emil Ludwig, *Bismarck, The Story of a Fighter*, 1939)

The first prominent, boots-on-the-ground leftist to recognize that Marxism would not work "in praxis" was a German labor activist namedd Ferdinand Lassalle. He was a brilliant and colorful character, and one of a long list of Karl Marx's early comrades upon whom he turned on with a vengeance in later years. Saul K. Padover describes Lassalle thusly in one of the "explanatory notes" in his book *The Letters of Karl Marx.*

A brilliant jurist, orator, scholar, and labor organizer, Lassalle, as a young man, was close to Marx and his communist circle (although never a communist himself) in Brussels and Cologne. Subsequently, while Marx lived in penurious exile in London, Lassalle pursued his triumphant, albeit flamboyant, career in Germany, culminating in his founding of the first German national labor party—*Allgemeiner Deutsche Arbeiterverein*—in 1863. Later, the *Arbeiterverein* merged with other labor organizations to form Germany's powerful, Marxist-oriented Social-Democratic Party. At the age of thirty-nine, Lassalle, after a long-standing relationship with a loyal older woman, Countess von Hatzfeldt, was killed in a duel—which Marx and Engels considered silly—over a nineteen-year-old girl.

Marx's attitude toward Lassalle, who was seven years his junior, was characterized by love-hate feelings. While Lassalle admired and helped

Marx whenever asked, the latter was clearly jealous of the power, fame, influence, and wealth achieved by Lassalle through sheer talents and guts. Deeply envious, and yet admiring, Marx indulged in scathing anti-Semitic remarks about Lassalle ("Nigger-Jew," etc.) in his private letters.[1]

In a letter to Marx immediately after Lassalle's death, Engels described their relationship thusly:

> You can imagine how the news surprised me. Personally, historically, scientifically, Lassalle may have been what he was, but politically he was surely one of the most outstanding fellows in Germany. For us he was uncertain friend in the present, quite certainly an enemy in the future, but nevertheless it hits one hard to see how Germany destroys all moderately capable men of the extreme party[2]

The "enemy in the future" line refers to three factors. First, Lassalle was out there in the real world selling socialism to real live workers and risking imprisonment or worse at the hands of the Prussian police. This meant he had a very good chance of becoming Europe's leading socialist philosopher and political leader, while Marx was invisibly ensconced in the British museum, nursing his boils and his hatreds, and writing his crackpot theories down in a book that might never be read.

Second, and even more importantly, the dream that Lassalle was pitching was very different from Marx's withering away of government. Lassalle's theory was unadulterated nonsense, of course, but it was no more so than Marx's. It was based on the "iron law of wages," a phrase he coined for a theory first advanced by the British economist Thomas Malthus, namely that a worker's wage could not exceed the bare minimum for subsistence for himself and for a small family. The extremely tortured reasoning behind this theory went as follows: an increase in wages will prompt the worker to have more children, which will expand the labor force and result in a decrease in wages. A cut in wages will result in smaller families, thus reducing the labor force and causing an increase in wages. Simply stated, Lassalle's answer to this gloomy conundrum was to form a partnership with government that would finance and promote workers' cooperatives, which, with enhanced universal suffrage, would strengthen the government.

Finally, there was Lassalle's budding, behind-the-scenes relationship with none other than Otto von Bismarck, the most powerful, conservative, anticommunist, antisocialist, monarchist politician in all of Europe. David Footman described the origins of this unlikely alliance of interests thusly in his book *Ferdinand Lassalle, Romantic Revolutionary.*

> The Bismarck-Lassalle correspondence (discovered in Berlin in 1927) starts with the original invitation, with corrections in Bismarck's own hand, dated the 11 May 1863: "In connexion with current deliberations on working-class conditions and problems I wish to obtain considered opinions from independent quarters. I would, therefore, be glad to have your views on these issues."
>
> This note was brought personally by [Carl Ludwig] Zitelmann, one of Bismarck's staff, who was charged to arrange an early meeting. Lassalle acknowledged the note the same day, and the first meeting took place within forty-eight hours. Fifteen years later (September 1878) Bismarck was pressed by [August] Bebel [a socialist critic of Bismarck] in the Reichstag to give an account of his relations with Lassalle. The Chancellor made the following statement:
>
> I saw him, and since my first conversation. I have never regretted doing so. I did not see him three or four times in that first week: I saw him

perhaps three or four times altogether. There was never the possibility of our talks taking the form of political negotiations. What could Lassalle have offered me? He had nothing behind him. In political negotiations the principle of *do ut des* is always present, though politeness may prevent it being voiced. He, as a minister, could have given me nothing. But he attracted me as an individual. He was one of the most intelligent and likeable men I had ever come across. He was very ambitious and by no means a republican. He was very much a nationalist and a monarchist. His ideal was the German Empire, and here was our point of contact. As I have said he was ambitious, on a large scale, and there is perhaps room for doubt as to whether, in his eyes, the German Empire ultimately entailed the Hohenzollern or the Lassalle dynasty ... Our talks lasted for hours and I was always sorry when they came to an end ... I am sorry that our positions did not allow a more extended intercourse. I would have been glad to have as a neighbor a man of such intellect and talent.[3]

Of course, Bismarck would not have requested a meeting with Lassalle if the socialist radical truly had nothing to offer. For the fact of the matter is that Bismarck was deeply involved at the time in the most important project of his life, namely the unification of Germany. And he needed Lassalle's support against their common foe, Germany's growing middle class, which was antagonistic to both the monarchy and to Prussian militarism, as well as, in Lassalle's mind at least, the interests of the proletariat workers. The English historian Robert Gildea explains it this way:

> The enemy was the liberal middle class; and Bismarck was prepared to enter into nego-

tiations with one section of the organized working class. This was the General German Workers' Union which was founded at Leipzig in May 1863, and led by the lawyer, writer, and gallant, Ferdinand Lassalle. Hostile to a bourgeoisie which was shored up by a property franchise and was ruthlessly exploiting the workers, Lassalle demanded universal suffrage and a producers' co-operative, and looked to Bismarck's state to finance them.[4]

The Swiss historian Emil Ludwig's discussion of the relationship in his classic biography of Bismarck dovetails with Gildea's. To wit:

The thing that brought the two men together was the fight against the bourgeoisie. Bismarck wanted power to use against the constitution; Lassalle wanted to mobilise the masses. Bismarck had weapons in his hands, weapons with which he forcibly equipped men; Lassalle had men at his disposal, men who were vainly clamouring for weapons. Each of them essentially desired a dictatorship under his own guidance; each of them detested free trade in goods and ideas, and detested no less the champions of free trade, the liberals.[5]

Bismarck, of course, hated socialism and fought against it his entire life. But he clearly saw some interesting possibilities for neutralizing the growing power of the bourgeoisie in Lassalle's government-sponsored and subsidized labor cooperatives along with his demand for universal suffrage. In fact, while Lassalle did not live to see it, in 1866 when Bismarck founded the Confederation of Northern Germany, he did so on the basis of universal suffrage, which, in the opinion of the French historian Élie *Halévy* in his 1941 book *The Era of Tyrannies*, had been a direct result of Lassalle's influence.[6]

In any case, while Lassalle is often described as the father of German socialism, Bismarck is just as often given credit for being the father of the German welfare state, which appears to be a distinction without a difference. And therein lies the beginning of the fascinating story of Bismarck's strange battle with socialism. To wit:

> Bismarck was the most charismatic, brilliant, visionary, and ruthless politician of his age. He annexed Schleswig to Prussia in 1865 by joining with Austria in a war against Denmark, and shortly thereafter humiliated the Austrians in the Seven Weeks War, in which he famously telegraphed general on crossing the Elbe into Austrian territory, "Treat them as fellow countrymen, homicidally if necessary."[7]
>
> He provoked an attack by the French in July 1870, as part of his plan to draw the German states in Southern Germany into an alliance with the North German Confederation, which Prussia dominated. The war was effectively over in early September when Napoleon III's forces were defeated at the Battle of Sedan. When news of the defeat reached Paris, a provisional government was established. Its leaders refused to surrender. Bismarck sieged the city. Three months later its citizens were starving. The new French government sent an emissary to negotiate a peace with Bismarck. Bismarck refused both to recognize the legitimacy of the new government and to lift the siege. The emissary asked, "Are you not afraid of making our resistance even fiercer." Bismarck's response was classic.
>
> Your resistance! You have no right—please listen to me carefully—you have no right, before man and God, for the sake of so pitiable a thing as military renown, to give over to famine a town

with a population of more than two millions?
Don't talk of resistance. In this case it is a crime.[8]

France surrendered. Germany was unified.

Now, historians have argued for years about Bismarck's motives for supporting various socialistic efforts to provide government benefits to workers. But his reasons were actually fairly simple.

His concern was that the widespread unrest among Germany's laboring class, which Lassalle had effectively united, would lead to the kind of revolutionary activities that swept Europe in 1848. His plan was to continue to play the proletariat and the bourgeoisie against each other, as he had with Lassalle's help, for as long as he could get away with it. In the meantime, he planned to try to convince the laboring class that their best hope for achieving a better life was in partnership with the monarchy against the industrialists and the bourgeoisie.

The first element of this plan was to continuously express his understanding and sympathy with the notion that the government had a responsibility to do more for the working man. Ludwig offers the following quotes, the first made in 1871 and the second ten years later, that highlight Bismarck's continuous public relations program designed to undercut the socialists' claims that the government was not concerned about the needs of the workingman.

> It is time for us to realise what parts of the socialist demands are reasonable and right, and to what extent these reasonable elements can be incorporated into the extant State system.
>
> The State must take the matter in hand, since the state can most easily provide the requisite funds. It must provide them, not as alms, but in fulfillment of the workers' right to look to the State for help in matters where their own good will can achieve nothing more. Why should not the labour soldier receive a pension, just as much as the man who has been disabled or has grown old in the army of the civil service?

KNOW THINE ENEMY

Ludwig then notes the motive behind these warm statements. "They are nothing more than the old calculations, the old ciphering, which sound especially cruel when he is setting them forth as the foundations of his 'practical Christianity.'" To wit:

> One who can look forward to an old-age pension is far more contented and much easier to manage. Contrast a man in private service with one who serves at the chancellery, or at court; the two latter must be far more accommodating and obedient than the former, for they have their pensions to think of ... A great price is not too much, if therewith we can make the disinherited satisfied with their lot ... Money thus spent is well invested; it is used to ward off a revolution which ... would cost a great deal more.[9]

In late 1881, Bismarck realized that he had to offer more than just words, and this carrot took the form of his "practical Christianity" speech to the Reichstag in which he proposed a series of insurance programs for workers. The first of these to gain his signature was the Sickness Insurance Law of 1883. It was following the next year by the Accident Insurance Law.

These had no meliorating effect on either the demands or the rapid growth in the socialist ranks. Gildea explained it this way: "The package was meaner than it appeared," in that "only about fifteen per cent of the claims for accident insurance were honoured [and] sick pay was about half the working wage and not available to domestic servants or agricultural workers."[10]

Not surprisingly then, in 1887, after an assassination attempt on the new emperor Wilhelm II by a radical socialist, the strength of the socialist movement became so threatening that the Reichstag passed a new Antisocialism Law, which, among other things, banned any group whose aim was to spread socialist principles, outlawed trade unions, and closed forty-five leftist newspapers. This stick was followed in 1889 by another carrot in the form of the Old Age and

Disability Insurance Law, which was later described by the great Austrian economist Ludwig von Mises in his classic 1922 book, *Socialism*, as "a more momentous pioneering on the way towards socialism than was [Lenin's] expropriation of the backward Russian manufacturers."[11]

Momentous? Yes. But too little to hold back the socialist tide. For, as Gildea notes, this pension plan was as sadly lacking in appeal as the aforementioned accident and sick pay packages, since it was payable only at seventy, after forty-eight years of contributions, and could not be passed on to widows or children in the event of a male worker's death.[12]

Bismarck's reaction was to bring out a bigger stick. The threat was too great to ignore. Unfortunately for him, the new Kaiser Wilhelm II, who had succeeded his grandfather in 1888, decided, against the Iron Chancellor's wishes, to attempt to placate the socialists even further. Bismarck's dismissal was inevitable. The impetus for this is highlighted by Ludwig as follows:

> There is a miners' strike, and the emperor [Wilhelm II] wants to treat it idealistically, whereas the chancellor wants to fight it with blood and iron ... he wants to turn this strike to account against the Reds, to use it for electoral purposes. But the emperor, "unexpectedly, spurs clinking", turns up at the meeting of the cabinet, declares that the mine owners are to blame, says that he has ordered them to pay better wages, failing which he will withdraw his soldiers. We see that the young man dreads the revolution, and wishes to avert it by reforms; the old man wants the revolutionists to show themselves, so that he can shoot them down. ...
>
> "I want to repeal the present Anti-socialist law for I need stronger measures," says the old statesman, and the young emperor is alarmed. Again a crown council is held. The emperor

announces his intention to have labour-protection laws passed. His dream is to avert the threatening revolt, to summon a congress, to address his people "in inspired language" on his birthday.

[Bismarck's friend, agricultural minister] Lucius [von Ballhausen] writes: "We sat there with growing astonishment, wondering who had blown these ideas into his mind." ... Bismarck is the first who is asked to give an opinion. With assumed quietude, he advises postponement, says that if the emperor carries out his plan it will have a bad effect upon the elections, for the possessing classes will be annoyed, while the workers will be encouraged. The emperor makes a civil answer. He says that his main desire is that the anti-socialist Law shall be rendered milder, and he adds that loyal advisers have urged this course upon him. Thereupon Bismarck growls out: "I cannot prove that Your Majesty's yielding policy will have disastrous consequences, but the experience of many years leads me to feel sure that it will ... If we give ground now, we shall not subsequently be able to dissolve the Reichstag, and shall have to await more serious happenings. If the law remains unsettled, there will be a vacuum, and then collisions may ensue!"

The emperor, irritably: "Unless extreme necessity arises, I shall avert such catastrophes, instead of staining the first year of my reign with the blood of my subjects!"

Bismarck: "That would be the fault of the revolutionists; matters will not be settled without bloodshed. That would be a capitulation! It is my duty, in virtue of my experience of these matters, to advise against the course you propose. Since the days of my entry into the government, the

> royal power has been steadily increasing ... This
> voluntary retreat would be the first step in the
> direction of parliamentary government, which
> might be convenient for the moment but would
> prove dangerous in the end. If your Majesty
> is unable to accept my advice, I do not know
> whether I can remain in office."[13]

At this point, we should note that Wilhelm II had an important ally within the German intellectual hierarchy for his attempt to reduce the Left's support among the laboring class by offering governmental handouts. His name was Gustav von Schmoller, a Prussian monarchist who worked tirelessly to promote "social reform" throughout and well beyond the Bismarckian era, and whose leftist legacy plagued Germany well into the twentieth century.

We will begin our account of Schmoller's influence by noting that the publication in 1776 of Adam Smith's *An Inquiry into the Nature and Causes of the Wealth of Nations* had spawned a new intellectual discipline that came to be called "economics." One of the first prominent practitioners of this new "science" was the Englishman David Ricardo. According to the American economist and historian Robert Heilbroner, the writings of this urbane and wealthy man made the topic of "political economy" so popular in England that "ladies who hired governesses inquired whether they could teach its principles to their children."[14]

Naturally, by the middle of the nineteenth century, there were economists all over Europe, exchanging ideas, developing new ones, melding their thoughts with other branches of the soft sciences, such as philosophy, sociology, and politics, and offering theories as to how these relationships might be manipulated in such a way as to benefit society. Not surprisingly, this new field was a matter of great interest to the leftist revolutionaries of the day, who were wont to translate their economic thoughts and theories into elaborate social hypotheses and political slogans designed to rally the masses to rise up against their "oppressors."

After all, were not these "brilliant" practitioners of the new science of economics saying much the same thing as they were? Namely, that being poor and miserable was not an act of God, or the result of some unfathomable force, such as those that cause floods, hurricanes, and plagues, but the result of the actions of men, and that it followed from this that men could change things for the better if they chose?

As might be expected, Germany not only had its full share of revolutionaries at the time, it had a fair number of economists also. Unfortunately for that nation, it had the worst of both worlds; that being several of the period's most persuasive and energetic revolutionaries and, without question, some of the worst economists to ever practice what Thomas Carlyle had already famously described as the "dismal science."

The first German economist of note was Friedrich List. He was a brilliant man, who offered many useful insights into the emerging world of economics. He was also, however, a strong advocate of government intervention in economic matters and a critic of the free trade doctrines of Smith, Ricardo, and the great French economist of the day Jean-Baptiste Say. These positions of List laid the groundwork for the errors of his successors.

The best known of these was Wilhelm Roscher, who was for nearly fifty years a professor of economics at Leipzig University. He is generally regarded as the founder of what is today known as the German Historical School of economics. The other two most prominent members of this "school" were Bruno Hildebrand and Karl Knies.

What distinguished the members of this "school" from their counterparts elsewhere was that they denied the existence of universal, theoretical economic truths, such as those that had been and were being developed in England and France by such groundbreaking early economists as Smith, Ricardo, Say, Malthus, John Stuart Mill, and Nassau Senior.

Briefly stated, these German economists believed that abstract deductions from ideal postulates were of little use; that economic actions were unique from society to society; that indeed, even within a given society, the people of any historical period would have operated under their own peculiar economic realities. Thus, they proposed that economics be studied not for the purpose of finding universal "laws," but from the perspective of the history of the society in question.

None of these three men actually did much to turn these ideas into practical action. This was left to Schmoller, a supremely egotistical Prussian who wore many hats. He taught at the University of Berlin, was the founder of the *Younger* German Historical School of economics, and, as *the* economist of Imperial Germany, he controlled virtually every important academic appointment in economics in that nation. Indeed, he was so influential that he could honestly refer to himself and his colleagues as the "intellectual bodyguard of the House of Hohenzollern" (e.g., the royal family of Prussia). Of course, he had the ear of Bismarck.

Schmoller's direct contribution to the discipline of economics was the accumulation, organization, study, and publication of vast amounts of historic/economic data. He conducted exhaustive studies of the history of the Weavers Guild of Strasburg, the guilds in seventeenth- and eighteenth-century Brandenburg and Prussia, the Prussian silk industry in the eighteenth century, Prussian financial policy, German towns in general, and Strasburg in particular. He studied the history and formation of social classes, as well as the history of mercantilism.

The idea behind all of this was that an intense study of the past, taking into account sociological, political, demographic, and geographical realities and trends, would reveal the unique motives behind the economic activities of the day. Eventually, this would lead to a significantly better and more nuanced understanding of the economic forces at work in the world than could be provided by the so-called "universal laws" of economics that were being sought by economists in other countries. The absolute volume of Schmoller's output was stunning but largely meaningless.

Of course, as we said above, he wore many hats. One of them was to provide powerful intellectual support for Germany's steady and fateful march toward the creation of a deeply socialistic society in Germany. You see, while Schmoller despised and feared the revolutionary socialism of Marx and Lassalle, and was thus a so-called "right-wing Hegelian," he actually shared the same view of the state as the "left-wing Hegelians." That being, as Hegel himself had put it, that it is "the course of God through the world that constitutes the State" and that in dealing with the State one must contemplate "the Idea, God as actual on earth."[15]

In 1873, Schmoller and several other social reformers, called *Sozialpolitiker* (policy-ers), formed a group of like-minded intellectuals known as the *Verein für Sozialpolitik* to refine and publicly promote their views, which, naturally, were supportive of Bismarck's efforts. Of course, Schmoller and his associates eschewed the socialist label arguing, along with Bismarck in those days, that they were simply trying to placate the laboring class in order to avoid socialism.

Of course, not all their critics recognized the distinction, and they began to refer to them collectively as the *Kathedersozialist*, or socialists of the chair. This was intended to be a derogatory label, but the *Verein* soon adopted as a badge of honor. A somewhat kinder, oft-used label for their ideology was "socialism of the cultivated."

While the passage of the Old Age and Disability Insurance Law in 1889 was the highlight of Bismarck's campaign for social reform, the *Verein* crowd was just getting started. Indeed, they went into high gear when Wilhelm II became emperor and stayed at the stormy center of German politics well into the twentieth century. Once again, Schmoller's role was decisive. Indeed, his historically most significant action as the leading economist in Germany involved his successful fight to keep the nation in the dark about the economic truths that were emerging at the time from universities throughout Europe.

This antagonism toward other "schools" of economic thought manifested itself in the famous *Methodenstreit*, or "struggle of methods" between Schmoller and Carl Menger, the illustrious founder of the now-famous Austrian School of Economics, which subsequently produced some of history's most innovative economists, including Friedrich von Wieser, Eugen von Bohm-Bawerk, Ludwig von Mises, and Friedrich Hayek.

This dispute began in 1871 when Menger, a professor at the University of Vienna, published his *Principles of Economics*, which set forth a general theory of value that attempted to explain all prices, including interest rates, wages, and rents, by the same principle. He dedicated the book to none other than Wilhelm Roscher and concluded his preface with a flattering greeting to German economists, to whose debate on "value" he hoped to make a major contribution.

Schmoller snubbed the book. Not only did it challenge the central idea behind his studies, but it was written by an Austrian, and as such was considered by the aristocratic Schmoller to be below his contempt. This prompted Menger to write another book, the first two sections of which, as explained in the dust jacket of the English translation, "constitute a polemic against the claims of the historical school to an exclusive right to treat economic problems and a positive exposition of the nature of theoretical economic analysis."[16]

Schmoller fired back with a condescending review, and Menger countered with a polemic diatribe entitled *The Errors of Historicism in German Economics*. This was published in 1884, which was thirteen years after the publication of Menger's first book set the famous quarrel in motion.

Now it would be comforting to be able to say that while the Historical School was teaching nonsense, it was harming no one except its unfortunate followers. But the fact is that its legacy was enormously damaging, not only to Germany but to the United States as well. You see, several of America's leading Progressive Era economists studied in Germany during the height of Schmoller's reign. And much like the conquistadors who brought syphilis home to Europe from the New World, these men brought two poisonous ideas home with them when they returned to America; the first was that laissez-faire economics is socially and spiritually unsound, and the second was the Hegelian notion that the state is God's chosen tool to achieve his ends.

We will discuss America's unfortunate experience with Schmoller's economics in a later chapter. In the meantime, Germany bore the brunt of this folly. In fact, many students of that period maintain that his ideas helped to pave the way to Hitler's National Socialism. And while this may be too harsh, it is not too harsh to argue that Schmoller's vehement attacks on all economic theories having to do with what he called "monetarism" played a major part in Germany's inability to deal with the hyperinflation of the early

1920s. The Norwegian economist Daastøl, Arno Mong put it this way:

> It is nowadays generally agreed that Schmoller's influence on the development of the economic sciences in Germany was rather unfortunate: it contributed to the neglect of economic theory in Germany for a full half century.[17]

Jurg Niehans offered an even more critical assessment in his authoritative *History of Economic Theory*, published in 1990. To wit:

> The closing of the German academic market to adherents of Carl Menger by Gustav Schmoller ... set back German economics for seventy years, indirectly perhaps to the present day.[18]

It is worth noting that marking off seventy years from the opening shot in the *Methodenstreit* would bring us to 1941, the year that America entered the World War II against Germany.

Let's let the poets in on the fun.

> Song of the Bell
> Freedom and Equality! one hears proclaimed,
> The peaceful citizen is driven to arms,
> The streets are filling, the halls,
> The vigilante-bands are moving,
> Then women change into hyenas
> And make a plaything out of terror,
> Though it twitches still, with panther's teeth,
> They tear apart the enemy's heart.
> Nothing is holy any longer, loosened
> Are all ties of righteousness,
> The good gives room to bad,
> And all vices freely rule.

Dangerous it is to wake the lion,
Ruinous is the tiger's tooth,
But the most terrible of all the terrors,
That is the mensch when crazed.
Woe to those, who lend to the eternally-blind
Enlightenment's heavenly torch!
It does not shine for him, it only can ignite
And puts to ashes towns and lands.
Friedrich von Schiller, 1798

Chapter 8

England: The Fabians and
the Bloomsburies

*Ever since the triumphant conclusion of the
Napoleonic Wars they [the English] had seemed to
be arbiters of the world's affairs, righting a balance
here, dismissing a potentate there, ringing the earth
with railways and submarine cables, lending money
everywhere, peopling the empty places with men of
the British stock, grandly revenging wrongs, converting pagans, discovering unknown lakes, setting up
dynasties, emancipating slaves, winning wars, putting down mutinies, keeping Turks in their place
and building bigger and faster battleships.* (James
Morris, *Pax Britannica*, 1992)

England's contribution to the history of the Left during the nineteenth century was almost entirely intellectual. Yes, there was a brief
period of social unrest in the first half of the century, but the government reacted in much the same way that Bismarck would act several
decades later. That is, by enacting measures designed to mollify the
unhappy workers.

The first of these was the Reform Act of 1832, which extended
the franchise to a greater number of citizens. This was a minimal
concession, but it met which very stiff resistance by the old guard.

Indeed, Brinton noted that "the ageing Wordsworth declared that, if the Bill were passed, he would retire to a safe and conservative country like Austria."[1]

Of course, Wordsworth did not move to Austria following the passage of the bill. Yet the threat of violence became so intense during the debate that when the House of Lords refused to ratify the measure the new king, William IV had to threaten the lords with putting a virtual end to their authority by appointing eighty pro-reform peers to their ranks. The lords relented and let the bill pass by abstaining from a vote, which drastically diminished their influence and thus destroyed the harmony of the existing order by leaving the gentry without a truly meaningful voice in the government.

Five years later, a radical organization called the Chartists, named after their "People's Charter of 1838," began to raise considerable hell over six issues that they claimed were not addressed in the 1832 law. Parliament rejected their proposals by a vote of 235 to 46. Disappointed radicals tried to organize a general strike and were arrested. When a mob marched on a prison demanding their release, British troops killed twenty-four of them and wounded many more.

This was an inauspicious start to reform, but keep in mind that this was several years before Marx and his buddies began meeting at Hippel's Weinstube and railing against the neglect of the working classes. When the dust settled, Parliament passed two more reform acts; and by the time the bloody revolutions of 1848 swept across Europe, England was relatively quiet on that front.

In any case, the real action was taking place among the upper-class intellectuals and scholars. You see, nineteenth-century England was overflowing with brilliant men of ideas: philosophers, economists, historians, political scientists, mathematicians, biologists, anthropologists, sociologists, accomplished statesmen, and a fair share of gadflies. Collectively, they created a vibrant, homegrown leftist presence that featured some of the most famous of a new breed of "respectable" "reformists" who would lead the leftist assault on Christendom long after the scruffy radicals had left the field and the barricades had been taken down.

These men engaged in active correspondence with each other as well as with their fellow "explorers of ideas" in other countries, especially Germany. They met at various prestigious clubs and royal societies to share and exchange their discoveries, thoughts, dreams, philosophies, beliefs, adventures, and plans for dealing with the unprecedented and startling demographic and economic changes that were occurring throughout Europe. Not only did these occasions result in considerable cross-pollination of their ideas, but quite often, one or another of these men would erect a new intellectual structure or theory upon the platform of another's work. Brinton sets the scene as follows.

> The revolutions of the late 18th century— the American, the French, and the industrial revolutions—had struck the western mind with a sense of catastrophe ... Men as far apart as St. Simon and Maistre set out consciously to rebuild an authority and a faith which all men might accept. Something essential, men felt, had been destroyed, and there was as yet nothing to put in its place. Quite ordinary people could agree with [the English socialist William] Morris that "we not only are but we feel ourselves to be living between the old and the new." The nineteenth century was consciously an age of transition, an age of groping. It was sometimes quite romantically proud of the fact, and invented a phrase, the *mal du siècle*, to consecrate its uncertainties.[2]

For the most part, these men were esteemed members of society who managed to be regarded as "reformists" rather than a "radicals." While this was a distinction without a difference, it was a popular delusion that afforded them considered freedom to discuss matters that once were considered not just gauche but treasonous.

Wisely, they did not engage in attacks on Christianity or Christians, or personal assaults on the ruling class. Yes, they were a bit radical, but after all, their ideas were philosophical and scientific in nature, designed to improve the social order and intended to be studied and implemented with the cooperation of the public. In short, they gave the English Left a new visage of propriety and respectability. This cleared the way for the discussion in polite company of such things as the religious skepticism of Hume, who had had to be careful about advertising his views on religion, and the atheism of Godwin, who, as noted earlier, came close to being prosecuted for blasphemy.

Jeremy Bentham was the first of this new breed of respectable leftists "reformers." The centerpiece of his hedonistic theory was what he called utilitarianism, which *The Oxford Companion to Philosophy* defines as follows:

> An approach to morality that treats pleasure of desire-satisfaction as the sole element in human good and that regards the morality of actions as entirely dependent on consequences or results for human (or sentient) well-being.[3]

In philosophical terms, this is called a teleological moral system, as contrasted to a deontological one, which is characterized primarily by adherence to an independent code of moral rules, say, for example, the Decalogue.

Bentham first developed his model in 1780 when he was thirty-two years old, but it was not published until 1789, and even then it enjoyed only limited circulation. In fact, in the early years, a French translation seems to have gained wider readership than the English version. We use the term "his model" because the notion of utilitarianism can be traced back to early in the third-century BC in the inscription above the entrance to Epicurus's garden school that read, "Stranger, here you will do well to tarry; here our highest good is pleasure."

Bentham published his approach to the subject under the title *Introduction to the Principles of Morals and Legislation*. He based it largely on the work of the Italian jurist and philosopher Cesare

Beccaria and, to a lesser degree, on Hume. As noted above, it went largely unnoticed for many years, but by 1823, Bentham had become a leading figure among the English reformists, at which point he published a greatly revised version of *Principles*, which became the standard.

Bentham was a child prodigy who is said to have begun reading Paul de Rapin's *History of England* and studying Latin at the age of three. He came from a wealthy family of lawyers and had intended to practice law himself, but as noted in the *Oxford Companion of Philosophy*, he became "disgusted with the current state of English law ... and turned instead to a study of what the law might be." In the course of this study, he became determined to lay the theoretical foundations for a perfect, dare we say utopian, system of law and government; that is, a system that would not simply create a well-ordered society but would actually change man's nature. This, the *Oxford Companion* notes, required "a measure of perfection, or of value." Hence, the name utilitarianism.[4]

Now Bentham lived eighty-four years, and given that his family wealth kept him from having to earn a living, he was thus able to devote his entire life to his philosophical inquiries. And given that he began his intellectual career at the age of four, and given that he was exceptionally bright, it is not surprising that he managed to make a significant contribution to the canon of Western intellectual thought.

But having said that, it should be noted that he was, like so many leftist geniuses before him, often out of touch with reality; a dreamer, a dabbler in fantasy worlds. Brinton alluded to this when he claimed that the poet, literary scholar, and author Robert Southey's description of Bentham as a "metaphysico-critico-politico-patriotico-phoolo-philosopher" was justified.[5]

The result was that Bentham's theory of utilitarianism was, like "scientific Marxism," fraught with what can only be described as ridiculous notions, mostly related to how it could be "praxised" from a philosophical theory to an actual model for social change. For example, as part of his theory of ascribing all human decision making to pleasure and pain, Bentham developed a "felicific calculus" to measure occurrences of pleasure and pain by their "intensity, duration, certainty and uncertainty, propinquity or remoteness, and when their long-run tendency is considered, by their fecundity and purity." We will let Brinton take it from there:

> Bentham lists fourteen simple pleasures, those of sense, wealth, skill, amity, good name, power, piety, benevolence, malevolence, memory, imagination, expectation, association, and relief; and twelve simple pains, those of privation, sense, awkwardness, enmity, ill name, piety, benevolence, malevolence, memory, imagination, expectation, and association. These, in turn, are subdivided. The pleasures of sense, for instance, include those of taste, intoxication, smell, touch, ear, eye, sex, health, and novelty. All are elaborated, worked out and illustrated ... his "sample" of the "pleasures of a country prospect," [are] listed under ii., 2, as "the idea of innocence and happiness of the birds, sheep, cattle, dogs, and other gentle of domestic animals."[6]

This was twaddle, of course, but it was highly popular twaddle among the reformers of the time. So much so that three years after Bentham's death in 1832, Benjamin Disraeli singled out the Utilitarians for special criticism in his book *A Vindication of the English Constitution*, which paved the way for his entry into British politics. Reflecting his famous mordant wit, he described Bentham's theory thusly:

> This waste of ingenuity on nonsense is like the condescending union that occasionally occurs between some high-bred steed and some long-eared beauty of the Pampas: the base and fantastical embrace only produces a barren and mulish progeny.[7]

Now, we cannot say with certainty that this nonsense would have eventually been universally recognized as such. But it doesn't matter, because fortunately for Bentham's theory, it was the ideological starting point for a man of even greater genius who was destined to become one of England's most famous philosophers. His name was John Stuart Mill. He was the son of Bentham's best friend James Mill, who was himself a prominent Scottish economist and philosopher.

Like Bentham, Mill was a child prodigy, who is said to have learned Greek by the age of three and to have read much of the classic literary canon by the age of eight. His father and Bentham educated him with the specific expectation, according to *The Cambridge Dictionary of Philosophy*, "that he would become a defender of the principles of the Benthamite school."[8] Partially true to this charge, Mill was respectful of Utilitarianism in his treatises on the subject and in his most famous book *On Liberty*, which was published in 1859. Yet he did come to question the practicality of a system that did not take into account the complex moral and social issues that were central to his thoughts about the importance of liberty.

In the process of exploring the deficiencies of Bentham's work, he began a lengthy correspondence with the Comte, who, as we mentioned earlier, had been a protégé of St. Simon and the founder of Positivism. Briefly stated, Positivism was, according to Comte, the third stage in the history of human thought. He claimed to have based this stage entirely on science, which he claimed was "the only authentic knowledge." The first stage was religion, which he said was based on superstition. The second was metaphysical, which was an improvement over the first but still speculative. Comte claimed that this third, scientific stage had evolved over time, moving from astronomy to physics to the various forms biology and finally to the "human science" of sociology. This new "science" was rooted in the leftist belief that societies operate according to the same types of general laws that govern the physical world.

Like his mentor, St. Simon, Comte was not wrapped too tight. In fact, like St. Simon, he spent some time in a mental hospital, failed in an attempt to commit suicide (by jumping off a bridge), and finally took on the task of developing a secular religion that was arguably even wackier than St. Simon's. Called the "Religion of Humanity, it encompassed a complete system of belief and ritual, with liturgy and sacraments, priesthood and pontiff, all organized around the public veneration of humanity, the *Grand Etre* (Great Being), later to be supplemented in a positivist trinity by the *Grand Fétich* (the Earth) and the *Grand Milieu* (Destiny)."[9]

Now Comte had garnered a significant following in Europe and the United States with his Positivism. In fact, he is recognized today as the "father of sociology." But his Religion of Humanity had a dampening effect on his reputation as a great thinker and thus on his relationship with Mill, who, when writing about Comte later, distinguished between the "good Comte" and the "bad Comte," the dividing line being the introduction of the Religion of Humanity, which Mill described as "ineffably ludicrous."[10]

Of course, Mill was not alone in this opinion. The biologist Thomas Huxley famously described Comte's religion as "Catholicism minus Christianity,"[11] a notion that we will encounter later when we take up the subject of fascism. As if that were not ridicule enough, Huxley added that he "would as soon worship a wilderness of apes as Comte's rationalized conception of humanity."[12] Under the category of being called ugly by a frog, Engels described it to Marx as "excrement."[13]

Historians differ as to how important Comte was to Mill's work. Hayek claims that Mill relied heavily on Comte for the entire chapter on "moral sciences" in his second most famous book *A System of Logic*, which was published in 1843.[14] Others are less charitable to Comte, although there is little question that Comte's fundamental thesis that social issues needed to be addressed scientifically were certainly evident in Mill's work.

In any case, the central thesis of *On Liberty* was that if men were left to the pursue their own utilitarian motives rather than being bullied by the government or by the mores, morals, customs, and ancient prejudices of his fellow citizens, the world would be a much better place. Relative to these morals, customs, etc., he anticipated Nietzsche by describing them as nothing more than tools of the "tyranny of the majority," which he described as "the tendency of society to impose, by other means than civil penalties, its own ideas and practices as rules of conduct on those who dissent from them."[15] Russell Kirk said this about that.

> It was Mill's extreme secularism, rather than his particular political ideas, which made him the enemy of all discerning conservatives. For he was eager to sweep the veneration out of social life, replacing it with the "religion of humanity," in which man would adore himself, found his moral system upon utilitarian reason, and consider every prescriptive custom of mankind simply as an "experiment in living." Man would mold his universe closer to his heart's desire. Poverty, disease, vicissitudes of fortune, every other ill from which men suffer—these may be eradicated by the rational plan of the new society. "All the grand sources, in short, of human suffering are in a great degree, many of them almost entirely, conquerable by human care and effort," Mill writes in *Utilitarianism*. These superior human beings, as they progress toward material perfection, will cease to require the childish comforts of religious consolation; present suffering abolished, they will shrug their shoulders at the prospect of eternal life. Mill is the harbinger of the twentieth-century socialists' lavish hopes for material comfort.[16]

Immediately upon publication, Mill's book was widely read, discussed, praised, and attacked. Relative to the latter, the lawyer and journalist James Fitzjames Stephen provided, in his classic 1873 book *Liberty, Equality, Fraternity*, what is widely regarded as the most thorough job of pointing out the practical and philosophical weaknesses of Mill's work and of providing an excellent and studied conservative response. Stephen was a remarkably interesting character. He was big, energetic, and not all that congenial. He was an ascetic, bullheaded, evangelical moralist who believed that "to be weak is wretched, that the state of nature is a state of war, and *Vae Victis* the great law of nature." He regarded English criminal law as the "Second Table of the Ten Commandments" and once described a Judge of the High Court as "the organ of the moral indignation of mankind." As such, he argued that Mill's notion of doing away with virtually all restraints on behavior leads not to liberty but to social chaos, and that true liberty can exist only within the boundaries of morals and laws.[17]

On Liberty quickly became one of the most important works in the canon of liberal political thought, and remains there today. As noted above, it was published in 1859, which brings us to another of England's famous nineteenth-century secular intellectuals. For it was in this same year that Charles Darwin placed another weapon in the hands of the Left by claiming that man was not made in God's image but was nothing more than an improved model of the ape.

As every schoolboy knows, Darwin developed the basis for his thesis during a five-year-long trip around the world on the HMS *Beagle* during which time he studied geological formations and collected specimens of animals and plants. After returning to England, he spent the next twenty-three years writing and lecturing on natural history and considering the ramifications of the material that he gathered on his trip. This led to the publication of his classic *On the Origin of Species*, in which he held that man had emerged from a long evolutionary period that was governed solely by chance, free of any design. He called this process "natural selection" and theorized that man, apes, and monkeys have a common ancestor. He put it this way:

> As many more individuals of each species are born than can possibly survive; and as, consequently, there is a frequently recurring struggle for existence, it follows that any being, if it vary however slightly in any manner profitable to itself, under the complex and sometimes vary-

ing conditions of life, will have a better chance of surviving, and thus be naturally selected. From the strong principle of inheritance, any selected variety will tend to propagate its new and modified form.[18]

Now, the word "controversial" does not even begin to describe the impact of this theory. Its ramifications spread into every nook and cranny in the worlds of science, sociology, philosophy, theology, and, of course, politics. From the perspective of the history of the Left, it served as a vital link between leftist ideology and Nietzsche's atheism.

You see, the Left had already rejected the Christian faith. From Voltaire to Kant, from Comte to Marx and Mill and all those in between, Christ's divinity was either rigorously questioned or denied. But many leftists had not yet abandoned Christian morality. Indeed, T. S. Eliot would observe some years later in an essay on the poet Matthew Arnold that many people, "the vanishing of whose religious faith has left behind only habits," had come to place "an exaggerated emphasis on morals."[19] Emile Faguet explained this phenomenon as follows in his 1918 book *On Reading Nietzsche*:

> The more the [Christian] dogma was relegated into oblivion, the more one felt bound to honour, to practice and especially to extol morality, to prove how one could be virtuous without being a Christian. There are atheists whose chief moral incentive is their very atheism, so anxious are they to prove that an atheist may be a good man and to what extent he may be one. The trouble is that if one detaches one's self from Christianity in that way, one becomes more Christian than ever and more than ever a propagandist and vulgarizer of the Christian idea. This shadow of Christianity is still hovering above the world.[20]

Then along came Darwin, who maintained that science—yes, *science*—supported the belief that life is, at its heart, nothing more than a struggle for existence. And at about the same time, Nietzsche entered the lists, and he argued that if Darwin were correct, success in this contest rested on strength not kindness, pride not humility, resolute action not altruism. Thomas Nagel described Nietzsche's view on this subject as follows in a series of essays published under the title *Secular Philosophy and the Religious Temperament.*

> He regarded modern morality, which speaks with the voice of the community or even of humanity as a whole, as particularly dangerous, because it requires suppression of the cruelty and recklessness that distinguishes the strong individual. The height of self-realization cannot be reached by someone who is too concerned with the reactions of others, or his effects on them. There is a fundamental conflict between the pursuit of individual creativity and perfection and the claims of the general welfare.[21]

Suddenly the Left had an excuse to discard such Christian virtues as humility, kindness, and restraint, reasoning, à la Nietzsche, that these debilitating tenets were preventing Western Civilization from reaching the sacred goal of a secular Utopia, peace on earth, universal happiness, and justice. The savior then would not be Christ, but a new kind of man, a strong, resolute man untethered by religious superstition, an Übermensch. Somewhere in the mists of time, Satan smiled and began preparing the way for Mussolini, Hitler, Lenin, Stalin, Mao, and many other lesser heralds of a world devoid of faith and justice.

In keeping with our above observation about the seers of nineteenth-century building on each other's work, we should point out that Darwin drew the inspiration for his theory of evolution from the British economist Thomas Malthus's famous 1796 "Essay on the Principle of Population." And Malthus had written this essay for the purpose of challenging the utopian notion of the perfectibility of man being advanced at the time by Godwin and Condorcet.

The gloomy gist of Malthus's article was that human population multiplies geometrically while the food supply increases arithmetically. The result, he said, was that population growth would be constantly controlled by a combination of famine, disease, misery, vice, and war. As an Anglican cleric, he argued that this insurmountable problem was God's way of promoting virtuous behavior. Furthermore, he argued that any attempts to alleviate this condition would only make matters worse, which, the story goes, prompted the Scottish historian Thomas Carlyle famously to label economics the "dismal science."

Contrary to his subsequent critics, Malthus was not an advocate of any sort of population control as a means of mitigating the problem he describes. In fact, the only significant reference he made to the subject was in direct response to Condorcet's observations concerning breeding improvements in animals and plants. Relative to this, Malthus admitted that it does not "seem impossible that by an attention to breed, a certain degree of improvement similar to that among animals, might take place among men." However, he then added the following, first critical and then humorous, observation.

> Whether intellect could be communicated may be a matter of doubt: but size, strength, beauty, complexion, and perhaps even longevity are in a degree transmissible. The error does not seem to lie in supposing a small degree of improvement possible, but in not discriminating between a small improvement, the limit of which is undefined, and an improvement really unlimited. As the human race, however, could not be improved in this way, without condemning all the bad specimens to celibacy, it is not probable that an attention to breed should ever become general; indeed, I know of no well-directed attempts of this kind, except in the ancient family of the

> Bickerstaffs, who are said to have been very suc-
> cessful in whitening the skins and increasing the
> height of their race by prudent marriages, par-
> ticularly by that very judicious cross with Maud,
> the milk-maid, by which some capital defects in
> the constitutions of the family were corrected.[22]

Bickerstaff was a pseudonym for the great Irish satirist Richard Steele, who wrote some seventy-five years earlier of his fictional ancestor's attempt to better the family's lot through selective breeding, which seemed always to lead to unexpected problems, one which was the "unlucky accident" of the birth of the hump-backed and high-nosed Richard II, which was, Bickerstaff wrote, "astonishing, because none of his forefathers ever had such a blemish, nor indeed was there anyone in the neighborhood of that make, except the butler who was noted for round shoulders and a Roman nose."[23]

Unfortunately for Malthus, not only did his population theory prove to be wrong, but, despite his attempt to make light of the prospect of improving men's lives through selective breeding, he came to be widely and viciously accused of heaping terrible wrongs upon the poor. In 1829, for example, the radical, leftist agitator William Cobbett described Malthus as a "monster" and charged that he considered men to be nothing but "mere animals."[24] Worse yet, in 1843, Dickens mocked Malthus in the famous character of Scrooge, who replies to a plea for Christmas charity for the poor this way: "If they would rather die, they had better do it, and decrease the surplus population."[25]

Darwin, on the other hand, was no critic of Malthus. Instead, he cited him thusly as the inspiration for his principle theory.

> In October 1838, that is, fifteen months after
> I had begun my systematic enquiry, I happened
> to read for amusement "Malthus on Population,"
> and being well prepared to appreciate the strug-
> gle for existence which everywhere goes on from
> long-continued observation of the habits of ani-

mals and plants, it at once struck me that under these circumstances favourable variations would tend to be preserved, and unfavourable ones to be destroyed. The result of this would be the formation of new species. Here then I had at last got a theory by which to work.[26]

Just as Malthus's work had influenced Darwin, Darwin's work brought the great philosopher and sociologist Herbert Spencer into the conversation, when he realized upon reading Darwin that his findings were highly similar in nature to ones that he himself had proposed seven years earlier, which were, not surprisingly, also inspired in part by Malthus. Spencer's observations on the principles of evolution were contained in an essay entitled "A Theory of Population, Deduced from the General Law of Animal Fertility." He put it this way.

And here it must be remarked, that the effect of pressure of population in increasing the ability to maintain life, and decreasing the ability to multiply, is not a uniform effect, but an average one. In this case, as in many others, Nature secures each step in advance by a succession of trials, which are perpetually repeated, and cannot fail to be repeated, until success is achieved. ... For as those prematurely carried off must, in the average of cases, be those in whom the power of self-preservation is the least, it unavoidably follows, that those left behind to continue the race are those in whom the power of self-preservation is the greatest—are the select of their generation.[27]

Needless the say, because their thoughts about evolution were startlingly similar, the public quickly got them mixed up even though their conclusions were quite different. You see, Darwin viewed the Malthusian struggle for existence as the biological process, which, through "natural selection," led to the emergence of new species that were neither better nor worse than their antecedents, but simply more adaptable to existing conditions. As Stephen Jay Gould noted in his classic *Ever Since Darwin*, Darwin held that "evolution has no direction; that it does not lead inevitably to higher things; that organisms become better adapted to their local environments, and that is all. The 'degeneracy' of the parasite is as perfect as the gait of a gazelle."[28]

Spencer, on the other hand, saw the struggle as a social process that led to the strengthening of the existing population by promoting the "survival of the fittest." He put it this way in the above-cited essay on population.

> It is clear, that by the ceaseless exercise of the faculties needed to contend with them [i.e., the complexities of society], and by the death of all men who fail to contend with them successfully, there is ensured a constant progress towards a higher degree of skill, intelligence, and self-regulation—a better co-ordination of actions—a more complete life.[29]

At this point, a new seer appears, from stage Left of course. His name is Friedrich Leopold August Weismann. He is a brilliant German biologist who holds the title of Director of the Zoological Institute and the first Professor of Zoology at the University of Freiburg. He will expand and expound on the Spencerian notion that the process of evolution is not limited to species but is actually *a major factor in the improvement of mankind.* Oxford University Professor Marc Stears explains his contribution thusly in his book *Progressives, Pluralists, and the Problems of the State.*

> The original Darwinians argued that evolution was dependent upon struggle: progress was reliant on the potentially brutal "survival of the fittest" and competition was thus the dominant

tendency in all forms of natural life. As the nineteenth century aged, though, a latter generation
began to argue that the obsession with struggle
as a *means* had obscured the quite different *direction* that such evolution was taking: a direction of
which Darwin himself had expressed ignorance
but which more "recent empirical researches"
were supposed to have discovered.

These new biologists, led by August
Weismann, were convinced that if one investi-
gated carefully it became apparent that although
evolution did indeed progress through natural
selection, through the "survival of the fittest," its
result actually consisted in a trend towards ever
more sophisticated models of *social interaction*
and *communal cooperation*. The individuals or
groups that survived through the evolutionary
process were, on this account, those whose lives
had become "integrative"; those who survived
were those who had learnt to "work more in
co-operation and less in competition with each
other."[30]

At almost exactly the same time, the editors of the new *Ninth
Edition of Encyclopedia Britannica* had arrived at the same conclusion. In *Three Rival Versions of Moral Enquiry*, Macintyre notes that
the secular adaptation of the notion of progress so impressed these
eminent scholars that they made it the centerpiece of the new Ninth
Edition. Published between 1875 and 1889, it featured the claim
that progress was not exclusive to the natural sciences, but extended
to the human sciences as well, and cited the work of the editors themselves as irrefutable evidence of this. As MacIntyre put it, these men
concluded that the "sciences concerned with the distinctively human
were taken to reveal to us a law-governed history whose climax so far
is their own emergence." Then he mordantly added, "Where once
the savage, the primitive, and the superstitious prevailed, there are

now [the editors] Adam Gifford, Thomas Spencer Baynes, and Agnes Mary Clerke."[31]

All of this was nonsense, of course. However, it became a widely-accepted theory among the new class of "respectable" leftists and lent an additional element of scientific respectability to their efforts, as had the social theories of Bentham, Mill, Darwin, and Spencer. Nevertheless, as the esteemed British philosopher and radical reformer T. H. Green stated, with some satisfaction, these efforts were directed at "the same old cause of social good against class interests, for which, under altered names, liberals are fighting now as they first did years ago."[32]

So it came to pass, that two years after Green's death, a new movement for "the same old cause" appeared in the form of a politically and socially powerful community of respectable left-wing "reformers" whose congeniality toward atheism and rejection of moral norms would, in the coming century, severely undermine Jolly Old England's traditional Judeo-Christian society and open its doors to socialism.

Called the Fabian Society, it was founded in January 1884 by author and "psychic researcher" Frank Podmore; poet Edith Nisbit and her husband, Hubert Bland, a bank clerk; stockbroker Edward Pease; and the truly wacky "sexologist" Havelock Ellis.

The movement grew quickly and soon included such notables as social reformers Sidney and Beatrice Webb (who eventually took control of the organization); author H. G. Wells; mystic and women's right activist Annie Besant; psychologist Graham Wallas; Labour Party politician Sydney Olivier; physicist Oliver Lodge; Labour Party politician and later Prime Minister Ramsay MacDonald; leader of the British suffragette movement Emmeline Pankhurst; playwright George Bernard Shaw; author Virginia Woolf; and Virginia's husband, Leonard.

It is very important at this point to note that none of the above-mentioned "intellectuals" could claim to have any special understanding or training in the field of economics, yet all of them pretended in their rhetorical flourishes to have extensive knowledge of this subject, which, after all, was the foundation of their entire project.

This may not have been the beginning of the prominence of pseudo-experts in Western society. But it certainly marked an important milestone in its growth. Today, it is commonplace, especially in the United States, for celebrities and self-proclaimed gurus to have enormous influence over the outcome of public debates over issues about which their understanding is superficial at best. In fact, it is not a stretch to say that a vast majority of the Americans today rely extensively on the television news personalities who are trained in public relations and journalism, to provide them with both the facts of any given matter and how they should interpret these facts.

Commenting on this phenomenon, the conservative Harvard Professor Irving Babbitt told the story of the French butcher who had a legal problem and, after reviewing the qualifications of the various lawyers, chose the fattest one.[33] Durant put it this way: "Men prepare themselves with life-long study before becoming authorities in physics or chemistry or biology, but in the field of social and political affairs every grocer's boy is an expert, knows the solution, and demands to be heard."[34] But Hayek drove the point home in a paper entitled "The Intellectuals and Socialism," which was published in the spring 1949 issue of the *University of Chicago Law Review*. To wit:

> The typical intellectual need ... not possess special knowledge of anything in particular, nor need he even be particularly intelligent, to perform his role as intermediary in the spreading of ideas. What qualifies him for his job is the wide range of subjects on which he can readily talk and write, and a position or habits through which he becomes acquainted with new ideas sooner than those to whom he addresses himself. ...
>
> Until one begins to list all the professions and activities which belong to the class, it is difficult to realize how numerous it is, how the scope for activities constantly increases in modern society, and how dependent on it we all have become. The class does not consist of only

journalists, teachers, ministers, lecturers, publicists, radio commentators, writers of fiction, cartoonists, and artists all of whom may be masters of the technique of conveying ideas but are usually amateurs so far as the substance of what they convey is concerned. The class also includes many professional men and technicians, such as scientists and doctors, who through their habitual intercourse with the printed word become carriers of new ideas outside their own fields and who, because of their expert knowledge of their own subjects, are listened with respect on most others. ...

There is little that the ordinary man of today learns about events or ideas except through the medium of this class; and outside our special fields of work we are in this respect almost all ordinary men, dependent for our information and instruction on those who make it their job to keep abreast of opinion. It is the intellectuals in this sense who decide what views and opinions are to reach us, which facts are important enough to be told to us, and in what form and from what angle they are to be presented. Whether we shall ever learn of the results of the work of the expert and the original thinker depends mainly on their decision. ...

And it is specially significant for our problem that every scholar can probably name several instances from his field of men who have undeservedly achieved a popular reputation as great scientists solely because they hold what the intellectuals regard as "progressive" political views; but I have yet to come across a single instance where such a scientific pseudo-reputation has been bestowed for political reason on a scholar of more

conservative leanings. This creation of reputations by the intellectuals is particularly important
in the fields where the results of expert studies are
not used by other specialists but depend on the
political decision of the public at large. There is
indeed scarcely a better illustration of this than
the attitude which professional economists have
taken to the growth of such doctrines as socialism
or protectionism. There was probably at no time
a majority of economists, who were recognized as
such by their peers, favorable to socialism (or, for
that matter, to protection).[35]

In any case, according to Shaw, these English intellectuals were,
"from the start," "warlike" in their opinions. They "denounced the
capitalists as thieves" and talked "among ourselves" of revolution
and anarchism "on the tacit assumption that the object of our campaign … was to bring about a tremendous smash-up of existing society, to be succeeded by complete Socialism." Eventually, however, he
notes that they realized that insurrection and anarchism was not their
cup of tea, so to speak. After all, they met in each other's "drawing
rooms," which as Shaw put it, "undoubtedly prevented working-men
from joining" the organization.[36]

Needless to say, then, their alternative path to socialism was
peaceful in nature. The Fabians made no charges against the upper
classes but soothingly claimed only to seek their help and advice in
making England a better place for all citizens. Moreover, they were
vocally patriotic, which manifested in their support for a robust imperialism that was based on the recognition of the need for foreign markets and for ultimately friendly control over the subject nations so as
to keep them under the wing of England. The gist of this position
was that the small nations of the world were an anachronism in the
twentieth century. Consequently, they felt that "the partition of the
greater part of the globe among such Powers is, as a matter of fact
that must be faced approvingly or deploringly, now only a question
of time." The only question was "whether England is to be the centre

and nucleus of one of those Great Powers of the future, or to be cast off by its colonies, ousted from its provinces, and reduced to its old island status."[37]

They directly and intentionally reflected this friendly approach to socialism in their name, which was taken from Quintus Fabias Maximus, a Roman general who developed the so-called Fabio strategy of warfare, which avoided frontal assaults in favor of a war of attrition involving small skirmishes and constant harassment. This strategy did not work all that well for General Fabius in the Second Punic War, largely because the Roman public wanted action. However, it proved enormously successful against the English aristocracy in late nineteenth-century and early twentieth-century England. An early Fabian pamphlet describes their organization as follows:

> THE FABIAN SOCIETY consists of men and women who are Socialists, that is to say, in the words of its "Basis," of those who aim at the reorganization of society by the emancipation of Land and Industrial Capital from individual and class ownership, and the vesting of them in the community for the general benefit. ... For the attainment of these ends the Fabian Society looks to the spread of Socialist opinions, and the social and political changes consequent thereon. It seeks to promote these by the general dissemination of knowledge as to the relation between the individual and society in its economic, ethical, and political aspects. The Society welcomes as members any persons, men or women, who desire to promote the growth of Socialist opinion and to hasten the enactment of Socialist measures.[38]

The economist Joseph Schumpeter described this strategy as applied by the Fabians as follows in his classic *Capitalism, Socialism, and Democracy.*

Most of them were not straight enemies of the established order. All of them stressed willingness to cooperate much more than hostility. They were not out to found a party and greatly disliked the phraseology of class war and revolution. Whenever possible they preferred making themselves useful to making themselves a nuisance ... They were not personally ambitious. They liked to serve behind the scene. Action through the bureaucracy whose growth in numbers and in power they foresaw and approved fitted in very well with the general scheme of their democratic state socialism ... From their standpoint it would have been nothing short of madness to rouse the bourgeois quarry into awareness of danger by talking about revolutions and class wars. The awakening of class consciousness was precisely what they wanted to avoid, at least at first, since it would have rendered impossible the peaceful but effective spread of their principles throughout the political and administrative organs of bourgeois society.

Thus, though it might be said with truth that, in the matter of class war as in others, Fabianism is the very opposite of Marxism, it might also be held that the Fabians were in a sense better Marxists than Marx himself. To concentrate on the problems that are within practical politics, to move in step with the evolution of things social, and to let the ultimate goal take care of itself is really more in accord with Marx's fundamental doctrine than the revolutionary ideology he himself grafted upon it. To have no illusions about an imminent catastrophe of capitalism, to realize that socialization is a slow process which tends to transform the attitudes of *all*

classes of society, even spells superiority in fundamental doctrine.[39]

Of course, Schumpeter was correct when he said that the
Fabians eschewed the rhetoric of class war. But then again, no one
would ever mistake them for egalitarians. For they were dyed-in-the-
wool racists. Sidney Webb put it this way:

> In Great Britain at this moment, when
> half, or perhaps two-thirds of all the married
> people are regulating their families, children are
> being freely born to the Irish Roman Catholics
> and the Polish, Russian and German Jews, and
> to the thriftless and irresponsible—largely the
> casual laborers and the other denizens of the
> one-roomed tenements and our great cities—on
> the other. Twenty-five percent of our parents, as
> Professor Karl Pearson keeps warning us, is pro-
> ducing 50 percent of the next generation. This
> can hardly result in anything but national dete-
> rioration; or, as an alternative, in this country
> gradually falling to the Irish and the Jews.[40]

Of course, their racism did not stop with criticism and pejorative. They were also enthusiastic supporters of the new science
of eugenics, which was the culmination of the long journey from
Malthus's theory on population to Spencer's theory of the "survival
of the fittest," and finally to Francis Galton's coining of the term
eugenics.

Who was Galton, you ask? Well, he was a brilliant scientist,
inventor, explorer, geographer, meteorologist, mathematician, statesmen, and friend of Beatrice Webb, who became interested in the
process of heredity as a result of reading his cousin Darwin's *The
Origin of* Species. He began his study with the three conclusions.
The first was that one did not need to know the process by which
parents pass on certain traits to their children to know that it, in fact,

does happen. The second was that, generally speaking, superior people pass on superior qualities to their offspring. Finally, he put forth the following disquieting observation, laced in the kind of specious empathy for the poor suffering "unfits" that would become the hallmark of the American eugenics movement.

> Man is gifted with pity and other kindly feelings; he has also the power of preventing many kinds of suffering. I conceive it to fall well within his province to replace Natural Selection by other processes that are more merciful and not less effective.
>
> This is precisely the aim of eugenics. Its first object is to check the birth-rate of the Unfit, instead of allowing them to come into being, though doomed in large numbers to perish prematurely. The second object is the improvement of the race by furthering the productivity of the Fit by early marriages and healthful rearing of their children. Natural Selection rests upon excessive production and wholesale destruction; Eugenics on bringing no more individuals into the world that can be properly cared for, and those only of the best stock.[41]

Thus, the Fabians were the first of all the leftist movements to combine the "progressive" ideology of socialism with the relatively new "science" of eugenics. We say "the first" because Marxism held that the classes were a product of social and economic rather than hereditary factors. Moreover, Marx was counting on the proletariat to overthrow the rich and the powerful. In contrast, the Fabians attributed class differences to biologics and thus regarded the poor of all races to be an undesirable form of humanity while viewing the rich and powerful as genetically superior and therefore the best suited to the task of breeding.

Naturally then, the Webbs wanted to scrap the old Poor Law, arguing that it "had undesirable results from the eugenic point of view ... because it surrendered the idea of intelligent, purposeful selection."[42] Then there was H. G. Wells: "I believe ... it is in the sterilisation of failure, and not in the selection of successes for breeding, that the possibility of an improvement of the human stock lies."[43] And of course, George Bernard Shaw: "The notion that persons should be safe from extermination as long as they do not commit willful murder, or levy war against the Crown, or kidnap, or throw vitriol, is not only to limit social responsibility unnecessarily, and to privilege the large range of intolerable misconduct that lies outside them, but to divert attention from the essential justification for extermination, which is always incorrigible social incompatibility and nothing else."[44] Finally, there is the famed "sexologist" Havelock Ellis: "Eventually, it seems evident, a general system, whether private or public, whereby all personal facts, biological and mental, normal and morbid, are duly and systematically registered, must become inevitable if we are to have a real guide as to those persons who are most fit, or most unfit to carry on the race."[45] Ellis's sexuality was, by the way, so unconventional for that period that it is likely that he would have been among those who were deemed unfit to "carry on the race" had he provided the saturnine facts of his own sex life to a "general system."

Thus, for the Fabians, socialism was in many ways the means to achieve their ends, not the end itself. Of course, many of these ends had nothing whatsoever to do with traditional leftist ideology. Imagine, if you will, Babeuf, Bakunin, Weitling, or even Marx, explaining, as Sydney Webb did in a pamphlet dated June 1896 entitled "The Difficulties of Individualism," that one of the principle benefits of a planned socialist state would be its ability to eliminate "wrong production," not just of commodities but of "human beings," which occurs as a result of the "breeding of degenerate hordes of a demoralized 'residuum' unfit for social life," or as he described it later, the "indiscriminate multiplication of the unfit."[46]

Then there is the extensive work that the Fabians did on population statistics, which had little or nothing to do with socialism, but was specifically designed to promote eugenics and was always presented in such a way as to raise fears of what would happen if something were not done to limit the breeding of the undesirables and the feeble-minded.

The Fabians never succeeded in converting their eugenics policies into law. They did, however, establish the British Labour Party in 1900 and founded and financed the London School of Economics in 1895, which was enormously successful in carrying on their work of educating and training an elite, leftist workforce to pursue their other schemes of socialist reform.

It is said that when the *Baltimore Sun* asked H. L. Mencken to review the obituary that had been prepared for his eventual demise, he asked the newspaper to add the sentence: "As he got older, he got worse."[47] We mention this because this would be an even more fitting obituary for the Fabians. You see, they went from a group of citizens who were devoted to the peaceful promotion of socialist and communist principals in England in the nineteenth century, to become Joseph Stalin's most powerful support group in the West during the post–World War I period, at the very same time that this psychopath was committing murder on a scale never before witnessed in the world. In fact, some of the accolades that leading Fabian figures showered on Stalin during this period provide an insight into the origins of the phrase that he and Lenin were said to have used to describe these very people, that is, "useful idiots."

The Webbs, for example, were impressed by the spirituality of the Soviet leadership. After their trip to Russia in 1932, they wrote the following:

> The marvel was not that there should be parks, hospitals, factories; after all, these could be found in England as well. The marvel was that they should all be inspired by a collective ideal, a single moral purpose ... The new rulers professing a crude scientific materialism, have done more for the soul than the body.[48]

H. G. Wells was one of the most gullible of the many leftist dupes, who were plentiful during the interregnum. He met Stalin personally in 1934, by which time the "Man of Steel" had the blood of millions on his hands and had struck terror even in the hearts of his family, and described him as follows:

> I have never met a man more candid, fair and honest, and to these qualities it is, and to nothing occult and sinister, that he owes his tremendous undisputed ascendancy in Russia. I had thought before I saw him that he might be where he was because we were afraid of him, but I realize that he owes his position to the fact that no one is afraid of him and everybody trusts him.[49]

In *United in Hate: The Left's Romance with Tyranny and Terror*, Jamie Glazov provides numerous, other sickening examples of this delusional madness. Among other things, she notes George Bernard Shaw's visit to Russia in 1931 during a deadly famine that was the direct result of Stalin's decision to collectivize agriculture by executing tens of thousands of the nation's most successful farmers, the Kulaks, and confiscating their property. To wit:

> Before the train crossed the Soviet border, [Shaw] threw a supply of food out of the train in order to demonstrate his conviction that the reports of food shortages in the Soviet Union were capitalist propaganda. Upon arriving in the Soviet utopia, Shaw was so overwhelmed with ecstasy that *everything* he saw impressed him—especially Soviet prisons. Arranged just for him in Potemkin fashion ... [he noted following upon return home] "in England a delinquent enters [the jail] as an ordinary man and comes out as a 'criminal' type," whereas in Russia he enters ... as a criminal type and would come out an ordi-

nary man but for the difficulty of inducing him to come out at all. As far as I could make out they could stay as long as they liked.[50]

Malcolm Muggeridge was one of a very few Western visitors to Moscow in those days who attempted to inform the world of the horrors that were taking place in the name of collectivism. As the Moscow correspondent of the *Manchester Guardian*, he described the famine as "one of the most monstrous crimes in history, so terrible that people in the future will scarcely be able to believe that it happened."[51] On a more general note, he provided one of the best accounts of the wages of communism every written. "It destroys everything, and everyone; is the essence of destruction—in towns, a darkness, a paralysis; in the country, a blight, sterility; shouting monotonously its empty formula—a classless, socialist society—it attacks with methodical barbarity, not only men and classes and institutions, but the soul of a society. It tears a society up by the roots and leaves it dead. 'If we go,' Lenin said, 'we shall slam the door on an empty house.'"[52] Needless to say, Muggeridge's missives were not greatly appreciated at home, and he eventually quit the newspaper in disgust.

Needless to say, the same fate awaited the truths about the nature of Russian communism that were revealed in so starkly in Arthur Koestler's remarkable 1941 novel *Darkness at Noon*, which exposed the moral disgrace of Stalin's murderous show trials, George Orwell's great 1949 novel *1984*, and numerous other similar works.

Interestingly, no one to our knowledge has ever explained how these financially well-off, well-educated men and women could have become so attracted to the ludicrous, utopian dream of socialism and communism, even to the point of falling hook, line, and sinker for Comrade Stalin's callous lies, despite overwhelming evidence, readily available at the time, that he was engaged in the deliberate starvation and wholesale slaughter of his own citizens.

Or to put this in another way, how these "intellectuals" could have become classic examples of the most ignorant cultists, impervious to facts, historical evidence, and logic; indeed, highly antagonistic and even tribally aggressive toward anyone who challenged their peculiar assumptions and beliefs.

Some have speculated that one of the characteristics of the intellectually gifted is an intense desire to gain esoteric knowledge. According to this theory, this causes them to skip over that part of the learning process that deals with common sense, that is, that bank of insights that provides average people with the means of dealing successfully with situations in which they have little or no expertise. To put it in another way, that quality that gave rise to the expression heard frequently among ordinary mortals that goes, "Any damn fool could figure that out."

Paul Johnson offered an alternative theory in *Modern Times*. To wit: "If the decline of Christianity created the modern political zealot—and his crimes—so the evaporation of religious faith among the educated left a vacuum in the minds of Western intellectuals easily filled by secular superstition."[53]

Babbitt described its origin thusly:

> If we attend carefully to the psychology of the persons who manifest such an eagerness to serve us, we shall find that they are even more eager to control us. What one discovers, for example, under the altruistic professions of the leaders of a typical organization for humanitarian crusading ... is a growing will to power and even an incipient terrorism.[54]

The longshoreman philosopher Eric Hoffer took the subject head-on in his powerful but short 1951 classic entitled *The True Believer*, in which he attempted to explain the "peculiarities common to all mass movements," with a particular emphasis on the enthusiasm and self-sacrifice that Hitler and Stalin were able to generate among their followers. We cannot do justice here to his highly insightful handling of the topic, but essentially, he claimed that the fanaticism and self-righteousness that are an integral part of all mass movements, as contrasted with "the appeal of a practical organization," are rooted in self-hatred, self-doubt, and insecurities. To wit:

> Faith in a holy cause is to a considerable extent a substitute for the lost faith in ourselves. The less justified a man is in claiming excellence for his own self, the more ready is he to claim all excellence for his nation, his religion, his race or his holy cause.
>
> A man is likely to mind his own business when it is worth minding. When it is not, he takes his mind off his own meaningless affairs by minding other people's business. This minding of other people's business expresses itself in gossip, snooping and meddling, and also in feverish interest in communal, national and racial affairs. In running away from ourselves we either fall on our neighbor's shoulder or fly at his throat.
>
> The burning conviction that we have a holy duty toward others is often a way of attaching our drowning selves to a passing raft. What looks like giving a hand is often a holding on for dear life. Take away our holy duties and you leave our lives puny and meaningless.[55]

Of course, if these explanations are not satisfactory, one can always turn to Bertold Brecht's comment upon hearing that Nikita Khrushchev had produced evidence in 1956 that confirmed the fact that Stalin was a mass murderer. Brecht, who had just won the "Stalin Peace Prize" and had been a stooge for Stalinism since the end of World War II, allowed as how it made no difference to him what the papers revealed. He explained his indifference this way.

> I have a horse. He is lame, mangy and he squints. Someone comes along and says: but the horse squints, he is lame and, look here, he is

> mangy. He is right, but what use is that to me? I
> have no other horse. There is no other. The best
> thing, I think, is to think about his faults as little
> as possible.[56]

We should stress here that at no time was the Fabian community large enough to have a meaningful and immediate impact on individual political matters in nineteenth-century England. As we said earlier, the defenders of Albion stood their ground throughout most of the century.

So all's well that ends well, right? Well, no. The bad news is that the presence within English society of a large number of respected and well-educated authors, poets, political writers, jurists, and socialites, who publicly and unapologetically sang the praises of socialism, communism, and even atheism, set the stage for the ascendance of a politically powerful, socialist labor movement in the immediate aftermath of World War I. The *Harper Dictionary of Modern Thought* put it this way.

> By accepting a constitutional approach [the
> Fabians] helped to make socialist ideas respect
> able in Britain ... its direct influence was not
> very great (its membership was 640 in 1893 and
> under 3,000 in 1914), but it established a mode
> of approach to social questions, based on socialist
> ideas and a study of social problems, which had a
> lasting impact on politics in Great Britain.[57]

Now, no examination of the "lasting impact" that the turn-of-the-century leftists had on England would be complete without a brief discussion of the Bloomsbury Group. This was a collection of left-wing intellectuals, most of whom were either members of the Fabian Society or friends of Fabians, who began to meet to discuss literature, art, philosophy, and politics around 1905 and reached the height of their notoriety during the interregnum.

These meetings originated when Cambridge student Thoby Stephen began inviting some friends from the university to his house on Thursday evenings to discuss art and politics. Most of these individuals were members of the Cambridge Apostles, a "secret discussion society" made up of undergraduates, dons, and ex-students. Because Stephen held the meetings at his home, his sisters Virginia and Vanessa were allowed to sit in. They impressed the other guests with their "boldness and skepticism" and were quickly accepted by them as equals and welcomed into their august debates.[58]

While each of the so-called Bloomsburies eventually became known for his or her social and professional positions, the group itself became famous for its public celebration of unconventional sexual behavior. Of course, one can be quite certain that they did nothing to or with one another that had not been done to or with others since the beginning of time. What these folks brought to the party was the apparent belief that their unconventional sexual antics and their accompanying dismissal of prevailing morals, mores, and religious teachings were not only deserving of much public airing but also meritorious as a means of bringing ridicule on the Victorian virtues that they regarded as outdated and lacking the benefit of "reason."

The British philosopher Roger Scruton described their antics thusly in an article in the October 2009 *American Spectator* entitled "A Dark Horse."

> [This "new upper class"] adopted the habit of flaunting its effete sexuality. Lytton Strachey, whose *Eminent Victorians*, debunking the icons of the old moral order, appeared in 1918, advocated what he called "the higher sodomy," in which the promiscuity of the public-school dormitory was combined with high romantic attachments designed to shock the few remaining advocates of marriage. The works of Freud, which were being translated by Lytton's brother James, seemed to authorize all breaches of the old sexual customs, and—in the wake of the First World War—the

culture of inversion acquired a sudden glamour. Homosexuality had been a hot topic ever since the pseudo-scientific explorations of [the extremely eccentric British physician and psychologist] Havelock Ellis and the trial of Oscar Wilde. But it enjoyed a kind of endorsement from the new elite that made it into a badge of membership, and a sign of moral distinction ... Many of its leading figures were Communist sympathizers, many more were romantic socialists of the H. G. Wells and George Bernard Shaw variety. Among French intellectuals leftist ideology, anti-patriotism, and prancing homosexuality were as frequent as they were in England—witness Jean Cocteau, Max Jacob, André Gide. But in France the cultural and the political elite were distinct. Politics was conducted on the *rive droite*, culture on the *rive gauche* of the city, and they were divided from each other by the vast and unfrequented monument of Nôtre Dame. In England the very people who were dominating the arts were shaping politics. They could join the political discussion through the hereditary House of Lords, and the public school system meant that the intoxicating Hellenism imbibed by those who joined the bohemian circles of Soho and Bloomsbury was imbibed also by those who went into Parliament, and by those—a surprisingly large number—who inhabited both milieus: J. M. Keynes, for instance, Bertrand Russell, Leonard Woolf.[59]

Relative to the war between the Right and the Left, the presence in early twentieth-century England of this publicly licentious group of self-proclaimed intellectuals is comparable to the appearance of the pus-filled sacs that signal the onset of the pox. Or to mix our metaphors here, that the socialist parasite had burrowed beyond the political and was beginning to eat away at the laws, customs, mores, social rhythms, attitudes, and traditions that formed the foundations of the ancient British society.

There was no formal membership involved in the Bloomsbury Group, so reports vary as to who was and who was not a regular at these meetings. Among the best known participants were Virginia Spencer Woolf and her husband, Leonard; Vanessa Spencer Bell and her husband, Clive; E. M. Forster, the novelist; Lytton Strachey, the essayist and critic; John Maynard Keynes, the economist and one-time boyfriend of Strachey; Duncan Grant, the painter and one-time lover of both Strachey and Keynes; Roger Fry, the noted art critic and lover of Vanessa Bell; Vita Sackville-West, author, poet, wife of Harold George Nicolson, and promiscuous lesbian lover of seemingly dozens of notable ladies of the day, including Virginia Woolf; and Harold George Nicolson, diplomat, author, Vita's husband, and bisexual bon vivant.

Finally, there was the philosopher G. E. Moore, whose 1903 book *Principia Ethica* formed the basis of the group's secular "religion" and who personally became so central to the group's early discussions that his biographer Paul Levy describes him as the "father of Bloomsbury."

Moore was one of the founders of something called the "analytic tradition" in philosophy. He is also known for something called "common sense concepts." Our interest of his philosophical musings is limited to his part in the development and favorable promotion of something called emotivism, which was defined by MacIntyre in his remarkable book *After Virtue* as the belief that "all evaluative judgments and more specifically all moral judgments are *nothing but* [emphasis in the original] expressions of preference, expressions of attitude or feeling."[60] Other philosophers are more closely associated with emotivism, but MacIntyre credits Moore with having moved the idea from the realm of philosophy to the drawing rooms of the radicals, where it became a foundation principle of the Left and remains so today. He put it this way:

For it at once might be objected to my thesis that emotivism has been after all propounded in a variety of time, places and circumstances, and hence that my stress upon Moore's part in generating emotivism is mistaken. To this I should reply that ... whenever something like emotivism is found to flourish it generally is the successor theory to views analogous to Moore's or [H.A.] Prichard's.[61]

Keynes recalled the overwhelming influence of Moore on the Bloomsbury crowd in an essay entitled "My Early Beliefs," which he wrote in 1938.

I went up to Cambridge at Michaelmas 190 2, and Moore's *Principia Ethica* came out at the end of my first year ... of course, its effect on us, and the talk which preceded and followed it, dominated, and perhaps still dominates everything else ... Indeed, in our opinion, one of the greatest advantages of his religion, was that it made morals unnecessary—meaning by "religion" one's attitude towards oneself and the ultimate and by "morals" one's attitude towards the outside world and intermediate ... In short, we repudiated all versions of the doctrine of original sin, of there being insane and irrational springs of wickedness in most men.[62]

In short, then, Moore provided philosophical grounds for the brilliant, but poorly socialized and emotionally stunted young men and women in the Group to convince themselves that their aberrational lifestyles were ethically and morally superior. Thus, between the Fabians and the Bloomsburies, England produced a prominent new force in the advancement of the Left, which Hal Draper would later describe in his classic 1966 pamphlet "The Two souls of

Socialism" as "socialism from above." He contrasted it with "social-ism from below" as follows:

> What unites the many different forms of Socialism-from-Above is the conception that socialism (or a reasonable facsimile thereof) must be *handed down* to the grateful masses in one form or another, by a ruling elite which is not subject to their control in fact. The heart of Socialism-from-Below is its view that socialism can be realized only through the self-emancipa-tion of activized masses in motion, reaching out for freedom with their own hands, mobilized "from below" in a struggle to take charge of their own destiny, as actors (not merely subjects) on the stage of history.[63]

Draper favored "socialism from below" and supported this posi-tion by citing the first sentence in the Rules Written for the First International by Marx. To wit: The emancipation of the working classes must be conquered by the working classes themselves.

His explanation and discussion of the "two souls of socialism" is crucial to understanding the phenomena, but it was Wyndham Lewis, in what is widely regarded as his best novel, *The Revenge for Love*, who most vividly illustrated the gap between the leftist intellec-tuals and Marx's proletariat.

The scene is a welcome home party for a communist who has just returned from the Spanish Civil War. The guests are bourgeois "reds," "socialists from above." Margot and her husband, Victor, are poor reds, dirt-poor, charter members of the proletariat. Margot feels uncomfortable at the party but is happy to be there because of the food, particularly "that great delicacy, the salmon, which was con-sumed by one guest after another, who came up and looked round to see what he could find to devour (simply for the sake of eating, not because they were hungry)."

Margot understood that no bridge existed across which she could pass to commune as an equal with this communist "lady" ... Nor did she wish to very much, because—for Victor's sake—she dreaded and disliked all these false politics, of the sham underdogs (as she felt them to be), politics which made such a lavish use of the poor and the unfortunate, of the "proletariat"—as they call her class—to advertise injustice to the profit of a predatory Party, of sham-underdogs athirst for power; whose doctrine was a universal Sicilian Vespers, and which yet treated the real poor, when they were encountered, with such overweening contempt, and even derision. She could not fathom the essence of this insolent contradiction: but association with such inhuman sectaries could be of no profit to any pukka underdog what ever, she saw that.[64]

In closing, we should mention that the subject of the above-quoted article by Roger Scruton's was the great South African poet Roy Campbell, whose autobiography was entitled *Light on a Dark Horse*. Regarded by Eliot as one of the finest poets of his day, his most famous poem is "The Georgiad," a long and scathing satire on the Bloomsburies, which he wrote after discovering that his wife, Mary Garmen, an artist and member of the Group, had been having a heated affair with Vita Sackville-West, much to the chagrin not only of Campbell but of Virginia Woolf, who was Vita's other lover at the time.

So naturally, our end-of-chapter poem is an excerpt from "The Georgiad." The "Russell" mentioned in the poem is the well-known Cambridge philosopher, religious skeptic, and pacifist, Bertrand Russell, who was not a "member" of the Bloomsbury Group but, like Moore, he was closely associated with it through both his work and his friendship with all the various members.

Let's let the poets in on the fun.
Excerpt from "The Georgiad":

> Hither flock all the crowd whom love has wrecked
> Of intellectuals without intellect
> And sexless folk whose sexes intersect:
> All who in Russell's burly frame admire
> The "lineaments of gratified desire,"
> And of despair have baulked the yawning precipice
> by swotting up his melancholy recipes
> for "happiness"—of which he is the cook
> And knows the weight, the flavour, and the look,
> Just how much self-control you have to spice it with:
> And the right kind of knife you ought to slice it with:
> How to "rechauffe" the stock-pot of desire
> Although the devil pisses on the fire.
> Roy Campbell, 1933

Chapter 9

France: Dreyfus, Maurras, Sorel

Thus the French Revolution, and the train of revolutions in its wake, signified more than simply a rearrangement of the political system of the day: it signified the collapse of an entire world-order, indeed, of a cosmology that the great majority of Europeans had regarded as inviolable. While old worlds must die in order that new worlds can be born, their dissolution, even when gradual, is always an unsettling experience for those who remain attached to former modes of thought. The downfall of familiar and beloved symbols threatens our sense of who and what we are. Feudalism was unjust, but the sacral kingdoms of the Christian Middle Ages at least supplied an identity in a hierarchical scheme of things for even the most lowly members of society. (Alan Davies, *Infected Christianity, At Study of Modern Racism*, 1988)

Paris was the most exciting and dramatic front in the street wars between the radicals and the monarchists in the nineteenth century. The first revolution there occurred in 1830 when Louis XVIII's successor Charles X had to flee to England under the "nom de flight" "Count of Ponthieu," after making a clumsy attempt to increase his power. The second came in 1848 when Charles's successor, King Louis-Phillip, the "bourgeois monarch," fled to England as "Mr. Smith." He was replaced by Louis Napoléon Bonaparte, who assumed the title of President, then changed it to President for Life, and finally to Emperor Napoleon III. After losing the war to Germany in 1871, he followed the lead of his two successors and went to live in England.

At that time, French radicals, made up of Jacobins, Proudhonists, and Blanquists, reacted to the loss of the war by seizing control of Paris and establishing the Paris Commune, which lasted for ten weeks in the spring of 1871. They replaced the Republican tricolor flag with the red socialist one, established a ninety-two-member "communal conference," and then proceeded to get the hell beat out them by the French army in a sweep that resulted in the death of an estimated seven thousand men, women, and children, as well as the imprisonment and deportation of upward of thirty thousand.

When the dust settled, the monarchists won the postwar election. However, they could not agree on who would be king, so the Republicans assumed leadership of the so-called Third Republic. They were representative of what passed for the Right in France at the time. However, they were opposed to the return of the monarchy, to the privileges of what remained of the landed aristocracy, and to any renewal of the political power of the Church. The latter was important because many among the bourgeois and the peasant classes feared the possibility of a restoration of Church lands.

These Republicans were not popular. Historian Michael Curtis notes that they faced opposition on two fronts: "those for whom the Revolution had been a calamity and desired above all a return to the past, and those for whom the task of the revolution had not been completed." In effect then, everyone was unhappy. How could they not be? None of the numerous revolutions and insurrections that had rocked the nation during the past century had delivered anything but bloodshed, more poverty, and hard feelings. The British had beaten the hell out of Napoleon I, and the Germans had done the same to Napoleon III. The economy was stagnant. Corruption and inefficiency abounded. Society was undisciplined, unmotivated, and fearful of all sorts of real and imagined bugbears ranging from the Jesuits to the Freemasons. In short, while another revolution was not in the cards anytime soon, a good, knock-down, drag-out political fight was long overdue. A small spark, and the French people would once again be at each other's throats.

Oddly enough, this spark came from the Army. We say "oddly enough" because the Army stood somewhat aloof from the ongoing factional conflicts. In the wake of its humiliating defeat at the hands of the Germans, the Republicans had substantially expanded, rebuilt, and retrained it for the sole purpose of exacting revenge. In the process, the officer corps had gradually become a separate social class with no particular loyalty to any one faction and a snobbish distaste for the Republican notion of the "sovereignty of a people."

The historian Jean-Denis Breden describes these officers as "moving in an extremely restricted circle of relations, removed from the lower classes but also from the governing elites, having developed a culture of their own, which, quite naturally, was intent on preserving the 'male sentiments' and 'virile habits' of devotion, daring, and bravery." In short, they kept to themselves and ran the Army with little interference from the political class.[1]

Of course, the Army was not without its own problems. One was a sizable number of Jewish officers. These men came largely from middle to upper middle-class families that had fled from extensive persecution in Poland, Russia, Germany, and other European nations to France during the revolution, which had granted full rights of citizenship to Jews. Their large presence in French officer corps was due in part to the limited opportunities for Jews in other professions.

The Christian component in the officer corps was composed, for the most part, of lower-to-lower-middle-class rural Catholics where the highly anti-Semitic Jesuits dominated the Church. These officers were accusing the Jews of "blocking paths of advancement, populating the École Polytechnique, taking the place of Catholics, and preparing the terrain for treason."[2] As Breden notes, the animosity toward Jews was so intense among the Catholic officers that several, high-profile duels took place in 1892 between Jewish officers and French anti-Semites.

So it happened that one morning in 1894, a Jewish captain named Alfred Dreyfus was summarily charged with selling military secrets to the Germans. He was quickly convicted and given a life term on Devil's Island in French Guiana. His family, which was quite wealthy, mounted a campaign to clear his name, and the affair turned into a highly heated, extremely polarizing, twelve-year-long, political struggle over Dreyfus's guilt.

On one side, there was the Army and a large contingent of nationalists backed by the Church. The other side featured a mélange made up of Dreyfus's family members, a handful of influential Jews, a few Christians who were outraged by the blatant anti-Semitism and corruption in the highest ranks of the Army, and, eventually, the leaders of the socialist parties. The latter had been reluctant to enter the fray because public opinion was so adamantly against Dreyfus. But they finally realized that it provided an opportunity to weaken the establishment Republicans.

These "Dreyfusards" made little headway during the first two years. Then, the chief of the Army's intelligence section, Colonel Georges Picquart, discovered that documents used in the prosecution had been falsified by a fellow officer named Ferdinand Walsin Esterhazy. Senior army officials warned Picquart to keep his mouth shut, but he bravely ignored the threats and surreptitiously passed the information on to several Dreyfusards. They, in turn, gained the support of the esteemed vice president of the Senate, August Scheurer-Kestner, who, after much deliberation, publicly announced that Dreyfus was innocent, and openly accused Esterhazy.

A military court opened the case against Esterhazy on January 10, 1898, and acquitted him of wrongdoing on the second day, after which the Army brought more charges against Dreyfus based on more false information that had been concocted by Colonel Hubert-Joseph Henry, a subordinate of Picquart. Bredin notes the following reaction to the acquittal of Esterhazy:

> Applause broke out in the room, along with shouts of "Long live the Army!" "Long live France!" "Death to Jews!" and "Death to the syn-

dicate!" [the latter being a reference to the widely
held belief that a nasty cabal of rich Jews were
behind the traitorous activities of Dreyfus] ...
Esterhazy found it hard to make his way through
the crowd ... the officers wanted to carry him
aloft in triumph ... At the threshold of the prison,
a loud voice proclaimed "Hats off to the martyr
of the Jews ... The next day, Colonel Picquart
would be arrested, confined to a fortress ... That
same day in the Senate Scheurer-Kestner would
be stripped of his vice presidency.[3]

End of story. Right? Dreyfus had been railroaded and no one
cared.

Well, no. The day after the trial, the wealthy and highly popular French author Émile Zola bravely took up Dreyfus's cause by
publishing a letter entitled "J'accuse!" in the radical socialist Georges
Clemenceau's newspaper *Aurore* summarizing the case against the
prosecution and accusing the highest levels of the French Army of
obstruction of justice.

It was a showstopper, a revolution on paper. Not only did it inject
new life into the defense of Dreyfus, it was a no-holds-barred attack
by a man of unimpeachable character on the Army, the Catholic
Church, and the Republicans, or as Bredin put it: "an indictment of
the forces and virtues of traditional France, its religious passion, military spirit, and hierarchies." In short, Zola single-handedly turned
the Dreyfus affair from a legal issue into the political melee that we
said earlier was long overdue.

Zola knew he would be prosecuted. In fact, he said he welcomed it as a means to bring evidence before the public of the
corruption in the military. "My fiery protest is but the cry of my
soul," he said. "Let me then be brought before a criminal court
and let the inquest take place in broad daylight."[5] He had his day
in court, so to speak. Naturally, he was found guilty, and when
sentenced to one year in prison, he fled to England during the
appeals process.

Then, in August of 1898, a new Minister of War, Jacques Marie Eugène Godefroy Cavaignac, discovered evidence of forgery. During a subsequent inquiry, both Esterhazy and Henry confessed. Esterhazy was placed on a pension and fled to England. Henry was jailed, and the next day he was found with this throat slit. Oddly enough, he had had no razor with him when he entered the cell, but the case was ruled a suicide because, after all, he had been distraught after having confessed to a serious crime and thrown in jail.

At that point, it was evident that Dreyfus was innocent, and it was widely assumed that he would be retried and acquitted. Had that happened, the entire event might have gone down in history as nothing more than another sad example of the rampant anti-Semitism that permeated French society at the turn of the century. The French people would have shrugged their shoulders and moved on. But that was not to be.

Suddenly, in early September 1898, another showstopper appeared. Seemingly out of nowhere, a newspaper article by a thirty-year-old, largely unknown journalist named Charles Maurras came to the defense of the Army, the Church, and France. It was entitled "The First Blood," and dramatically proclaimed that Colonel Henry's forgery was a noble, patriotic act committed solely for the purpose of saving France from a nefarious Jewish "syndicate" that was out to destroy both the Army and the nation. He declared that Henry was both a hero and a martyr. To wit:

> The energetic plebian [Henry] had fabricated it for the public good, confiding in no one, not even the superiors whom he loved, agreeing to take a risk, but alone ... National sentiment will awaken; it will prevail and avenge you. In life and in death you have led from the front. Your unfortunate "forgery" will be counted amongst you finest military acts.[6]
>
> Colonel, there is not a drop of your precious blood, which does not steam still wherever the heart of the Nation beats ... We were not able to

give you the great funeral that your martyrdom deserved. We should have waved your bloody tunic and sullied blades down the boulevards; marched the coffin, hoisted the mortuary banner like a black flag. If will be our shame not to have attempted as much. ... But the national sentiment will awaken to triumph and avenge you. Before long from the country's soil, in Paris, in your little village, there will arise monuments to expiate our cowardice. ... In life as in death, you marched forward. Your unhappy forgery will be counted among your best acts of war.[7]

The article was pure fabrication. There had never been a "syndicate" of traitorous Jews. Nevertheless, the claim provided the anti-Dreyfus forces with a new platform from which to continue the fight, which they did with remarkable intensity. Nolte described the resulting atmosphere as follows: "The warring parties ceased to be opponents, they became enemies, with no quarter given or expected ... society became polarized in two hostile blocs accusing each other of criminal plots."[8]

On September 9, 1899, a military court once again found Dreyfus guilty of treason and sentenced him to ten years in prison. On September 19, French president Émile Loubet realized that Dreyfus could not get a fair trial and pardoned him. This decided the legal matter, but the ambiguity of the resolution aggravated the rifts that permeated French society and assured that combatants would continue the fight on the political front, which was already a hotbed of anger and controversy between and among all parties, including the Left. Thus, the stage was set in France for another major chapter in the history of the Left, namely the appearance of a new version of Marxism, which would eventually morph into fascism and Nazism.

You see, as noted earlier, the industrial revolution had rendered Marxism sadly out-of-date even before Marx had finished setting forth its principles in *Das Kapital* in 1867. Proudhon had recognized this as far back as the 1840s when he dismissed Marxism entirely and stated that no government at all would be preferable. Lassalle had put the frosting on the cake in the 1860s, when he joined with Bismarck in a partnership that resulted in the first successful experiment in abandoning the notion of a revolution in favor of working within the existing system.

The result of this Lassallian revision was to split the Left into the two warring camps mentioned above. The fight debuted publicly during the meetings of the Second International, which opened in Paris on July 14, 1889, the hundredth anniversary of the fall of Bastille. It continued to be a hot topic of debate among the participants at the various meetings of the Congress for the next ten years. Then, in January 1899, Edward Bernstein took it public via the publication of a book entitled *Evolutionary Socialism*. Among other things, he boldly stated that it was not only time to drop the pretense of Marx's intellectual omnipotence, but specifically said that it was time to abandon the whole notion of an upcoming grand proletarian revolution.

Now Bernstein was no slouch when it came to leftist dogma. He had been one of the most ardent Marxist activists in Germany, where he was exiled by Bismarck, and in Switzerland, from which he fled to England in 1888, five years after the death of Karl Marx. While in London, he had become so closely associated with Engels that he was the executor of his estate in 1895. However, during his stay, he also became enamored of the Fabians, and following Engels's death, he became a leading spokesman for the revisionists.

Naturally, the book hit the European leftist establishment like a bombshell. In fact, in the preface to the first English edition, Bernstein himself noted that Karl Kautsky, his friend and fellow Marxist, also known as the "pope of Marxism," had denounced it as an abandonment of the fundamental principles and conception of "scientific socialism." The following discussion of the controversy that this book created comes from the introduction to a 1961 paperback edition by the American philosopher Sidney Hook.

Three things account for the startling, and
to the orthodox, terrifying impact of Bernstein's

book. First, it broke sharply with the apocalyptic conception that capitalism would collapse by virtue of inherent economic tendencies which would cause such widespread misery among the working classes that they would rise in revolutionary wrath, destroy the existing state, and introduce collective ownership of all major means of production, distribution, and exchange. Bernstein argued that the economic tendencies, upon which Marx predicted the collapse of capitalism, had not been fulfilled. The poor were not becoming poorer and the rich, richer. The doctrines of the increasing misery of the working class, the constant growth in size of the mass army of unemployed, the uninterrupted development of monopolies defying all social regulation, were not established by the facts. Bernstein's explanation for the failure of Marx's predictions to materialize is that Marx had underestimated the economic and social consequences of the operation of a free political system upon its mode of production.

[According to Bernstein] the socialist movement must, in the formulation of its program, purge itself of the remaining elements of Utopianism. It must stop conceiving of itself as fulfilling "a final goal," and constantly realize itself in the myriad daily tasks, small or large, which confront the movement towards greater democratization ... The sentence which infuriated Bernstein's socialist colleagues most was the one in which he declared that the socialist *movement* meant everything to him and what was usually called *final aim* of socialism, nothing.

In taking these positions Bernstein was doing little more than describing and approving the actual behavior, as distinct from the dogmatic declarations of the German Social Democratic movement and other Western socialist parties. But in demythologizing the socialist outlook, in pointing to the disparities between its holiday rhetoric and daily practice, in calling for greater empirical sobriety and less terminological pieties, Bernstein was criticizing not only the trappings of faith but its substance as well.[9]

Not surprisingly, everyone then joined in the fray, including Lenin, who had just been released from his exile in Siberia and was beginning his career as a Marxist organizer, touring European capitals, meeting with fellow Marxists, and writing political pamphlets. One of the first of these pamphlets, entitled "What Is to Be Done?" was in direct response to Bernstein. It called for the formation of a "vanguard party" to lead the reluctant proletariat to revolution.[10]

Bernstein's book was particularly relevant in France, where the socialists finally had their first opportunity since the Commune had fallen to defeat the Republicans. Not only had the Republicans been badly weakened by the Dreyfus affair, but the socialists had won the right to form workers' organizations such as trade and craft unions and the so-called syndicates, which the anarchists had turned into bases from which to launch strikes and sabotage. The bad news for the leftists was that they were in the midst of an epic, internecine fight between the dedicated Marxists, the revisionists, and the anarchists.

At this point, our interest focuses on Maurras. He was an outlier, a political rebel. He is routinely labeled as a "right wing" ideologue by historians on the Left, which may have some validity if one understands that if one moves far enough to the Right he arrives at the Left. But be that as it may, from the perspective of the history of the Left, he was a highly important figure in its upcoming painful and dark transformation from an ideology that professed to improve mankind's condition to a murderous nightmare of totalitarianism as practiced by Hitler, Stalin, Mao, and their imitators and successors.

With the Right, Maurras argued that the French Revolution was a travesty, and that Marxism and socialism were standing in the way of a return to the good old days when a king, a strong Army, and the Catholic Church provided order. He was also a fan of Hegel's contention that "the nation state [das Volk als Staat] is the spirit in its substantial rationality and immediate actuality, and is therefore the absolute power on earth."[11] Naturally then, he also shared Hegel's antipathy for subjective freedom unless it is exercised within the context of an orderly society.

With the Left, he was an atheist and a fan of Comte's Positivism. His support for the Catholic Church had nothing to do with its religious significance, but focused entirely on its secular role in keeping society orderly, as a partner with the Army, so to speak. His religion was, as with Comte, "Catholicism minus Christianity."[12] A friend and fellow French nationalist Maurice Barrès explained it this way: Maurras "accepts the Church and not the evangelist. He wants the Pope, not Christ."[13]

Here's Nolte:

> His Catholicism is anti-Christian ... Maurras made little effort to hide the fact that he really wants to attack Christ and regards Catholicism [favorably we should note] as un-Christian precisely because to him Catholicism is the incomparable masterpiece of pagan and secular wisdom which by a hierarchical system of mediators makes the church the spokesman of man and eliminates both Father and Son.[14]

His anti-Semitism was of the left-wing variety, meaning that, in keeping with his antagonism toward Christianity, he did not hate Jews for having "killed Christ," but for their "invention" of monotheism, which was responsible for individualism, which he regarded as responsible for all the disorder and evil that plagued Europe. The historian Michael Sutton explains this idea as follows:

> Monotheism, for Maurras as for Comte, was typically anarchic or individualistic because

it fostered in the believer an egotistic concern with his own spiritual welfare and his relationship to the intangible supreme deity, to the detriment of his ties with his fellow men and their past; in directing the individual to cultivate his own conscience with a heady concern for a supposed supernatural, monotheism posited a view of man's nature and end utterly at variance with his social character ... it dissolves societies, and constitutes, according to the fine definition of Auguste Comte, sedition by the individual against mankind.[15]

Maurras himself put it this way in one of his earliest articles, entitled "Three Political Ideas."

It is a case of knowing whether the idea of God, present in the consciousness, is always a beneficent and politic idea ... If, in this naturally anarchist consciousness, the feeling is allowed to germinate that it can establish direct relations with the absolute, infinite, and all-powerful being, then the idea of this invisible and distant master will quickly deprive the consciousness of the respect it owes to its visible and nearby masters; it will prefer to obey God rather than men.[16]

Not surprisingly then, Maurras hated all the "Jewishly-inspired" principles of Western society. These included some of the "enlightenment" values, such as natural rights, liberty, democracy, individualism, Hegel's "subjective freedom," and Rousseau's dual notions of a "social contract" and a "general will" of the people. These, Maurras believed, were not only to blame for the French Revolution but represented an ever-present threat of revolution. As evidence of this, he cited Jeremiah 22:1–5. To wit: "Thus saith the LORD; Go down to the house of the king of Judah, and speak there this word, And say,

Hear the word of the LORD, O king of Judah, that sittest upon the throne of David."[17]

Maurras singled out the notion of freedom as particularly offensive. He put it this way:

> The level of this indeterminate freedom is pitched so low that men bear no other label but that which they share with every plant or animal: individuality. Individual liberty, social individualism, such is the vocabulary of progressive doctrine. How ironical it is. A dog, a donkey, even a blade of grass are all individuals. Naturally, the jostling throng of disorganized "individuals" will willingly accept from the revolutionary spirits its dazzling promises of power and happiness: but if the mob falls for these promises, it is the task of reason to challenge them and of experience to give them the lie. Reason foresees that the quality of life will decline when the unbridled individual is granted, under the direction of the state, his dreary freedom to think only of himself and to live only for himself.[18]

These complaints against the evils of monotheism were, of course, behind his desire to return to monarchism. Yet as with his support for the Church, this also was nuanced, having nothing to do with loyalty to any particular royal family, but solely to his conviction that someone had to be in charge, and the worst possible way of choosing whom that should be was to ask the people to decide. He argued that an individual who is chosen by "the people" would be beholden to them, while a king drew his power from his position, not his person. A king, he claimed, would eliminate the creation of parties, which weaken the nation. In short, he was looking for a philosopher king.

Naturally, he shared some of Bernstein's notions. One of these was that one of the biggest problems with Marxism was the fallacious belief that some sort of brotherly bond existed between the all the "workers of the world," and that this bond would cause them to unite in a monumental class war to overthrow their capitalist exploiters.

Maurras understood that no such bond existed, that the "workers" in France did not give a hoot about the "workers" in Germany, or anywhere else for that matter. Indeed, he knew that they hated both the German workers and the English workers. Moreover, he understood that the changes brought on by the industrial revolutions over the preceding decades had actually created a bond between the proletariat and bourgeoisie that transcended class. Here we come to an important ingredient in Maurras's template for change.

Marx's enemy was the bourgeoisie, the capitalists if you will. His solution was for the proletariat to eliminate them in a class war. Maurras agreed with Bernstein that this war was not going to happen. His solution was to drop the nonsense about an international brotherhood of workers and substitute something called "nationalisme integral."

Now, this was not your mother's nationalism. It demanded absolute obedience from its citizens on all matters—social, economic, and spiritual. In a sense then this was not a denial of the Marxist notion of class warfare. It was a forceful resolution of it. All classes would be welcome, including the industrialists, whom Maurras called "the active and fortunate producers," as opposed to the poor, whom he called the "greedy consumers."[19] The sole criterion for acceptance would be patriotism, *as defined and enforced by the Monarch.*

In short then, Maurras revered the classical Greek sense of ethical order, harmony, and community. In his view, Christianity had destroyed this ideal by creating modern man's obsession with his own personal welfare over the state. Marx was aware of this friction between the individual and communal interest but finessed it by maintaining that the individual rights of the proletariat would become unimportant when all distinctions between ruler and ruled disappeared. By default then, Marx opted for totalitarianism. Maurras embraced it openly.

Of course, Maurras's idea of an omnipotent boss man—whether king, pope, dictator, or President for Life—acting on behalf of a weak-kneed proletariat, fit in well with the Babeuf/Buonarroti understanding of a "temporary dictatorship" of "wise and courageous citizens," who would handle postrevolutionary matters until "the people" were ready to take over. So naturally, both ideas became a standard feature in all leftist movements, including Mussolini's fascism, Hitler's National Socialism, and Lenin's communism, as well as a goal for America's liberals.

Finally, there was Marx's fallacious notion that the proletariat revolution would happen spontaneously, in response to the natural and inevitable collapse of capitalism. Maurras understood that this was nonsense. So he formed a gang of thugs called the Camelots du Roi (street vendors of the king), who were charged with the task of intimidating political foes with acts of violence, to hurry the "inevitable" along, so to speak. Mussolini's counterpart were Blackshirts, Hitler's were the Brownshirts. Lenin's were Chekas, and Mao's the Red Guards. American liberalism favored labor union plug-uglies and numerous classes of "victims of capitalism" that they created and exploited for propaganda purposes, such as "Black Lives Matter."

This hint of violence brings us to Sorel, author of the 1908 political classic *Reflections sur la Violence*. He was a highly successful engineer who turned to studying and writing about political philosophy as an avocation. At one time or another, he was an admirer of Marx, Maurras, and Lenin, but he was never able to find a comfortable intellectual home within any of various contemporary leftist schools of thought.

Sorel was not a practicing Christian, but he shared Maurras's understanding that the secular role of the Catholic Church as a defender of social values was crucial to the future of civilization. In fact, one of the most interesting and important elements of his ideology was his agreement with the historian Ernest Renan that the declining influence of Christianity was alarming, and that the disappearance of religion from the world was a harbinger of "an immense moral, and perhaps intellectual, degeneracy."[20] He put it this way in words that are startlingly close to the views of some of America's leading Christian moralists today, including one of the greatest of that exalted profession, Alasdair McIntyre.

France has lost its morals. Not that, as a matter of fact, the men of our generation are worse than their fathers. ... When I say that France has lost its morals I mean that it has ceased to believe in the very principles of morality, a very different thing. She has no longer moral intelligence or conscience, she has almost lost the idea of morals itself; as a result of continual criticism we have come to this melancholy conclusion: that right and wrong, between which we formerly thought we were able to distinguish dogmatically, are now vague and indeterminate conventional terms; that all these words. Right, Duty, Morality, Virtue, etc., of which the pulpit and the school talk so much, serve to cover nothing but pure hypotheses, vain Utopias, and unprovable prejudices; that thus ordinary social behaviour, which is apparently governed by some sort of human respect or by convention, is in reality arbitrary.[21]

With Proudhon, he blamed this growing decadence on "bourgeois society and its intellectual, moral, and political values." These included "Cartesian rationalism, optimism, utilitarianism, Positivism, and intellectualism; the theory of natural rights and all the values inherited from the civilization of the Enlightenment as generally associated, at the turn of the twentieth century, with liberal democracy"[22]

As a fan of the eighteenth-century Italian philosopher Giambattista Vico, he believed that Christianity's decline was part of the natural historic process of decay and rebirth. Nevertheless, he was not entirely wedded to historicism, for he believed that the ongoing decadence could be halted by replacing religiosity with socialism, which he described as "the highest moral ideal ever conceived by man." He put it this way:

This time it is not a new religion which is shaping itself underground, without the help of

the middle-class thinkers, it is the birth of a virtue, a virtue which the middle-class Intellectuals
are incapable of understanding, a virtue which
has the power to save civilisation, as Renan hoped
it would be saved—but by the total elimination
of the class to which Renan belonged.[23]

Of course, Sorel's socialism and his proposed means for achieving it were unorthodox.
As a long-time admirer of Proudhon, he was an
anarchist at heart. He disliked and distrusted
both the old-line Marxists and the revisionists,
complaining, among other things, that their
incessant and tedious chattering was not only a
waste of time but damaging to the cause.

The fundamental economic notion behind Sorel's views was
that the proletariat should own the means of production, with no
interference from the state. Sternhell describes his proposed system as
"revolutionary capitalism," that is, "a capitalism of producers, hostile
to the plutocracy and high finance, the stock exchange, the middle-
men, and the money grubbers ... strongly attached to the market
economy, to competition, and to the nonintervention of the state in
economic activity."[24] Sorel put it this way:

The proletariat must be preserved from
the experience of the Germans who conquered
the Roman Empire; they were ashamed of their
barbarism and put themselves to school with the
rhetoricians of Latin decadence; they had no reason to congratulate themselves for having wished
to be civilized! [25]

He was, of course, aware of and disturbed by the fact that time
had blurred the line between the proletariat and the bourgeoisie; that
indeed, bourgeois democracy had increasingly corrupted the prole-

tariat, which explains his brief attraction to Maurras's *"nationalisme integral."* But he was greatly encouraged by the formation of labor syndicates and the large number of often violent strikes that were going on across Europe.

In 1906, for example, some 438,000 French Workers (one in every sixteen) engaged in a strike, and as Sternhell noted, many more were in solidarity with the idea. As evidence of their commitment, Sternhell points out that some of these strikes came at enormous cost to the workers and their families. Some lasted for weeks, and at least one resulted in bloodshed when the army was called in to stop it.[26] Of course, this violence was causing concerns among the socialists who were attempting to become part of the system. Sorel dismissed these anxieties with words reminiscent of Robespierre, and which one day the likes of Hitler, Lenin, Stalin, Mao, and other leftist murders would parrot. To wit:

> We are thus led to ask ourselves whether certain criminal acts could not be considered heroic, or at least meritorious, if we were to take into account the happy consequences for their fellow-citizens anticipated by the perpetrators, as the result of their crimes. Certain individual criminal attempts have rendered such great services to democracy that the latter has often consecrated as great men those who, at the peril of their lives, have tried to rid it of its enemies.[27]
>
> Proletarian violence, carried on as a pure and simple manifestation of the sentiment of the class war, appears thus as a very fine and very heroic thing ; it is at the service of the immemorial interests of civilisation ; it is not perhaps the most appropriate method of obtaining immediate material advantages, but it may save the world from barbarism.[28]

As indicated in this quote, Sorel's advocacy of violence was not driven by revenge or hatred, but by utility. Violence incites enthusiasm, heroics, a sense of purpose, a willingness to sacrifice for the cause. As for the bosses, Sorel put this way:

> Proletarian violence confines employers to their role as producers and tends to restore the class structure just when they seemed on the point of intermingling in the democratic morass. ... Thus proletarian violence has become an essential factor in Marxism. Let us add once more that, if properly conducted, it will have the result of suppressing parliamentary socialism, which will no longer be able to pose as the leader of the working classes and as the guardian of order."[29]

Finally, he notes, "the obsessed and frightened administration nearly always intervenes with the masters and forces an agreement upon them, which becomes an encouragement to the propagandists of violence."[30] In his 1908 book, *The Illusions of Progress*, he cites none other than Madame de Staël as an ally in this theory of violence, quoting her thusly from her book, *De La Literature*.

> Although strong passions lead to crimes indifference would never have caused, there are circumstances in history in which these passions are necessary to revive the mainsprings of society. Reason, with the help of the centuries, takes hold of some of the effects of these great moments. But there are certain ideas that are revealed by passions and that would be unknown without them. Violent jolts are necessary to expose the human mind to entirely new objects: these are the earthquakes and subterranean fires that show men the riches time alone could not have revealed.[31]

At this point then he had the makings of a revolutionary move-ment led by syndicalists, who could convincingly wield the threat of a violent "general strike," which, Sorel believed, would bring all production to a halt and result in the takeover of the means of pro-duction. Now, understand that it was the "myth" of the general strike that Sorel addressed, not the strike itself. That does not mean that Sorel would not have welcomed a general strike. It simply means that his focus was on the glorious idea of myth as a means to motive workers to action and to instill fear in the capitalists. From that view-point, it did not need to happen. It needed only to attract and inspire heroes to the cause. He put it this way:

> Socialists must be convinced that the work to which they are devoting themselves is a seri-ous, formidable and sublime work; it is only on this condition that they will be able to bear the innumerable sacrifices imposed on them by a propaganda, which can produce neither honours, profits nor even immediate intellectual satisfac-tion. Even if the only result of the idea of the general strike was to make the socialist concep-tion more heroic, it should on that account alone be looked upon as having an incalculable value.[32]

The problem, from Sorel's perspective, was that the ongoing strikes were motivated by demands for better working conditions and higher wages rather than by a desire to place control of the means of production in the hands of syndicates. This meant that, in effect, every victory by the strikers was a defeat for the cause.

Sorel's solution to this problem *became one of the most important weapons in the leftist arsenal going forward; that being the creation and promotion of myths, which Sorel claimed were much more persuasive than truth, reason, economic theories, and obtuse philosophical discus-sions.* Indeed, he noted, workers grasped myths intuitively, so there was no need for a Leninist élite schooled in the scientific theory of

Marxism. Moreover, myths stood their ground against all skeptics. He put it this way.

> I thus put myself in a position to refuse any discussion whatever with the people who wish to submit the idea of a general strike to a detailed criticism, and who accumulate objections against its practical impossibility ... The intellectualist philosophy finds itself unable to explain phenomena like the following—the sacrifice of his life which the soldier of Napoleon made in order to have had the honour of taking part in "immortal deeds and of living in the glory of France, knowing all the time that" he would always be "poor man;" then, again, the extraordinary virtues shown by the Romans who resigned themselves to a frightful inequality and who suffered so much to conquer the world.[33]

Finally, Sorel noted that myths were behind all the great movements and events in history. He used Christianity as an example. To wit:

> Catholics have never been discouraged by even the hardest trials because they have always pictured the history of the Church as a series of battles between Satan and the hierarchy supported by Christ; every new difficulty which arises is only an episode in a war which must finally end in the victory of Catholicism. ... If Catholicism is in danger at the present time, it is to a great extent owing to the fact that the myth of the Church militant tends to disappear ... to these educated Catholics the myth of the struggle with Satan then appears dangerous, and they point out it ridiculous aspects; but they do not

in the least understand its historical bearing. ...
The intellectualist philosophy would have vainly
endeavoured to convince the ardent Catholics,
who for so long struggled successfully against
the revolutionary traditions, that the myth of the
Church militant was not in harmony with the
scientific theories formulated by the most learned
authors according to the best rules of criticism; it
would never have succeeded in persuading them.
It would not have been possible to shake the
faith that these men had in the promises made
to the Church by any argument; and so long as
this faith remained, the myth was, in their eyes,
incontestable.[34]

Now Plato had stated centuries earlier in *Phaedrus* that "from
opinion comes persuasion and not from truth."[35] But Sorel had
pieced together his formula from numerous contemporary sources.
As noted earlier, one of these was Renan, who said this in *The English
Christian*: "People die for *opinions* and not for *certitudes* because they
believe and not because they know ... whenever beliefs are in question and the greatest testimony and the most efficacious demonstra-
tion is to die for them."[36]

Then there was the French philosopher Henri Bergson, who,
among many other things, introduced Sorel to the idea of "intuition," which, when integrated with the science and reason produced a higher understand of men's motivates. Sorel put it this way:
"Bergson has taught us that it is not only religion which occupies the
profounder region of our mental life; revolutionary myths have their
place there equally with religion."[37]

Unfortunately, for Sorel at least, World War I prevented the
efficacy of the myth of the general strike from being finally determined. However, along with those of Maurras, his ideas lived on in
the immoral and criminal acts of Mussolini, Hitler, Lenin, Stalin,
Mao, American liberalism, and countless other totalitarian ideologies. We will address this further in a future chapter. In the mean-

time, we will close with a paragraph from Thomas Mann's classic novel *Dr. Faustus*, which dramatically portrays Germany's decline into madness during the interregnum.

> [Sorel's] relentless prognostication of war and anarchy, his characterization of Europe as the war-breeding soil, his theory that the peoples of our continent can unite only in the one idea, that of making war—all justified its public calling it *the book of the day*. But even more trenchant and telling was its perception and statement of the fact that in this age of the masses parliamentary discussion must prove entirely inadequate for the shaping of political decisions; that in its stead the masses would have in the future to be provided with mythical fictions, devised like primitive battle-cries, to release and activate political energies. This was in fact the crass and inflaming prophecy of the book; that popular myths or rather those proper for the masses would become the vehicle for political actions; fables, insane visions, chimeras, which needed to having nothing to do with truth or reason or science in order to be creative, to determine the course of life and history, and thus to prove themselves dynamic realities. Not for nothing, of course, did the book bear its alarming title; for it dealt with violence as the triumphant antitheses of truth.[38]

Postscript: Maurras met his downfall shortly after the end of World War II. You see, while he hated Germans, he hated Jews more. So when the Nazis occupied France, he threw his support behind the Vichy government and became a champion of the campaign to round up French Jews and send them to Auschwitz. He was tried for collaboration with the enemy in 1945 and sentenced to life in prison. He was seventy-seven at the time. In 1952, he was released to a clinic in Tours, where, after living his life as a self-professed atheist, he asked for and received his last rites and died.

Let's let the poets in on the fun.

> Eldorado
> Gaily bedight,
> A gallant knight,
> In sunshine and in shadow,
> Had journeyed long,
> Singing a song,
> In search of Eldorado.
> But he grew old—
> This knight so bold—
> And o'er his heart a shadow
> Fell, as he found
> No spot of ground
> That looked like Eldorado.
> And, as his strength
> Failed him at length,
> He met a pilgrim shadow—
> "Shadow," said he,
> "Where can it be—
> This land of Eldorado?"
> "Over the Mountains
> Of the Moon,
> Down the Valley of the Shadow,
> Ride, boldly ride,"
> The shade replied,—
> "If you seek for Eldorado!"
> Edgar Allen Poe, 1849

Part III

Capitalism, Socialism, Progress, Decay

"The time has come," the Walrus said,
"To talk of many things:
Of shoes—and ships—and sealing-wax—
Of cabbages—and kings—
And why the sea is boiling hot—
And whether pigs have wings."
"But wait a bit," the Oysters cried,
"Before we have our chat;
For some of us are out of breath,
And all of us are fat!"
"No hurry!" said the Carpenter.
They thanked him much for that.
(Lewis Carroll, *Through the Looking-Glass*, 1871)

The time has come to take a four-chapter break from our narrative to prepare the way for a lengthy discussion of the Left's invasion of the United States. We will begin with a brief history of capitalism, that great and noble progeny of Christianity and one of the pillars upon which Western Civilization stands. We will then review the warnings of several wise and gifted men about the dangers and consequences of collectivism, and offer a few thoughts of our own on the subject. We will then explore the notion of human "progress," that seemingly innocent idea that we described earlier as the *fourth principle in all leftist models*. And finally, we will briefly explore the death of nations.

Let's let the poets in on the fun.

How Doth the Little Crocodile
How doth the little crocodile
Improve his shining tail,
And pour the waters of the Nile
On every golden scale!
How cheerfully he seems to grin
How neatly spreads his claws,
And welcomes little fishes in,
With gently smiling jaws!
Lewis Carroll, 1865

Chapter 10

On Capitalism

Again, how immeasurably greater is the plea-sure, when a man feels a thing to be his own; for surly the love of self is a feeling implanted by nature and not given in vain, although selfishness is right censured; this, however, is not the mere love of self, but the love of self in excess, like the miser's love of money; for all, or almost all, men love money and other such objects in a measure. And further, there is the greatest pleasure in doing a kindness or service to friends or guests or companions, which can only be rendered when a man has private property. These advantages are lost by excessive unification of the state ... No one, when men have all things in com-mon, will any longer set an example of liberality or do any liberal action; for liberality consists in the use which is made of property.

Such legislation may have a specious appear-ance of benevolence; men readily listen to it, and are easily induced to believe that in some wonderful manner everybody will become everybody's friend, especially when someone is heard denouncing the evils now existing in states, suits about contracts, convictions for perjury, flatteries of rich men and

> *the like, which are said to arise out of the possession*
> *of private property. These evils, however, are due to*
> *a very different cause—the wickedness of human*
> *nature. Indeed, we see that there is much more quar-*
> *relling among those who have all things in common,*
> *though there are not many of them when compared*
> *with the vast numbers who have private property.*
> (Aristotle, *Politics*, 350 BC)

We will begin our discussion of capitalism by noting that it is not an ideology. It is not "the opposite" of socialism, as some people seem to think. In its simplest form, capitalism is nothing more than a method used to facilitate the exchange of goods. It traces its origins back to the time when the first hominid fashioned a stick into a club and declared it to be "his" by virtue of the capital (in this case time, energy, and ingenuity) that he invested in its manufacture, and other hominids recognized his claim as valid, either formally or informally, grudgingly or willingly. The ban against theft and the evidence of trade between individuals in every human society known to history is a testament to the recognition among even the most primitive human species of the existence of the notion of the private ownership of property, and thus the existence of capitalism, in its simplest form.

Somewhere along the line, human societies began to impose rules and restrictions regarding the possession and transfer of material objects and real estate. Of course, some societies preferred a high degree of communal ownership, while others favored the ownership of "everything" by one individual or group of individuals. Yet even these societies recognized the need for a practical method involving the ownership of property to reward those persons who were more enthusiastic and effective than others in investing their time and energy into the communal enterprise.

The ancient Greeks and the early Christians are a case in point. They frowned upon individual ownership, but still recognized capitalism as an unavoidable evil. Deirdre McCloskey's *The Bourgeois Virtues* put it this way.

Plato's Socrates declares in *The Republic* that "the more men value money-making, the less they value virtue." Aristotle says of retail trade that it is "justly to be censured, because the gain in which it results is not natural made, but is made at the expense of other men." By "natural made" he means grown from plants and animals. Aristotle is exhibiting here a hardy physiocracy that views only agriculture as "productive." Late in the *Politics,* he says that "the life of mechanics and shopkeepers ... is ignoble and inimical to goodness." In 44 B.C. Cicero declares to his son Marcus that "trade, if petty, is to be considered vulgar; but if wholesale and on a large scale ... it is not to be greatly criticized ... but of all the gainful occupations none is better than cultivation of the soil, none more fruitful, none more sweet, none more appropriate to a free man."

For all their actual immersion in a market economy, the two founts of virtue-talk in Athens—Plato the literal aristocrat and his graduate student Aristotle, the son of a physician in the Macedonian court and himself tutor to royal Alexander—did not view business people as capable of true virtue. Julius Caesar likewise attributes the bravery of the Belgians to their distance from cultivation and refinement and to their lack of commerce with merchants whose goods tend to the effeminization of the spirit (*ad animos effeminandos*). Seneca the Stoic in a commercial Rome was contemptuous of the idea that businessmen could have honor, though it is among his many self contradictions that he was born into an extremely rich family and himself lent money at interest.[1]

ON CAPITALISM

Jerry Z. Muller, in *The Mind and the Market, Capitalism in Western Thought*, agrees and includes the early Christians among those who are unsympathetic to trade and capitalism.

> If classical Greek thought was suspicious of trade and of merchants, the Christian Gospels and the early Fathers of the Church were actively and intensely hostile. The Gospels warned shrilly and repeatedly that riches were a threat to salvation. "Do not lay up for yourselves treasure on earth," Jesus is reported to have preached in this Sermon on the Mount. "For where your treasure is, there will your heart be also." ... Paul reiterated these lessons, and added that "the love of money is the root of all evils"
>
> Closely intertwined with this disparagement of wealth was the suspicion of merchants and the pursuit of profit. "Jesus entered the temple of God and drove out all who sold and bought in the temple, and he overturned the tables of the moneychangers and the seats of those who sold pigeons." ... Referring to these verses, the early canon *Ejiciens Dominus* declared that the profession of merchant was scarcely ever agreeable to God. It was later incorporated into the *Decretum*, the great collection of canon law compiled by Gratian in the middle of the twelfth century, and encapsulated the Church's view of commerce as expressed in law and ritual. Gratian condemned trade and its profits absolutely.[2]

Heilbroner expands on Muller's observations about medieval Christianity's views of commerce thusly in his classic *The Worldly Philosophers*.

As long as the paramount idea was that life on earth was only a preamble to Life Eternal, the business spirit neither was encouraged nor found spontaneous nourishment.

Kings wanted treasure, and for that they fought wars; the nobility wanted land, and since no self- respecting nobleman would willingly sell his ancestral estates, that entailed conquest, too. But most people—serfs, village craftsmen, even the master of the manufacturing guilds—wanted to be left alone to live as their fathers had lived and as their sons would live in turn.

The absence of the idea of gain as a normal guide for daily life—in fact the positive disrepute in which the idea was held by the Church—constituted one enormous difference between the strange world of the tenth to sixteenth centuries and the world that began, a century or two before Adam Smith, to resemble our own.

But there was an even more fundamental difference. The idea of "making a living" had not yet come into being. Work was not yet a means to an end—the end being money and the things it buys. Work was an end in itself, encompassing, of course, money and commodities, but engaged in as a part of a tradition, as a natural way of life. In a word, the great social invention of 'the market' had not yet been made.[3]

Heilbroner explains that this happened sometime in the thirteent century, when the notion of "capital" as an ingredient, consciously accumulated and applied in economic affairs, and the related concept of "economic man," as we understand that term today, began to take form. Moreover, he notes that the subsequent six-century-long transition to modern-day capitalism was a tortured one involving many different social forces.[4] A major step occurred in 1679 when the great British philosopher John Locke offered a Christian argument in favor of private property in his famous Second Treatise of Civil Government, upon which America's founding fathers relied heavily.

God, who hath given the world to men in common, hath also given them reason to make use of it to the best advantage of life, and convenience. The earth, and all that is therein, is given to men for the support and comfort of their being. And tho' all the fruits it naturally produces, and beasts it feeds, belong to mankind in common, as they are produced by the spontaneous hand of nature; and no body has originally a private dominion, exclusive of the rest of mankind, in any of them, as they are thus in their natural state: yet being given for the use of men, there must of necessity be a means to appropriate them some way or other, before they can be of any use, or at all beneficial to any particular man. ...

Though the earth, and all inferior creatures, be common to all men, yet every man has a property in his own person: this no body has any right to but himself. The labour of his body, and the work of his hands, we may say, are properly his. Whatsoever then he removes out of the state that nature hath provided, and left it in, he hath mixed his labour with, and joined to it something that is his own, and thereby makes it his property. It being by him removed from the common state nature hath placed it in, it hath by this labour something annexed to it, that excludes the common right of other men: for this labour being the unquestionable property of the labourer, no man but he can have a right to what that is once joined to, at least where there is enough, and as good, left in common for others.[5]

Muller too cites the thirteenth century as a time of change, noting that at that time Thomas Aquinas and his successors provided a slightly more religiously benign view of commercial life, by distinguishing the evils of dishonesty and fraud in trade from commerce itself.

> Aquinas, John Duns Scotus (ca. 1266–1308) and San Bernardino of Siena (1380–1444) all recognized that merchants played a positive role in supplying their customers with wares from distant places, and were entitled to some remuneration for their services. Yet this more positive view of commerce remained highly qualified. Although trade was accepted as a permanent institution, commerce for the sake of profit was generally disdained as unworthy of those who pursued a virtuous life, and the motivations of those who engaged in trade continued to meet with mistrust on a variety of grounds.[6]

Of course, historians disagree over the influence and importance of the various forces behind the formation of organized capitalism, but the one thing that seems clear to virtually everyone is that this transition cannot be understood outside the context of the Judeo-Christian culture in which it occurred. For example, the Crusades became an important catalyst for the emergence of capitalism because they spurred the trade and exchange of goods across national borders, which in turn required an increase in the production of goods beyond the immediate needs of the community, which in turn required a commitment of "capital."

Nevertheless, the Church remained generally skeptical of the changes that were occurring as a result of increased trade, capital investment, and the resulting accumulation of wealth, if for no other reason that it seemed to promote a concomitant increase in the occurrence of each of the seven deadly sins, namely wrath, greed, sloth, pride, lust, gluttony, and envy.

Thomas More's classic, *Utopia,* provides a marvelous example of the anger and fear that these changes brought to some Christian leaders of the day. The year was 1515, and More was highly concerned about the practice of "enclosure," a trend that had accelerated during the reign of the Tudors, in which wealthy individuals claimed ownership over communal pastures and peasant tillages. The purpose was to engage in large-scale sheep farming to supply the wool for England's emerging textile industry. Yet one result was widespread impoverishment and the disappearance of rural villages. Another was the advent of large estates run by men with great wealth in the presence of extreme poverty.

In *Utopia,* a word that More coined from Latin meaning "noplace," he described a society that was free from the things that were troubling him, not the least of which was money. In the process of the narrative, one of his characters, a world traveler and philosopher Raphael Hythloday, contrasts the ways of Utopia with More's Europe, and says the following:

> "But that's not the only thing that compels people to steal. There are other factors at work which must, I think, be peculiar to your country." "And what are they?" asked the cardinal.
>
> "Sheep," I told him. "These placid creatures, which used to require so little food, have now apparently developed a raging appetite and turned into man-eaters. Fields, houses, towns, everything goes down their throats. To put it more plainly, in those parts of the kingdom where the finest and most expensive wool is produced, the nobles and gentlemen, not to mention several saintly abbots, have grown dissatisfied with the income that their predecessors got out of their estates. They're no longer content to lead lazy

lives, which do no good to society—they must actively do it harm, by enclosing all the land they can for pasture, and leaving none for cultivation. They're even tearing down houses and demolishing whole towns—except, of course, for the churches, which they preserve for use as sheepfolds. As though they didn't waste enough of your soil already on their coverts and game-preserves, these kind souls have started destroying all traces of human habitation, and turning every scrap of farmland into a wilderness.

So what happens? Each greedy individual preys on his native land like a malignant growth, absorbing field after field, and enclosing thousands of acres with a single fence. The result is that hundreds of farmers are evicted. They're either cheated or bullied into giving up their property, or systematically so ill-treated that they're finally forced to sell. Whichever way it's done, out the poor creatures have to go, men and women, husbands and wives, widows and orphans, mothers and tiny children, together with all their employees—whose great numbers are not a sign of wealth, but simply of the fact that you can't run a farm without plenty of manpower. Out they have to go from the homes that they know so well, and they can't find anywhere else to live ... For the same reason, grain is much dearer in many districts. The price of wool has also risen so steeply that your poorer weavers simply can't afford to buy it, which means a lot more people thrown out of work ... Thus a few greedy people have converted one of England's greatest natural advantages into a national disaster. For it's the high price of food that makes employers turn off so many of their servants—which

> inevitably means turning them into beggars or thieves. ... To make matters worse, this terrible poverty is linked with expensive tastes. Servants, tradesmen, even farm-laborers, in fact all classes of society are recklessly extravagant about clothes and food. Then think how many brothels there are, including those that go under the names of wine-taverns or ale-houses.[7]

Needless to say, the tension between the Church and embryonic capitalism was high. Then, just one year after More published his *Utopia*, another notable Christian named Martin Luther nailed his famous "95 Theses" on the door of the All Saints Church in Wittenberg. This began the Reformation, which the great sociologist Max Weber would describe in this classic book, *The Protestant Ethic and the Spirit of Capitalism*, as a pivotal point in the growth and acceptance of capitalism.

According to Weber, this boon to capitalism was prompted by Luther's identification of the theological concept of a "calling"; that is, the understanding that because man's talents are a gift from God, man has an obligation to Him to use these talents to the best of his ability. Weber further noted that this belief stands in direct contrast to the prevailing Catholic view at the time (and thus More's) that (citing Thomas Aquinas) "labor is only necessary *naturali ratione* for the maintenance of individual and community ... where this end is achieved, the precept ceases to have any meaning."[8] Weber explained it this way:

> Luther developed [this concept] in the course of the first decade of his activity as a reformer. At first, quite in harmony with the prevailing tradition of the Middle Ages, as represented, for example, by Thomas Aquinas, he thought of activity in the world as a thing of the flesh, even though willed by God. It is the indispensable natural condition of a life of faith,

but in itself, like eating and drinking, morally neutral. But with the development of the conception of *sola fide* [justification by faith] in all its consequences, and its logical result, the increasingly sharp emphasis against the Catholic *consilia evangelica* [monastic vow] of the monks as dictates of the devil, the calling grew in importance. The monastic life is not only quite devoid of value as a means of justification before God, but he also looks upon its renunciation of the duties of this world as the product of selfishness, withdrawing from temporal obligations. In contrast, labor in a calling appears to him as the outward expression of brotherly love ... That this moral justification of worldly activity was one of the most important results of the Reformation, especially of Luther's part in it, is beyond doubt, and may even be considered a platitude.[9]

According to Weber, Luther did not put too fine a point on this theory. In fact, he emphatically states that Luther "cannot be claimed for the spirit of capitalism in the sense in which we have used that term above, or for that matter in any sense whatever."[10] That honor, he says, goes to John Calvin, who made it one of the central themes of his religious teachings, which he outlined in detail in 1536 in his seminal work *Institutes of Christian Religion*. To wit:

Let this be our principle, that we err not in the use of the gifts of Providence when we refer them to the end for which their author made and destined them, since he created them for our good, and not for our destruction. No man will keep the true path better than he who shall have this end carefully in view. Now then, if we consider for what end he created food, we shall find that he consulted not only for our necessity, but also for our enjoyment and delight. Thus, in clothing, the end was, in addition to necessity, comeliness and honour; and in herbs, fruits, and trees, besides their various uses, gracefulness of appearance and sweetness of smell.

Were it not so, the Prophet would not enumerate among the mercies of God "wine that maketh glad the heart of man, and oil to make his face to shine." The Scriptures would not everywhere mention, in commendation of his benignity, that he had given such things to men. The natural qualities of things themselves demonstrate to what end, and how far, they may be lawfully enjoyed. Has the Lord adorned flowers with all the beauty which spontaneously presents itself to the eye, and the sweet odour which delights the sense of smell, and shall it be unlawful for us to enjoy that beauty and this odour? What? Has he not so distinguished colours as to make some more agreeable than others? Has he not given qualities to gold and silver, ivory and marble, thereby rendering them precious above other metals or stones? In short, has he not given many things a value without having any necessary use? [11]

Weber explains Calvin's reasoning as follows:

The world exists to serve the glorification of God and for that purpose alone. The elected Christian is in the world only to increase this glory of God by fulfilling His commandments to the best of his ability. But God requires social achievement of the Christian because He wills that social life shall be organized according to His commandments, in accordance with that purpose. The social activity of the Christian in the world is solely activity in *majorem gloriam Dei*. This character is hence shared by labor in a calling which serves the mundane life of the community. Even in Luther we found specialized labor in callings justified in terms of brotherly love. But what for him remained an uncertain, purely intellectual suggestion became for the Calvinists a characteristic element in their ethical system. Brotherly love, since it may only be practiced for the glory of God and not in the service of the flesh, is expressed in the first place in the fulfillment of the daily tasks given by the *lex naturae*; and in the Process this fulfillment assumes a peculiarly objective and impersonal character, that of service in the interest of the rational organization of our social environment.

For the wonderfully purposeful organization and arrangement of this cosmos is, according both to the revelation of the Bible and to natural intuition, evidently designed by God to serve the utility of the human race. This makes labor in the service of impersonal social usefulness appear to promote the glory of God and hence to be willed by Him. The complete elimination of the theodicy problem and of all those questions about the meaning of the world and of life, which have tortured others, was as self-evident to the Puritan as, for quite different reasons, to the Jew, and even in a certain sense to all the non mystical types of Christian religion.[12]

Now Calvinism, or the "Reformed" movement as Calvin himself preferred it to call it, had a rough time in continental Europe, where the Catholic Church declared open war on all forms of Protestantism. These vicious and bloody "wars of religion" began in

1524 and went on for a century and a half, ending with a series of treaties signed at the Congress of Westphalia, which was held in Osnabrück and Münster in 1648.

While these wars were sparked by myriad economic and social trends that were part of the long and tortuous breakdown of the old feudal system, they contained a strong religious element. Hence their collective name. Belfort Bax described this relationship as follows in *The Peasants War in Germany, 1525–1526.*

> The religious movement inaugurated by Luther met and was absorbed by all these [economic and social] elements of change. It furnished them with a religious flag, under cover of which they could work themselves out. This was necessary in an age when the Christian theology was unquestioningly accepted in one or another form by well-nigh all men, and hence entered as a practical belief into their daily thoughts and lives.[13]

The German Peasant's War was the first of these wars. It lasted for two years and resulted in the death of an estimated one hundred thousand peasants. Another highly bloody event occurred in 1572 when the French Catholics slaughtered some seventy thousand French Huguenots on Saint Bartholomew's Day. Then, of course, there was the Thirty Years War, which took place between 1618 and 1648. Most of the actual fighting in this war took place in Germany, but it involved virtually every other major power in Europe, including Austria, Denmark, France, Spain, the Netherlands, and Sweden. Tens of thousands died in this conflict. Germany was devastated. No reliable statistics are available, but Cicely Veronica Wedgwood notes the following in *The Thirty Years War.*

> Whether Germany lost three-quarters of her population, or a small percentage, it is certain that never before, and possibly never since, in her

history had there been so universal a sense of irre-
trievable disaster, so wide-spread a consciousness
of the horror of the period which lay behind ...
"I would not have believed a land could have
been so despoiled had I not seen it with my own
eyes," declared Gernal Mortaigne in Nassau.[14]

She then describes the hostile reaction by both sides in the conflict to the peace treaties that called an end to the slaughter.

> At Lissa in Poland the Bohemian Protestant
> exile Comenius wrote: "They have sacrificed us
> at the treaties of Osnabrück ... I conjure you by
> the wounds of Christ, that you do not forsake us
> who are persecuted for the sake of Christ." From
> the Vatican, Innocent X solemnly condemned the
> peace as "null, void, invalid, iniquitous, unjust,
> damnable, reprobate, inane, empty of meaning
> and effect for all time." After thirty years of fight-
> ing extreme Catholics and the extreme Protestants
> were left still unsatisfield ... After the expendi-
> ture of so much human life to so little purpose,
> men might have grasped the essential futility of
> putting the beliefs of the mind to the judgment
> of the sword. Instead, they rejected religion as an
> object to fight for and found others ... Its effects,
> both immediate and indirect, were either nega-
> tive or disastrous. Morally subversive, econom-
> ically destructive, socially degrading, confused
> in its causes, devious in its course, futile in its
> results, it is the outstanding example in European
> history of meaningless conflict.[15]

In the end, the Reformists managed to set down roots in
Switzerland, the Netherlands, Germany, France, Hungry, Poland,
and Sweden. However, their influence on the histories and customs

of these nations was limited since none could claim even a semblance of a victory for the hearts and minds of a majority of their fellow citizens.

In contrast, the Reform movement found fertile soil in England where, in 1534, Henry VIII began the process of breaking away from the Catholic Church, thus setting the stage for the eventual emergence of the English Calvinists (i.e., the Puritans) as a major political force. Then, in 1649, these Puritans beheaded King Charles and installed their leader Oliver Cromwell, known as Old Ironsides, as Lord Protector of the Commonwealth of England, Scotland, and Ireland. This, in turn, created a circumstance described by the prominent nineteenth-century American historian John Fiske as one of those moments of "stupendous significance" when "the dominant religious sentiment" in a country "came to be enlisted on the side of political freedom." Reflecting on this circumstance, he said the following.

> As often as we reflect upon the general state of things at the end of the seventeenth century—the dreadful ignorance and misery which prevailed among most of the people of continental Europe, and apparently without hope of remedy—so often must we be impressed anew with the stupendous significance of the part played by self-governing England in overcoming dangers which have threatened the very existence of modern civilization. It is not too much to say that in the seventeenth century the entire political future of mankind was staked upon the questions that were issue in England. Had it not been for the Puritans, political liberty would probably have disappeared from the world. If ever there were men who laid down their lives in the cause of all mankind, it was those grim old Ironsides, whose watch-words were texts of Holy Writ, whose battle-cries were hymns of praise.[16]

There is, of course, an element of hyperbole in this assertion by Fiske. But there is little question that the Calvinist's claim that God required hard work found favor among the energetic Islanders played a large part in the subsequent emergence of Great Britain as the world's greatest economic power and trailblazer for the industrial revolution.

Moreover, the sometimes violent Catholic pushback on the English Protestant community in the early seventeenth century, particularly by Queen Mary and James I, resulted in the migration to America of thousands of ascetic Protestants who took with them to the New World their Godly admonition to use God's gifts in a manner that would honor Him. And this, gentle reader, eventually, turned into a secularized prescription for individual achievement and prosperity, unlike anything the world had ever seen. Weber famously described this as the "Protestant work ethic," which was quickly secularized in America by the teachings of, among others, Benjamin Franklin ("a penny saved is a penny earned," "early to bed, early to rise," etc.).

Now, having offered these observations and theories, based on Weber's scholarship, we would note that by far the greatest influence of Judeo-Christian beliefs on the emergence of capitalism was the fundamental tenet of both religions, namely the equality of all souls before God.

Elie Wiesel stated it this way in the introduction to his classic *Night*, "that every one of us has been entrusted with a sacred spark from the Shekinah's flame; that every one of us carries in his eyes and in his soul a reflection of God's image."[17]

Hegel asserted in his *Lectures on the Philosophy of Law* that "this idea came into the world through Christianity in which it is that the individual, *as such*, has an *infinite worth*, as being aim and object of the love of God, and destined, consequently, to have his absolute relation to God as spirit, to have this spirit dwelling in him." He further noted the following:

> Entire quarters of the globe, Africa, and
> the East, have never had, and have not yet, this

idea ... this notion of freedom as such, freedom on its own account. ... The Greeks and Romans, Plato and Aristotle and the Stoics, had it not. On the contrary, they conceived only that a man by his birth (as Athenian or Spartan citizen, &c), or by strength of character, by education, by philosophy (the wise man is free even when a slave or in chains), only so did they conceive a man to be free."[18]

The point here is that Western society produced capitalism, as we know it today, within the framework of the Judeo-Christian ethic. This close association with Christianity helped to keep its predatory aspects from deteriorating into a totalitarian nightmare, while the system of laws slowly came into being as a helpmate. And it is the combination of these two today, law and a time-honored body of moral and ethical beliefs, that keeps capitalism functioning smoothly in Western societies. One without the other would inevitably lead to a nightmare of totalitarianism.

Adam Smith, who first identified and explained the principles of capitalism, was acutely aware of this. Indeed, both of his major volumes on the subject, *The Theory of Moral Sentiments* (1759) and *The Wealth of Nations* (1776), are filled with admonitions that corruption among businessmen is the greatest threat to the social and economic benefits of free markets, and that a combination of law and a moral society are necessary to protect against this threat.

This is not to say that capitalism can only function in a society based on Judeo-Christian principles. It is simply to note that capitalism will only work efficiently in a society that respects the freedom of individuals to act in their own best interests, that honors the right of individuals to retain the fruits of their labor, and that encompasses a strong moral framework as a supplement to its legal system. He explained this notion in both the above-mentioned books. In the first, he utilizes the parable of the "Ambitious Poor Man's Son." A truncated version goes as follows:

The poor man's son, whom heaven in its anger has visited with ambition, when he begins to look around him, admires the condition of the rich. He finds the cottage of his father too small for his accommodation, and fancies he should be lodged more at his ease in a palace. He is displeased with being obliged to walk a-foot, or to endure the fatigue of riding on horseback. He sees his superiors carried about in machines, and imagines that in one of these he could travel with less inconveniency. He feels himself naturally indolent, and willing to serve himself with his own hands as little as possible; and judges that a numerous retinue of servants would save him from a great deal of trouble. He thinks if he had attained all these, he would sit still contentedly, and be quiet, enjoying himself in the thought of the happiness and tranquility of his situation. He is enchanted with the distant idea of this felicity. It appears in his fancy like the life of some superior rank of being, and in order to arrive at it, he devotes himself for ever to the pursuit of wealth and greatness.

To obtain the conveniences which these afford, he submits in the first year, nay in the first month of his application, to more fatigue of body and more uneasiness of mind than he could have suffered through the whole of his life from the want of them. He studies to distinguish himself in some laborious profession. With the most unrelenting industry, he labours night and day to acquire talents superior to all his competitors. He endeavours next to bring those talents into public view, and with equal assiduity solicits every opportunity of employment. For this purpose he makes his court to all mankind; he serves those whom he hates, and is obsequious to those whom he despises. Through the whole of his life he pursues the idea of a certain artificial and elegant repose which he may never arrive at, for which he sacrifices a real tranquility that is at all times in his power, and which, if in the extremity of old age he should at last attain to it, he will find to be in no respect preferable to that humble security and contentment which he had abandoned for it. It is then, in the last dregs of life, his body wasted with toil and diseases, his mind galled and ruffled by the memory of a thousand injuries and disappointments which he imagines he has met with from the injustice of his enemies, or from the perfidy and ingratitude of his friends, that he begins at last to find that wealth and greatness are mere trinkets of frivolous utility, no more adapted for procuring ease of body or tranquility of mind than the tweezer-cases of the lover of toys; and like them too, more troublesome to the person who carries them about with him than all the advantages they can afford him are commodious.

Yet, Smith asserts,

And it is well that nature imposes upon us in this manner. It is this deception which rouses and keeps in continual motion the industry of mankind. It is this which first prompted them to cultivate the ground, to build houses, to found cities and commonwealths, and to invent and improve all the sciences and arts, which ennoble and embellish human life; which have entirely changed the whole face of the globe, have turned the rude forests of nature into agreeable and fertile plains, and made the trackless and barren ocean a new fund of subsistence, and the great high road of communication to the different nations of the earth ...

The rich only select from the heap what is most precious and agreeable. They consume little more than the poor, and in spite of their natural selfishness and rapacity, though they mean only their own conveniency, though the sole end which they propose from the labours of all the thousands whom they employ, be the gratification of their own vain and insatiable desires, they divide with the poor the produce of all their improvements. They are led by an invisible hand to make nearly the same distribution of the necessaries of life, which would have been made, had the earth been divided into equal portions among all its inhabitants, and thus without intending it, without knowing it, advance the interest of the society, and afford means to the multiplication of the species.[19]

In the *Wealth of Nations*, he put the same thought this way:

But the annual revenue of every society is always precisely equal to the exchangeable value of the whole annual produce of its industry, or rather is precisely the same thing with that exchangeable value. As every individual, therefore, endeavours as much as he can both to employ his capital in the support of domestic industry, and so to direct that industry that its produce may be of the greatest value; every individual necessarily labours to render the annual revenue of the society as great as he can. He generally, indeed, neither intends to promote the public interest, nor knows how much he is promoting it. By preferring the support of domestic to that of foreign industry, he intends only his own security; and by directing that industry in such a manner as its produce may be of the greatest value, he intends only his own gain, and he is in this, as in many other cases, led by an invisible hand to promote an end which was no part of his intention. Nor is it always the worse for the society that it was no part of it. By pursuing his own interest he frequently promotes that of the society more effectually than when he really intends to promote it. I have never known much good done by those who affected to trade for the public good. It is an affectation, indeed, not very common among merchants, and very few words need be employed in dissuading them from it.

What is the species of domestic industry which his capital can employ, and of which the produce is likely to be of the greatest value, every individual, it is evident, can, in his local situation, judge much better than any statesman or lawgiver can do for him. The statesman who should attempt to direct private people in what manner they ought to employ their capitals would not only load himself with a most unnecessary attention, but assume an authority which could safely be trusted, not only to no single person, but to no council or senate whatever, and which would nowhere be so dangerous as in the hands of a man who had folly and presumption enough to fancy himself fit to exercise it.[20]

As for the importance of the ownership of private property, Muller, in *Adam Smith in His Time and Ours*, notes that Smith strongly believed that mankind's ceaseless quest for "justice" should never include an effort to allocate possessions according to some universally shared criteria since there are no such criteria. The following quote from Smith's friend the philosopher David Hume's *Enquiry Concerning the Principles of Morals* beautifully explains the theory underlying this contention by Smith and provides one of the most precise and insightful condemnations of American liberalism's dream of wealth redistribution ever written.

> We shall suppose that a creature, possessed of reason, but unacquainted with human nature, deliberates with himself what rules of justice or property would best promote public interest, and establish peace and security among mankind: His most obvious thought would be, to assign the largest possessions to the most extensive virtue, and give every one the power of doing good, proportioned to his inclination. In a perfect theocracy, where a being, infinitely intelligent, governs by particular volitions, this rule would certainly have place, and might serve to the wisest purposes:
>
> But were mankind to execute such a law; so great is the uncertainty of merit, both from its natural obscurity, and from the self-conceit of each individual, that no determinate rule of conduct would ever result from it; and the total dissolution of society must be the immediate consequence. Fanatics may suppose, *that dominion is founded on grace*, and *that saints alone inherit the earth*; but the civil magistrate very justly puts these sublime theorists on the same footing with common robbers, and teaches them by the severest discipline, that a rule, which, in speculation, may seem the most advantageous to society, may yet be found, in practice, totally pernicious and destructive.[21]

Finally, relative to the importance of a moral framework to capitalism, Smith maintained in *The Theory of Moral Sentiments* that "upon the tolerable observance" of such duties as politeness, justice, trust, chastity, and fidelity, "depends the very existence of human society, which would crumble into nothing if mankind were not generally impressed with a reverence for these important rules of conduct."[22] In keeping with this thought, Smith agreed with Aristotle that the social order is not spontaneous or automatic, but is founded on institutions that promote self-control, prudence, gratification deferral, respect for the lives and property of others, and some concern for the common good. With this in mind, it should come as no surprise that the greatest challenge to Western Civilization, and thus to capitalism, would come in the form of an attack on the fundamental beliefs of Judaism and Christianity.

Let's let the poets in on the fun.

> Chicago
> HOG Butcher for the World,
> Tool Maker, Stacker of Wheat,
> Player with Railroads and the Nation's Freight Handler;
> Stormy, husky, brawling,
> City of the Big Shoulders:
> They tell me you are wicked and I believe them, for I
> have seen your painted women under the gas lamps
> luring the farm boys.
> And they tell me you are crooked and I answer: Yes, it
> is true I have seen the gunman kill and go free to
> kill again.
> And they tell me you are brutal and my reply is: On the
> faces of women and children I have seen the marks
> of wanton hunger.
> And having answered so I turn once more to those who
> sneer at this my city, and I give them back the sneer
> and say to them:
> Come and show me another city with lifted head singing
> so proud to be alive and coarse and strong and cunning.
> Flinging magnetic curses amid the toil of piling job on
> job, here is a tall bold slugger set vivid against the

little soft cities;
Fierce as a dog with tongue lapping for action, cunning
as a savage pitted against the wilderness,
Bareheaded,
Shoveling,
Wrecking,
Planning,
Building, breaking, rebuilding,
Under the smoke, dust all over his mouth, laughing with
white teeth,
Under the terrible burden of destiny laughing as a young
man laughs,
Laughing even as an ignorant fighter laughs who has
never lost a battle,
Bragging and laughing that under his wrist is the pulse.
and under his ribs the heart of the people,
Laughing!
Laughing the stormy, husky, brawling laughter of
Youth, half-naked, sweating, proud to be Hog
Butcher, Tool Maker, Stacker of Wheat, Player with
Railroads and Freight Handler to the Nation.
Carl Sandburg, 1916

Chapter 11

On Communism and Socialism

We Socialists were, I think, profoundly wrong to ignore the depth and generality of the drive toward property, and therefore exchange of property, in man. Walt Whitman was profoundly wrong when he said in his famous hymm of praise to the animals: "Not one is demented with the mania of owning things." Ownership is not a mania, but a robust instinct extending far and wide in the animal kingdom. Even the birds stake out with their songs an area that belongs to them, attacking fiercely any intruder upon it. Less lyrical beasts serve notice by depositing distinctive odors on the boundaires of their domain. People who keep watch dogs can hardly deny the range and ferocity of the proprietary instinct. It was fully developed even among the nomads with their tents of different sizes. For settled and civilized man, there can never be a paradise, I fear, or even a sane and peaceful habitat, where this deep wish is unsatisfied. It has been neglected in utopias because their authors were guided rather by the Christian evangel of sainthood than by a study of the needs of average men. (Max Eastman, *Reflections on the Failure of Socialism*, 1955)

As noted earlier, in this chapter, we are going briefly to explore the views of several highly intelligent men who share a criticism of collectivism and end with some thoughts of our own on where this evil ideology is taking us. Our guests on the journey are the political scientist Alexis de Tocqueville; the French economist Frédéric Bastiat; two popes, Pius IX and Leo XIII; the English sociologist and polymath Herbert Spencer; the philosopher Friedrich Nietzsche; the French leftist Georges Sorel; the French political scientist Bertrand de Jouvenel; two great American authors, George Orwell and Aldous Huxley; and the political theorist Hanna Arendt.

These folks hail from various places, periods, and positions of historic importance. Yet it is our contention, that if you, gentle reader, want to venture forth in defense of capitalism, freedom, the sanctity of the individual, the importance of private property, and God's role in man's existence, you will benefit from studying their thoughts on these important subjects. Of course, we cannot do any of them justice in this short chapter. However, we can whet your appetite in hopes of spurring you to further study.

We will begin with Tocqueville's *Memoir on Pauperism*, a short work that resulted from a visit he took to England in 1833 to study the effects of the expansion of suffrage, which had been the centerpiece of the Reform Act of 1832. As noted in a previous chapter, English society was in turmoil at the time. In fact, Tocqueville had even heard rumors that the nation was on a verge of a revolution, and while he discovered that this was unlikely, he soon became deeply involved in discussions with various political figures about ongoing efforts to reform the "poor laws," which were widely believed to be one of the causes of the social unrest.

These laws represented the Western world's first public welfare system. They dated back to the sixteenth century, but Queen Elizabeth formalized them in 1601, partially in response to her father's destruction of the Roman Catholic monasteries and religious orders in England, which had previously looked after the needs of the poor. Not surprisingly, the problems created by the poor laws were under discussion before Tocqueville entered the conversation.

In 1798, for example, the much-maligned Thomas Malthus had written the following:

> The poor laws of England may therefore be said to diminish both the power and the will to save among the common people, and thus to weaken one of the strongest incentives to sobriety and industry, and consequently to happiness.[1]

In 1828, the great French economist Jean-Baptiste Say added this:

> England is the country that has most havens available to the unfortunate, and it is perhaps the one where most unfortunates demand aid. Let public welfare or private associations open, a hundred, a thousand others—all—will be filled; and there will remain in society equally as many unfortunates who will request permission to enter or who will claim it as a right if one recognized it as such.[2]

Tocqueville began his work by praising private charity, which he noted is the willing act of man to provide for his fellow man, sharing voluntarily from his wealth to enable and empower his less-fortunate neighbor. This, he said, "private charity establishes valuable ties between the rich and the poor," a "deed [that] itself involves the giver in the fate of the one whose poverty he has chosen to alleviate." Moreover, he said, "the latter ... feels inspired by gratitude."

In contrast, he says, the involvement of government in this transaction destroys both the inherent nobility of charity and the bond that would otherwise exist between giver and receiver. Public charity, he says, serves simply to "inflame society's sores," to create class envy and hatred, and to lay the foundation for what we know today as "class warfare." He put it this way:

Any measure that establishes legal charity on a permanent basis and gives it an administrative form thereby creates an idle and lazy class, living at the expense of the industrial and working class. This, at least, is its inevitable consequence, if not the immediate result. It reproduces all the vices of the monastic system, minus the high ideals of morality and religion that often went along with it. Such a law is a bad seed planted in the legal structure ... The number of illegitimate children and criminals grows rapidly and continuously, the indigent population is limitless, the spirit of foresight and of saving becomes more and more alien to the poor. While throughout the rest of the nation education spreads, morals improve, tastes become more refined, manners more polished—the indigent remains motionless, or rather he goes backward. He could be described as reverting to barbarism. Amid the marvels of civilization, he seems to emulate savage man in his ideas and his inclinations. ...

The law strips the man of wealth of a part of his surplus without consulting him, and he sees the poor man only as a greedy stranger invited by the legislator to share his wealth. The poor man, on the other hand, feels no gratitude for a benefit that no one can refuse him and that could not satisfy him in any case ... Far from uniting these two rival nations, who have existed since the beginning of the world and who are called the rich and the poor, into a single people, it breaks the only link which could be established between them. It ranges each one under a banner, tallies them, and, bringing them face to face, prepares them for combat.

Finally, he said this:

> I am deeply convinced that any permanent,
> regular administrative system whose aim is to
> provide for the needs of the poor will breed more
> miseries than it can cure, will deprive the pop-
> ulation that it wants to help and comfort, will
> in time reduce the rich to being no more than
> the tenant-farmers of the poor, will dry up the
> sources of savings, will stop the accumulation of
> capital, will retard the development of trade, and
> will benumb human industry and activity, and
> will culminate by bringing about violent revo-
> lution in the State, when the number of those
> who receive alms will have become as large as
> those who give it, and the indigent, no longer
> being able to take from the impoverished rich the
> means of providing for his needs, will find it eas-
> ier to plunder them of all their property at one
> stroke than to ask for their help.[3]

Next, we will turn to Bastiat. He was an intellectual, a politician, and a member of the French Liberal School of economists,
which was made up of antisocialist supporters of the established
bourgeois order. Marx referred to them as the "vulgar" economists.
He wrote countless articles and books, including *Economic Sophisms*,
one of only two humorous economics books that readily come to
mind, the other being *Dialogues on the Commerce of Grains* by the
eighteenth-century Italian moralist abbé F. Galiani, about whom
Voltaire is supposed to have said, "No one has ever made famine so
amusing."[4] Heilbroner describes Bastiat as follows:

> An eccentric Frenchman, who lived from
> 1801 to 1850, and who in that short space of
> time and an even shorter space of literary life—
> six years—brought to bear on economics that

most devastating of all weapons, ridicule. Look at this madhouse of a world, says Bastiat. It goes to enormous efforts to tunnel underneath a mountain in order to connect two countries. And then what does it do? Having labored mightily to facilitate the interchange of goods, it sets up customs guards on both sides of the mountain and makes it as difficult as possible for merchandise to travel through the tunnel.[5]

Bastiat is most remembered today for having debunked the notion that there was some economic benefit from a broken window because it provides work to the glazier. He argued that while this was true to some degree, the money spent on replacing the window could have been used for a more productive purpose. However, he did not stop there. He noted that the same argument might be made against those who believe that war is good for the economy since it reduces unemployment and increases production, noting that the costs of war come at the expense of other more useful purposes.

With that said, we will concentrate on what Bastiat had to say about "fraternity," which is the word that the French Left used for what leftists today call compassion. These quotes come from a paper entitled "Justice and Fraternity," which was first published in 1848 in the *Journal des Economistes*, which happens to be the same year that Marx's Communist Manifesto hit the streets. The paragraphs come from a much longer text and are not necessarily in order.

We too, believe us, are filled with fervent emotion when we hear the word fraternity, handed down eighteen centuries ago from the top of the holy mountain and inscribed forever on our republican flag. We too desire to see individuals, families, nations associate with one another, aid one another, relieve one another in the painful journey of mortal life. We too feel our hearts stir and our tears welling up at the recital of noble deeds, whether they add luster to the lives of simple citizens, join different classes together in close union, or accelerate the onward movement of nations chosen by destiny to occupy the advanced outpost of progress and civilization.

But we have not been shown that fraternity can be imposed. If, indeed, wherever it appears, it excites our sympathy so keenly, that is because it acts outside of all legal constraint. Either fraternity is spontaneous, or it does not exist. To decree it is to annihilate it. The law can indeed force men to remain just; in vain would it try to force them to be self-sacrificing.

[Every socialist] has a plan designed to make mankind happy, and they all have the air of saying that if we oppose them, it is because we fear either for our property or for other social advantages. No; we oppose them because we consider their ideas to be false, because we believe their proposals to be as naive as they are disastrous. If we could be shown that happiness could be brought forever down to earth by an artificial social organization, or by decreeing fraternity, there are some among us, even though we are economists, who would gladly sign that decree with the last drop of their blood.

Certainly we should like very much to grant that numerous political theorists who ... appear so pitiless toward what they call individualism, who incessantly repeat the words "devotion," "sacrifice," "fraternity," are themselves actuated exclusively by those sublime motives that they recommend to others, that they practice what they preach, that they have been careful to put their own conduct to harmony with their doctrines.

We should indeed like to take them at their word and believe that they are full of disinterestedness and charity; but, in the last analysis, we may venture to say that we do not fear comparison in this regard.

[The socialists declare] that the state owes subsistence, well-being, and education to all its citizens; that it should be generous, charitable, involved in everything, devoted to everybody; that its mission is to feed the infants, instruct the young, assure employment to the able-bodied, provide pensions for the disabled; in a word, that it should intervene directly to relieve all suffering, satisfy and anticipate all wants, furnish capital to all enterprises, enlightenment to all minds, balm for all wounds, asylums for all the unfortunate, and even aid to the point of shedding French blood, for all oppressed people on the face of the earth.

Who would not like to see all these benefits flow forth upon the world from the law as from an inexhaustible source? ... But is it possible? ... Whence does [the state] draw those resources that it is urged to dispense by way of benefits to individuals? Is it not from the individuals themselves? How, then, can these resources be increased by passing through the hands of a parasitical and voracious intermediary? Is it not clear, on the contrary, that the whole apparatus of government is of such a nature as to absorb many useful resources and to reduce the share of the workers proportionately? Is it not also evident that the latter will thereby lose a part of their freedom, along with a part of the well-being?

If socialists mean that under extraordinary circumstances, for urgent cases, the state should set aside some resources to assist certain unfortunate people, to help them adjust to changing conditions, we will, of course, agree. This is done now; we desire that it be done better. There is however, a point on this road that must not be passed; it is the point where governmental foresight would step in to replace individual foresight and thus destroy, it. It is quite evident that organized charity would, in this case, do much more permanent harm than temporary good.[6]

Now we will turn to Pius IX. The year is 1846. He has been on the Throne of Saint Peter for just under five months. These are dark days. The Church is under assault from revolutionary forces spreading Godless ideologies across the entire European landscape, including a powerful movement within the Papal States themselves demanding, among other things, a constitutional government and the entire laicization of the ministry. Pius has made numerous concessions to the revolutionaries at home, but these have simply encouraged them to increase their demands.

On November 9, he issues his first encyclical entitled *Qui Pluribus* (On Faith and Religion) in which he speaks of the multiplicity of threats to the Church. In the process, he specifically mentions communism, thus marking the Church's first formal recognition of its ancient enemy in the newly acquired costume of a "reason-based" ideology. To wit:

> Each of you has noticed, venerable brothers, that a very bitter and fearsome war against the whole Catholic commonwealth is being stirred up by men bound together in a lawless alliance ... In order to easily mislead the people into making errors, deceiving particularly the imprudent and the inexperienced, they pretend that they alone know the ways to prosperity. They claim for themselves without hesitation the name of

"philosophers." They feel as if philosophy, which is wholly concerned with the search for truth in nature, ought to reject those truths which God Himself, the supreme and merciful creator of nature, has deigned to make plain to men as a special gift ... So, by means of an obviously ridiculous and extremely specious kind of argumentation, these enemies never stop invoking the power and excellence of human reason; they raise it up against the most holy faith of Christ, and they blather with great foolhardiness that this faith is opposed to human reason ... *To this goal also tends the unspeakable doctrine of Communism, as it is called, a doctrine most opposed to the very natural law. For if this doctrine were accepted, the complete destruction of everyone's laws, government, property, and even of human society itself would follow.* [Emphasis added] [7]

As detailed in previous chapters, the Left made considerable progress in its march across the political landscape of Europe during Pius's thirty-two-year-long tenure as pope. One of many people who found these gains to be distressing was none other than Herbert Spencer.

As mentioned in a previous chapter, Spencer was the author of the term "survival of the fittest." But he was much more than that. In fact, he was widely recognized during his lifetime as one of the Western world's leading polymaths, which means that he did not simply know a little bit about a great many things, but in fact knew a great deal about a great many things.

In his book *The Great Illusion*, the historian Oron J. Hale notes that in Britain and the United States, "Spencer's disciples had not blushed to compare him with Aristotle."[8] Among other things, he contributed significantly to the discussions of the day on such subjects as philosophy, ethics, religion, anthropology, economics, biology, sociology, and psychology. On top of that, he was nominated for the Nobel Prize for Literature in 1902.

In any case, our particular interest in Spencer at this point relates to his common-sense warnings of the ill effects of creating a dependent class in order to prop up the least fit. He did this in 1884 in an essay entitled "The Coming Slavery." To wit:

> The kinship of pity to love is shown among other ways in this, that it idealizes its object. Sympathy with one in suffering suppresses, for the time being, remembrance of his transgressions. The feeling which vents itself in "poor fellow!" on seeing one in agony, excludes the thought of "bad fellow," which might at another time arise. Naturally, then, if the wretched are unknown or but vaguely known, all the demerits they may have are ignored; and thus it happens that when the miseries of the poor are dilated upon, they are thought of as the miseries of the deserving poor, instead of being thought of as the miseries of the undeserving poor, which in large measure they should be. Those whose hardships are set forth in pamphlets and proclaimed in sermons and speeches which echo throughout society, are assumed to be all worthy souls, grievously wronged; and none of them are thought of as bearing the penalties of their misdeeds. ...
>
> But surely we are not without responsibilities, even when the suffering is that of the unworthy?" If the meaning of the word "we" be so expanded as to include with ourselves our ancestors, and especially our ancestral legislators, I agree. I admit that those who made, and modified, and administered, the old Poor Law, were responsible for producing an appalling amount of demoralization, which it will take more than one generation to remove. I admit, too, the partial responsibility of recent and present law-mak-

ers for regulations which have brought into being a permanent body of tramps, who ramble from union to union; and also their responsibility for maintaining a constant supply of felons by sending back convicts into society under such conditions that they are almost compelled again to commit crimes. Moreover, I admit that the philanthropic are not without their share of responsibility; since, that they may aid the offspring of the unworthy, they disadvantage the offspring of the worthy through burdening their parents by increased local rates. Nay, I even admit that these swarms of good-for-nothings, fostered and multiplied by public and private agencies, have, by sundry mischievous meddling, been made to suffer more than they would otherwise have suffered. Are these the responsibilities meant? I suspect not. ...

It is said that when railways were first opened in Spain, peasants standing on the tracks were not unfrequently run over; and that the blame fell on the engine-drivers for not stopping: rural experiences having yielded no conception of the momentum of a large mass moving at a high velocity.

The incident is recalled to me on contemplating the ideas of the so-called "practical" politician, into whose mind there enters no thought of such a thing as political momentum, still less of a political momentum which, instead of diminishing or remaining constant, increases. The theory on which he daily proceeds is that the change caused by his measure will stop where he intends it to stop. He contemplates intently the things his act will achieve, but thinks little of the remoter issues of the movement his act sets up, and still less its collateral issues ... [W]hen Mr. Pitt said, "Let us make relief in cases where there are a number of children a matter of right and honour, instead of a ground for opprobrium and contempt," it was not expected that the poor-rates would be quadrupled in fifty years, that women with many bastards would be preferred as wives to modest women, because of their incomes from the parish, and that hosts of ratepayers would be pulled down into the ranks of pauperism. ...

Failure does not destroy faith in the agencies employed, but merely suggests more stringent use of such agencies or wider ramifications of them. The extension of this policy, causing extension of corresponding ideas, fosters everywhere the tacit assumption that Government should step in whenever anything is not going right ... "Surely you would not have this misery continue!" exclaims someone, if you hint a demurrer to much that is now being said and done. Observe what is implied by this exclamation. It takes for granted, first, that all suffering ought to be pre-vented, which is not true: much of the suffering is curative, and prevention of it is prevention of a remedy. In the second place, it takes for granted that every evil can be removed: the truth being that, with the existing defects of human nature, many evils can only be thrust out of one place or form into another place or form—often being increased by the change. The exclamation also implies the unhesitating belief, here especially concerning us, that evils of all kinds should be dealt with by the State. There does not occur the inquiry whether there are at work other agencies capable of dealing with evils, and whether the evils in question may not be among those which are best dealt with by these other agencies. And obviously, the more numerous governmental interventions become, the more confirmed does this habit of thought grow, and the more loud and perpetual the demands for intervention ... A comparatively small body of officials, coherent, having common interests, and acting under central authority, has an immense advantage over an incoherent public which has no settled policy, and can be brought to act unitedly only under strong provocation. Hence an organization of officials, once passing a certain stage of growth, becomes less and less resistible; as we see in the bureaucracies of the Continent. ...

The hard-worked and over-burdened who form the great majority, and still more the incapables perpetually helped who are ever led to look for more help, are ready supporters of schemes which promise them this or the other benefit of State-agency, and ready believers of those who tell them that such benefits can be given, and ought to be given. They listen with eager faith to all builders of political air-castles, from Oxford graduates down to Irish irreconcilables; and every additional tax-supported appliance for their welfare raises hopes of further ones. Indeed the more numerous public instrumentalities become, the more is there generated in citizens the notion that everything is to be done for them, and nothing by them. Each generation is made less familiar with the attainment of desired ends by individual actions or private combinations, and more familiar with the attainment of them by governmental agencies; until, eventually, governmental agencies come to be thought of as the only available agencies ... Moreover, every additional

State-interference strengthens the tacit assumption that it is the duty of the State to deal with all evils and secure all benefits. Increasing power of a growing administrative organization is accompanied by decreasing power of the rest of the society to resist its further growth and control. The multiplication of careers opened by a developing bureaucracy, tempts members of the classes regulated by it to favour its extension, as adding to the chances of safe and respectable places for their relatives. The people at large, led to look on benefits received through public agencies as gratis benefits, have their hopes continually excited by the prospects of more. A spreading education, furthering the diffusion of pleasing errors rather than of stern truths, renders such hopes both stronger and more general. Worse still, such hopes are ministered to by candidates for public choice, to augment their chances of success; and leading statesmen, in pursuit of party ends, bid for popular favour by countenancing them. ...

A druggist's assistant who, after listening to the description of pains which he mistakes for those of colic, but which are really caused by inflammation of the caecum, prescribes a sharp purgative and kills the patient, is found guilty of manslaughter. He is not allowed to excuse himself on the ground that he did not intend harm but hoped for good. The plea that he simply made a mistake in his diagnosis is not entertained. He is told that he had no right to risk disastrous consequences by meddling in a matter concerning which his knowledge was so inadequate. The fact that he was ignorant how great was his ignorance is not accepted in bar of judgment. It is tacitly assumed that the experience common to all should have taught him that even the skilled, and much more the unskilled, make mistakes in the identification of disorders and in the appropriate treatment; and that having disregarded the warning derivable from common experience, he was answerable for the consequences.

We measure the responsibilities of legislators for mischiefs they may do, in a much more lenient fashion. In most cases, so far from thinking of them as deserving punishment for causing disasters by laws ignorantly enacted, we scarcely think of them as deserving reprobation. It is held that common experience should have taught the druggist's assistant, untrained as he is, not to interfere; but it is not held that common experience should have taught the legislator not to interfere till he has trained himself. Though multitudinous facts are before him in the recorded legislation of our own country and of other countries, which should impress on him the immense evils caused by wrong treatment, he is not condemned for disregarding these warnings against rash meddling. Contrariwise, it is thought meritorious in him when—perhaps lately from college, perhaps fresh from keeping a pack of hounds which made him popular in his county, perhaps emerging from a provincial town where he acquired a fortune, perhaps rising from the bar at which he has gained a name as an advocate—he enters Parliament; and forthwith, in quite a light-hearted way, begins to aid or hinder this or that means of operating on the body politic. In this case there is no occasion even to make for him the excuse that he does not know how little he knows; for the public at large agrees with him in thinking it needless that he should know

anything more than what the debates on the proposed measures tell him. And yet the mischiefs
wrought by uninstructed lawmaking, enormous
in their amount as compared with those caused
by uninstructed medical treatment, are conspicuous to all who do but glance over its history. ...

One might have expected that whether
they observed the implications of these domestic
failures, or whether they contemplated in every
newspaper the indications of a social life too
vast, too varied, too involved, to be even vaguely
pictured in thought, men would have entered
on the business of law-making with the greatest
hesitation. Yet in this more than anything else
do they show a confident readiness. Nowhere
is there so astounding a contrast between the
difficulty of the task and the unpreparedness of
those who undertake it. Unquestionably among
monstrous beliefs one of the most monstrous is
that while for a simple handicraft, such as shoe-
making, a long apprenticeship is needful, the sole
thing which needs no apprenticeship is making a
nation's laws! [9]

Now we will turn to Pius IX's successor, Leo XIII. In the early
years of his papacy, he made considerable gains in mending fences
with the various radical factions within the Church while at the same
time continuing the Church's battle against the forces of atheism and
nihilism as manifested in the growing socialist movement.

In 1891, he issued the great encyclical on capital and labor,
Rerum Novarum, which set out the Church's views of the rights and
duties of property owners and the relations between employer and
employee. According to the *Catholic Encyclopedia*, no other papal
pronouncement on the social question has had so many readers or
exercised such a wide influence.[10] When reading the following from
this encyclical, reflect upon the fact that very little has been said in

the intervening 125 years that improves upon this understanding of the evils of the contagion we call the Left.

The contention, then, that the civil government should at its option intrude into and exercise intimate control over the family and the household is a great and pernicious error. True, if a family finds itself in exceeding distress, utterly deprived of the counsel of friends, and without any prospect of extricating itself, it is right that extreme necessity be met by public aid, since each family is a part of the commonwealth. In like manner, if within the precincts of the household there occur grave disturbance of mutual rights, public authority should intervene to force each party to yield to the other its proper due; for this is not to deprive citizens of their rights, but justly and properly to safeguard and strengthen them. But the rulers of the commonwealth must go no further; here, nature bids them stop. Paternal authority can be neither abolished nor absorbed by the State; for it has the same source as human life itself. "The child belongs to the father," and is, as it were, the continuation of the father's personality; and speaking strictly, the child takes its place in civil society, not of its own right, but in its quality as member of the family in which it is born. And for the very reason that "the child belongs to the father" it is, as St. Thomas Aquinas says, "before it attains the use of free will, under the power and the charge of its parents." The socialists, therefore, in setting aside the parent and setting up a State supervision, act against natural justice, and destroy the structure of the home. And in addition to injustice, it is only too evident what an upset and disturbance there would be in all classes, and to how intoler-able and hateful a slavery citizens would be sub-jected. The door would be thrown open to envy, to mutual invective, and to discord; the sources of wealth themselves would run dry, for no one would have any interest in exerting his talents or his industry; and that ideal equality about which they entertain pleasant dreams would be in real-ity the leveling down of all to a like condition of misery and degradation. Hence, it is clear that the main tenet of socialism, community of goods, must be utterly rejected, since it only injures those whom it would seem meant to benefit, is directly contrary to the natural rights of mankind, and would introduce confusion and disorder into the commonweal. The first and most fundamental principle, therefore, if one would undertake to alleviate the condition of the masses, must be the inviolability of private property. ...

It must be first of all recognized that the condition of things inherent in human affairs must be borne with, for it is impossible to reduce civil society to one dead level. Socialists may in that intent do their utmost, but all striving against nature is in vain. There naturally exist among mankind manifold differences of the most important kind; people differ in capacity, skill, health, strength; and unequal fortune is a neces-sary result of unequal condition. Such unequality is far from being disadvantageous either to indi-viduals or to the community. Social and public life can only be maintained by means of various kinds of capacity for business and the playing of many parts; and each man, as a rule, chooses the part which suits his own peculiar domestic condi-tion. As regards bodily labor, even had man never

fallen from the state of innocence, he would not
have remained wholly idle; but that which would
then have been his free choice and his delight
became afterwards compulsory, and the painful
expiation for his disobedience. "Cursed be the
earth in thy work; in thy labor thou shalt eat of it
all the days of thy life." ...

The great mistake made in regard to the
matter now under consideration is to take up
with the notion that class is naturally hostile to
class, and that the wealthy and the working men
are intended by nature to live in mutual conflict.
So irrational and so false is this view that the
direct contrary is the truth. Just as the symmetry
of the human frame is the result of the suitable
arrangement of the different parts of the body, so
in a State is it ordained by nature that these two
classes should dwell in harmony and agreement,
so as to maintain the balance of the body politic.
Each needs the other: capital cannot do without
labor, nor labor without capital. Mutual agreement results in the beauty of good order, while
perpetual conflict necessarily produces confusion
and savage barbarity. Now, in preventing such
strife as this, and in uprooting it, the efficacy of
Christian institutions is marvelous and manifold.
First of all, there is no intermediary more powerful than religion (whereof the Church is the
interpreter and guardian) in drawing the rich and
the working class together, by reminding each of
its duties to the other, and especially of the obligations of justice.[11]

And lest anyone believe that there was nothing about which any
pope and Nietzsche could agree, we present the following from the

godless philosopher himself, taken from his 1878 book of aphorisms, *Human, All Too Human.*

> Socialism is the visionary younger brother of an almost decrepit despotism, whose heir it wants to be. Thus its efforts are reactionary in the deepest sense. For it desires a wealth of executive power, as only despotism had it; indeed, it outdoes everything in the past by striving for the downright destruction of the individual, which it sees as an unjustified luxury of nature, and which it intends to improve into an expedient *organ of the community.* Socialism crops up in the vicinity of all excessive displays of power because of its relation to it, like the typical old socialist Plato, at the court of the Sicilian tyrant; it desires (and in certain circumstances, furthers) the Caesarean power state of this century, because, as we said, it would like to be its heir. But even this inheritance would not suffice for its purposes; it needs the most submissive subjugation of all citizens to the absolute state, the like of which has never existed. And since it cannot even count any longer on the old religious piety towards the state, having rather always to work automatically to eliminate piety (because it works on the elimination of all existing *states),* it can only hope to exist here and there for short periods of time by means of the most extreme terrorism. Therefore, it secretly prepares for reigns of terror, and drives the word "justice" like a nail into the heads of the semieducated masses, to rob them completely of their reason (after this reason has already suffered a great deal from its semieducation), and to give them a good conscience for the evil game that they are supposed to play.

Socialism can serve as a rather brutal and forceful way to teach the danger of all accumulations of state power, and to that extent instill one with distrust of the state itself. When its rough voice chimes in with the battle cry "As *much state as possible,*" it will at first make the cry noisier than ever; but soon the opposite cry will be heard with strength the greater: "As *little state as possible.*"[12]

Now we will turn our attention to our old friend Georges Sorel. Aside from having created his theory of the power of the myth, he was a brilliant and insightful critic of the leftists who took control of the French government in the wake of the Dreyfus Affair. He called them "parliamentary socialists" and said this about them.

O Whole pages could be filled with the bare outlines of the contradictory, comical, and quack arguments which form the substance of the harangues of our great men; nothing embarrasses them, and they know how to combine, in pompous, impetuous, and nebulous speeches, the most absolute irreconcilability with the most supple opportunism.[13]

O Politicians have nothing to fear from the Utopias which present a deceptive mirage of the future to the people, and turn [in the words of Clemenceau] "men towards immediate realizations of terrestrial felicity, which anyone who looks at these matters scientifically knows can only be very partially realized, and even then only after long efforts on the part of several generations." The more readily the electors believe in the magical forces of the State, the more will they be disposed to vote for the candidate who promises marvels; in the electoral struggle each candidate tries to outbid the others; in order that the Socialist candidates may put the Radicals to rout, the electors must be credulous enough to believe every promise of future bliss; our

Socialist politicians take very good care therefore, not to combat these comfortable Utopias in any very effective way.[14]

O Enfeebled classes habitually put their trust in people who promise them the protection of the State, without ever trying to understand how this protection could possibly harmonize their discordant interests; they readily enter into every coalition formed for the purpose of forcing concessions from the Government; they greatly admire charlatans who speak with a glib tongue ... The political general strike [as opposed to the real "general strike"] presupposes that very diverse social groups shall possess the same faith in the magical force of the State; this faith is never lacking in social groups which are on the downgrade, and its existence enables windbags to represent themselves as able to do everything. The political general strike would be greatly helped by the stupidity of philanthropists, and this stupidity is always a result of the degeneration of the rich classes. Its chances of success would be enhanced by the fact that it would have to deal with cowardly and discouraged capitalists.[15]

O Wise Socialists desire two things: (1) to take possession of this [great State] machine so that they may improve its works, and make them run to further their friends' interests as much as possible, and (2) to assure the stability of the Government which will be very advantageous for all business men ... Socialist financiers ... understand instinctively that the preservation of a highly centralized, very authoritative and very democratic State puts immense resources at their disposal, and protects them from proletarian revolution. The transformations which their friends, the Parliamentary Socialists, may carry out will always be of a very limited scope, and it will always be possible, thanks to the State, to correct any imprudences they may commit. Therefore, the authors of all enquiries into modern socialism are forced to acknowledge that the latter implies the division of society

into two groups: the first of these is a select body, organized as a political party, which has adopted the mission of
thinking for the thoughtless masses, and which imagines
that, because it allows the latter to enjoy the results of its
superior enlightenment, it has done something admirable.
The second is ... whole body of the producers. The select
body of politicians has no other profession than that of
using its wits, and they find that it is strictly in accordance
with the principles of immanent justice (of which they are
sole owners) that the proletariat should work to feed them
and furnish them with the means for an existence that only
distantly resembles an ascetic's.[16]

O The masses believe that they are suffering from the iniqui-
tous consequences of a past that was full of violence, ignorance, and wickedness; they are confident that the genius
of their leaders will render them less unhappy; they believe
that democracy, if it were only free, would replace a malev-
olent hierarchy by a benevolent hierarchy. The leaders who
foster this sweet illusion in their men, see the situation
from quite another point of view; the present social organization revolts them just in so far as it creates obstacles
to their ambition; they are less shocked by the existence
of the classes than by their own inability to attain to the
positions already acquired by older men; when they have
penetrated far enough into the sanctuaries of the State, into
drawing-rooms and places of amusement, they cease, as a
rule, to be revolutionary and speak learnedly of "evolution." Politicians ... argue about social conflicts in exactly
the same manner as diplomats argue about international
affairs; all the actual fighting apparatus interests them very
little; they see in the combatants nothing but instruments.
The proletariat is their army, which they love in the same
way that a colonial administrator loves the troops which
enable him to bring large numbers of negroes under his
authority; they apply themselves to the task of training the
proletariat, because they are in a hurry to win quickly the

great battle which will deliver the State into their hands; they keep up the ardour of their men, as the ardour of troops of mercenaries has always been kept up, by promises of pillage, by appeals to hatred, and also by the small favours which their occupancy of a few political places enables them to distribute already. But the proletariat for them is food for cannon, and nothing else, as Marx said in 1873. The reinforcement of power of the State is at the basis of all their conceptions; in the organizations which they at present control, the politicians are already preparing the framework of a strong, centralized and disciplined authority, which will not be hampered by the criticism of an opposition, which will be able to enforce silence, and that will give currency to its lies.[17]

O   Religions constitute a very troublesome problem for the intellectualists [read: Parliamentary Socialists], for they can neither regard them as being without historical importance nor can they explain them.[18]

O   To most people the class war is the principle of Socialist tactics. That means that the Socialist party founds its electoral successes on the clashing of interests which exist in an acute state between certain groups, and that, if need be, it would undertake to make this hostility still more acute; their candidates ask the poorest and most numerous class to look upon themselves as forming a corporation, and they offer to become the advocates of this corporation; they promise to use their influence as representatives to improve the lot of the disinherited ... Socialism makes its appeal to the discontented without troubling about the place they occupy in the world of production; in a society as complex as ours, and as subject to economic upheavals, there is an enormous number of discontented people in all classes—that is why Socialists are often found in places where one would least expect to meet them. Parliamentary Socialism speaks as many languages as it has types of clients. It makes its appeal to workmen, to small employers of labour, to peasants; and in spite of Engels, it aims at reaching the farmers; it is at times patriotic; at other times it declares against the Army. It is stopped by no contradiction, experience having shown that it is possible, in the course of an electoral campaign, to group together forces, which, according to Marxian conceptions, should normally be antagonistic ... In the end the term 'proletariat' became synonymous with oppressed; and there are oppressed in all classes.[19]

O   He [Jaurès] saw that this upper middle class was terribly ignorant, gapingly stupid, politically absolutely impotent; he recognized that with people who understand nothing of the principles of capitalist economics it is easy to contrive a policy of compromise on the basis of an extremely broad Socialism; he calculated the proportions in which it is necessary to mix together flattery of the superior intelligence of the imbeciles whose seduction was aimed at, appeals to the disinterested sentiments of speculators who pride themselves on having invented the ideal, and threats of revolution in order to obtain the leadership of people void of ideas.[20]

We will now turn our attention to Bertrand de Jouvenel's powerful and groundbreaking book *The Ethics of Redistribution*, in which he addresses the destructive consequences of governmental efforts at wealth redistribution. This is an especially important topic at this time because the forced redistribution of wealth by the federal government has, during the past century, become the Left's favored weapon in its assault on the "inviolability of private property," being easier and less violent than outright confiscation. As we shall see in a later chapter, this effort began in earnest in the United States with the introduction of a graduated income tax.

De Jouvenel begins his critique by noting the following arguments used by the Left to justify an aggressive redistribution of wealth. To wit: "the government should be centrally involved in the relief of poverty"; "economic inequality is itself unjust or evil";[21] "the richer would feel their loss less than the poorer would appreciate their gain"; and government bureaucrats know "how to achieve the maximum sum of individual satisfactions capable of being drawn from a given flow of production, which must always be assumed to be unaffected."[22] Of course, as he asserts, all these assertions are not only bogus but damaging to all involved. He explains it this way:

> The State sets up as trustee for the lower-income group and doles out services and benefits. In order to avoid the creation of a "protected class," a discrimination fatal to political equality, the tendency has been to extend the benefits and services upward to all members of society, to cheapen food and rents for the rich as well as the poor, to assist the well-to-do in illness equally with the needy. ...
>
> The more one considers the matter, the clearer it becomes that redistribution is in effect far less a redistribution of free income from the richer to the poorer, as imagined, than a redistribution of power from the individual to the State.
>
> Insofar as the State amputates higher incomes, it must assume their savings and investment functions, and we come to the centralization of investment. Insofar, as the amputated higher incomes fail to sustain certain social activities, the state must step in, subsidize these activities, and preside over them.
>
> This results in a transfer of power from individuals to officials, who tend to constitute a new ruling class ... This leads the observer to wonder how far the demand for equality is directed against inequality itself and is thus a fundamental demand, and how far it is directed against a certain set of "unequals" and is thus an unconscious move in a change of elites.[23]

There is much more to de Jouvenel's book than that. The British philosopher John Gray did a wonderful job of compressing some of its other most important points in an introduction to the Liberty Press edition, which we will turn to now:

— A subsistence minimum cannot be derived solely, or even primarily, from taxation of the rich. Such resources must be extracted from the middle classes, who are also the beneficiaries of income-transfer schemes ... [de Jouvenel] further notes that a policy of redistribution is bound to discriminate against minorities, since it will inevitably favor the preferences and interests of the majority—a fact remarked upon also by Hayek. ...

— The regime of high taxation inseparable from the redistributionist state has the further undesirable consequences of diminishing the sphere of free services in which people engage in convivial relations without the expectation of payment—and thereby corroding the culture of civility that sustains liberal civilization.

— The modern welfare state is not defensible by reference to any coherent set of principles or purposes. It has not significantly alleviated poverty but has instead substantially institutionalized it. This is the upshot of path breaking studies such as Charles Murray's *Losing Ground*. A generation of welfare policy has inflicted on its clients such disincentives and moral hazards as to leave their last state worse than their first ... If any social group benefits, it is likely to be the middle class majority rather than the poor.

— The institution of the family is disprivileged under any redistributionist regime: "To such views, families are disturbing; for within a family occur transfers that upset the favored distribution.[24]

Now, in a sane world, these many observations would militate against the horrors they describe. Yet these warnings and thousands of other similar ones have been and continue to be powerless against the Left's beguiling promise of a world of milk and honey. In fact, when confronted with the extraordinary success that the Left has enjoyed throughout the world during the past two hundred years, one can begin to truly appreciate Nietzsche's claim that Rousseau was "the greatest revolutionizing force of the modern era," and Carlyle's observation that he "set the world on fire."

All of which begs the question, "to what end is this leading?"

We will explore this question in some depth later. In the meantime, it is instructive to look at what others have said on the subject, beginning with Tocqueville, who was not addressing any particular threat present at the time but simply commenting on the nature of man and government, about which he had an uncanny understanding. To wit:

> I seek to trace the novel features under which despotism may appear in the world. The first thing that strikes the observation is an innumerable multitude of men, all equal and all alike incessantly endeavoring to procure the petty and paltry pleasures with which they glut their lives. Each of them, living apart, is as a stranger to the fate of all the rest; his children and his private friends constitute to him the whole of mankind. As for the rest of his fellow citizens, he is close to them, but he does not see them; he touches them, but he does not feel them; he exits only in himself and for himself alone; and if his kindred still remain to him, he may be said at any rate to have lost his country.
>
> Above this race of men stands an immense and tutelary power, which takes upon itself alone to secure their gratifications and to watch over their fate. That power is absolute, minute, regular, provident, and mild. It would be like the authority of a parent if, like that authority, its object was to prepare men for manhood; but it

seeks, on the contrary, to keep them in perpetual childhood; it is well content that the people should rejoice, provided that they think of
nothing but rejoicing. For their happiness such a
government willingly labors, but it chooses to be
the sole agent and the only arbiter of their necessities, facilitates their pleasures, manages their
principal concerns, directs their industry, regulates the descent of property, and subdivides their
inheritances; what remains, but to spare them all
the care of thinking and all the trouble of living?
Thus it every day renders the exercise of the free
agency of man less useful and less frequent; it cir-
cumscribes the will within a narrower range and
gradually robs a man of all the uses of himself.
The principle of equality has prepared men for
these things; it has predisposed them to endure
them and often to look on them as benefits.[25]

Then, of course, Aldous Huxley and George Orwell each took
a stab at it: Huxley in 1932 with his novel *Brave New World*, and
Orwell in 1949 with *Nineteen Eighty-Four*. Unlike Tocqueville, who
was calmly contemplating the long-term future of this new creature
called the United States, Huxley and Orwell were dealing with very
specific threats to the social order. The problem is that they did not
agree with each other. Orwell's vision of the future was of a brutal,
totalitarian nightmare.

There will be no loyalty, except loyalty
towards the Party. There will be no love, except
the love of Big Brother. There will be no laughter, except the laugh of triumph over a defeated
enemy. There will be no art, no literature, no science. ... There will be no curiosity, no enjoyment
of the process of life. All competing pleasures will
be destroyed. But always ... always there will be

the intoxication of power, constantly increasing and constantly growing subtler. Always, at every moment, there will be the thrill of victory, the sensation of trampling on an enemy who is helpless. If you want a picture of the future, imagine a boot stamping on a human face—forever.[26]

Huxley's prophecy involved a "benevolent" dictatorship of ten "World Controllers" who would manage all human activity including the creation and raising of the children in "hatcheries" and "conditioning centers." He spoke of the differences between their respective outlooks in a letter he wrote to Orwell shortly after reading *Nineteen Eighty-Four*. To wit:

> Whether in actual fact the policy of the boot-on-the-face can go on indefinitely seems doubtful. My own belief is that the ruling oligarchy will find less arduous and wasteful ways of governing and of satisfying its lust for power, and these ways will resemble those which I described in *Brave New World*. ... Within the next generation I believe that the world's rulers will discover that infant conditioning and narco-hypnosis are more efficient, as instruments of government, than clubs and prisons, and that the lust for power can be just as completely satisfied by suggesting people into loving their servitude as by flogging and kicking them into obedience. In other words, I feel that the nightmare of Nineteen Eighty-Four is destined to modulate into the nightmare of a world having more resemblance to that which I imagined in *Brave New World*. The change will be brought about as a result of a felt need for increased efficiency.[27]

As Huxley said, the boot in the face has not turned out to be a practical, long-term solution to the problem of keeping order, especially since a combination of technological spying, multiple layers of taxes, thousands of laws and regulations, and vast dependency on the welfare state have provided government with many more effective means to exercise control.

Hanna Arendt has offered a somewhat different and interesting take on the use of terror. To wit:

> A fundamental difference between modern dictatorships and all other tyrannies of the past is that terror is no longer used as a means to exterminate and frighten opponents, but as an instrument to rule masses of people who are perfectly obedient. Terror as we know it today strikes without any preliminary provocation, its victims are innocent even from the point of view of the persecutor.[28]

What is undeniable is that there is no apparent limit to the acquisitiveness of an all-powerful government, which has to protect its turf constantly from virtually any form of organization outside the state. This protection entails, a la Orwell, the destruction, nullification, or the annexation of all the institutions that traditionally compete with the government in providing both physical and social comfort to the people. These include the family, religion, outside charities, and independent news and entertainment providers. Another key requirement is a constant drumbeat of trouble, turmoil, and pain, which keeps the masses restless, fearful, and in need of assurances from the government that all will be well.

Orwell drives this point home by portraying Oceania as uninterested in creating a happy and contented community but one that perpetuates despondency and suffering. In 1948, despairing of the failure of England's postwar socialist government to bring order, he said this: "This is an age of an unresolved dilemma, of the struggle which never slows down and never leads to a decision. It is as though the world were suffering from a disease which is simultaneously acute, chronic, and not fatal ... a state of almost continuous crises, like one of those radio serials in which the hero falls over a precipice at the end of each installment."[29] A few years later, Hanna Arendt put it this way: "They can remain in power only so long as they keep moving and set everything around them in motion ... instability is indeed a functional requisite of total domination."[30]

The crux of the matter then is that while the Left promises a utopia, it draws its energy from turmoil, fear, and war. The fly in the ointment is that governments such as these are highly inefficient. Capital becomes a political tool rather than a natural and crucial element in the functioning of a modern economy. It is mismanaged, stolen, and counterfeited. Relative to this latter, we should note that just as surely as the miracle of compound interest promises financial gain, the miracle of fiat currency promises bankruptcy.

At which time, as is evident today in nations such as Venezuela and, eventually, cities like Chicago, the government will eventually find that it is unable to meet its many responsibilities. In short, it loses its status as a source of assurance. People are forced to depend on their own private resources for food and, most especially, security. Those who were most dependent on the government will suffer the most. Civil unrest will ensue in the least stable regions. Power will move from the central government to a variety of local communities and associations that share a common interest based on such factors as regional pride, religious affiliation, race, wealth, poverty, and security. Out of these crises, new governments and new leaders will emerge.

Let's let the poets in on the fun.

Excerpt from "Choruses from the Rock":

> The Eagle soars in the summit of Heaven,
> The Hunter with his dogs pursues his circuit.
> O perpetual revolution of configured stars,
> O perpetual recurrence of determined seasons,
> O world of spring and autumn, birth and dying!
> The endless cycle of idea and action,

Endless invention, endless experiment,
Brings knowledge of motion, but not of stillness;
Knowledge of speech, but not of silence;
Knowledge of words, and ignorance of the Word.
All our knowledge brings us nearer to our ignorance,
All our ignorance brings us nearer to death,
But nearness to death no nearer to GOD.
Where is the Life we have lost in living?
Where is the wisdom we have lost in knowledge?
Where is the knowledge we have lost in information?
The cycles of Heaven in twenty centuries
Bring us farther from *GOD* and nearer to the *Dust*.
T. S. Eliot, 1934

Chapter 12

On Decay

In the second century of the Christian Aera, the empire of Rome comprehended the fairest part of the earth, and the most civilized portion of mankind. The frontiers of that extensive monarchy were guarded by ancient renown and disciplined valor. The gentle but powerful influence of laws and manners had gradually cemented the union of the provinces. Their peaceful inhabitants enjoyed and abused the advantages of wealth and luxury. The image of a free constitution was preserved with decent reverence: the Roman senate appeared to possess the sovereign authority, and devolved on the emperors all the executive powers of government. During a happy period of more than fourscore years, the public administration was conducted by the virtue and abilities of Nerva, Trajan, Hadrian, and the two Antonines. It is the design of this, and of the two succeeding chapters, to describe the prosperous condition of their empire; and after wards, from the death of Marcus Antoninus, to deduce the most important circumstances of its decline and fall; a revolution which will ever be remembered, and is still felt by the nations of the earth. (Edward

Gibbon, *The History of the Decline and Fall of the Roman Empire*, 1776)

Many brilliant books, articles, and historical narratives have explored the decline and fall of empires, nations, and civilizations. One of the most moving accounts can be found in the descriptions by both Appian and Polybius of the great Roman General Scipio the Younger standing on a hill watching while his army destroys Carthage in 146 BC, slaughtering its defenders, enslaving its citizens, and burning its buildings. Appian describes the scene as follows in *Punica*.

> Scipio, beholding this city, which had flourished 700 years from its foundation and had ruled over so many lands, islands, and seas, as rich with arms and fleets, elephants and money as the mightiest empires, but far surpassing them in hardihood and high spirit (since when stripped of all its ships and arms, it had sustained famine and a mighty war for three years), now come to its end in total destruction—Scipio, beholding this spectacle, is said to have shed tears and publicly lamented the fortune of the enemy.
>
> After meditating by himself a long time and reflecting on the inevitable fall of cities, nations, and empires, as well as of individuals, upon the fate of Troy, that once proud city, upon that of the Assyrian, the Median, and afterwards of the great Persian empire, and most recently of all, of the splendid empire of Macedon, either voluntarily or otherwise the words of the poet [Homer] escaped his lips:
>
> The day shall come in which our sacred Troy And Priam, and the people over whom Spear-bearing Priam rules, shall perish all.

Being asked by Polybius in familiar conversation (for Polybius had been his tutor) what he meant by using these words, Polybius says that he did not hesitate frankly to name his own country, for whose fate he feared when he considered the mutability of human affairs. And Polybius wrote this down just as he heard it.[1]

And here is Polybius's own account in his famous *Histories*.

But all things are subject to decay and change. This is a truth so evident, and so demonstrated by the perpetual and the necessary course of nature, that it needs no other proof. ... For when a state, having passed with safety through many and great dangers, arrives at the highest degree of power, and possesses an entire and undisputed sovereignty, it is manifest that the long continuance of prosperity must give birth to costly and luxurious manners, and that the minds of men will be heated with ambitious contests, and become too eager and aspiring in the pursuit of dignities.

And as those evils are continually increased, the desire of power and rule, and the imagined ignominy of remaining in a subject state, will first begin to work the ruin of the republic; arrogance and luxury will afterwards advance it; and in the end the change will be completed by the people; when the avarice of some is found to injure and oppress them, and the ambition of others swells their vanity, and poisons them with flattering hopes.

For then, being inflamed with rage, and following only the dictates of their passions, they no longer will submit to any control, or be contented with an equal share of the administration, in conjunction with their rules; but will draw to themselves the entire sovereignty and supreme direction of all affairs. When this is done, the government will assume indeed the fairest of all names, that of a free and popular state; but will in truth be the greatest of all evils, the government of the multitude.[2]

Polybius was, of course, prescient. When Carthage fell, Rome became an unrivaled world power; and thirteen years later, it began its long period of military, economic, and spiritual decline, kicked off by Tiberius Gracchus's parliamentary effort to force rich Roman landowners to divide their properties with the landless Romans. According to Plutarch, Gracchus's plea went as follows:

The wild beasts that roam over Italy, have every one of them a cave or lair to lurk in; but the men who fight and die for Italy enjoy the common air and light, indeed, but nothing else; houseless and homeless they wander about with their wives and children. And it is with lying lips that their imperators exhort the soldiers in their battles to defend sepulchers and shrines from the enemy; for not a man of them has an hereditary altar, not one of all these many Romans an ancestral tomb, but they fight and die to support others in wealth and luxury, and though they are styled masters of the world, they have not a single clod of earth that is their own.[3]

Tiberius Gracchus was assassinated by wealthy Roman senators. His brother Caius took up the cause and eventually led a sanguinary revolt on behalf of the Roman poor during which he either fell on his sword when he knew he was about to be killed or was murdered, depending on which historian one believes. As we mentioned in an earlier chapter, the fiery French revolutionary leader, François-Noël Babeuf, honored the Gracchi almost one thousand years later by adopting the *nom de guerre* Gracchus Babeuf.

Unlike Carthage, the Eternal City didn't fall on a specific date. Its trip across the rivers Styx and Acheron took several centuries. But August 24, 410, holds a predominant place in this historic journey. On that day, the Visigoth king Alaric breached the city's walls and sacked it. It was the first time that this had happened in eight hundred years. The Western Empire's weird little emperor at the time, Flavius Honorius, was hiding in Ravenna when this occurred. His reaction to hearing of Rome's fall is illustrative of the extent to which decay had engulfed the once-proud empire by that time. The historian Procopius of Caesarea gives the following account:

> At that time they say that the Emperor Honorius in Ravenna received the message from one of the eunuchs, evidently a keeper of the poultry, that Rome had perished. And he cried out and said, "And yet it has just eaten from my hands!" For he had a very large cock, Roma by name; and the eunuch comprehending his words said that it was the city of Rome which had perished at the hands of Alaric, and the emperor with a sigh of relief answered quickly, "But I, my good fellow, thought that my fowl Roma had perished."[4]

Edward Gibbon provided a remarkably detailed account of the process of this decay in his justly famous, seven-volume tome on the history of the fall of Rome. Space does not allow us to do justice to his many perceptive insights, but the following provides interesting support to Polybius's observations.

> A long period of calamity or decay must have checked the industry, and diminished the wealth, of the people; and their profuse lux-

ury must have been the result of that indolent despair, which enjoys the present hour, and declines the thoughts of futurity. The uncertain condition of their property discouraged the subjects of Theodosius from engaging in those useful and laborious undertakings which require an immediate expense, and promise a slow and distant advantage. The frequent examples of ruin and desolation tempted them not to spare the remains of a patrimony, which might, every hour, become the prey of the rapacious Goth. And the mad prodigality which prevails in the confusion of a shipwreck, or a siege, may serve to explain the progress of luxury amidst the misfortunes and terrors of a sinking nation.[5]

It should be noted that Gibbon began his history with the death in the year AD 180 of one of Rome's finest emperors, the great stoic philosopher Marcus Aurelius, and the ascent to the throne of one of its most licentious, demented, and insane emperors, Marcus's son Commodus. And with all due respect to Gibbon, by this time the rot had already penetrated so deeply into Roman society that there was no hope of turning back. Indeed, Aurelius's temperate and morally sound rule, along with that of his four predecessors, was so out of sync with the times that they are described by historians today as the "five good emperors," in juxtaposition to the bad ones that appeared not just after, but also before.

Numerous other great historians have offered accounts of Rome's earlier years. Livy's original *History of Rome* covers the period from the founding of the city in the eighth century BC to a decade after the death of Caesar in 44 BC, although a substantial portion of his work has been lost. It is notable that a decline in morality of the Roman people is one of the key factors in Livy's understanding of the decay that was already in evidence at the time of his death in AD 17. Indeed, he emphasizes this in the preface to his work, thusly.

I invite the reader's attention to the much more serious consideration of the kind of lives our ancestors lived, of who were the men and what the means, both in politics and war, by which Rome's power was first acquired and subsequently expanded; I would then have him trace the process of our moral decline, to watch, first, the sinking of the foundations of morality as the old teaching was allowed to lapse, then the rapidly increasingly disintegration, then the final collapse of the whole edifice, and the dark dawning of our modern day when we can neither endure our vices nor face the remedies needed to cure them.[6]

Suetonius, Tacitus, and several others took up the story from there and provided excellent insights into the moral and economic decline of which Livy had spoken. Besides noting the recurring debasement of the currency, they provide grotesque portraits of some of the most demented early Caesars, such as Caligula and Nero, who are often accused of having caused the fall of Rome rather than being symptoms of the true reasons. Considering this charge, one is reminded of Kipling's observation that while the beehive is destroyed by the invasion of the wax moth, the fault lies not with the wax moth, but with the bees themselves. He put it this way: "Wax moths only succeed when weak bees let them in ... that never happen till the stock's weakened."[7]

Of course, anyone attempting to offer a comprehensive explanation for the fall civilizations, empires, nations, or states must integrate a vast array of complex social, economic, military, and governmental matters. But when viewing the many attempts that have been made over the years to accomplish this task, it becomes apparent that all seem to arrive at one common conclusion, that being that decay sets in when the population loses its interest in and love for the religious beliefs, traditions, mores, and moral values that had first joined them together in community. The groundbreaking French psychologist Gustave Le Bon recognized this truth in his classic 1895 book *The Crowd*.

> History tells us that from the moment when the moral forces on which a civilization rested have lost their strength, its final dissolution is brought about by those unconscious and brutal crowds known, justifiably enough, as barbarians. Civilizations as yet have only been created and directed by a small intellectual aristocracy, never by crowds. Crowds are only powerful for destruction. Their rule is always tantamount to a barbarian phase. A civilization involves fixed rules, discipline, a passing from the instinctive to the rational state, forethought for the future, an elevated degree of culture—all of them conditions that crowds, left to themselves, have invariably shown themselves incapable of realizing. In consequence of the purely destructive nature of their power, crowds act like those microbes which hasten the dissolution of enfeebled or dead bodies. When the structure of a civilization is rotten, it is always the masses that bring about its downfall. It is at such a juncture that their chief mission is plainly visible, and that for a while the philosophy of numbers seems the only philosophy of history.[8]

Lord Patrick Devlin, a Fellow of the British Academy, put it this way in his classic 1965 book *The Enforcement of Morals*.

> Without shared ideas on politics, moral, and ethics no society can exist ... If men and women try to create a society in which there is no fundamental agreement about good and evil they will fail; if, having based it on common

agreement, the agreement goes, the society will disintegrate. For society is not something that is kept together physically; it is held by the invisible bonds of common thought. If the bonds were too far relaxed the members would drift apart. A common morality is part of the bondage. The bondage is part of the price of society; and mankind, which needs society, must pay its price.[9]

More recently, in the aforementioned book, *Holding Up a Mirror, How Civilizations Decline*, Glyn-Jones discusses and describes the process by which a society turns away from its ideological beliefs to what she describes as a "sensate" or materialistic formulation, which is the predecessor to outright decay. The dust jacket of her books describes this transformation as follows:

> History shows that Empires rise as they turn away from religion to science, but then decline because without an underpinning of religious belief, the morality that holds society together inevitably falls away. In the West today the triumph of materialist philosophies has transformed living standards, but declining moral standards are destroying what has been achieved, as crime escalates and personal relationships (especially between the sexes) turn sour, encompassing the inevitable spread of sexually transmitted diseases and the breakdown of families. In a secular society the arts turn increasingly to sensationalism, until violence and explicit sex coalesce in the amalgam of pornography. Despair and disgust ride rampant, and in a final gesture of evolutionary futility, communities cease even to reproduce themselves.[10]

In the book, she describes such a society as follows:

> In a society in which materialism is the
> only reality recognized, the purpose of life is
> fulfillment in the here and now, the pursuit of
> happiness, which is increasingly interpreted in
> material terms ... Europe and America since the
> eighteenth century clearly exemplify this trend,
> as did Greece of the third and subsequent cen-
> turies BC. Roman writers themselves identified
> the second century BC as the period when values
> of their own society began to shift towards what
> we would now call consumerism. The pursuit of
> happiness is worthless unless each individual can
> pursue his own definition of what for him consti-
> tutes happiness; thus individualism is a marked
> characteristic of hedonistic societies. In the early
> phases of the evolution from a society based on
> otherworldly tenets, a vestigial absolute moral
> order may remain, but absolutes give way to rel-
> atives. Law is brought into conformity with the
> demand for maximum choice in the pursuit of
> personal fulfillment, subject only to constraints
> where conduct might lead to unhappiness for
> others.[11]

Glyn-Jones relied heavily on the work of Pitirim Sorokin, who emigrated from Russia to the United States in 1922, taught at the University of Minnesota until 1930 when Harvard President Lawrence Lowell asked him to come to Harvard to Chair the University's First Department of Sociology. In fact, Glyn-Jones says in the preface that she wrote her book in the hope of bringing his ideas to a new generation. In his greatest work, *Social and Cultural Dynamics*, Sorokin described the origin of a sensate society as follows.

A regime professing Sensate ideals will approve anything that increases the sum total of Sensate enjoyment; and that leads to man's control over nature and over other men, as the means of satisfying ever-expanding needs. Of a special importance in such a state of society is the search for material objects which under the circumstances are particularly efficient in bringing satisfaction. As one of the most efficient means has always been *material wealth*, in a Sensate society it is the *alpha* and *omega* of comfort, of the satisfaction of all desires, of power, prestige, fame, happiness. With it everything can be bought, everything can be sold, and everything can be gratified. Therefore, it is quite comprehensible that the striving for wealth is inevitably one of the main activities of such a culture, that wealth is the standard by which almost all other values are judged, that it is, in fact, the supreme value of values. *Pecuniary value thus becomes the measuring stick* of scientific, artistic, moral, and other values. [emphasis in original] [12]

Finally, we would be remiss not to cite the views on this subject of Orestes Brownson, the remarkable nineteenth-century Catholic social commentator and essayist.

A nation of atheists were a solecism in history. A few atheists may, perhaps, live in society, and even serve it for a time, where the mass of the people are believers and worshippers, but an entire nation of real atheists was never yet founded, and never could subsist any longer than it would take to dissipate the moral wealth acquired while it was as yet a religious nation. It was well said by the Abbé de La Mennais, before his unhappy fall:

> "Religion is always found by the cradle of nations, philosophy only at their tombs"—meaning, as he did, philosophy in the sense of unbelief and irreligion; not philosophy in the sense of the rational exercise of the faculties of the human mind on divine and human things, aided by the light of revelation. The ancient lawgivers always sought for their laws not only a moral but a religious sanction, and where the voice of God does not, in some form, speak to men's consciences, and bid them obey the higher power, government can subsist only as a craft or as a sheer force, which nobody is bound to respect or obey.[13]

Now, when one considers the totality of this commentary on the fall of civilizations, one fact becomes apparent; that being, as we stated earlier, that the ongoing war between the Right and Left is not simply a contest between alternative governing systems, but a life-or-death battle to determine fate not only of the United States but of Western Civilization itself.

This is, of course, not a novel idea on our part. In fact, Washington stated the case in his First Inaugural Address when he noted "that the foundation of our national policy will be laid in the pure and immutable principles of private morality" and brought it up again in his Farewell Address to the American people as president. To wit:

> Of all the dispositions and habits which lead to political prosperity, religion and morality are indispensable supports. In vain would that man claim the tribute of patriotism, who should labor to subvert these great pillars of human happiness, these firmest props of the duties of men and citizens. The mere politician, equally with the pious man, ought to respect and to cherish them. A volume could not trace all their connec-

tions with private and public felicity. Let it simply be asked: Where is the security for property, for reputation, for life, if the sense of religious obligation desert the oaths which are the instruments of investigation in courts of justice? And let us with caution indulge the supposition that morality can be maintained without religion. Whatever may be conceded to the influence of refined education on minds of peculiar structure, reason and experience both forbid us to expect that national morality can prevail in exclusion of religious principle.[14]

With that in mind and with apologies to T. S. Eliot, who maintained that it is not only "silly, but damnable" to offer utilitarian rather than faith-based arguments on behalf of Christianity,[15] we would argue that anyone who has a stake in the future of the United States as a free nation and is not religious, who is lukewarm to religiosity, or who hates and fears formal, organized religion should nevertheless enthusiastically applaud and support those who keep the flame of Christianity and Judaism alive in the United States. For, like it or not, these people represent the front line of defense against the spread of radical utopian ideologies, whether they be communism, socialism, fascism, or the excesses of American liberalism. For these ideologies spell death to justice and freedom.

Let's let the poets in on the fun.

> Stay with Me, God
> Stay with me, God. The night is dark,
> The night is cold: my little spark
> Of courage dies. The night is long;
> Be with me, God, and make me strong.
> I love a game; I love a fight.
> I hate the dark; I love the light.
> I love my child; I love my wife.
> I am no coward. I love Life,

Life with its change of mood and shade.
I want to live. I'm not afraid,
But me and mine are hard to part;
Oh, unknown God, lift up my heart.
You stilled the waters at Dunkirk
And saved Your Servants. All Your work
Is wonderful, dear God. You strode
Before us down that dreadful road.
We were alone, and hope had fled;
We loved our country and our dead,
And could not shame them; so we stayed
The course, and were not much afraid.
Dear God that nightmare road! And then
That sea! We got there-we were men.
My eyes were blind, my feet were torn,
My soul sang like a bird at dawn!
I knew that death is but a door.
I knew what we were fighting for:
Peace for the kids, our brothers freed,
A kinder world, a cleaner breed.
I'm but the son my mother bore,
A simple man, and nothing more.
But-God of strength and gentleness,
Be pleased to make me nothing less.
Help me, O God, when Death is near
To mock the haggard face of fear,
That when I fall-if fall I must—
My soul may triumph in the Dust.
Anonymous, 1942

Chapter 13

On Progress

*No single idea has been more important than,
perhaps more important as, the idea of progress in
Western Civilization for nearly three thousand years.
Other ideas will come to mind, properly: liberty,
justice, equality, community, and so forth. I do not
derogate from one of them. But this must be stressed:
throughout most of Western history, the substratum
of even these ideas has been a philosophy of history
that lends past, present, and future to their importance. Nothing gives greater importance or credibil-
ity to a moral or political value than belief that it
is more than something cherished or be cherished;
that it is an essential element of historical movement
from past through present to the future. Such a value
can then be transposed from the merely desirable to
the historically necessary. Simply stated, the idea of
progress holds that mankind has advanced in the
past—from some aboriginal condition of primitive-
ness, barbarism, or even nullity—is now advancing,
and will continue to advance through the foresee-
able future.* (Robert Nisbet, *History of the Idea of
Progress*, 1980)

W e will begin the discussion of "progress" by noting that the prevailing belief among the citizens of mankind's earliest civilizations was that the social conditions in which they lived had always been as they were then and would always be so. One consequence of this was that men spent little time thinking about or trying to improve upon the future. The Egyptologist Henri Frankfort describes this tendency in ancient Egypt some five thousand years ago as follows in *The Birth of Civilization in the Near East*:

> Egyptians had very little sense of history or of past and future. For they conceived their world as essentially static and unchanging. It had gone forth complete in the hands of the Creator. Historical incidents were, consequently, no more than superficial disturbances of the established order, or recurring events of never-changing significance. The past and the future—far from being a matter of concern—were wholly implicit in the present.[1]

Heraclitus challenged this view of a static world some 2,500 years later when he began his famous discussion of the constancy of "change." "All things come into being through opposition, and all are in flux like a river," he said. He then added this: "Upon those who step into the same rivers flow other and yet other waters."[2]

These ideas of Heraclitus survived in popular form over the centuries in two phrases: "everything is in flux, nothing is at rest" and "no man ever steps in the same river twice." These seem today to be rather commonplace observations, yet according to Karl Popper, the "greatness" of the discovery of universal flux "cannot be overrated." Citing Wilhelm Nestle's work on the pre-Socratic philosophers, Popper notes that this notion "has been described as a terrifying one, and its effect has been compared with that of an earthquake in which everything seems to sway."[3]

Why was it so terrifying? Because Heraclitus was challenging the widespread and comforting belief that the future would not be different from the past at a highly tumultuous period of social revolution, during which the ancient Greek tribal aristocracies were yielding to the demands of the demos. Moreover, he was saying that the people had no control over the nature of the "change" that was occurring, that it was being regulated by "a cosmic order" or, as Popper put it, "an inexorable and immutable law of destiny."[4]

Aristotle took some of the mystery out of this notion of inevitable change when he soothingly discussed the development of the polis from its origin in the family to groups of families, to the appearance of villages, and finally to federations of states. He also raised the idea of historical cyclicality when he toyed with the notion that time itself might be cyclical rather than linear, which prompted him to make the following intriguing comment in *Problems*:

> If then human life is a circle, and a circle has neither beginning nor end, we should not be prior to those who lived in the time of Troy nor they prior to us by being nearer to the beginning.[5]

Polybius helped this along with his analysis of the rise and fall of civilizations. However, as Nisbet notes in *History of the Idea of Progress*, neither man made an effort to link the evolution of societies and the rise and fall of nations with the idea that humans were progressing toward some identifiable end.[6] The Greek poets and playwrights, for example, sang repeatedly of their dependence on the winds and of the helplessness of human beings in the grasp of impersonal fates. Peter Bernstein put it this way in *Against the Gods: The Remarkable Story of Risk*.

> The Greeks believed that order is to be found only in the skies, where the planets and stars regularly appear in their appointed places with an unmatched regularity. To this harmonious performance, the Greeks paid deep respect,

and their mathematicians studied it intensely. But the perfection of the heavens served only to highlight the disarray of life on earth. Moreover, the predictability of the firmament contrasted sharply with the behavior of the fickle, foolish gods who dwelt on high.[7]

Of course, the Jews and Christians fashioned their own novel twist by introducing the promise of a future age of perfection. In the case of the Jews, this age would commence with the arrival of a Messiah, a secular king; in the case of the Christians, it would be marked by the return of Jesus Christ. In the meantime, Christians and Jews were in much the same situation as the Greeks, marching toward an unknown and unknowable temporal future.

Saint Augustine's reaction to this troubling fact was to dismiss it as inconsequential. He argued that the catalog of day-to-day historical events, which he described as "profane history," had neither direction nor meaning. In his view, the only history that mattered to a Christian was the one that moves steadily in one direction, that being toward the Christian eschaton, or the "end times." Bryan S. Turner described this history as "the revelation of grace through the creation and fall of man, the advent, death and resurrection of Christ, the lives of the saints and the Church, and ultimately the creation of the Second Kingdom."[8]

This Christian view that profane history was little more than a series of ups and downs with no rational meaning or predictability continued well into the Renaissance. Nisbet attributes this to the fact that while Renaissance scholars held the Greek and Roman civilizations in high regard, they felt that the intervening thousand years had been void of anything meaningful. This ruled out any theory of a linear progression of mankind. He put it this way:

> Their theory of history was a simple one: the Greeks brought civilization into being; the Romans added to it. Then, however, came the fall of Rome, caused by the external bar-

barians sprung from Germany's forests and by the Christians within Rome. The result, in the Renaissance mind, was a thousand years of desuetude, of sterility and drought, and worse, of a vast thicket of ignorance, superstition, preoccupation with the hereafter, and unremitting ecclesiastical tyranny.[9]

Nisbet cites Machiavelli's view as representative.

> Not for this extraordinary mind any belief in long run, irreversible progress for mankind. Men, he writes, are "readier to evil than to good," and the result of this is *a fixed oscillation in history between the bad and the good*, but with the bad in control more often and over longer periods of time. ... Fortune "turns states and kingdoms upside down as she pleases; she deprives the just of the good that she freely gives to the unjust."[10]

Later in the Renaissance what is perhaps the single most useful aspect of history was voiced by Bishop Jaques Amyot in the preface to his 1572 French translation of Plutarch's *Lives of the Noble Grecians and Romans*; that being that it is valuable as a means of identifying the mistakes of the past in order to avoid them in the future. He put it this way:

> [History] is a certaine rule and instruction, which by examples past, teacheth us to judge of things present, and to foresee thinges to come, so as we may know what to like of, and what to follow; what to mislike, and what to eschew ... These things it doth with much greater grace, efficacie, and speede, than the books of morall Philosophy doe: forasmuch as examples are of more force to move and instruct, than are the

arguments and proofes of reason, or their precise precepts, bicause examples, be the very formes of our deeds and accompanied with all circumstances ... To be short, it may be truely sayd, that the reading of histories is the schole of wisedom, to facion mens understanding, by considering advisedly the state of the world that is past.[11]

In 1543, the century-and-a-half-long Scientific Revolution opened with the publication of Nicolaus Copernicus's *On the Revolutions of the Celestial Spheres*, which, among other things, placed the Sun at the center of the universe rather than Earth. Other great scientists followed with other truly great revelations, including Galileo Galilei, Johannes Kepler, René Descartes, and Francis Bacon.

Our immediate interest is in Bacon, whose classic *Novum Organum Scientiarum*, published in 1620, gave one of the first hints of the notion of progress, or, in his case, scientific progress. Translated, the title of his book means a "new instrument of science," the "new" being a reference to Aristotle's classic book on logic, *Organon*. And lest the title didn't fully explain his desire to replace what he considered to be the sterility of Aristotle's methods of inquiry and the false finality he bestowed on the results, the picture on the title page of Bacon's book depicts a galleon passing between the mythical Pillars of Hercules, which stand on either side of the Strait of Gibraltar, marking the exit from familiar waters of the Mediterranean into the Atlantic Ocean. And the Latin tag at the bottom of the page is taken from *Daniel 12:4:* "Many will travel and knowledge will be increased."

Briefly stated, Bacon criticized Aristotle for his syllogistic methods and proposed a new "Baconian" approach based on empirical observation and experimentation. But more importantly from our perspective, he introduced the then-novel notion that scientific knowledge of the kind that he was advocating is cumulative, that each subsequent generation would necessarily know more than its predecessor, and that this progress would lead to new discoveries that would benefit mankind.

Although historians disagree about the actual beginning and ends of various periods, for our purposes, the Scientific Revolution began its fusion with the Age of Enlightenment with the publication of Isaac Newton's *Principia* in 1687.

Naturally then, by the opening of the eighteenth century, the amazing scientific advances made during the previous century and a half had everyone talking about the notion of progress. One of the most prominent of these was the aforementioned German polymath and eternal optimist Gottfried Leibniz, who viewed the amazing discoveries as well as the changes that they had brought about as a sign of genuine progress toward "greater improvement." He stopped at "greater improvement" because he believed that the consequences of original sin would put the brakes on the progress at some time, and he wasn't qualified to say when that might be. He put it this way.

> Further, to realize in its completeness the universal beauty and perfection of the works of God, we must recognize a certain perpetual and very free progress of the whole universe, such that it is always going forward to greater improvement. So even now a great part of our earth has received cultivation and will receive it more and more. And although it is true that sometimes certain parts of it grow wild again, or again suffer destruction or degeneration, yet this is to be understood in the way in which affliction was explained above, that is to say, that this very destruction and degeneration leads to some greater end, so that somehow we profit by the loss itself. And to the possible objection that, if this were so, the world ought long ago to have become a paradise, there is a ready answer. Although many substances have already attained a great perfection, yet on account of the infinite divisibility of the continuous, there always remain in the abyss of things slumbering parts which have yet to be awakened, to grow in

size and worth, and, in a word, to advance to a more perfect state. And hence no end of progress is ever reached.[12]

A few years later, a disciple of Bacon's scientific method and Professor of Rhetoric at the University of Naples named Giambattista Vico finally ventured an opinion as to where all this progress was headed. He began with a short essay published in 1714 entitled *On the Ancient Wisdom of the Italians*, in which he took a page out of Bacon's book and argued that the Cartesian method of employing science and mathematics to discover truth was not suitable for exploring human behavior and social change. He put it this way:

> To introduce geometrical method into practical life is "like trying to go mad with the rules of reason," attempting to proceed by a straight line among the tortuosities of life, as though human affairs were not ruled by capriciousness, temerity, opportunity, and chance. Similarly, to arrange a political speech according to the precepts of geometrical method is equivalent to stripping it of any acute remarks and to uttering nothing but pedestrian lines of argument.[13]

Fifteen years later, he would once again borrow an idea from Bacon and name his great and lasting masterpiece, *The New Science*, the "New" in this case not referring to Aristotle's Organon, but to Descartes's rationalism and emphasis on the geometric method. And indeed, his "new" approach, went far beyond Descartes's beloved science and mathematics by considering such factors as "vicissitude and probability—languages, poetry, eloquence, history, jurisprudence, politics."[14]

Löwith would describe *The New Science* as "the first empirical construction of universal history—of religion, society, governments, legal institutions, and languages—on the philosophical principle of an eternal law of providential development which is neither progressive and redemptive nor simply cyclical and natural."[15] Voegelin, whose own classic *The New Science of Politics* was named after both Bacon and Vico's books, would call it "the magnificent beginning of a modern philosophy of history and politics."[16]

Briefly stated, Vico made the then-remarkable claim that societies progress along three understandable and distinct stages during which social, civil, and political order develops from barbarism to civilization. He called the first stage "the age of gods." This period, he said, is marked by the Hobbesian war of man against man. It leads to the formation of "families" and then communities and societies for the purpose of mutual protection. The second stage is the "age of heroes." It features conflict between patricians and plebeians, the latter wishing to change the state and the nobles seeking to preserve it as it is. The final stage is "the age of man," during which the warring parties reach a mutually acceptable social order.

As with Leibniz, Vico's belief in the doctrine of original sin prevented him from forecasting mankind's progress beyond a certain point. Instead, he noted that the age of man would eventually run its course and society would return to barbarism, and begin the process all over again. He described this regression as follows (as summarized by the distinguished philosophy professor and Vico scholar Max Harold Fisch).

> The discipline, respect for law, and social solidarity of the patrician orders gave way to a humane and easy tolerance. Philosophy took the place of religion. Equality led to license. There was dispersion of private interests and decline of public spirit. Birth was first displaced by wealth as the sign of fitness to rule, since to acquire or retain it implied industry, thrift, and foresight. But in time, even the property qualification was swept away, and political power was extended to those who lacked the leisure or the will to exercise it wisely. The meanest citizen could press the public force into the service of his appetites

and whims, or sell his vote to the highest bidder among faction leaders and demagogues. The external symptoms of the process of disintegration were abated by the rise of bureaucratic monarchies, for the most part even more "humane" than the democracies, yet relieving nobles and plebeians alike of public responsibility. In this last phase of "the age of men," the humanization and softening of customs and laws continued, until breakdown within or conquest from without brought on a reversion to barbarism, and a new cycle of the three ages began.[17]

So it was that the powerful idea that history is progressing toward some sort of earthly paradise had to wait for Kant in Germany, Hume in England, and Voltaire and the philosophes in France to set the stage for the appearance early in the eighteenth century of the theists and atheists, whose optimism concerning the future wasn't constrained by the "myth" of original sin. The list of distinguished individuals who participated in this popular parlor game includes such distinguished characters as Godwin, Condorcet, Comte, Saint-Simon, Fourier, and Owen.

But it was Hegel, during his lectures on the philosophy of history in the 1820s, who first posited the claim that history was inexorably *progressing toward a specific and positive goal.* Moreover, it was Hegel who finessed the problem concerning original sin by proclaiming that such beliefs "belong to an earlier stage in the Christian world," which are "no longer of interest to us." And he assured readers that they "have no reason to be ashamed of our ancestors, for whom religious notions such as these were of supreme importance."[18]

Of course, Marx recognized the potential that Hegel's fanciful but vaguely defined view had as a great propaganda tool. For as Löwith put it, "what is cheaper than the faith that over the long course of history, everything that has ever happened, with all its consequences, must have a meaning and a purpose."[19] The result was his creation of a fairy-tale eschaton that would appeal to his beloved "proletariat" (i.e., a worker's' paradise), and that he would then turn into a centerpiece of his "scientific" theory of history and economics. And once again, the world changed forever.

Naturally, not everyone bought into Hegel's optimistic theory of progress. One of the earliest critics was, as previously noted, the economist of gloom, Thomas Malthus. Then there was Hegel's great bête noire, Schopenhauer, who concluded that the nihilism and social discontent that engulfed Europe during the nineteenth century were conclusive proof that the idea of progress was bogus. Schopenhauer, who was a vociferous opponent of the entirety of Hegel's philosophical hodgepodge of ideas, was especially critical. His argument went as follows:

> The true philosophy of history lies in perceiving that, in all the endless changes and motley complexity of events, it is only the self-same unchangeable being which is before us, which to-day pursues the same ends as it did yesterday and as it ever will. The historical philosopher has accordingly to recognize the identical character in all events, of the ancient and the modern world, of the East and the West; and in spite of all the variety of special circumstances, of costume, and of manners and customs, has to see everywhere the same humanity. This self-same element, which persists through all change, consists in the fundamental qualities of heart and head—many bad, a few good. The motto of philosophy in general must run: *Eadem sed aliter*. [Always the same, but different] To have read Herodotus is, from a philosophical point of view, to have studied enough history. For in him you already find everything that makes subsequent history— the acts and pursuits, the life and destiny of the human race, as they flow from the aforesaid qualities in conjunction with physical conditions.[20]

Nietzsche summed up his views as follows in 1865 in an essay entitled "Schopenhauer as Educator."

> How does the philosopher of our time regard culture? Quite differently, I assure you, from the professors who are so content with their new state. He seems to see the symptoms of an absolute uprooting of culture in the increasing rush and hurry of life, and the decay of all reflection and simplicity. The waters of religion are ebbing, and leaving swamps or stagnant pools: the nations are drawing away in enmity again, and long to tear each other in pieces. The sciences, blindly driving along, on a laissez faire system, without a common standard, are splitting up, and losing hold of every firm principle. The educated classes are being swept along in the contemptible struggle for wealth. Never was the world been more worldly, never poorer in goodness and love.[21]

Another critic of progress was the great German poet Johann Goethe. He had more than a passing interest in the subject, having been involved in a lifelong study of the development of plants and animals, and having written a book on the subject in 1790 entitled *Metamorphosis of Plants*, which was favorably mentioned by Darwin in the introduction of the fourth edition of *Origin*. He added nothing substantive to the philosophical discussion of progress, but probably summed up the view of a large plurality of people then and now as follows:

> And even if you were able to study and examine all the sources, what would you find? Nothing else than a great truth which has long been known, for whose confirmation one does not have far to look—the truth that men have

been miserable in all lands and in all ages. Men have always been troubled, and worried, they have tortured and martyred each other; they have made their brief lives bitter for themselves and for others, and have been unable either to see or to enjoy the beauty of the world and the sweetness of existence which the world offers them. Only a few have been comfortable and happy. The majority, having experienced life for a while would rather leave the scene than begin over again. That which gave or gives them still some hold on life was and is only fear of death. Thus it is today; thus it has always been; thus it will probably always be. That is simply the lot of man. What further evidence do we need?[22]

Another of the great poets of this period, Charles Baudelaire, arrived at a similar conclusion. He put it this way in his diary, which was published after his death in 1867.

Belief in progress is a doctrine of the slothful ... it is the individual who relies on his neighbors to tend to his affairs. There can be no progress (true, that is, moral) save in the individual and by the individual himself. It is impossible to glance through any newspaper at all, no matter of what day, what month, what year, without finding in every line the most frightful signs of human perversity, together with the most astonishing boasts of probity, of goodness, of charity, and the most shameless affirmations in regard to the progress of civilization. What more absurd than progress since man, as is proven by everyday fact, is always like and equal to man, that is to say, always in the savage state! [23]

Then there was the Swiss historian Jacob Burckhardt, who was a friend and colleague of Nietzsche at the University of Basle, and one of first prominent historians to question the idea progress. Like Nietzsche, Burckhardt was intensely interested in art and culture, which he argued were the building blocks of civilization. He viewed history as a marvelous story of human creativity, artistic and literary beauty, and the achievements of the human spirit that transcend politics and economics. However, he maintained that it had no direction discernable by man. Löwith summarizes Burckhardt's view as follows:

> Philosophy and theology of history have to deal with first beginnings and ultimate ends, and the profane historian cannot deal with either of them. The one point accessible to him is the permanent center of history: "man as he is and was and ever shall be," striving, acting, suffering. ... However creative great upheavals and destructions may turn out to be, evil remains evil and we cannot fathom the economy of the world's history. If there is anything to be learned from the study of history, it is a sober insight into our real situation: struggle and suffering, short glories and long miseries, wars and intermittent periods of peace. All are equally significant, and none reveals an ultimate meaning in a final purpose.[24]

Now, as we said earlier, one of the reasons we are discussing this somewhat arcane subject is that the idea of "progress" toward an earthly paradise was as important to the development of the ideology of the Left as Rousseau's belief in the perfectibility of man. What we did not say was it was *also the portal through which the Left successfully entered Christian America.* And with that said, we will proceed to that story.

Let's let the poets in on the fun.

> Sonnets from China XV
> As evening fell the day's oppression lifted;
> Far peaks came into focus; it had rained:
> Across wide lawns and cultured flowers drifted
> The conversation of the highly trained.
> Thin gardeners watched them pass and priced their shoes;
> A chauffeur waited, reading in the drive,
> For them to finish their exchange of views;
> It seemed a picture of the way to live.
> Far off, no matter what good they intended,
> The armies waited for a verbal error
> With all the instruments for causing pain.
> And on the issue of their charm depended
> A land laid waste, with all its young men slain,
> Its women weeping, and its towns in terror.
> W. H. Auden, 1938

Part IV

The Left in America

Religion in America takes no direct part in the government of society, but it must be regarded as the first of their political institutions; for if it does not impart a taste for freedom, it facilitates the use of it. Indeed, it is in this same point of view that the inhabitants of the United States themselves look upon religious belief. I do not know whether all Americans have a sincere faith in their religion— for who can search the human heart?—but I am certain that they hold it to be indispensable to the maintenance of republican institutions. This opinion is not peculiar to a class of citizens or to a party, but it belongs to the whole nation and to every rank of society. In the United States, if a politician attacks a sect, this may not prevent the partisans of that very sect from supporting him; but if he attacks all the sects together, everyone abandons him, and he remains alone.

The Americans combine the notions of Christianity and of liberty so intimately in their minds that it is impossible to make them conceive the one without the other; and with them this conviction does not spring from that barren, traditional faith which seems to vegetate rather than to live in the soul. (Alexis de Tocqueville, *Democracy in America, Volume II,* 1840)

M ost accounts of the Left in America begin around 1865 when the first wave of European laborers came to the country to participate in the phenomenal, post–Civil War industrialization and began to demand better working conditions under the banner of European socialism. Technically, this is true, and we will do the same. But first, we need to briefly discuss some developments in an earlier period that prepared the way, so to speak.

We will begin this exercise in 1734, the same year that Voltaire and Émilie were playing wet nurse to the Left in Europe. America at that time was home to a hodgepodge of competing Protestant denominations that had migrated to the New World in the seventeenth century to get away from the widespread religious discrimination in Europe. Roughly speaking, these can be divided into two groups, the Old Lights and the New Lights. The Old Lights were the mainline Anglicans, Lutherans, and Presbyterians. The New Lights were the evangelicals (i.e., the Congregationalists, Methodists, Baptists, and reform Presbyterians).

The New Lights were unhappy about what they believed was a waning of Christian belief among the general public and an increased interest in Deism, Unitarianism, and universalism among the educated population. They blamed this situation on the stodginess and formalism of the Old Lights, and decided that they had to act to restore the piety that was the mark of seventheenth-century America.[2] Thus began a Christian revivalist movement that would become known as the First Great Awakening, which "extended the reach and scope of religion to the poor, to blacks who had been spurned by the established sects, to people in newly settled areas, and to women who were attracted to the new style of preaching."[3]

The leaders of this undertaking were brilliant theologians who inspired Americans in much the same way as Voltaire, Rousseau, Diderot, et al. were about to inspire the French. Their approach to worship was vastly different from the ritually oriented practices of the Old Lights, as was their message, which was highly personal; intensely focused on spiritual growth, redemption, introspection, salvation, faith; and a personal commitment to high moral standards. They drew enormous crowds along with intense criticism from the Old Lights, who ridiculed them as frauds and hucksters. At one point, the controversy became so heated that it created a formal breakup among the synods of the Presbyterian Church.

The three most famous evangelical ministers involved in this movement were Jonathan Edwards, whom the *Stanford Encyclopedia of Philosophy* would describe as "widely acknowledged to be America's most important and original philosophical theologian";[4] John Wesley, the founder of Methodism and one of America's first abolitionists; and the charismatic George Whitefield. Whitefield's oratorical powers were so great that the actor David Garrick said, "He could make people weep merely by his enunciation of the word Mesopotamia, or by the pathos with which he could read a bookseller's catalogue." Dr. Johnson agreed, saying he "would be followed by crowds were he to wear a nightcap in the pulpit, or were he to preach from a tree."[5]

Of course, nothing can last forever, and in the 1740s, enthusiasm became to wane. But it had planted the seeds of evangelism in fertile soil, and in 1790, the Second Great Awakening sprang to life in the wake of the American Revolution.

Like the first one, this one involved charismatic preachers, thunderously enthusiastic revival meetings, healing crusades, church rallies, and a focus on bringing sinners back to the Christ. Our interest is focused on the strong emphasis that this movement placed on postmillennialism, that being the understanding that Christ's return to earth would be preceded by a long, possibly a thousand-year-period during which all of humanity would be converted to Christianity and society would reach a perfect state that would welcome the return of the Lord.

This belief traced it roots to something called the Savoy Declaration of 1658, which was a list of amendments that the Congregationalists had tacked on to Westminster Confession, which had been adopted in 1646 by the Church of the England as its formal statement on doctrine, church governance, and worship. The amendment in question reads as follows:

> As the Lord in his care and love towards his Church, hath in his infinite wise providence exercised it with great variety in all ages, for the good of them that love him, and his own glory; so according to his promise, *we expect that in the latter days,* antichrist being destroyed, the Jews called, and the adversaries of the kingdom of his dear Son broken, *the churches of Christ being enlarged, and edified through a free and plentiful communication of light and grace, shall enjoy in this world a more quiet, peaceable and glorious condition than they have enjoyed.*[6]

The Second Great Awakening lasted well into the 1840s. It added millions of members to the rolls of the evangelical churches and, due to its emphasis on postmillennialism, fostered the growth of a wide spectrum of political reform movements designed to speed the arrival of the coveted millennium period.

In short, over a century and a half before Hegel formulated his theory of history, and Marx adopted it as a key element of Marxism, nonconformist Christians in America had developed a Hegelian-like belief in progress, a Marxist-like belief in the inevitable arrival of a secular paradise, and an acclaimed need for human assistance to ease the "birth pangs" of this arrival. All of which, as we shall see, set the stage for the creation of America's own homegrown version of Christian socialism, which would do battle with the versions imported from Europe in the wake of the Civil War.

Let's let the poets in on the fun.

> The New Colossus
> Not like the brazen giant of Greek fame,
> With conquering limbs astride from land to land;
> Here at our sea-washed, sunset gates shall stand
> A mighty woman with a torch, whose flame
> Is the imprisoned lightning, and her name
> Mother of Exiles. From her beacon-hand
> Glows world-wide welcome; her mild eyes command
> The air-bridged harbor that twin cities frame.
> "Keep, ancient lands, your storied pomp!" cries she
> With silent lips. "Give me your tired, your poor,
> Your huddled masses yearning to breathe free,
> The wretched refuse of your teeming shore.
> Send these, the homeless, tempest-tost to me,
> I lift my lamp beside the golden door!"
> Emma Lazarus, 1883

Chapter 14

The European Left Comes to America

People who attend to their own business, tread the routine their fathers trod, and attempt to discharge in peace and quiet the practical duties of their state, little suspect what is fermenting in the heated brains of this nineteenth century. They know next to nothing of what is going on around them. They look upon the doctrines contained in the works like the one before us [The Communist Manifesto] as the speculations of a few insane dreamers, and are sure that the good sense of mankind will prevent them from spreading, and confine their mischief to the misguided individuals who put them forth. They regard them as too ridiculous, as too absurd, to be believed. They can do no harm, and we need not trouble our heads about them. This is certainly a plausible view of the subject, but unhappily, there is nothing too ridiculous or too absurd to be believed, if demanded by the dominant spirit or sentiment of an age or country; for what is seen to be demanded by that spirit or sentiment never appears ridiculous or absurd to those who are under its influence.
(Orestes Brownson, "Notes on Socialism and the

Church," *Brownson's Quarterly Review*, January 1849)

Of course, the United States could not forever avoid the leftist turmoil that had plagued Europe throughout the nineteenth century. The trouble started shortly after the end of the Civil War when a phenomenal number of new inventions and technologies began to transform the nation from an almost entirely agricultural society to one of largest manufacturing countries in the world.

Enormous commitments of capital were required to produce the materials necessary for this expansion: iron, coal, copper, silver, lumber, electrical power, petroleum, and other products, and to create a system of railroads, bridges, tunnels, highways, and river ports large enough to move the materials and finished products. This, in turn, demanded large numbers of workers, and indeed, between 1866 and 1915, twenty-five million immigrants entered the United States.

Naturally, men with the vision and the courage to gamble huge amounts of money on such risky ventures expected and received large returns. The result was that many became fabulously rich and powerful. They included such names as Paul Warburg, Jacob Schiff, J. P. Morgan, John D. Rockefeller, Andrew Mellon, Andrew Carnegie, Cornelius Vanderbilt, John Jacob Astor, Henry Clay Frick, and E. H. Harriman, some of whom acted in close partnership with the European Rothschild colossus, which had vast sums available and a desire to loan it.

These men were wheelers and dealers, driven by a will to power. They had the intelligence, courage, and vision to raise and invest the capital that built the railroads, the telegraph lines, the steel mills, the petroleum cartels, the chemical plants, and the power companies, which resulted in the most broadly-based prosperity that the world had ever known. In the early years, they and their organizations clashed repeatedly with each other in the worlds of finance and commerce. But over time they came to a tacit understanding that, as John D. Rockefeller put it, "competition is a sin," and slowly began to divide up the spoils in a more orderly and friendly fashion. In his classic, *Tragedy and Hope*, Carroll Quigley describes them thusly:

> They lived a life of dazzling splendor. Sailing the ocean in great private yachts or traveling on land by private trains, they moved in a ceremonious round between their spectacular estates and townhouses in Palm Beach, Long Island, the Berkshires, Newport, and Bar Harbor; assembling from their fortress-like New York residences to attend the Metropolitan Opera under the critical eye of Mrs. Astor; or gathering for business meetings of the highest strategic level in the awesome presence of J. P. Morgan himself.
>
> The structure of financial controls created by the tycoons of "Big Banking" and "Big Business" in the period 1880–1933 was of extraordinary complexity, one business fief being built on another, both being allied with semi-independent associates, the whole rearing upward into two pinnacles of economic and financial power, of which one, centered in New York, was headed by J. P. Morgan and Company, and the other, in Ohio, was headed by the Rockefeller family. When these two cooperated, as they generally did, they could influence the economic life of the country to a large degree and could almost control its political life, at least on the Federal level. …
>
> The influence of these business leaders was so great that the Morgan and Rockefeller groups acting together, or even Morgan acting alone, could have wrecked the economic system of the country merely by throwing securities on the stock market for sale, and, having precipitated a

stock-market panic, could then have bought back
the securities they had sold but at a lower price.[1]

Not surprisingly, many of the folks who provided the labor necessary for these ventures believed that their input was not being fairly
valued, given the vast fortunes that the capital side of the equation
was producing. This tension was natural to the process of industrialization. In fact, without the wealth disparities, the industrialization
could not have occurred.

Arguably, if the process had been allowed to run its course, the
wealth would have spread naturally to the workers when high returns
were no longer needed to attract the capital to keep the process
going. Of course, this did not happen, and the nation experienced a
long, difficult period of labor unrest, as well as the formation of labor
unions.

The two most successful coalitions of unions were the Noble and
Holy Order of the Knights of Labor and the American Federation of
Labor, both of which were led by men who were openly and vocally
opposed to socialism. The first of these was founded in 1869. It
began slowly but became more successful after Terence Powderly
became the Grand Master Workman in 1879. He was an advocate
of a populist notion called producerism, which extolled the "enno-
bling virtues" of those who earn their living by producing something.
This group included not only laborers but also small businessmen
and entrepreneurs. The enemies in Powderly's view of the world
were parasitical elements at the extremes of the social structure. At
one end were the large, politically connected corporations that the
Knights charged were stifling free competition, avoiding taxes, and
using their political power to strangle their smaller competitors. At
the other end were the unproductive poor, who live off the charity of
others. Powderly's solution to the problem was to abandon the wage
system in favor of a network of cooperatives.

The AFL was founded in 1886 as an alliance of craft unions
that were disaffected from the Knights. Samuel Gompers, one of
the founders, led the organization from that year until his death in
1924. He disagreed with Powderly's claim that the interests of labor

and capital were the same, but he was just as hostile to socialism as Powderly was and believed strongly that the expansion of the capitalist system was the best path to the betterment of labor. This left the large and rapidly growing European immigrant community without an organizational voice, given that very few of them had the skill required for membership in the trade unions and virtually all of them had leftist political views that rendered them unwelcome to either labor organization.

As fate would have it, this was when Marx moved the headquarters of the First International to New York City to keep it safely out of the reach of Bakunin, who, as already noted, was battling Marx for control of the organization. The move kept Bakunin away, but not his followers. The result was that the fight continued within the International between the Marxist "Reds," who favored union organization as a prelude to revolution, and Bakunin's "Blacks," who advocated immediate violent action to overthrow the government.

The result was the breakup of the First International in 1876 and the formation a few days later by Marxist splinter groups of the Workingmen's Party of the United States, which later became the Socialist Labor Party of America. The SLP was reasonably successful at first at keeping the various leftist factions in line. However, the railway strikes of 1877 turned bloody, especially in Missouri, Maryland, Pennsylvania, and Illinois; and this energized the anarchists within the SLP.

In fact, a group of SLP members in Chicago formed an organization called the *Lehr und Wehr Verein* (Educational and Defense Society), which—according to an article in the July 20, 1886, *New York Times*—was specifically charged with training and drilling union members to "get ready for the great conflict between capital and labor which agitators of that class have for many years declared imminent."[2]

In order to keep the anarchists in line, the SLP leadership ordered all its members to disassociate themselves with any and all such radical organizations. This marked the end of the importance of the SLP, although it lingered on in one form or another until officially closing its New York office in 2008, which allowed it to claim the title of the "oldest socialist political party in the United States."

In 1880, a New York group left the SLP and formed an organization known as the Social Revolutionary Club. Shortly thereafter, other Social Revolutionary Clubs sprung up in Boston, Philadelphia, Milwaukee, and Chicago, which, it is fair to say, opened up a new and highly violent chapter in the American labor movement. The Chicago Club was the most powerful. Its leaders were Albert R. Parsons, the most prominent Native American Socialist personality in the Midwest, and August Spies, a German-born worker who joined the socialist movement after the 1877 Railroad Strike and soon became one of America's leading Socialist orators and journalists.

In 1881, the New York Club attended a conference in London where it affiliated with the International Working People's Association (IWPA), which was an anarchist group founded by Bakunin and also called the Black International. They returned to the states infatuated with Kropotkin's doctrine of the "propaganda of the deed" and the idea that conspiratorial action and individual terror against the ruling class was the only way to rouse the masses to revolt.[3]

Their first order of business was to call for a meeting in Chicago of all the other Clubs in hopes of establishing an American branch of the IWPA. This did not happen, but the Clubs did adopt the name Revolutionary Socialist Party and agreed to a platform that stated that the chief weapon that they would use to combat the capitalist system was "the armed organizations of workingmen who stand ready with the gun to resist encroachments upon their rights."[3]

Not much happened in the first year, but in 1882, Johann Most arrived in New York and provided much needed individual leadership to the anarchists clubs. He was a small German man with a deformed face. He had been a leader in Germany's socialist movement, repeatedly arrested for his advocacy of violent action, exiled to France, and exiled from there to London, where he had just served a sixteen-month stint in prison for praising in print the assassination of Tsar Alexander II. Morris Hillquit describes his reception in New York as follows in his *History of Socialism in the United States*:

For the members of the revolutionary clubs, or the "Social Revolutionists," as they styled themselves, Most was no mean acquisition. A forceful and popular speaker, a brilliant journalist, and a "martyr" to the cause, he was the ideal man to gather the disheartened and demoralized elements in the socialist movement of America under the banner of revolt and destruction.

The great mass-meeting arranged for his reception in the large hall of Cooper Union Institute in December, 1882, turned into a veritable ovation for the "victim of bourgeois justice," and his tour through the principle cities of the country in the early part of 1883 resembled a triumphant procession. His meetings were large and enthusiastic, they were extensively reported by the press, and a number of anarchistic "groups" were organized as a result of his agitation.[4]

Among Most's best-known acolytes were Emma Goldman and Alexander Berkman, who met one night at a lecture given by Most. The historian Barbara Tuchman describes that night as follows in her book *The Proud Tower*. "From the 'tension and fearful excitement' of Most's speech about the martyrs, Emma sought 'relief' in Sasha's [Berkman] arms and subsequently her enthusiasm led her to Most's arms as well. The tensions of this arrangement proved no different from those of any bourgeois triangle."[5]

For a year or so, Most traveled the country preaching anarchism, and published an anarchist newspaper *Freiheit*, which openly extolled workers to violence. In her autobiography *Living My Life*, Goldberg described her education at the hands of Most as follows:

He opened up a new world to me, introduced me to music, books, the theatre. But his own rich personality meant far more to me—the alternating heights and depths of his spirit, his hatred of the capitalist system, his vision of a new society of beauty and joy for all. Most became my idol. I worshipped him … I had great talent, he said, and I must begin soon to recite and speak in public. He would make me a great speaker—"to take my place when I am gone," he added.[6]

Then in 1883, Most called a meeting of anarchists in Pittsburg, during which he united the Clubs and other anarchist groups under the umbrella of IWPA. By that time, the Chicago club had five to six thousand members and published five different newspapers; so naturally, Parsons and Spies were among the IWPA's leaders, which made their downfall three years later at a labor rally on May 4, 1886, in Chicago's Haymarket Square all the more important.

The roots of this occasion dated to a resolution passed by the AFL in 1884, establishing May 1, 1886, as the date by which the eight-hour workday would become standard. Of course, this dead-line was not met, and in response to this failure, labor unions all over America staged strikes and rallies in protest. The tension was particularly high in Chicago where thousands of workers were already in the midst of a highly acrimonious strike against McCormick Harvesting Machines. On May 1, Parsons, accompanied by his wife and children, led a parade of eighty thousand people down Michigan Avenue.

On May 3, Spies was holding a rally in support of striking workers in Haymarket Square when the police arrived and told them to break it up. During the argument, someone threw a bomb and killed a policeman. The policemen started shooting into the crowd, and when the dust settled, eight policemen were dead (some, possibly all, by "friendly fire"), and no one knows how many demonstrators were killed. Estimates range from five to sixty. In the subsequent trial, four of the anarchists, including Spies and Parson, were found guilty and eventually hanged.

The trial's fairness is debatable. On the side of the government, there was little question that the defendants were dangerous people with serious plans to do harm. Michael Schaack provides a comprehensive account of these plans in his 1889 book *Anarchy and*

Anarchists, including the following from subsequent testimony of one of the *Lehr und Wehr Verein* members.

> Our only hope for a victory lay in the torch and dynamite. When Chicago would be surrounded by fire and destroyed, these "beasts," he said, would be obliged to take refuge on the prairies, and there it would be very easy for us to master them by our unmerciful proceedings. If this was done, other cities, like New York, St. Louis, Pittsburg, etc., would follow our example. Then all eyes would be centered on the Anarchists of Chicago, and therefore we would proclaim the Commune.[7]

The defendants argued, rather convincingly, that that state could not prove that any of them had actually killed anyone and that under US law they had a right to express their views in public. Moreover, they claimed that it was impossible to find an impartial jury in the atmosphere of rage, hatred, and fear that prevailed in the aftermath of the event. We have no dog in this fight, but we would cite two rulings in the case simply to point up the stark difference between the treatment of terrorists in the late nineteenth century and today. The first will be Judge Joseph E. Gary's declaration as to the limits to one's right to hold forth on unpopular beliefs. To wit:

> Each man has the full right to entertain and advocate by speech and print such opinions as suits himself, and the great body of the people will usually care little what he says. But if he proposes murder as a means of enforcing he puts his own life at stake. And no clamor about free speech or the evils to be cured or the wrongs to be redressed, will shield him from the consequences of his crime. His liberty is not a license to destroy. The toleration that he enjoys he must

extend to others, and not arrogantly assume that the great majority are wrong and may rightfully be coerced by terror, or removed by dynamite. It only remains that for the crime you have committed, and of which you have been convicted after a trial unexampled in the patience with which an outraged people have extended to you every protection and privilege of the law which you derided and defied, that the sentence of that law be now given. In form and detail that sentence will appear upon the records of the Court. In substance and effect it is that the defendant Neebe be imprisoned in the State Penitentiary at Joliet at hard labor for the term of fifteen years. And that each of the other defendants, between the hours of ten o'clock in the forenoon and two o'clock in the afternoon of the third day of December next, in the manner provided by the statute of this state, be hung by the neck until he is dead. Remove the prisoners.[8]

The second ruling came during an appeal in which the defendants argued that some of the jurors were not impartial, that many had actually publicly expressed a dislike for anarchism, communism, and socialism. To which the Illinois Supreme Court responded that such opinions do not disqualify a juror but reflect "merely a prejudice against crime."[9]

The next big event in the anarchist's tragic adventure in America was Berkman's highly publicized assassination attempt on the life of Andrew Carnegie's plant manager Henry Clay Frick, who had violently put down the bloody strike in 1892 at Carnegie's giant steel plant in Homestead, Pennsylvania. Berkman spent fourteen years behind bars for that crime, during which he wrote his memoirs, from which the following comes:

"Fr—," I begin." The look of terror on his face strikes me speechless. It is the dread of the conscious presence of death. "He understands," it flashes through my mind. With a quick motion I draw the revolver. As I raise the weapon, I see Frick clutch with both hands the arm of the chair, and attempt to rise. I aim at his head. "Perhaps he wears armor," I reflect. With a look of horror he quickly averts his face, as I pull the trigger. There is a flash, and the high-ceilinged room reverberates as with the booming of cannon. I hear a sharp, piercing cry, and see Frick on his knees, his head against the arm of the chair. I feel calm and possessed, intent upon every movement of the man. He is lying head and shoulders under the large armchair, without sound or motion. "Dead?" I wonder. I must make sure. About twenty-five feet separate us. I take a few steps toward him, when suddenly the other man, whose presence I had quite forgotten, leaps upon me. I struggle to loosen his hold. He looks slender and small. I would not hurt him: I have no business with him. Suddenly I hear the cry, "Murder! Help!" My heart stands still as I realize that it is Frick shouting. "Alive?" I wonder. I hurl the stranger aside and fire at the crawling figure of Frick. The man struck my hand, —I have missed! He grapples with me, and we wrestle across the room. I try to throw him, but spying an opening between his arm and body, I thrust the revolver against his side and aim at Frick, cowering behind the chair. I pull the trigger. There is a click—but no explosion! By the throat I catch the stranger, still clinging to me, when suddenly something heavy strikes me on the back of the head. Sharp pains shoot through my eyes. I sink to the floor, vaguely conscious of the weapon slipping from my hands. "Where is the hammer?

Hit him, carpenter!" Confused voices ring in my ears. Painfully I strive to rise. The weight of many bodies is pressing on me. Now—it's Frick's voice! Not dead? ... I crawl in the direction of the sound, dragging the struggling men with me. I must get the dagger from my pocket—I have it! Repeatedly I strike with it at the legs of the man near the window. I hear Frick cry out in pain— there is much shouting and stamping—my arms are pulled and twisted, and I am lifted bodily from the floor. Police, clerks, workmen in over- alls, surround me. An officer pulls my head back by the hair, and my eyes meet Frick's. He stands in front of me, supported by several men. His face is ashen gray; the black beard is streaked with red, and blood is oozing from his neck. For an instant a strange feeling, as of shame, comes over me; but the next moment I am filled with anger at the sentiment, so unworthy of a revolutionist. With defiant hatred I look him full in the face.[10]

However, the anarchist's greatest spectacle occurred on September 14, 1901, when an anarchist named Leon Czolgos assassinated President McKinley while he was shaking hands with well-wishers at the Pan-American Exposition in Buffalo, New York. Czolgos was an American who was born in Detroit of Polish parents. He was a small, twenty-eight-year-old, unemployed recluse who had spent a lot of time reading socialist and anarchist newspapers and going to anarchist meetings. The following comes from the official report entitled "The Trial, Execution, Autopsy and Mental Status of Leon F. Czolgosz, Alias Fred Nieman, the Assassin of President McKinley":

By his own admissions, Czolgosz was a devout Anarchist and a firm believer in the principles of "Free Society," as taught by Emma

Goldman—of whom he was an ardent admirer—and others. These were the beliefs which furnished the motives for the murderous deed ... He further said that he had been an ardent student of the doctrine of Anarchy, and had attended many "circles" where these subjects were discussed. He had attended a meeting of Anarchists "about six weeks ago," and also in July; had met and talked with an Anarchist in Chicago "about ten days ago;" that he belonged to a "circle" in Cleveland which had no name. "They called themselves Anarchists."

The report contains the following direct quotes from Czolgosz: "I have done my duty, I don't believe in voting; it is against my principles. I am an Anarchist." "I planned to kill the President three or four days ago, after I came to Buffalo." "I don't believe in the Republican form of government, and I don't believe we should have any rulers. I had that idea when I shot the President, and that is why I was there." "McKinley was going around the country shouting prosperity when there was no prosperity for the poor man. I am not afraid to die. We all have to die sometime." And finally, his last words a few seconds before dying in the electric chair: "I killed the President because he was the enemy of the good people—the good working people. I am not sorry for my crime. I am sorry I could not see my father."[11]

Needless to say, the Haymarket affair, the attempt on Frick's life, and the assassination of McKinley were not helpful to the reputation of the union movement. So with their back to the wall, a veritable rogue's gallery of the nation's most prominent socialists and radical union leaders gathered in Chicago in June 1905 and founded the Industrial Workers of the World, better known as the Wobblies. History books, encyclopedias, etc. generally describe the Wobblies as socialists, but this isn't entirely accurate. Technically, they were syndicalists in the mold of Georges Sorel. Their professed goal was to unite all workers into one organization, to eliminate capitalism, and to form a structure to carry on production after the capitalists were overthrown. As to the means for achieving this, they subscribed to Sorel's notion of the "general strike," which is a shutdown of all economic activity, which would bring the government to its knees, and to be replaced by a network of union syndicates. And it goes without saying that violence was regarded as an acceptable tool.

The Wobbly membership was made up, for the most part, of a motley crew of miners, lumberjacks, longshoremen, and itinerant agricultural laborers, who were considered unskilled rabble by Gomper's AFL, which was the backbone of the American labor movement at that time.

Wobbly organizers included "Big Bill" Haywood, a union plug-ugly who had earned his spurs in the bloody labor riots in 1900 involving the Western Federation of Miners; Daniel De Leon, a Marxist gadfly who had taken control of the all-but-defunct SLP and had unsuccessfully tried to use it as a springboard for a political career; Lucy Parsons, a fiery, well-known anarchist/social revolutionary activist and the wife of Albert Parsons, the native American who was executed for participation in the Haymarket riot; and "Mother" Mary Harris Jones, another noisy, well-known labor organizer, who specialized in organizing the wives and children of striking workers.

Then, of course, there was Eugene Debs, who was at the time a member of the SLP. He was, unquestionably, the best-known union organizer in America. Not only had he run for president in 1900 as a socialist, he had been head of the powerful American Railway Union in 1894 when it joined a wildcat strike of workers at the Pullman Palace Car Company, which eventually involved some 250,000 workers in twenty-seven states and considerable violence.

That strike had been broken when President Cleveland sent in twelve thousand US Army troops to put it down, declaring that it was interfering with the delivery of the US mail and posed a threat to public safety. The government convinced a federal court to issue an injunction against the strikers that was so broad in its application that the *New York Times* referred to it as a "Gatling gun on paper."[12] It then proceeded to charge Debs with conspiring "to interfere with the transportation of the mails and to violate the Sherman Anti-Trust Act of 1890, which prohibited any collaborative action in restraint of trade or commerce among the several states." Debs spent six months in jail after a highly-publicized trial at which he was represented by none other than Clarence Darrow.

The IWW made big waves in the world of workers during the next couple decades in the face of heavy and often violent resistance from other unions that objected to its extremist views, from local anti-union, vigilante groups, and from the federal government itself. The Wobblies' quarrel with Washington reached a crescendo in November 1916 when it took a page from the Second International's playbook and voted to not participate in Wilson's war, maintaining that it was strictly a capitalist affair in which the working poor would die at the hands of other workers.

When the war came, the organization eschewed public anti-war demonstrations but advised its members of simply requesting an exemption from the draft based. Nevertheless, the organization became highly unpopular during the war with both the public at large and with the federal government, which launched a veritable storm of federal prosecutions against it and its members, based on the Espionage Act of 1917, which made it illegal to "willfully utter, print, write, or publish any disloyal, profane, scurrilous, or abusive language about the form of the Government of the United States" or to "willfully urge, incite, or advocate any curtailment of the pro-duction" of the things "necessary or essential to the prosecution of the war." Naturally, Debs openly violated this law and was finally arrested for giving a speech urging resistance to the draft just two months before the fighting stopped. He was sentenced to ten years in prison, where he made his fourth run for the presidency and received more than one million votes.

Let's let the poets in on the fun.

> The International
> Arise ye workers from your slumbers
> Arise ye prisoners of want
> For reason in revolt now thunders
> And at last ends the age of cant.
> Away with all your superstitions

THE EUROPEAN LEFT COMES TO AMERICA

Servile masses arise, arise
We'll change henceforth the old tradition
And spurn the dust to win the prize.
So comrades, come rally
And the last fight let us face
The Internationale unites the human race.
No more deluded by reaction
On tyrants only we'll make war
The soldiers too will take strike action
They'll break ranks and fight no more
And if those cannibals keep trying
To sacrifice us to their pride
They soon shall hear the bullets flying
We'll shoot the generals on our own side.
No saviour from on high delivers
No faith have we in prince or peer
Our own right hand the chains must shiver
Chains of hatred, greed and fear
E'er the thieves will out with their booty
And give to all a happier lot.
Each at the forge must do their duty
And we'll strike while the iron is hot.
A member of the Paris Commune, 1871

Chapter 15

America's Homegrown Left

Not only is a democratic people led by its own taste to centralize its government, but the passions of all the men by whom it is governed constantly urge it in the same direction. It may easily be foreseen that almost all the able and ambitious members of a democratic community will labor unceasingly to extend the powers of government, because they all hope at some time or other to wield those powers themselves. It would be a waste of time to attempt to prove to them that extreme centralization may be injurious to the state, since they are centralizing it for their own benefit. Among the public men of democracies, there are hardly any but men of great disinterestedness or extreme mediocrity who seek to oppose the centralization of government; the former are scarce, the latter powerless. (Alexis de Tocqueville, *Democracy in America*, Volume II, 1840)

Historians generally agree that the so-called Progressive Era in the United States began in the 1890s. However, as we noted earlier, its roots go back a half century to the First and Second Great Awakenings. In any case, progressivism was a social movement made up of tens of thousands of Americans from both political parties who were fixated on the use of the federal government to solve the many problems that had been brought on by industrialization, urbanization, immigration, and corruption.

While it lacked any type of centralized, formal organization, progressivism somewhat resembled Fabianism. Its approach was stealthy, unthreatening, and peaceful. Its underlying political focus was on the reorganization of the existing society rather than revolution. Its leaders were generally well educated and regarded as respectable citizens. It concentrated on problems that were, theoretically at least, within the realm of practical politics. Finally, while many of its advocates were sympathetic with the leftists who were involved in the often-violent battles between labor and capital, the majority were not.

Many of these drew their inspiration from the numerous utopian communities that were established in the United States during the early to mid-nineteenth century by followers of Fourier, Owen, and another European utopian socialist named Étienne Cabe. Others were attracted to an impressive blueprint for a peaceful and just society formulated by Laurence Gronlund, a Dane, who moved to the United States in 1867 at the age of twenty-one and practiced law in Chicago. He was prominent in the early American labor movement but is so little known today that he does not even rate a mention in the *Cambridge Biographical Dictionary*. His fabled fifteen minutes of fame was as the author in 1884 of *The Cooperative Commonwealth in Its Outline: An Exposition of Modern Socialism*, which posits an omnipotent administrative state in which the workers control production and an elite group of intellectuals run the government. Draper describes it thusly.

> Gronlund is so up-to-date that he does not say he rejects democracy—he merely "redefines" it; as "Administration by the Competent," as against "government by majorities," together with a modest proposal to wipe out representative government as such as well as all parties.

All the "people" want, he teaches, is "administration—good administration." They should find "the right leaders," and then be "willing to thrust their whole collective power into their hands." Representative government will be replaced by the plebiscite. He is sure that his scheme will work, he explains, because it works so well for the hierarchy of the Catholic Church. Naturally, he rejects the horrible idea of class struggle. The workers are incapable of self-emancipation, and he specifically denounces Marx's famous expression of this First Principle. The Yahoos will be emancipated by an elite of the "competent," drawn from the intelligentsia; and at one point he set out to organize a secret conspiratorial American Socialist Fraternity for students.[1]

The book was a big hit, selling over one hundred thousand copies. However, its real claim to fame is having inspired Edward Bellamy to write his classic utopian tome, *Looking Backward*. This book, which was published in 1887, is still in print today and is widely regarded as having spread the seeds of socialism among a vast number of ordinary Americans who were troubled at the time by the America's many growth pains. (For trivia fans, Edward's first cousin Francis composed America's Pledge of Allegiance in 1892.)

Bellamy's book was a fantasy about a young Bostonian, Julian West, who falls into a deep sleep in 1887 and awakens in 2000 to a world of peace and plenty, in which there is neither squalor nor injustice. Life is regimented and hierarchical, ruled by an elite. Most significantly, private capitalism has disappeared. Everyone works for one big capitalist organization, the state. The vision of the book is a perfectly organized industrial system that, because of the close interlocking of its wheels, works with a minimum of friction and a maximum of wealth and leisure to all. Upon waking, Julien is curious as to the reasoning behind all the changes that had occurred while he slept. The following excerpt tells much about the answers he received to his many questions.

Dr. Leete ceased speaking, and I remained silent, endeavoring to form some general conception of the changes in the arrangements of society implied in the tremendous revolution which he had described.

Finally, I said, "The idea of such an extension of the functions of government is, to say the least, rather overwhelming."

"Extension!" he repeated, "where is the extension?"

"In my day," I replied, "it was considered that the proper functions of government, strictly speaking, were limited to keeping the peace and defending the people against the public enemy, that is, to the military and police powers."

"And, in heaven's name, who are the public enemies?" exclaimed Dr. Leete. "Are they France, England, Germany, or hunger, cold, and nakedness? In your day governments were accustomed, on the slightest international misunderstanding, to seize upon the bodies of citizens and deliver them over by hundreds of thousands to death and mutilation, wasting their treasures the while like water; and all this oftenest for no imaginable profit to the victims. We have no wars now, and our governments no war powers, but in order to protect every citizen against hunger, cold, and nakedness, and provide for all his physical and mental needs, the function is assumed of directing his industry for a term of years. No, Mr. West, I am sure on reflection you will perceive that it was in your age, not in ours, that the extension of the functions of governments was extraordinary.

Not even for the best ends would men now allow
their governments such powers as were then used
for the most maleficent."[2]

The following is a brief description of Bellamy's fantasy world
from the foreword written by Erich Fromm to the Signet Classic
paperback edition dated 1960.

> Everyone receives the same amount of
> money, regardless of the amount of work he does.
> Everyone has the right to a decent human life not
> because he excels in this or that, but because he
> is a man ... All means of production are in the
> hands of the state, and there is no private owner of
> capital or business. Both the kind and the extent
> of work anyone does is determined by individual
> choice. Bellamy's good society is one the aim of
> which is not luxury and consumption per se, but
> the good life; and work, while freely chosen, is
> not the aim of life either. After the age of forty
> five, everyone is exempt from further economic
> service to the nation, with the exception of the
> very specialized professional and administrative
> jobs which give pleasure and require a great deal
> of experience. It is Bellamy's basic principle that
> the system is "entirely voluntary, the logical out-
> come of the operation of human nature under
> rational conditions." One of the striking fea-
> tures of Bellamy's utopia is the fact that people
> not only live better materially, but that they are
> different psychologically. There is no individual
> antagonism, but a sense of solidarity and love.
> Their principle is that one accepts only those ser-
> vices one is willing to return. They are frank and
> they do not lie, and there is complete equality of
> the sexes, with no need for deceit and manipula-

tion. In other words, it is a society in which the religion of brotherly love and solidarity has been realized.[3]

By any measure, Bellamy's little fairy tale makes *Alice in Wonderland* look like a National Geographic Special. Yet millions of Americans were captivated by this book. And why not? Economic growth, while substantial, had been marred since the end of the Civil War by periodic recessions known to historians today as the Panic of 1873, the Panic of 1893, and the Panic of 1896. Banks and business failures were habitual. Unemployment rose to 14 percent at times. Open warfare between the labor unions and the capitalists had resulted in numerous violent and economically damaging strikes. Cities were bursting at the seams as workers flooded in for the new industrial jobs. The population of Chicago, for example, went from 30,000 in 1850, to 300,000 in 1870, and 1.1 million by 1890. The result was shocking poverty and squalor. All of which had turned the United States into a playground for the communists and anarchists who were a commonplace among the hordes of immigrants who were entering the country in search of work.

Then, amidst this political and economic turmoil and uncertainty, there came Bellamy's entertaining, easily understood, and fun-to-read novel of a world free from these nagging problems; a novel that explained how peace could be achieved by the imposition of a collectivist order, run by men of principles and intelligence.

In reality, of course, it was a horror story about a totalitarian government that had stolen the humanity, the freedom, the individuality, and the god of its citizens. Yet, as noted above, a great many Americans were in need of such dreams and began to look with sympathy on the notion of some form of forced political order.

Americans bought millions of copies. In fact, as Fromm notes, it was the third most popular book in the nation at the turn of the century after *Uncle Tom's Cabin* and *Ben-Hur*. Moreover, Fromm points out, It stimulated utopian thinking to such an extent that from 1889 to 1900, forty-six other utopian novels were published in the United States, and between 1890 and 1891 one hundred and sixty-five "Bellamy Clubs" sprang up across the country, "devoted to the discussion and propagation of the aims expressed in *Looking Backward*."[4] Nor was this a passing fad. Indeed, these clubs dotted the American landscape throughout the presidency of Franklin Roosevelt. So crucial was the widespread interest in *Looking Backward* to the left-wing drift of the nation in late nineteenth century that Draper describes Bellamy as "the leading figure" at the "wellsprings of American 'native socialism.'"[5]

In short, Bellamy's book provided Americans with an inviting, nonthreatening view of socialism, which helped to clear the way for the reforms that the Progressives were promoting. Douglas Steeples, Professor of History Emeritus at Mercer University, and David O. Whitten, Professor of Economics at Auburn, described this slow but sure attitudinal change as follows in *Democracy in Desperation: The Depression of 1893*.

> Hard times intensified social sensitivity to a wide range of problems accompanying industrialization by making them more severe. Those whom depression struck hardest, as well as much of the general public and major Protestant churches, shored up their civic consciousness about currency and banking reform, regulation of business in the public interest, and labor relations. Although nineteenth-century liberalism and the tradition of administrative minimalism that it favored remained viable, *public opinion began to swing toward the governmental activism and interventionism associated with modern, industrial societies, erecting in the process the intellectual foundation for the reform impulse that was to be called Progressivism in twentieth-century America.* Most important of all, these opposed tendencies in thought set the boundaries within which Americans for the next century debated the most vital questions of their shared experience. The

depression was a reminder of business slumps, commonweal above avarice, and principle above principal. [Emphasis added] [6]

Leslie Fishbein, associated professor at Rutgers, put it this way in her award-winning book *Rebels in Bohemia: The Radicals of the Masses, 1911–1917.*

In the Progressive era socialism no longer seemed as distinctive and as threatening as it once had been. The Socialist party attracted to its ranks such urban reformers as [newspaper publisher] Joseph Medill Patterson, [author] Upton Sinclair, [wealthy philanthropist] J. G. Phelps Stokes, [wealthy labor reformer] William English Walling, [wealthy social reformer] Robert Hunter, and [Pulitzer Prize-winning muckraker] Charles Edward Russell, and it grew increasingly respectable. The capitalist press opened its pages to news about socialism. The *New York Times* and the *New York Evening Post* interviewed [founder and leader of the Socialist Party of America] Morris Hillquit during his 1906 congressional campaign, and William Randolph Hearst's *New York Journal* invited the Milwaukee socialist Victor Berger to write a series of articles. This leftward drift resulted in the unexpected conversion of the *Metropolitan Magazine*, a popular monthly that announced early in 1912 that it would "give socialism a hearing."[7]

Despite progressivism's similarities to Fabianism, it was very different in many respects from all other leftist constructs due largely to the fact that Christianity and capitalism were still profoundly influential in the United States in the late nineteenth and early twentieth century. As such, Progressives did not claim that religion was one of the bad social institutions that stood in the way of reform. In fact, early on there was a strong conservative, Christian-based element within the Movement that focused attention on a number of issues. These included widespread corruption by the Democratic political machines in the nation's big cities, and the social problems related to alcohol abuse. Over the longer term, however, the movement was taken over by reformist democrats, who shifted the focus to the evils of big business. Roughly speaking, the progressive movement consisted of five distinct camps, although there was considerable overlap between and among them.

1. The first of these consisted of thousands of ordinary community activists and reformers who were, for the most part, organized into small, local movements that were driven by the simple desire to help the less fortunate among them and to improve the community in which they lived. Their many and diverse projects involved ferreting out corruption in state and local governments, fighting for restrictions on child labor, workplace reforms, and minimum wage laws, battling against predatory business practices and moral decay, and building settlements homes in urban locations to provide food, education, and other services to the poor. The first of these homes was the Neighborhood Guild, which was founded in New York City in 1886. By early in the twentieth century, four hundred settlement houses were scattered across the nation, staffed by ambitious and energetic volunteers who became a prolific source of future leaders of the American leftist community.

2. The second group was comprised of a large array of proto-socialists who fought a propaganda war on a wide front, attacking the status quo, promoting "justice," and building a leftist infrastructure. Their ranks included intellectuals, artists, writers, poets, politicians, feminists, journalists, college professors, lawyers, and a great many cranks.

One of the most famous of these individuals was Jack London, a muscular, assertive, creative, and energetic man who joined the Socialist Labor Party of Oakland in 1896 at the age of twenty and began "holding forth" to large crowds in City Hall Park, which earned him the title of "the boy socialist of Oakland."[8] He had dropped out of school when he was fourteen, and during the intervening six years, he had become an avid reader who studied the works of such men as Nietzsche, Marx, Darwin, Thomas Henry Huxley, and Spencer.

He had also worked as a sailor and an "oyster pirate," and had "tramped" extensively throughout the United States and Canada, during which time he joined the populist Jacob Coxey's march on Washington DC to protest President Grover Cleveland's labor and monetary policies. In 1905, by which time he was internationally famous for writing such books as *The Call of the Wild* and *The People of the Abyss*, he wrote a well-known essay in which he said that his experiences living among the poor as a tramp had given rise to his socialism.

Then there was Upton Sinclair, who became famous in 1906 for his novel, *The Jungle*, which exposed the unsanitary conditions in the US meatpacking industry. His socialism was, like London's, almost entirely homegrown. He had read Marx, Kropotkin, Bernstein, and Kautsky. Yet, by all accounts, his uniquely American brand of socialism came mostly from reading Bellamy; the gritty, all-American novels of London and Frank Norris; and, as if that were not American enough, from the words of Jesus Christ. You see, Sinclair was among a large number of socialists of the day who were great admirers of the "workingman of Nazareth." Sinclair described Christ as a "founder of socialism, a tramp and an outcast" and the man who imbibed him with "the spirit of social revolution" as a child.[9]

Besides influencing tens of thousands of Americans with their literary works and speeches, London and Sinclair took the lead in 1905 of establishing the Intercollegiate Socialists Society. Its purpose was to "promote an intelligent interest in Socialism among college men and women ... by the formation of Study Chapters in universities, colleges and high schools; by furnishing speakers, and placing standard Socialist books and periodicals in college libraries and reading rooms."[10]

Among the prominent New York leftist intellectuals who were present at the founding were the already famous attorney Clarence Darrow and William English Walling, who was a wealthy labor reformer and husband of the reportedly beautiful and vivacious feminist Anna Strunsky. She had previously been involved romantically with London, and her description of him after his death provides a valuable insight into the seriousness with which these folks viewed themselves and their socialist project.

> He is the outgrowth of the struggle and the suffering of the Old Order, and he is the strength and the virtue of all its terrible and criminal vices. He came out of the Abyss in which millions of his generation and the generation preceding him throughout time have been hopelessly lost. He rose out of the Abyss, and he escaped from the Abyss to become as large as the race and to be identified with the forces that shape the future of mankind ... Napoleon and Nietzsche had a part in him, but his Nietzschean philosophy became transmuted into Socialism—the movement of his time—and it was by the force of his Napoleonic temperament that he conceived the idea of an incredible success, and had the will to achieve it.[11]

While London did not go down in the history books as a peer of either Napoleon or Nietzsche, his part in the founding of the ISS was significant in the history of the Left in America. In fact, the importance of this organization to the overwhelming success that the Left enjoyed in the United States throughout the twentieth century cannot be overstated.

For starters, it provided the growing ranks of young leftist intellectuals in the nation's leading colleges and universities with a formal organization within which to develop and proselytize their socialist beliefs to other students. It also garnered them the intellectual and monetary support of an impressive array of benefactors and advisers, which was helpful in getting their local campus groups approved by the college administrators who were initially wary of their socialist roots.

Moreover, it created a powerful social network that allowed fellow travelers to identify and to assist each other after they left the academy and went forth to become the backbone not only of the progressive movement but also of Franklin Roosevelt's New Deal. Probably more importantly, it legitimized the discussion and study of socialism in the academy, which cleared the way for schools and departments to hire socialist professors.

3.   The third group of progressives consisted of the writers for the highly popular newspapers and magazines that fanned the flames of reform by exposing all manner of corruption, greed, and evil that they had uncovered in their investigative pieces. In a temporary fit of anger, Teddy Roosevelt, himself a leading reformer, branded these writers muckrakers. The reference was to the man in Bunyan's *Pilgrim's Progress* who was so engrossed with muckraking straws, small sticks, and dust from floor that he "could look no way but downward" toward earthly things, which, "when they are with power upon men's minds, quite carry their hearts away from God."[12] Teddy meant the term as a pejorative, but it quickly became a badge of honor for the journalists themselves.

McClure's Magazine led the way with articles beginning in October 1902 by Teddy's friend Lincoln Steffens, who wrote about corruption in city governments. Then there was Ida Tarbell, who focused on the evils of Standard Oil and John D. Rockefeller; Ray Stannard Baker, who specialized in financial corruption in the railroads and other enterprises, as well as racial lynchings in the South;

and David Graham Phillips, who wrote about corruption in the US Senate.

Of course, these journalists did not intend to provide a balanced look at the situation in question. Instead, they wanted to attract readers, and as such, the more sensational they were, the better. Not surprisingly, the quality varied widely. In fact, some were as fraudulent and intellectually corrupt as the stuff they claimed to be exposing. It is probably fair to say, however, that they served a legitimate social purpose.

Our interest in the subject focuses on a very specific conflict between the ideology of the Right and the Left that captured national attention via Tarbell's best-selling book, *The History of the Standard Oil Company*, which appeared in a nineteen-part series in *McClure's* between November 1902 and October 1904.

Her complaint centered on the unfairness of the fact that in a highly competitive marketplace some businesses are destined to fail. One of these was her father's oil operation, which fell at the hands of Standard Oil. The facts were quite simple. There were twenty-six refineries in Cleveland. Some three-quarters of them were very small. The competition was fierce. Rockefeller began to buy them out. According to Rockefeller, most were happy to sell because the price was fair and they were not performing well. Tarbell was off-put by the pain endured by those that felt they had to sell their business. She put it this way:

> The thing which a man has begun, cared for, led to a healthy life, from which he has begun to gather fruit, which he knows he can make greater and richer, he loves as he does his life. It is one of the fruits of his life. He is jealous of it—wishes the honor of it, will not divide it with another. He can suffer heavily by his own mistakes, learn from them, correct them. He can fight opposition, bear all—so long as the work is his. There were refiners in 1875 who loved their business in this way. Why one should love an oil refinery

the outsider may not see; but to the man who had begun with one still and had seen it grow by his own energy and intelligence to 10, who now sold 500 barrels a day where he once sold five, the refinery was the dearest spot on earth save his home. He walked with pride among its evil-smelling places, watched the processes with eagerness, experimented with joy and recounted triumphantly every improvement. To ask such a man to give up his refinery was to ask him to give up the thing which, after his family, meant most in life to him.[13]

This was, of course, an old complaint reminiscent of the opening days of the industrial revolution in England when the English Luddites made the same argument because they were losing their jobs to the advent of new technology in the textile industry. However, Ida would have none of this. In her eyes, her father was a victim of evil and that was all there was to it. Moreover, the perpetrator of that evil was John D. Rockefeller himself.

Her problem was twofold. First, there was very little legal ground upon which to base her attack. Congress had attempted to address this issue in 1890 with the Sherman Antitrust Act. However, this law was extremely vague and subject to a variety of interpretations. This left her with having to claim that his actions were, as noted above, evil rather than illegal. The problem here was that there were no outward signs that Rockefeller was an inherently evil person.

Indeed, Tarbell herself had to admit that he was a "good man" when measured against essentially all the Western standards of human behavior and virtue by which Christians had traditionally calculated their chances of enjoying a heavenly afterlife. She put it this way:

There was no more faithful Baptist in Cleveland than he. Every enterprise of that church he had supported liberally from his youth. He gave to its poor. He visited its sick. He wept with its suffering. Moreover, he gave unostentatiously to many outside charities of whose worthiness he was satisfied. He was simple and frugal in his habits. He never went to the theatre, never drank wine. He gave much time to the training of his children, seeking to develop in them his own habits of economy and of charity.

The result was she had to base her attack on the alleged presence within this man who had bested her father of a hidden, but deep-seated and dark disdain for both justice and popular opinion, coupled with overwhelming greed. To wit:

Yet he was willing to strain every nerve to obtain for himself special and unjust privileges from the railroads which were bound to ruin every man in the oil business not sharing them with him. He was willing to array himself against the combined better sentiment of a whole industry, to oppose a popular movement aimed at righting an injustice, so revolting to one's sense of fair play as that of railroad discriminations. Religious emotion and sentiments of charity, propriety, and self-denial seem to have taken the place in him of notions of justice and regard for the rights of others.[14]

Unfortunately for Rockefeller, a large number of Americans who were adversely affected by the massive social and economic changes that had been brought on by advances in technology, transportation, and manufacturing practices were looking for someone to blame, and Tarbell had served one such person up on a platter. Not surprisingly, they then lumped in all the other "crooked, rich bastards" with him, and suddenly the fights between the Right and Left became highly personal.

4. The fourth group consisted of a highly influential crowd of advocates of applied eugenics. As noted earlier, while the Fabians were intensely interested in eugenics as a means of creating a more perfect society, they were never successful in actually implementing any of their schemes. America's progressives had no such problem. Indeed, there was no place in their "utopia" for the "physically impaired" and the "feeble-minded" and they sought their removal with the kind of zeal that would not be duplicated until the Nazis came upon the scene several decades later.

5. Finally, we come to the fifth, most important and powerful element within the progressive movement. These were the followers of the so-called Social Gospel. They were the spawn of the Second Great Awakening, the folks who moved socialism from the streets into the centers of power by demanding, *in God's name*, that the federal government get intimately involved in the various reforms that the above-mentioned groups were advocating. These included but were not limited to poverty, alcoholism, crime, racial tensions, slums, and child labor. Oddly enough, despite their alleged dedication to Christian principles, many of them were also members of the above-cited eugenics crowd.

By far the most important Social Gospel member was Richard Ely. He was a prominent postmillennialist intellectual and a founder of the Christian Social Union of the Episcopal Church. He also just happened to be one of those previously mentioned economists who had studied in Germany, where he had become enamored with the Bismarckian welfare state and imbued with the pro-statists, anti-laissez-faire economics of Bismarck's "socialist of the chair," Gustav Schmoller's Historical School of Economics. Naturally then, he also subscribed to the dual notions that, in his own words, "God works through the states to carry out his purposes more universally than through any other institution" and that "Christianity which is not practical is not Christianity at all."[15]

This is a new twist for the Left. Yes, the Germans and the English had laid the foundations for the welfare state. But both did it as a means of combating socialism, and neither claimed that their newly found, governmental generosity had anything to do with Jesus Christ. Indeed, as we noted earlier in our comments about Pope Pius IX, Christianity in Europe had been engaged in an all-out war with communism and socialism for over a half a century, which had reached a pivotal point when the Danish philosopher and theologian Søren Aabye Kierkegaard expressed his concern that secular humanism would change the focus of Christianity away from God and toward the interests of mankind.

In any case, as a Professor of Economics at Johns Hopkins from 1881 to 1892, Ely drilled this drivel into hundreds of students including, most notably, Woodrow Wilson, whose ham-handed government-led intrusions into the economy and messianic approach to the presidency are easily traceable to his days as an Ely understudy. After leaving Hopkins, Ely spent thirty-three years at the University of Wisconsin, where he founded a new School of Economics, Political Science, and History. This served as the brain trust behind the state's governor Robert M. La Follette, who became such a powerhouse in the progressive movement that a 1982 survey of historians ranked him as tied for first place with Henry Clay as one of the greatest senators in US history.

Ely became acquainted with Teddy Roosevelt during this period and was fond of telling that once after a banquet in Madison, when someone "started to introduce me to Roosevelt," the president said, in the presence of all these people, "I know Dr. Ely. He first introduced me to radicalism in economics and then he made me sane in my radicalism."[16]

It was at Hopkins in 1885 that Ely began the above-noted assault on capitalism by joining with two other German-educated American economists in founding the American Economic Association, which he modeled on Schmoller's *Verein für Sozialpolitik*. His partners in this enterprise were John Bates Clark and Henry Carter Adams, both of whom had grown up in evangelical Protestant families. Adams was a professor at Cornell. Clark was a professor at Smith. It is worth noting here that the list of members of the first council of this group includes Woodrow Wilson, who, as a student of Ely's, wrote a paper supporting the notion that the Social Gospel could be used to find a happy medium between laissez-faire and socialism. The new Association's statement of principles put it this way:

> We regard the state as an educational and ethical agency whose positive aid is an indispensable condition of human progress. While we recognize the necessity of individual initiative in industrial life, we hold that the doctrine of laissez-faire is unsafe in politics and unsound in morals; and that it suggests an inadequate explanation of the relations between the state and the citizens ... We hold that the conflict of labour and capital has brought to the front a vast number of social problems whose solution is impossible without the united efforts of Church, State, and Science.[17]

Ely himself put it this way in a paper entitled "The Past and the Present of Political Economy."

> This younger political economy [the Historic School] no longer permits the science [of economics] to be used as a tool in the hands of the greedy and the avaricious for keeping down and oppressing the laboring classes. It does not acknowledge laissez-faire as an excuse for doing nothing while people starve, nor allow the all-sufficiency of competition as a plea for grinding the poor. It denotes a return to the grand principle of common sense and Christian precept. Love, generosity, nobility of character, self-sacrifice, and all that is best and truest in our nature have their place in economic life. For economists of

the Historical School, *the political economy of the present* [emphasis in original], recognize with Thomas Hughes that "we have all to learn somehow or other that the first duty of man in trade, as in other departments of human employment, is to follow the Golden Rule 'Do unto others as ye would that others should do unto you.'"[18]

Now, it is necessary to note here that laissez-faire was one of the most important pillars of the nineteenth-century view of economics, sociology, and even the culture of America. History professor Sidney Fine put it this way in his comprehensive history of the subject *Laissez Faire and the General-Welfare State*:

From 1865 to 1885 political economy and laissez-faire were virtually synonymous in the United States. Orthodoxy required that an economist be a believer in laissez-faire and in free trade; and as one economist declared, orthodoxy was the criterion to distinguish good and bad. If you were held to be unorthodox, it was a terrible indictment.

Moreover, most advocates of laissez-faire were as quick as Ely to defend their position by claiming that God was on their side. For example, the well-known businessman and economist Edward Atkinson noted that "there must be a higher law" that is "steadily, surely, and slowly working to the benefit of the great mass of the people ... slowly but surely securing to them ... a constantly larger and increasing share of a larger and larger annual product." Harvard economist Francis Bowen stated that laissez-faire means "things regulate themselves ... which means, of course, that God regulates them by his general laws, which always, in the long run, work to the good."

Julian M. Sturtevant, the founder and president of Illinois College, argued that the domain of economics was being "pervaded by all the contingencies which arise from human legislation, and human ignorance and folly," the consequence of which were "disasters, miseries and confusions," resulting from the violation of natural law.[19]

B. E. Fernow, a founder of the US Forest Service, explained the laissez-faire position as follows in a speech before the American Association for the Advancement of Science entitled "The Providential Functions of Government with Special Reference to Natural Resources."

> "The individualist ... will insist ... that this object, the good of the nation, is obtained by inactivity rather than by active exertion by the government, by allowing the individuals to work out their own salvation (or damnation) amid the free and unrestricted play of natural forces, rather than by making them do so. *Laissez-faire* instead of *faire-marcher!*" [emphasis in the original][20]

Moreover, not only was Adam Smith's "invisible hand" a staple of economic wisdom at the time, but Spencer's interpretation of Darwin's discoveries had added considerably to the appeal of the notion that the best approach to business was to let the big dog run.

Finally, a host of new theories involving mathematics and probability put the frosting on the laissez-faire cake. Now, a thorough exploration of these new mathematical theories is beyond the scope of this book. However, a brief review will help to provide an understanding of the widespread support for laissez-faire economics at the time and therefore the remarkability of Ely et al.'s successful attack on it.

We will begin this examination with the great French polymath Pierre-Simon Laplace, who is described in the Ninth Edition of the *Encyclopedia Britannica* as "one of the greatest mathematicians and physical astronomers who ever lived."[21] He was a protégé of d'Alembert, a professor at the École Militaire, where one of his students was Napoleon, and became a member of the French *Académie des sciences* at the age of twenty-four. His discoveries were legion. Our interest focuses on the one that became known as Laplace's Demon, described by the great Stephen Hawking in a lecture entitled "Does God Play Dice?" as the first publicly expressed idea of scientific determinism.[22]

As described by Louis Menand in his Pulitzer Prize–winning book, *The Metaphysical Club*, this theory held that "every event, including the actions of human beings, is the singular and inevitable consequence of a chain of antecedent events in which chance does not play a role."[23] Menand explains the significance of this to our particular interest as follows:

> In short, Laplace extended the application of probability from physics to people, with the promise that events that seem random and unpredictable … can be shown to obey hidden laws. People marry and letters get misaddressed for apparently subjective and unreproducible reasons, but statistics reveals that the total number of marriages or of dead letters every year gravitates, as if by necessity, around a mean value. The consistency of that value, Laplace thought, signified the operation of a natural law. "All events, even those which, by their insignificance, seem not to follow the great laws of nature, follow them as necessarily as the revolutions of the sun."[24]

Laplace's work inspired a Belgium sociologist named Adolphe Quetelet to apply statistical data to his discipline. In 1835, he published a two-volume work in which he noted that such things as crime, marriage, and suicide rates follow regular patterns, year in and year out, and from this, he posited the existence of social laws that are just as determinate as the law of gravity. For example, per Menand:

> "Man is born, grows up, and dies according to certain laws, which have never been studied," Quetelet began, and he printed a table showing that the annual number of murders reported in

France from 1826 to 1831 was relatively constant. This was not, perhaps, an unexpected finding. But Quetelet's table also showed that the proportion of murders committed with guns each year was also relatively constant, as were the proportions of murders committed using swords, knives, canes, stones, cutting and stabbing instruments, kicks and punches, strangulation, drowning, and fire. He concluded that although we may not know who will kill whom by what means, we do know, with a high degree of probability, that a certain number of murders of a certain type will happen every year in France.[25]

From this, he concluded:

> People who murder—like people who marry and people who commit suicide—are only fulfilling a quota that has been preset by social conditions.[26]

This brings us to the British historian Henry Thomas Buckle, whom Menand describes as Quetelet's "most zealous British disciple." In 1857, Buckle wrote his *History of Civilization in England*, which he described as the first history "written from an entirely statistical point of view."[27] Reflecting Quetelet's influence, Buckle's most notable conclusion was that the course of human progress is governed by laws as fixed and regular as those in the physical world.

We need not dwell on the complex, and some would say wacky, machinations by which he reached his conclusions. Simply stated, he claimed that the combination of climate, soil, food, and the "General Aspect of Nature" consorted to make Europe the only place on earth where man had, in the words of Menand, "really succeeded in taming the energies of nature, bending them to his own will, turning them aside from their ordinary course, and compelling them to minister to his happiness, and subserve the general purposes of human life."[28]

In case you're wondering why any of this matters, it is because the combined works of Smith, Laplace, Quetelet, and Darwin made it, according to Menand, "tempting to conclude that the world must be set up in such a way that things regulate themselves. And this was taken to confer a kind of cosmic seal of approval on the political doctrines of individualism and laissez-faire."[29] Buckle said this about that: "The great enemy of civilization is the protective spirit; by which I mean the notion that society cannot prosper unless the affairs of life are watched over and protected at nearly every turn by the state and the church."[30] So it was widely believed.

E. L. Godkin led the initial defense of traditional, laissez-faire economics against the assault by Ely and other members of the AEA. He was an Irish-born journalist who founded *The Nation*, was editor in chief of the *New York Evening Post*, and was one of most influential journalists of his day. William James said this of him:

> To my generation, he was certainly the towering influence in all thought concerning public affairs and indirectly his influence has certainly been more persuasive than that of any other writer of his generation, for he influenced other writers, who never quoted him, and determined the whole current of discussion.[31]

In *The Reconstruction of American Liberalism, 1865–1914*, Nancy Cohen said this about him and his defense of laissez-faire economics.

> Godkin, who had been attacking the German historical school since 1875 for "strengthening and diffusing amongst the vast mass of ignorant and unreflecting men who are now coming into possession of political power all over the world, the notion that wonderful changes may be effected in the conditions of human existence by the vigorous use of govern-

mental machinery," was alert to Ely's importation of the suspect theories. The review he solicited of Ely ... concluded that the German school economics was ... worthless."[32]

As a sign of the seriousness with which conservatives took the threat against laissez-faire, William Graham Sumner joined Godkin's crusade. He was another very big gun. He had been a professor of sociology at Yale for twelve years, during which time he had established himself as one of that college's most popular and influential professors, as the nation's leading opponent of socialism and imperialism, and as a staunch, unflinching proponent of Spencer's theory of the survival of the fittest. He put it this way:

> The fact that a man is here is no demand upon other people that they shall keep him alive and sustain him. He has got to fight the battle with nature as every other man has; and if he fights it with the same energy and enterprise and skill and industry as any other man, I cannot imagine his failing—that is misfortune apart.[33]

And this:

> Let every man be sober, industrious, prudent, and wise, and bring up his children to be so likewise, and poverty will be abolished in a few generation."[34]

The support of laissez-faire by Godkin, Sumner, et al. was reasonably successful in the short run. Ely, Adams, and many of their proto-socialist colleagues were either removed from their teaching posts or retained after heated fights that often ended in their being forced to disavow their public declarations of sympathy for socialism. However, these pietistic and socialistic economists managed to hang in there, as saying goes, and eventually to gain recognition for their socialist views of economics within the academy and within the profession.

In fact, they played a decisive role in the crucial deliberations that were beginning to take place over the government's responsibilities in the newly emerging industrial economy. And it was these deliberations that, in the words of Cohen, *set the boundaries of acceptable debate, especially about socialism, collectivism, and democratic collective action, on the cusp of the era when new liberalism, progressivism, and socialism were about to sweep transatlantic politics.*[35] [Emphasis added]

There are numerous reasons for the success of the anti-laissez-faire crowd, but one, posited by Merand, is worth keeping in mind as we move on to a discussion of the battles between the Right and the Left in the years to come. To wit:

> After all, which assumption offers a more promising basis for a field of inquiry: the assumption that societies develop according to underlying laws whose efficiency cannot be improved by public policies, or the assumption that societies are multivariable organisms whose progress can be guided by scientific intelligence? Professions come into existence because there is a demand for expertise. The expertise required to repeat, in every situation, "Let the market decide" (or as Sumner liked to say, "Root, hog, or die) is not great.[36]

Let's let the poets in on the fun.

> On the Big Rock Candy Mountain
> On a summer day in the month of May a burly bum came
>   hiking
> Down a shady lane through the sugar cane, he was looking
>   for his liking.

405

As he roamed along he sang a song of the land of milk and
honey
Where a bum can stay for many a day, and he won't need
any money
Oh the buzzin' of the bees in the <u>cigarette</u> trees near the
soda water fountain,
At the lemonade springs where the <u>bluebird</u> sings on the
Big Rock Candy Mountains
There's a lake of <u>gin</u> we can both jump in, and the hand-
outs grow on bushes
In the new-mown hay we can sleep all day, and the bars all
have free lunches
Where the mail train stops and there ain't no cops, and the
folks are tender-hearted
Where you never change your socks and you never throw
rocks,
And your hair is never parted
Oh the buzzin' of the bees in the cigarette trees near the
soda water fountain,
At the lemonade springs where the bluebird sings on the
Big Rock Candy Mountains
Oh, a farmer and his son, they were on the run, to the hay
field they were bounding
Said the bum to the son, "Why don't you come to the big
rock candy mountains?"
So the very next day they hiked away, the mileposts they
were counting
But they never arrived at the lemonade tide, on the Big
Rock Candy Mountains
Oh the buzzin' of the bees in the cigarette trees near the
soda water fountain,
At the lemonade springs where the bluebird sings on the
Big Rock Candy Mountains
One evening as the sun went down and the jungle fires
were burning,

Down the track came a hobo hiking, and he said "Boys,
     I'm not turning."
"I'm heading for a land that's far away beside the crystal
     fountains;"
"So come with me, we'll go and see the Big Rock Candy
     Mountains."
In the Big Rock Candy Mountains, there's a land that's fair
     and bright,
The handouts grow on bushes and you sleep out every
     night
Where the boxcars all are empty and the sun shines every
     day
On the birds and the bees and the cigarette trees,
The lemonade springs where the bluebird sings
In the Big Rock Candy Mountains
In the Big Rock Candy Mountains, all the cops have
     wooden legs
And the bulldogs all have rubber teeth and the hens lay
     soft-boiled eggs
The farmer's trees are full of fruit and the barns are full of
     hay
Oh I'm bound to go where there ain't no snow
Where the rain don't fall, the wind don't blow
In the Big Rock Candy Mountains
In the Big Rock Candy Mountains, you never change your
     socks
And little streams of *alcohol* come a-trickling down the
     rocks
The brakemen have to tip their hats and the railroad bulls
     are blind
There's a lake of stew and of *whiskey* too
And you can paddle all around 'em in a big canoe
In the Big Rock Candy Mountains
In the Big Rock Candy Mountains the jails are made of
     tin,
And you can walk right out again as soon as you are in

There ain't no short-handled shovels, no axes, saws or
    picks,
I'm a-goin' to stay where you sleep all day
Where they hung the jerk that invented work
In the Big Rock Candy Mountains
Harry "Haywire Mac" McClintock, 1920s

Chapter 16

Teddy's Medicine Show

In a fair distribution among a vast multitude, none can have much. That class of dependant pensioners called the rich is so extremely small that if all their throats were cut, and a distribution made of all they consume in a year, it would not give a bit of bread and cheese for one night's supper to those who labour, and who in reality feed both the pensioners and themselves. But the throats of the rich ought not to be cut, nor their magazines plundered; because, in their persons they are trustees for those who labour, and their hoards are the bankinghouses of these latter. Whether they mean it or not, they do, in effect, execute their trust—some with more, some with less fidelity and judgment. But on the whole, the duty is performed, and everything returns, deducting some very trifling commission and discount, to the place from whence it arose. When the poor rise to destroy the rich, they act as wisely for their own purposes as when they burn mills, and throw corn into the river, to make bread cheap. ... A perfect equality will indeed be produced; that is to say, equal want, equal wretchedness, equal beggary, and on the part of the partitioners, a woeful, helpless, and desperate disappointment. Such is the event of all compulsory equalizations. They pull down what is above. They never raise what is below: and they depress high and low together beneath the level of what was originally the lowest. (Edmund Burke, "Thoughts and Details on Scarcity," 1795)

It may seem odd from the perspective of the twenty-first century, but in the closing decade of the nineteenth century, the federal government had little direct interest in the day-to-day affairs of its citizens. There were no Departments of Commerce, Labor, Health and Human Services, Education, Energy, Housing, or Transportation. There was no OSHA, FBI, CIA, FEMA, or any of the thousands of lesser federal agencies, departments, offices, and bureaus that monitor and control virtually all aspects of the lives of Americans today.

To put a human face on this observation, we would simply note that in 1889 the South Fork Dam in Johnstown, Pennsylvania, collapsed, killing 2,209 people. Ninety-nine entire families died in the flood, including 396 children. One hundred twenty-four women and 198 men were widowed, ninety-eight children were orphaned. One-third of the dead, 777 people, were never identified. It was the worst flood to hit the US in the nineteenth century. Sixteen hundred homes were destroyed, $17 million in property damage levied, and four square miles of downtown Johnstown were completely destroyed.

Cleanup operations continued for years. Americans mobilized to help the victims. Food, clothing, medicine, and other provisions began arriving by rail. At its peak, the army of relief workers totaled about seven thousand. As for the Federal government's role, President Benjamin Harrison issued a statement of sympathy and prayer for the victims, and called for the establishment of a committee to "to speedily collect contributions of food in order that a train loaded with provisions might be dispatched to-night or in the early morning to these sufferers" and "to collect from your citizens such articles of clothing, especially bedclothing, as can be spared." He added that "now that the summer season is on, there can hardly be many households in Washington that cannot spare a blanket or a coverlid for the relief of the suffering ones."

In conclusion, he said the following: "As a temporary citizen of Washington it would give me great satisfaction if the national capital should so generously respond to this call of our distressed fellow-citizens as to be conspicuous among the cities of the land for its ample and generous answer ... on being first apprised of the need at Johnstown, I telegraphed to the mayor of that city my subscription."

In other words, the "total state" had not yet come into existence. That being the state that, several decades later, the German political economist Carl Schmitt would describe as one that "no longer knows anything absolutely nonpolitical." By which he meant, the state whose interests extend far beyond the mere protection of the property and lives of its citizens but has become a participant in the domestic disputes over the dreams, schemes, emotions, attitudes, and political health of its various partners in governance.[1]

Of course, this happy situation couldn't last. As already noted, the nation was experiencing severe growing pains related primarily to industrialization, urbanization, immigration, and corruption in government, which was prodigious and widespread. This was, after all, the Gilded Age, a term coined by Mark Twain meaning that it glittered on the surface but was deeply corrupt underneath. The most visible corruption was centered in the large cities, where political machines, like New York's Tammany Hall, were hotbeds of graft and outright theft. Naturally, center stage of this circus featured the federal government's role in dealing with these problems.

And who better to occupy center stage than Theodore Roosevelt, who became president of the United States upon the death of McKinley? Teddy was not just a progressive. In fact, he had been a key player in the reformist, anticorruption wing of the Republican Party for sixteen years, beginning when he became a member of the New York State Assembly at the age of twenty-four. More recently, as governor of New York, he had been so enthusiastic about cleaning up the state's corrupt political machine that the state's Republican Party boss, Senator Thomas Platt, had contrived to get him out of town by putting him on the ticket as President William McKinley's vice president in the 1900 election.

Ohio Senator Mark Hanna, who was McKinley's chief political adviser as well as chairman of the Republican National Committee, had been adamantly opposed to Roosevelt for a variety of reasons, including Teddy's reformist bent, which the establishment wing of the party detested. Hanna, after all, was a wealthy industrialist and a friend of John D. Rockefeller, whose Standard Oil Company had contributed $250,000 to the McKinley's campaign in 1896, which was equal to half of all Democratic contributions.[2]

Teddy was not certain he wanted the job, anyway, but when he got to the convention, the challenge of gaining it was too much to resist. Two famous quotes tell the tale. The first is from Secretary of State John Hay in a letter to a friend:

> Teddy has been here [at the convention], have you heard of it? It was more a fun than a goat. He came down with a somber resolution thrown on his strenuous brow to let McKinley and Hanna know once for all that he would not be Vice-President, and found to his stupefaction that nobody in Washington, except Platt, had ever dreamed of such a thing.[3]

The second is from Hanna:

> "Don't any of you realize that there's only one life between that madman and the Presidency?"[4]

As fate would have it, that "one life" was snuffed out on September 14, 1901, a date that should be noted on the timeline of the march of Left across the globe as prominently as the storming of the Bastille on July 14, 1789, and Lenin's arrival at Finland Station on April 3, 1917.

Why? Well, to be specific, Teddy's assault on the constitutional limits that the founding fathers placed on the executive branch would pave the way for turning the Office of the Presidency into a left-wing bastion of political overreach. Among other things:

- He coined the platitudes and gave the speeches that helped to convince the American public to sacrifice their precious freedom for the warm feeling that comes from having a "big brother" in Washington looking after their welfare.
- His misguided and corrupt "trust busting" fostered the federal government's massive intrusion into the business world, which led to the development of the largest, most inefficient and corrupt "trust" that the world has ever known. That being the US corporatist state, in which the government and big business collude to pursue ends that eschew competition, promote corruption, and impinge on traditional American freedoms.
- His peevish, sanctimonious railing against the "evil men of wealth" introduced the concept of class warfare into a land that had theretofore been largely free of this centerpiece of leftist ideology.

Now it is worth noting that Teddy did not set out to do any of these things, at least not specifically. Yes, he was a "progressive" and a "reformer." However, these were mutable terms at the time. That is, they did not bring to mind a clearly defined system of ideas, manifesto, or menu of goals, and certainly no grand and all-encompassing blueprint for action. In short, he was not an advocate of a canned ideology. His early ideas did not come from reading socialist tracts, from an enthusiastic commitment to the Social Gospel, from divine intervention, from any overriding concern for the working poor or the conditions of the immigrants, from anger at the ruling classes, or from any overarching loathing of big businesses or trusts.

He was an all-American boy who loved his country. He loved life. He meant well. He came from a rich family. He was a Harvard grad, a boxer, a hunter, a cowboy, a war hero, a corruption fighter, and a family man. He was nonpartisan when it came to labor disputes.

Indeed, to paraphrase the Wizard of Oz, a fictional contemporary of Teddy's, he was a very good man, he was just a very bad president.

His muse was his gigantic ego. He was a combination of a snake oil salesman, Meredith Wilson's Professor Harold Hill (another fictional contemporary), and Don Quixote. He was there to solve all the problems that were vexing folks, and a few more that they did not even know existed.

One of Teddy's finest biographers, Kathleen Dalton, maintains that he styled himself after the heroes in the books he read as a youth, men like James Fenimore Cooper's Leatherstocking and Francis Parkman's brave pioneers. To further illustrate this point, she comments favorably on Mark Twain's characterization of Teddy as suffering from "the Sir Walter disease," a reference to his "eagerness to emulate the knights of yore," as described by Sir Walter Scott. "He cast himself in heroic roles again and again," she notes, constantly "associating his own crusades with the heroics of Washington, Jackson, and Lincoln" and arguing that public service required a "healthy combativeness."[5]

When he was going after corruption in New York, he could do little harm. That kind of corruption was easy to identify, and the various cures available were tried and true. Suddenly, however, when he woke up one day as president of the United States, a veritable fairyland of new problems appeared as if out of nowhere. Moreover, the presidency provided him a big stick, much like Merlin's staff, with which to attack them.

His friend, the then well-known muckraker Lincoln Steffens, was one of the first individuals to visit him after he became president. He described his and Teddy's excitement at prospects for the future this way:

> So we reformers were up in the air when President McKinley was shot, took our bearings, and flew straight to our first president, T.R. And he understood, he shared, our joy ... His offices were crowded with people, mostly reformers, all day long. ... He strode triumphant around

among us, talking and shaking hands, dictating
and signing letters, and laughing. Washington,
the whole country, was in mourning, and no
doubt the President felt he should hold himself
down; he didn't; he tried to but his joy showed
in every word and movement. ... With his feet,
his fists, his face and his free words, he laughed at
his luck. He laughed at the rage of Boss Platt and
at the tragic disappointment of Mark Hanna ...
And he laughed with glee at the power and place
that had come to him.[6]

Now, most of the "problems" Teddy went after were little more
than growing pains that would have been resolved without doing
damage to the Constitution by a combination of the passing of time
and the actions of the nation's citizens themselves, the state governments, and the marketplace. Others were products of his quixotic
need for evil foes to slay.

Making matters worse, his overweening hubris rendered him
incapable of ascribing wisdom to the thoughts of anyone but himself, which diminished the mollifying effects of such niceties as the
Constitution's system of checks and balances, concern over setting
dangerous precedents, and the possibility of creating secondary and
tertiary problems that would prove worse than the original one. The
Spanish philosopher Ortega y Gasset provided an apt description of
Teddy's type some years later when he spoke of the "average man
who has learned to use much of the machinery of civilization, but
who is characterized by root-ignorance of the very principles of that
civilization."[7]

He opened his presidential tent show less than three months
into his presidency with an impassioned twenty-thousand-word message to Congress. In acknowledgment of a promise he had made to
Hanna to "go slow," he began with an obvious attempt to put his
Republican colleagues at ease by praising the glories of capitalism and
liberty in a way that Adam Smith himself would have found encouraging. He congratulated the "nation" for its "present abounding pros-

perity." He gave a big pat on the back to the "captains of industry who have driven the railway systems across this continent, who have built up our commerce, who have developed our manufactures, have on the whole done great good to our people." Without them, he said, "the material development of which we are so justly proud could never have taken place." Moreover, he said that Americans should recognize how important it is that we leave "as unhampered as is compatible with the public good the strong and forceful men upon whom the success of business operations inevitably rests."

In fact, he said, "the mechanism of modern business is so delicate that extreme care must be taken not to interfere with it in a spirit of rashness or ignorance." Then he added that "in facing new industrial conditions, the whole history of the world shows that legislation will generally be both unwise and ineffective unless undertaken after calm inquiry and with sober self-restraint." As for the workers themselves, he stated that their welfare must "rest on individual thrift and energy, resolution, and intelligence."

But then ... but then ... he woefully declared that all was not just ducky in the land of the free; that they, his fellow Americans, had trouble, trouble, my friends, I say trouble right here in America. Moreover, these were not ordinary troubles. No sir! They were big troubles, terrible, terrible, troubles, with a capital *T*, and it rhymes with *C*, and it stands for the Constitution. Yes, my friends, the Constitution of the United States of America was sadly out of date.

You see, he explained to the poor suckers in his audience, when the founding fathers wrote that document, they mistakenly "accepted as a matter of course that the several States were the proper authorities to regulate, so far as was then necessary, the comparatively insignificant and strictly localized corporate bodies of the day."

Of course, this was a forgivable error on their part, Teddy graciously and condescendingly admitted. After all, he said, "No human wisdom could foretell the sweeping changes, alike in industrial and political conditions, which were to take place by the beginning of the twentieth century." However, it was a shortfall nevertheless, and he was there to remedy it. "The conditions today are wholly different and wholly different action is called for," he said. "The old laws, and the old customs which had almost the binding force of law" are no longer sufficient "to regulate the accumulation and distribution of wealth."

To be more specific, he claimed that there was "widespread conviction" among the American people that "certain features and tendencies" of the "great corporations known as trusts" were "hurtful to the general welfare." He did not say explicitly whether he agreed with this claim, but he carefully noted that it did not spring from envy, uncharitableness, or ignorance on the part of the people, nor "from lack of pride in the great industrial achievements that have placed this country at the head of the nations struggling for commercial supremacy." It was based, he said, "upon sincere conviction that combination and concentration should be, not prohibited, but supervised and within reasonable limits controlled; and in my judgment this conviction is right."

Obviously, someone had to accomplish this purpose that "the people" had identified. And who better than he? For starters, he said, the country needed a new law that would, "without interfering with the power of the States in the matter itself," give the federal government "the power of supervision and regulation over all corporations doing an interstate business." And if such a law were to be found unconstitutional, he stated that "a constitutional amendment should be submitted to confer the power."

With this new power in hand, he said, "Artificial bodies, such as corporations and joint stock or other associations, depending upon any statutory law for their existence or privileges, should be subject to proper governmental supervision, and full and accurate information as to their operations should be made public regularly at reasonable intervals ... the Government should have the right to inspect and examine the workings of the great corporations engaged in interstate business."[8]

Now a careful reading of this speech reveals that nowhere did Teddy specify the exact nature of the "problems" that the trusts had supposedly created. He used phrases such as "crimes of cunning," "real and grave evils," "hurtful to the general welfare," "working to the public injury," and "baleful consequences." Yet he provided no specific examples of either the crimes or the victims. He said only that the government should "bring to light the issues" involving these trusts. Then, he prejudged these issues by stating that the study would have to "determine what remedies are needed" to address them.

Presumably, Teddy did not think that a discussion of the "problems" themselves was necessary. After all, when there is "widespread conviction," attention must be paid. Yet one cannot help but wonder why in a twenty-thousand-word speech filled with dark warnings of egregious harm, this pretentious blowhard did not choose to wave the bloody shirt of at least one poor victim of this evil.

We can only speculate. Yet it is worth noting that one of the "problems" that the trusts created was actually lower prices, brought on by a combination of intense competition and the extraordinary advances in transportation, technology, and manufacturing practices that were being utilized by the most enterprising of the industrial giants to promote the general welfare of the nation and the consumer. Jim Powell said this about that in his well-documented history, *Bully Boy: The Truth about Theodore Roosevelt's Legacy*:

> Far from being riddled with terrible problems caused by irresponsible, self-serving capitalists, the American economy was among the wonders of the world, a major reason why millions of people left their homes and traveled thousands of miles to pursue the American dream. …
>
> For more than two decades before Roosevelt became president, output had been expanding and prices had been falling—the opposite of what one would expect if there were a lot of monopolies. Despite Roosevelt's allegations about railroad monopolies, in the previous half century railroad mileage in the United States had increased more than 250-fold, and railroad rates were falling. Cheaper railroad rates undermined local monopolies by giving people the choice of buying economically priced goods from far

away. Supporters of antitrust laws pointed to the "great merger wave" of the late 1890s as evidence of monopolization, but in fact, the total the number of commercial and industrial firms in the United States increased from 1.11 million in 1890 to 1.17 million in 1900 and 1.51 million in 1910, according to the U.S. Bureau of the Census. The business failure rate among commercial and industrial firms, and the average liability per failure, actually declined between 1890 and 1910. Contrary to Roosevelt's claims, mounting evidence shows that monopolies are rare in free markets, as changing consumer tastes, changing business conditions, new technologies, and new competitors both foreign and domestic relentlessly challenge established companies.[9]

Of course, Teddy was not about to cite lower prices as the "problem" he intended to solve. Instead, he implied that his concern stemmed from some nonspecific, moral deficiency extant within the "money interests." Yet there was no evidence that Morgan, Rockefeller, Schiff, Harriman, Carnegie, et al. had broken any known "old laws," or "old customs" for that matter, and there was no reason whatsoever to believe that they were not always acting in what they deemed to be the best interests of their country.

Furthermore, Teddy's suggestion that the federal government's involvement in the day-to-day affairs of business would somehow add an element of virtue and competence to the enterprise was laughable. As for virtue, one of the most vociferous charges made by Teddy and his fellow "reformers" was that corruption was rampant within the government of virtually every large city in the country. Moreover, it was no secret that the federal government was a veritable playground for corrupt politicians.

As for the competence angle, just a few years earlier, Morgan had personally saved the nation from bankruptcy that was the direct result of a massive loss of confidence in the federal government to deal with the ongoing depression. Everyone, everywhere, had been trading in dollars for gold. Cleveland had floated two bond issues to help replenish the gold supply, but neither had solved the problem, in part because bankers were buying gold out of one treasury window to pay for the bonds at another. By January 1895, gold was pouring out of the Treasury at such a frightening rate that Cleveland was contemplating a third bond offering to the public, which would also have failed to solve the problem if Morgan had not stepped in to save the damn fools from his ignorance of finance.

Morgan demanded a meeting with Cleveland to explain that an unmediated sale of bonds in the highly distressed economic environment would do little more than recycle gold that was already in the United States. He further pointed out that this was no time for a government-sponsored sale of bonds anyway, noting that he personally knew that a $10 million draft by an unnamed party was about to be presented to the Treasury that very day. This, he said, would send the government into default by 3:00 p.m. since it had only $9 million in gold left in its vaults.

Cleveland reluctantly asked Morgan what he should do. Morgan replied that he would work with the Rothschild's London branch to sell $65 million of US government bonds to European buyers. The government could then use the money to buy 3.5 million ounces of gold, mostly from Europe, thus bringing fresh gold into the country.

According to the historian Thomas Kessner, Cleveland then made the "remarkable request" that Morgan guarantee that the European investors would not simply cash in *their* US securities for American gold to buy the new bond issue. According to Kessner, "backed by a banking empire that spanned two continents, Morgan answered simply, 'Yes, sir.'" He honored this pledge, and through various manipulations of the gold market, the powerful syndicate protected the country from European investors who wished to make quite a profit by selling their bonds back to the United States for gold when the price of the bonds quickly rose from $112.25 to $124.[10]

So here was Teddy, three months into his presidency, casting aspersions at the men who had turned the United States into one of most powerful economic forces in the world less than a half century after an economically devastating civil war that had resulted in the deaths of some 8 percent of the male population. One of whom had personally rescued it from bankruptcy just a few years earlier.

Then, to add insult to injury, on February 18, 1902, just one month after his speech, he filed an antitrust suit against the Northern Securities Company, a railroad trust that Morgan had put together in an attempt to end a bidding war between two railroad barons that Nathan Miller in *Theodore Roosevelt, A Life* described as a "disastrous financial panic."[11]

Of course, Morgan was unhappy. He had had no advance warning of the suit, which he felt was a serious breach of protocol. Moreover, the stock market had plunged on the news. Finally, he had no reason whatsoever to believe that the trust had violated any law or "old custom." And indeed, it had not. In fact, in 1904, the Supreme Court found that Northern had *not* engaged in any behavior that threatened commerce, but it ruled against the merger anyway because it constituted a "future threat" to freedom of commerce, which took the meaning of the law to an entirely new and legally absurd level that Morgan could hardly have anticipated.

In any case, Morgan's immediate concern was that he had recently put together US Steel, the largest company in the entire world with three times the annual revenue of the federal government, and in doing so had greatly increased the efficiency of the American steel industry. Naturally, he was worried about what this upstart president had in mind. Therefore, accompanied by Hanna and New York senator Chauncey Depew, who was also president of the New York Central Railroad, he went to the White House to meet with Teddy and Attorney General Philander Knox to see if they could find common ground.

For what it is worth, Knox was a very successful and wealthy attorney, who had handled high-profile cases and corporate business for Carnegie, Frick, Mellon, and Vanderbilt, and through his relations with Carnegie had been deeply involved with Morgan in putting together US Steel.

The meeting was not friendly. For starters, Morgan was not a hale fellow well-met kind of person. Teddy was bound to show that he could not be cowed by the notoriously intimidating titan of finance. Morgan opened the conversation with the blunt and now famous statement, "If we have done anything wrong, send your man (Knox) to my man (Morgan's lawyer Francis Stetson) and they can fix it up." To which both Teddy and Knox replied. Teddy stating, "That can't be done." And Knox saying, "We don't want to fix it up, we want to stop it." Morgan then asked, "Are you going to attack my others interests, the Steel Trust and others?" Teddy responded, "Certainly not, unless we find out that in any case they have done something that we regard as wrong."[12]

Most historians tend to believe that Teddy won the day. The idea is that his suit against Northern Securities accomplished its purpose, which was to make him a key player in the great world of business and finance. In addition, it increased his popularity with his reformist friends. Morgan, on the other hand, had had to acknowledge that despite all his wealth and influence, the federal government had the power to disrupt his world in a major fashion and that he would seriously have to consider the government's interests in the future. In *Corsair: The Life of J. Pierpont Morgan*, Andrew Sinclair bluntly maintained that Morgan had come out on the short end and was angry about it, that is, "he realized that in the President he had found an adversary more difficult than Cleveland at the end of the gold crisis. The White House people were no longer in his pocket. In fact, he might be in theirs."[13]

Our view is that Morgan actually won, and won big. And the country lost and lost big.

For the fact is, Teddy was way out of his league when he confronted Morgan. Of course, he could not help himself. His ego demanded that he show that he, the "accidental president," could stand toe to toe with the man known in the press as Jupiter. Of course, he believed that he had more than held his own. After the meeting, he told Knox, "Mr. Morgan could not help regarding me as a big rival operator, who either intended to ruin all his interests, or else could be induced to come to an agreement to ruin none."[14] The word for this is hubris, defined as foolish pride, dangerous self-confidence, the absence of humility. Eve suffered from this malady, as have virtually all of history and literature's most famous tragic figures, ranging from Oedipus and Antigone, to Othello and Hamlet, to Willy Loman.

Morgan, you see, was one of the most powerful, intelligent, and influential men in the entire world. He was a colossus, a force of nature. He had achieved this status by brains, courage, determination, and iron will. Henry Clews, the famous author of *Fifty Years on Wall Street*, described him as having "the driving power of a locomotive."[15] Sereno Pratt, editor of the *Wall Street Journal*, saw him as the Napoleon of Finance. Alexander Noyes, financial editor of the *Evening Post*, concluded, "No financial magnet ever occupied so extraordinary a position of prestige throughout all financial communities, home and foreign."[16] Needless to say, Morgan was not only an excellent judge of character but highly skilled at taking advantage of the flaws he uncovered in other men, and he saw many such flaws in Teddy that day.

Prior to their meeting, Morgan's interest in politics was largely perfunctory. He supported McKinley because McKinley was a Republican, and Republicans supported big business, which translated into a peaceful, orderly environment in which men like him could carry on their task of making America the leading industrial and financial power in the world. He had met with Hanna, told him what he expected from McKinley, contributed to McKinley's campaign, and McKinley had won handily. In her classic and best-selling biography, *Morgan: American Financier*, Jean Strouse put it this way:

> With McKinley in the Executive Office, Morgan had known more or less what to expect: minimal antitrust prosecution, regular consultation between Wall Street and Washington, virtual carte blanche to promote the market stability and economic policies favored by the conservative elite of both parties.[17]

Then McKinley died suddenly, and Teddy went off half-cocked. Hanna arranged a meeting with Roosevelt, and Morgan came face-to-face with a problem he had never had to consider. A fool was running the Republican Party. What must he do?

Historians report that Morgan went home angry and began writing a rude letter to Teddy, which his lawyers prevented him from sending. The specifics of this letter are not recorded, but we would venture to say that his anger was not directed at Teddy personally, but at the fact that Teddy was doing exactly what Hill and Harriman had done with their feud over the ownership of the Burlington line, that is, roiling the markets and violating Morgan's "sense of order."

You see, while neither Teddy nor anyone else recognized it at the time—or since then, for that matter—Morgan was as close as the American Left would ever come to the philosopher king whom they sought to rule Bellamy's socialist utopia where "life is regimented and hierarchical, ruled by an elite." He was, after all, an authoritarian who believed in the concentration of power. Indeed, he very much would have preferred just one great trust ruling all commerce. He valued order in business, in society, and in government. He was scrupulously honest and ethical because he believed that corruption was disorderly. Power, when used unjustly, was likewise disorderly. He had put together the Northern Securities to end the squabbling that was hindering the railroad business. He had formed the Steel trust because competition was disorderly. He had pulled Cleveland's coals out of the fire because the government's fiscal problems were disorderly. Now it had become clear that friction between the government and business was disorderly. Clearly, if Jupiter was to rule over an orderly world, he would have to personally assure that the government of that world was orderly.

George W. Perkins took control of this project. He was so senior a member of Morgan's inner circle that he was sometimes referred to as Morgan's secretary of state.[18] He had also been Teddy's friend and associate when Teddy was governor. Moreover, as Ron Chernow puts it in *The House of Morgan: An American Banking Dynasty and the Rise of Modern Finance*, Perkins recognized a harmony between the great financier and the Progressives that others did not see. He explains it this way:

Where Pierpont's theorizing was largely nonexistent, Perkins's was sophisticated ... He was an oddity at the world's most cryptic bank. He preached a gospel of industrial cooperation, contending that small-scale business depressed wages and retarded technological advance. Not Wall Street, he said, but steam engines and telephones produced trusts ... He drew a parallel Pierpont wouldn't admit to—that trusts, with their centralized production and distribution, were a form of private socialism. And unlike Pierpont, he saw that they acquired a public character, and he favored government licensing of interstate companies and extended work benefits, including profit sharing, social insurance and old-age pensions. This he boasted would be "socialism of the highest, best and most ideal sort." Although Teddy Roosevelt sometimes wondered whether Perkins simply rationalized a selfish Morgan agenda, there was a striking likeness between their views.

That a Morgan partner should advocate socialism is not so startling. After all, Pierpont, starting with his railway associations of the late 1880s, espoused industrial cooperation instead of competition. He liked his capitalism neat, tidy, and under bankers' control. The House of Morgan was banker to established enterprises—the great industrial planning system that favored stability over innovation, predictability over experimentation, and were threatened by upstart companies; so the bank had a heavy stake in the status quo.[19]

At this point in the narrative, Morgan et al. begin their metamorphosis from being aggressive supporters of laissez-faire economics to being proto-socialists who, along with their successors ad infinitum, would henceforth seek to take full advantage of this new partnership with the kleptocrats in Washington. This then set the stage for the emergence of the modern corporate state under the direction of Franklin Delano Roosevelt.

The courtship began in June 1902, just a few months after the aforementioned meeting, when Perkins called on the White House to ask Teddy if he could arrange for "some safe plan for us to adopt" a merger between several major American-flag shipping lines and British Leyland in order to better compete with the other leading British line, Cunard.[20] Teddy recognized this request for what it was, that is, a bid for détente, and he did not challenge the combination. Clearly, he thought he had Morgan where he wanted him.

A few weeks later, Perkins received a call from Rockefeller Jr. whose brother-in-law, one of three sons who inherited McCormick Harvesting Company, wanted to buy the firm's major competitors but had been warned that their plans could run afoul of the Roosevelt trustbusters. Perkins suggested that they should hire the House of Morgan to help with the transaction. They did, and, of course, the merger of five of the nation's six largest manufacturers of farm equipment into a firm called International Harvester went unchallenged by Roosevelt, just as Perkins had assured Rockefeller it would.

The following September, Teddy gave the speech in which he explained that his future actions against the various trusts would be entirely subjective, or more specifically, that he himself would judge the legality of trusts not on size but on whether or not they "behave badly."[21]

Of course, Teddy's newly found friends at Morgan were pleased that Teddy himself would decide which trusts were "good" and which were "bad," and their marriage of convenience subsequently flourished. Among other things, they joined forces in October 1902 to end a strike by 150,000 coal miners in Eastern Pennsylvania that threatened millions of city dwellers with a winter without heat. Then, sometime during the next year, Morgan became, to borrow a phrase from author Andrew Sinclair, "Roosevelt's bagman in the taking of the Panama Canal."[22]

To lend some administrative legitimacy to their arrangement, Roosevelt asked Perkins in 1903 to help push a bill through the Senate that would create a Department of Commerce, which would house an industry-friendly Bureau of Corporations that would have the authority to conduct investigations and provide "expert" advice to the president on the various trusts.

Strenuous opposition to the bill came from both those who wanted it to do more and those who did not want it all. Among those in the latter camp was one of Rockefeller's senior executives, John D. Archbold. To bolster public support for the plan, Teddy leaked opposition telegrams from Archbold, claiming that they came direct from Rockefeller himself. Miller notes that Teddy knew Archbold's name meant nothing to the public but that Rockefeller "personified the evils of the trusts." The ploy worked. "A storm of protest arose in Congress following the release of the telegrams," and the bill passed.[23] As a token of his appreciation, Teddy gave Perkins one of the pens that he used to sign it, and then named James R. Garfield, the son of President James A. Garfield and a close college friend of Morgan's top lawyer, the aforementioned Francis Stetson, to be the first Commissioner of Corporations.[24]

As is customary in large joint ventures such as this one, "honest money" was required, and lo, more than three-quarters of Teddy's $2.2 million reelection campaign fund in 1904 came from corporations and their owners. Among others, Morgan gave $150,000, Archbold gave $125,000, Harriman gave $50,000, and Frick gave $100,000.[25]

Of course, Teddy won big, taking 57 percent of the popular vote and 70 percent of the electoral vote. Nevertheless, this groundswell of popularity did not translate into an easy path for his agenda of moderate progressivism. For starters, he had to deal with the Old Guard Republicans, also known as the "stand patters." Their leaders were the most powerful political players in Washington, the iconic and crusty old House Speaker Joseph Cannon and the wealthy and socially prominent father-in-law of John D. Rockefeller Jr., Senate Majority Leader Nelson Aldrich. As defenders of the industrialists, they opposed all government interference with the growing influence of the trusts. But their principal task was defending the high tariffs, which protected these trusts from foreign competition at the expense of consumers who paid higher prices, and Southern farmers, who produced goods for export such as cotton and tobacco.

Teddy had a two-part plan for dealing with this crowd. First, he would continue to keep the tariff issue off the table, but to use it as a veiled threat. Second, he would convince them that his brand of "moderate" progressivism was all that stood between them and disaster at the hands of more radical progressives and socialists. Miller cites a letter from Teddy to Taft saying the following: "The dull purblind folly of the very rich men, their greed and arrogance … and the corruption of business and politics, have tended to produce a very unhealthy condition and excitement in the public mind, which shows itself in the great increase in socialist propaganda."[26]

This would be a tough sale, but Teddy could make a convincing argument that the radical socialists and anarchists were gaining ground. As previously noted, the most radical members of these two groups had "gone to cover" in the wake of the Haymarket riots and the McKinley assassination. And while they had been reasonably quiet ever since, they were increasingly aware that their left-wing cousins, the Progressives, viewed them more as an unwelcome and embarrassing stepchild than a partner in their efforts to construct a more just society.

Yes, the Progressives sided with the workers in the ongoing battle between labor and capital, but they were, as noted previously, elitists in the mold of the Fabians, who had little natural empathy for the working stiff himself. Moreover, they had no sympathy whatsoever for violence and little, if any, for the labor unions, which they viewed in the same way that they viewed big business, namely that they should be under the thumb of the government, or at least in partnership with it.

The socialist labor leader Eugene Debs was the titular head of this crowd. He had run for president against McKinley in 1900 and received one hundred thousand votes; and against Teddy in 1904, when he received four hundred thousand. He had been an early member and senior executive of the elitist Brotherhood of Locomotive

Firemen, whose membership excluded unskilled immigrants and non-whites. He quit the union 1893 to form the American Railway Union to represent unskilled workers in head-to-head battles with managements. The next year, the ARU joined a wildcat strike of workers at the Pullman Palace Car Company, which eventually involved some 250,000 workers in twenty-seven states and considerable violence. The strike was broken only when President Cleveland sent in twelve thousand US Army troops to put it down, declaring that it was interfering with the delivery of the US mail and posed a threat to public safety. Debs spent six months in jail after a highly publicized trial that brought more national attention and fame to his attorney Clarence Darrow, and he was readying himself for another go at the presidency in 1908.

In addition, Teddy could claim with some justification that his "moderate progressivism" was the "Old Guard's" best defense against the much more radical segment of the party's progressive movement under the leadership of the highly charismatic Republican governor of Wisconsin Robert La Follett. Also known as "Fighting Bob," as well as the "little giant," La Follette had single-handedly destroyed the deeply embedded and highly corrupt Republican Party in Wisconsin and had gained a national reputation when Steffens lavished praise on him in an article in *McClure's* in October 1904.

Steffens had initially traveled to Wisconsin to expose La Follette as a self-righteous fraud but discovered him to be an honest, ethical, and aggressive foe of tariffs, trusts, the railroads, the "bosses," and "vast corporation combinations."[27] Moreover, in partnership with the previously mentioned economist and Social Gospel leader Richard Ely, La Follette had developed what became known as the Wisconsin Idea, which described itself as the "laboratory of democracy," which promoted racial justice, popular governance, and a return to the Republican Party's populist roots.

So, comforted by his bargain with the "Old Guard," steeped in the sanctimony of the Social Gospel belief in the importance of government's role in improving mankind, and anxious to protect his leadership of the progressive movement from La Follette's challenge, Teddy became the progressive from hell.

He opened his second term by taking on what was arguably the most highly charged political issue of the day, stating in his Fourth Annual Message on December 6, 1904, that a law was needed that would allow the government to "supervise and regulate" railroad rates. Indeed, he said that such a law was "the only alternative to an increase of the present evils on the one hand or a still more radical policy on the other."[28]

Now, this seems like small potatoes today. However, the fact is that he who controlled the rails in those bygone days exercised massive control over not just the national economy but also that of the major cities and states. For the railroads were the principal fount of the power and wealth of the industrialists and bankers, "the scaffolding upon which worlds would be built," as Ron Chernow put it in *The House of Morgan*.[29]

Two months later, in a January 30, 1905, speech, he upped the ante, claiming that the government should have "the power over [rail] rates, and especially over rebates" in order to "protect alike the railroad and the shipper, and put the big shipper and the little shipper on equal footing."

Of course, it was Teddy's habit in every speech to anticipate criticism by maintaining early on that the very thing he was about to advocate was not what he was advocating. We noted earlier, for example, that he once said that the trusts and "the strong and forceful men upon whom the success of business operations inevitably rests" should be left "as unhampered as is compatible with the public good" just before he made the case for hampering them. So just before advocating the usurpation of the railroad owners' right to manage their own businesses, he said this:

> We are not trying to strike down the rich man; on the contrary, we will not tolerate any attack upon his rights. We are not trying to give an improper advantage to the poor man because he is poor, to the man of small means because he has not larger means; but we are striving to see that the man of small means has exactly as good a

chance, so far as we can obtain it for him, as the
man of larger means; that there shall be equality
of opportunity for the one as for the other.

So, why did the nation need this law? Well, a month earlier he
had said it was to prevent "present evils" from growing. Now, it was
to obtain justice for all. To wit:

> In some body such as the Interstate
> Commerce Commission there must lodged in
> effective shape the power to see that every shipper
> who uses the railroads and every man who owns
> or manages a railroad shall on the one hand be
> given justice and on the other hand be required
> to do justice.[30]

Ah, yes, "justice," that complex metaphysical notion that has
occupied the minds of some of the world's most learned philosophers
and theologians since the beginning of civilization. Now, he, Teddy
Roosevelt, would utilize "justice" to decide what rates the railroad
owners could charge their customers.

Once again, he offered no specific evidence of any "injustices"
that had been inflicted on the nation as a whole by the railroad owners. In fact, a review of the Congressional debates over the related
legislation reveals that the "justice" about which Teddy spoke had to
do with taking sides in a fight being waged by his fellow progressives
on behalf of small farmers and merchants, who wanted to protect
their local markets from the *lower-priced* and/or *higher-quality* goods
being shipped on the railroads from newly concentrated production
facilities.

The University of Miami law professor Fred S. McChesney put
it this way in *The Causes and Consequences of Antitrust: The Public-
Choice Perspective.*

> Rural cattlemen and butchers were espe-
> cially eager to have statutes enacted that would

thwart competition from the newly centralized
meat processing facilities in Chicago. The evidence on price and output in these industries,
moreover, does not support the conjecture that
these industries suffered from a monopoly in the
late nineteenth century, if monopoly is understood in the conventional neoclassical way as an
organization of industry which tends to restrict
output and raise prices. These industries were
fiercely competitive because of relatively free
entry and rapid technological advances such as
refrigeration.[31]

In response to Teddy's promise to avoid the tariff issue, Cannon
moved the railroad bill forward in the House, which passed it in the
closing days of the 58th Congress in March 1905. Teddy was elated.
However, House passage had come too late for the Senate to take it
up.

Teddy spent the spring, summer, and fall of 1905 pushing the
railroad measure, burnishing his progressive credentials, accelerating
his ham-handed, federal appropriation of millions of acres of land,
cataloguing the complaints of his fellow progressives all over the
nation, and generally setting the stage for the birth of the "regulatory
state." In fact, he delivered an average of ten speeches a month from
February to November, building up a head of steam for his infamous
fifth Annual Message on December 5, 1905, which was described by
the *New York World* as the "most amazing program of centralization
that any President of the United States has ever recommended."[32]

This characterization was an understatement. In fact, the twen-
ty-five-thousand-word document was actually a maniacal laundry list
of all the progressive causes that he had collected during his travels the previous summer. Not unlike the rantings of Saint-Simon,
Fourier, and Owen, it opened with a disjointed and tortured exposition of barbershop philosophy on all matters big and small. These
included the ebb and flow of prosperity, deserving and undeserving
members of the community, the wrath of the Lord, the follies of

mankind, panic brought on by speculative folly, the severity of the stoppage of welfare, the importance of high individual character, the presence of the rich in the world, of both good and bad men among the rich, the responsibilities of corporations, the fact that we are all in this together, and the need for government to supervise these various human activities and circumstances.

Teddy then addressed, at long length, the desperate need for federal control over virtually all aspects of the railroad business "to see that justice is done ... in a spirit as remote as possible from hysteria and rancor." And lest anyone should question whether this exercise might involve men just as "evil" as those they would oversee, he stated that these government men would be required "to possess a lofty probity which will revolt as quickly at the thought of pandering to any gust of popular prejudice against rich men as at the thought of anything even remotely resembling subserviency to rich men."

Finally, he offered a long-winded, disjointed hodgepodge of issues and thoughts, some big, some small, some banal, some detailed, and some almost ethereal: the power of the courts to issue injunctions in labor disputes, the conditions of child labor, the protection of children and dumb animals, the conditions of women in industry, the question of securing a healthy, self-respecting, and mutually sympathetic attitude as between employer and employee, the dangers of class spirit, the evils of plutocracy, the need for a man to show broad sympathy for his neighbor; the growth in the insurance business, corruption of a flagrant kind in business, budget deficits, Russian trade, abolishment of the office of Receiver of Public Moneys for the United States Land Office, the Panama Canal, the need for elasticity in the money supply, the need to keep the Navy strong, bribery and corruption in the election system, a new Hague convention, the war between Russia and Japan, the contraband of war, the Monroe Doctrine, immigration, public land laws, forestry, China, adulterated food and drugs, the dense black or gray smoke in the city of Washington, the great shaggy-maned wild ox, pensions to firemen and policemen in the nation's cities, the presence of bootleggers among American Indian tribes, the destruction by the rinderpest among the cattle on the Philippine islands, the fortification of Hawaii, citizenship for Puerto Ricans, an elective delegate from Alaska, an increase in the number of personnel at the Department of State, et cetera, et cetera, et cetera, ad nauseam.[33]

To say the least, the Old Guard was not excited about Teddy's ambitious agenda. However, Teddy was ready for a fight, which began almost immediately after the opening of the second session of the 59th Congress on March 3, 1906, with the reintroduction of his much-coveted railroad legislation.

Once again, the bill passed easily in the House. However, a group of "railroad senators" led by Aldrich pledged to defeat it in the Senate. This revolt from within his own party against his showpiece legislative initiative was both a surprise and a massive embarrassment to Teddy, especially given the agreement that he thought he had reached with them. Moreover, La Follette, who had recently arrived in town as a newly elected senator from Wisconsin, began immediately to criticize Teddy for not going far enough with his initiative.

At this point, the battle became highly intense. Miller notes that words like "liar," "unqualified falsehood," "betrayal" were flung back and forth and that Teddy told a friend "he would be happy to lend the Russian government several eminent statesmen if they would guarantee to place them where a bomb was likely to go off."[34]

As fate would have it, it was right at this time that William Randolph Hearst's *Cosmopolitan* magazine published a series of articles entitled "The Treason of the Senate" by the muckraker David Graham Phillips charging Aldrich and many of his buddies in the Senate with corruption and conflict of interest. To wit:

> No railway legislation that was not either helpful to or harmless against "the interests"; no legislation on the subject of corporations that would interfere with "the interests," which use the corporate form to simplify and systematize their stealing; no legislation on the tariff question unless it secured to "the interests" full and free license to loot; no investigations of wholesale robbery or of any of the evils resulting from it—

there you have in a few words the whole story of the Senate's treason under Aldrich's leadership, and of why property is concentrating in the hands of the few and the little children of the masses are being sent to toil in the darkness of mines, in the dreariness and unhealthfulness of factories instead of being sent to school; and why the great middle class—the old-fashioned Americans, the people with the incomes of from 2,000 to 15,000 a year—is being swiftly crushed into dependence and the repulsive miseries of "genteel poverty." The heavy and ever heavier taxes of "the interests" are swelling rents, swelling the prices of food, clothing, fuel, all the necessities and all the necessary comforts. And the Senate both forbids the lifting of those taxes and levies fresh taxes for its master.[35]

Here, gentle reader, we come to that Carlylean moment when our protagonist either earns the title of "hero," or is relegated to the ranks of those who sit on the sidewalk and cheer as the heroes pass by. Or as Robert Penn Warren would describe a similar situation years later, Teddy was "face to face with the margin of mystery where all our calculations collapse, where the stream of time dwindles into the sands of eternity, where the formula fails in the test tube, where chaos and old night hold sway and we hear the laughter in the ether dream."[36]

You see, Teddy knows that Phillips is correct when he says that Aldrich and his pals are corrupt. In fact, everyone knows it, and everyone knows that Teddy knows it. But Teddy wants his railroad bill badly, and he needs Aldrich's help. What to do? He, Teddy, is, after all, a great corruption fighter, a champion of the moral, a charter member of the sacred fraternity of Progressives, a foe of evil, a warrior for justice. Carlyle had set the standard for heroes sixty years earlier when noted that Luther had ridden into Worms unafraid. "Were there as many devils in Worms as there are roof-tiles, I would on."[37]

Again, what to do? Well. Our hero bent his knee. He lacked the courage to take to the battlefield when the war in which he had been a combatant for over two decades became too hot for him. Moreover, unlike the great Achilles, Teddy did not stay in his tent. He stood on the sidelines with the spectators and kibitzed.

In ringing tones of righteousness and hackneyed homilies, he spoke of the "urgent necessity for the sternest war" against the "many and grave evils" that exist in the economic and social body politic. Indeed, he said, "There should be relentless exposure of and attack upon every evil man, whether politician or business man, every evil practice, whether in politics, business, or social life," and said that he personally would "hail as a benefactor every writer or speaker, every man who, on the platform or in a book, magazine, or newspaper, with merciless severity makes such attack."

But ... ah yes, but ... he cautioned that there is a danger that the accuser could be lying, or employ "hysterical exaggeration," or, worse yet, could become, as we noted earlier, a "muckraker," "whose vision is fixed on carnal instead of spiritual things," who "also typifies the man who in this life consistently refuses to see aught that is lofty, and fixes his eyes with solemn intentness only on that which is vile and debasing." This could, he said, result in a "public calamity" by creating a morbid and vicious public sentiment, and at the same time act as a profound deterrent to able men of normal sensitiveness and tend to prevent them from entering the public service at any price." Thus, he said with great profundity, that while it is one's duty to "expose the crime, and hunt down the criminal," one must "remember that even in the case of crime, if it is attacked in sensational, lurid, and untruthful fashion, the attack may do more damage to the public mind than the crime itself."[38]

Oh my! Who knew?

It is not clear whether Aldrich, whose name Teddy never mentioned, felt vindicated by the speech or whether Phillips, who also went unnamed, felt chastised. Our guess is that Teddy lost considerable support on both sides by his pantywaisted take on the controversy.

In the end, Aldrich realized he did not have the clout to kill the railroad bill, so he tacked on several amendments involving judicial oversight that were designed to slow down or stall any future action by the ICC. The bill passed Congress, and Teddy signed it on June 29, 1906, calling it a "fine piece of constructive legislation."[39]

At the time, the Old Guard viewed this outcome as a victory. It turned out to be otherwise, for the courts ultimately refrained from any sort of comprehensive review of the ICC, which assured that the agency would become a powerful arm of the executive branch. Moreover, it opened the door to the plague-like proliferation of other regulatory agencies that continues unchecked today. Historian John Morton Blum put it this way: "Modest as the proposal was, it challenged the most cherished prerogative of private management, the most hoary tenet of free private enterprise—the ability freely to make prices."[40]

Of course, that was not known then. In fact, the progressives, who were already angry at Teddy's muckraker speech, felt additionally betrayed by his happy acceptance of the Aldrich amendments. As for the Old Guard, they had had enough of Teddy. Not only were they embarrassed by their failure to kill the railroad bill, they had also lost two bitter and heated fights over the Pure Food and Drug Act and the Meat Inspection Act, both of which expanded the powers of the government far beyond the role outlined for it in the Constitution.

Teddy signed the bills on June 30, and was naturally pleased, noting that these three important pieces of legislation marked a "noteworthy advance in the policy of securing Federal supervision and control of corporations." What he did not know was, as Miller put it, that that session of congress would be "the high water mark of his years in the White House."[41] You see, with both factions within his party less than happy with him, and his moral compass having grown increasingly out of kilter, it would become harder and harder for him to negotiate the troubled waters that divided the two sides.

The result was that a deeply frustrated Teddy became a peevish, sanctimonious scold, who spent his last two years in office tirelessly railing against the "evil" rich.

At first blush, it seems odd that one of Teddy's chosen foes would be the wealthy. After all, he came from an affluent family and his circle of friends was made up almost entirely of the same crowd. Moreover, he had no sympathy whatsoever for Marxism or for the labor union bosses and their threats of violence. Nor did his antagonism for the rich come from the Social Gospel movement. In fact, while the Social Gospel folks believed in government action to bring the society into harmony with heaven, they were not overly antagonistic to wealth or to inequality of income. According to the historian Dr. Luigi Bradizza, Ely himself believed that the obligation of the wealthy to help the poor, as called for in the requirement to "love my neighbor as myself," stopped at assuring that they had "necessities," and did not include supplying "comforts or luxuries."[42]

However, as we noted earlier, Teddy's ego demanded that he be constantly engaged in a battle against some evil force on behalf of some noble and righteous cause. And what more suitable an adversary could there be for the president of the United States than the richest, most powerful, and most successful men in the world?

Of course, he still had to placate the Old Guard. Hence, his lame differentiation between the "bad" rich and the "good" rich. In addition, of course, to make the fight worthy of his exalted opinion of himself, the "bad" rich had to be more than just bad; they had to be evil, sinful even, a threat not just to the nation but to mankind.

Naturally then, during the run up to the all-important Congressional elections in the fall of 1906, Teddy's ire against the "bad rich" reached a fever pitch. Gone were any opening words of praise for the hard work and genius that had turned the United States into the most successful experiment in self-government that the world had ever witnessed. Instead, just five hundred words into his speech in Harrisonburg, Pennsylvania, on October 4 to celebrate the happy dedication of a new capitol building, he began harping on the "evils" that "flourish" in the wake of the "extraordinary industrial changes of the last half-century."[43]

One month later, on November 18, Teddy's Justice Department filed his antitrust suit against Standard Oil, which, apparently, he had decided was a "bad trust." After all, the "Standard Oil people," as

Tarbell called them, had sided with Aldrich in the fight over railroad rates and had declined to donate to the Republicans in the recent midyear elections. Clearly, they were evil. Indeed, lest anyone disagree, he referred to them as "the biggest criminals in the country."[44]

Finally, in his December 3 message to Congress, he let the "bad rich" bastards really have it. He began by disassociating himself from those men "who seek to excite a violent class hatred against all men of wealth" by launching campaigns of "hysterical excitement and falsehood" aimed at inflaming "to madness the brutal passions of mankind" in the name of "doing away with the abuses connected with wealth." Then, of course, he did just that. To wit:

> In the end the honest man, whether rich or poor, who earns his own living and tries to deal justly by his fellows, has as much to fear from the insincere and unworthy demagog, promising much and performing nothing, or else performing nothing but evil, who would set on the mob to plunder the rich, as from the crafty corruptionist, who, for his own ends, would permit the common people to be exploited by the very wealthy. If we ever let this Government fall into the hands of men of either of these two classes, we shall show ourselves false to America's past. Moreover, the demagog and the corruptionist often work hand in hand. There are at this moment wealthy reactionaries of such obtuse morality that they regard the public servant who prosecutes them when they violate the law, or who seeks to make them bear their proper share of the public burdens, as being even more objectionable than the violent agitator who hounds on the mob to plunder the rich. There is nothing to choose between such a reactionary and such an agitator; fundamentally they are alike in their selfish disregard of the rights of others; and it is

natural that they should join in opposition to any movement of which the aim is fearlessly to do exact and even justice to all.

Of course, Teddy did not elaborate on how he set about to distinguish between the "wealthy reactionaries" and the good rich fellow who "earns his own living and tries to deal justly by his fellows." He simply said that everything would be fine if the "man of great wealth" would simply pay more taxes "in the spirit of justice." At which point he called on Congress to pass both a graduated tax on inheritance and another on income, all with the intent "to treat rich man and poor man on a basis of absolute equality."[45]

Of course, Congress did not get a chance to consider this means for assuring that "everything would be fine." In fact, by March 1907, Congress, Teddy, and everyone else had more pressing matters on their minds, namely a shaky stock market and a severe credit crunch. These combined to prevent towns and cities across the nation, including New York and Boston, from being able to float bond issues, and companies such as Westinghouse Electric, Interborough Metropolitan, and numerous other manufacturers from finding equity purchasers, which forced them into receivership.

Harriman quickly placed the blame on Teddy, which began a highly public quarrel between the two that called attention to the growing rift between Washington and the business community and made the situation worse. Then, on August 10, the stock market crashed again. The *New York Times* estimated the losses at $1 billion. In London, Morgan's son Jack blamed the crash on Teddy's attacks on big business. "Everyone is frightened to death by the actions of people like our fool Attorney General."[46]

On August 20, Teddy gave a speech in Provincetown, Massachusetts, in which he blamed the "present trouble with the stock market," at least in part, on the "certain malefactors of great wealth" who have combined "to bring about as much financial stress as possible in order to discredit the policy of the government and thereby secure a reversal of that policy so that they may enjoy the unmolested fruits of their own evil doing." Then he assured his listeners that "there will be no change in the policy we have steadily pursued," which he described as a "contest" over who will shall "rule," that is, the people or "a few ruthless and domineering men, whose wealth make them particularly formidable because they hide behind the breastworks of corporate organization."[47] Six weeks later, on October 19, a banking panic occurred when the Knickerbocker Trust, the third largest in the New York City, went belly up.

Our interest in the details of this financial mess, known as the Panic of 1907, is limited. Suffice it to say, once again, that Morgan saved the day. In the process, he arranged for US Steel to buy the Tennessee Coal, Iron and Railroad Company from a brokerage firm, Moore & Schley, which was about to collapse due to the sudden drop in price of the stock of TC&I. The acquisition by US Steel of the rich iron ore deposits of the TCC&I would almost certainly have come under fire as an antitrust violation. Of course, Morgan's men went to see Teddy. They told him that they were buying TC&I "out of sense of duty," that it would be of "little benefit" to US Steel. Moreover, they said, all would be lost if he did not give him approval. Of course, Teddy gave it. We will let Miller take it from there.

> Hostile criticism poured in … from every direction in the wake of the panic. The business world blamed his reform policies for the disaster; progressives saw betrayal in his response to the cries for help from Wall Street. They charged that he had allowed himself to be duped by Morgan's emissaries into scuttling his antitrust policy. Senator La Follette even claimed the bankers had created the panic for their own ends. Through the acquisition of Tennessee Coal, it was pointed out, U. S. Steel had for a bargain $45 million gained assets later valued at about $1 billion, which gave it control of 62 percent of the nation's steel-making capacity.[48]

Teddy, of course, claimed publicly that he had done the right thing. Of course, he knew better. The one rich person that he liked and trusted duped him. Naturally then, by January 1908, the rich were no longer simply dishonest, but "sinful" as well. Nor was Teddy's self-righteousness directed solely at the evildoers themselves. Those newspapers and reporters, speakers, and other degenerate believers in free speech were also to blame for this hideous wealth accumulation. Assuming the role of prosecutor, judge, and jury, phrases such as "sinister offenders," "wealthy criminals," "predatory wealth," "rotten-ness," and "criminal misconduct" flowed from his lips like ink from a squid.

The attacks by these great corporations on the Administration's actions have been given wide circulation throughout the country, in the newspapers and otherwise, by those Writers and speakers who, consciously or unconsciously, act as the representatives of predatory wealth—of the wealth accumulated on giant scale by all forms of iniquity, ranging from the oppression of wage-workers to unfair and unwholesome methods of crushing out competition, and to defrauding the public by stock jobbing and the manipulation of securities. Certain wealthy men of this stamp, whose conduct should be abhorrent to every man of ordinarily decent conscience, and who com-mit the hideous wrong of teaching our young men that phenomenal business success must ordinarily be based on dishonesty, have during the last few months made it apparent that they have banded together to work for reaction. Their endeavor is to overthrow and discredit all who honestly administer the law, to prevent any addi-tional legislation which would check and restrain them, and to secure if possible freedom from all restraint which will permit every unscrupulous wrongdoer to do what he wishes unchecked provided he has enough money. The only way to counteract the movement in which these men are engaged is to make clear to the public just what they have done in the past and just what they are seeking to accomplish in the present. ... The Federal Government does scourge sin; it does bid sinners fear, for it has put behind bars with impartial severity the powerful financial, the powerful politician, the rich land thief, and the rich contractor ... we strive to bring nearer the day when greed and trickery and cunning shall be trampled underfoot by those who fight for righteousness that exalted a nation.[49]

In short, Teddy ended his presidential days angrily fighting everyone and everybody who fought his plan for the "moral regeneration" of American business, which he wished to achieve by placing the world of commerce into the wise hands of the federal bureaucrats, and, of course, himself. The truth is that he need not have been angry, for he had paved the way for the continued and continuous destruction of the Constitution that stood in the path of his leftist vision of America. Moreover, he was by no means finished with this task. In fact, some of his finest days as an avatar of the Left were still to come.

Let's let the poets in on the fun.

> The Leaders of the Crowd
> They must to keep their certainty accuse
> All that are different of a base intent;
> Pull down established honour; hawk for news
> Whatever their loose phantasy invent
> And murmur it with bated breath, as though
> The abounding gutter had been Helicon
> Or calumny a song. How can they know
> Truth flourishes where the student's lamp has shone,

And there alone, that have no solitude?
So the crowd come they care not what may come.
They have loud music, hope every day renewed
And heartier loves; that lamp is from the tomb.
William Butler Yeats, 1918

Chapter 17

Taft: The Post Turtle

*It is obvious that a graduated tax is a direct
penalty imposed on saving and industry, a direct
premium offered to idleness and extravagance. It
discourages the very habits and qualities which it
is most in the interest of the State to foster. ... It
is at the same time perfectly arbitrary. When the
principle of taxing all fortunes on the same rate of
computation is abandoned, no definite rule or principle remains. At what point the higher scale is to
begin, or to what degree it is to be raised, depends
wholly on the policy of Governments and the balance of parties. The ascending scale may at first
be very moderate, but it may at any time, when
fresh taxes are required, be made more severe, till it
reaches or approaches the point of confiscation. ...
Highly graduated taxation realizes most completely
the supreme danger of democracy, creating a state of
things in which one class imposes on another burdens which it is not asked to share, and impels the
State into vast schemes of extravagance, under the
belief that the whole cost will be thrown upon others. Dishonest politicians ... will have no difficulty
in drawing impressive contrasts between the luxury*

of the rich and the necessities of the poor, and in persuading ignorant men that there can be no harm in throwing great burdens of exceptional taxation on a few men, who will still remain immeasurably richer than themselves. Yet, no truth of political economy is more certain than that a heavy taxation of capital, which starves industry and employment, will fall most severely on the poor ... Taxation is, ultimately, the payment which is made by the subject for the security and other advantages which he derives from the State. If the taxation of one class is out of all proportion to the cost of the protection they enjoy; if its members are convinced that it is not an equitable payment, but an exceptional and confiscatory burden imposed upon them by an act of power because they are politically weak, very many of them will have no more scruple in defrauding the Government than they would have in deceiving a highwayman or a burglar. (W. E. H. Lecky, *Democracy and Liberty*, Volume 1, 1896)

President William Howard Taft was a decent man to whom people should have listened when he said that he did not want to be president. All he wanted was to be on the Supreme Court. However, he agreed to run for president because his friend Teddy asked him to do so, and because his wife, Nellie, had wanted to be the nation's First Lady ever since she was seventeen, and had visited the White House with her father to visit his law partner President Rutherford Hayes.[1]

History books generally describe Taft as progressive, and sometimes as a conservative. In truth, he was neither. You see, both labels imply the presence of a governing philosophy, a passion of some sort. He was free of such qualities. He was the prototype of the turtle on the fence post as described by the country boy. "You know he didn't get up there by himself, he doesn't belong up there, and he doesn't know what to do while he's up there, and you just wonder what kind of a dumb ass put him up there to being with."

Of course, the dumb ass was Teddy. Having promised not to run for a third term, he assumed for himself the task of choosing his successor. His first pick was his friend the New York senator Elihu Root, who had been Secretary of War under McKinley and Teddy's secretary of state. Teddy described him as "without question the greatest living statesman," saying, "I would rather see him in the White House than any other man now possible." Root was, however, a well-known corporate lawyer with close ties to Wall Street, and Teddy did not think he could win the election. Root agreed.[2] Teddy's vice president Charles Fairbanks was never considered. Teddy did not like him. He described him as a "reactionary, machine politician."[3] A third possibility was New York governor Charles Hughes, whom Teddy also did not much like.[4] That left Taft.

Teddy assumed that Taft was a progressive whom he could count on to continue in his footsteps, which made sense because this was exactly what Taft intended to do. This strategy, however, turned out to be a mistake, because, as we noted earlier, the trail that Teddy blazed had become increasingly rocky and laden with both moral and practical hazards. Thus, it was that Taft stumbled through four years in the White House, doing almost as much to advance the cause of the Left in America than Teddy did, without ever knowing it.

The disaster that was Taft's presidency began immediately when he called a special session of Congress to fulfill a campaign promise he had made to the Progressives to lower tariffs. As noted earlier, this was such a hot-button issue that Teddy had intentionally avoided it. Not surprisingly, then, the fight between the Old Guard and the Progressives was extremely heated.

We have no interest in the details. Suffice it to say, the bill that passed in the House was marginally acceptable to the Progressives, but Aldrich did to it in the Senate just what he had done to Teddy's railroad rate legislation. He turned it into a farce. Not only did the final law make only a modest reduction in some tariffs, it actually raised others that were favored by the large trusts. Progressives were outraged and demanded that Taft veto it. But Taft, who was already way over his head just a few months into his presidency, not only signed the bill in August 1909 but one month later publicly declared in a speech that it was the best tariff law ever passed by the Republican Party. In effect then, his effort to lower tariffs raised eyebrows among the Old Guard, while his failure to do so had angered the progressives.

Yet, here is the rub. During the debate over the legislation, the Democrats introduced a proposal for a graduated income tax on individuals. Now, this was not a new idea. In fact, Congress had passed, and President Lincoln had approved a graduated income tax in 1862 to help pay for the huge costs being incurred by the Civil War. The rate was 3% on incomes between $600 and $10,000, and 5% on incomes over $10,000. Two years later the tax was increased to 5% on incomes between $600 and $5,000, 7.5% on incomes between $5,000 and $10,000, and 10% on those above $10,000. After the war, a fight occurred over whether to abolish or extend the tax. President Grant allowed it to expire in 1872.

Of course, the discussion over a need for an income tax continued, and finally in 1894, during Cleveland's second term, the pro-taxers won. Cleveland had run on a promise to cut tariffs, which he said were a "vicious, inequitable and illogical" tax that placed an unfair burden on every American. He said that they were the "the mother of trusts," and, finally, in a comment that placed him very high on a very short list of Democratic politicians with even a modicum of sense, he said that the government didn't need the money anyway. He put it this way:

> The public Treasury, which should only exist as a conduit conveying the people's tribute to its legitimate objects of expenditure, becomes a hoarding place for money needlessly withdrawn from trade and the people's use, thus crippling our national energies, suspending our country's development, preventing investment in productive enterprise, threatening financial disturbance, and inviting schemes of public plunder.[5]

The Democratic Congress succeeded in moderately lowering tariffs, but it tacked on a 2 percent tax on incomes above $4,000, ostensibly to make up for the lost revenue from the tariff reductions. Cleveland was disappointed with the bill, saying that the tariff reforms fell far short of what was needed. He famously proclaimed that any "true Democrat" who supports the bill is guilty of "party perfidy and party dishonor," and blamed the whole mess on "the trusts and combinations—the communism of pelf—whose machinations have prevented us from reaching the success we deserved."[6] Yet, after considerable bluster, he concluded that the reforms were a small improvement over the existing tariffs, so he let the bill become law without his signature.

The Supreme Court ruled the law unconstitutional the very next year in the case of Pollack vs. Farmers Loan & Trust Co. The decision was made on technical grounds. However, the real objection was that a graduated tax violated the uniformity clause in the Constitution. It reads: "The Congress shall have Power To lay and collect Taxes, Duties, Imposts and Excises, to pay the Debts and provide for the common Defence and general Welfare of the United States; but all Duties, Imposts and Excises shall be uniform throughout the United States."

The debate among the founders over this section was long, intense, and complicated. It involved two primary concerns, the first relating to the possible abuse of the power to tax, and the second involving the type of taxes that the federal government could use, given that the states would have to tax citizens also. Interestingly, the founders had many lengthy discussions over these issues, which encompassed everything from matters of punctuation to the use of federal funds to finance disaster relief in cases such as the great Savanna fire. Yet one finds not even a hint of disagreement over whether taxes for all citizens should be taxes at the same rate. In fact, the topic appears only once in the *Federalist Papers*, and then indirectly during Madison's discussion in Federalist #10 of the importance of preventing certain factions of society from acting in concert to "carry into effect schemes of oppression" against others. He put it this way:

The apportionment of taxes on the various descriptions of property is an act which seems to require the most exact impartiality; yet there is, perhaps, no legislative act in which greater opportunity and temptation are given to a predominant party to trample on the rules of justice. Every shilling with which they overburden the inferior number, is a shilling saved to their own pockets."[7]

With this clause in mind, Justice Stephen Johnson Field, writing for the majority in the Pollock case, said the following:

The present assault upon capital is but the beginning. It will be but the stepping stone to others larger and more sweeping, until our political contest will become a war of the poor against the rich; a war of growing intensity and bitterness. "If the court sanctions the power of discriminating taxation, and nullifies the uniformity mandate of the constitution," as said by one who has been all his life a student of our institutions, "it will mark the hour when the sure decadence of our present government will commence."

The legislation, in the discrimination it makes, is class legislation. Whenever a distinction is made in the burdens a law imposes or in the benefits it confers on any citizens by reason of their birth, or wealth, or religion, it is class legislation, and leads inevitably to oppression and abuses, and to general unrest and disturbance in society.[8]

Now, this should have put the matter to rest. After all, in 1896, McKinley won back the White House for the Republicans on a platform that featured high tariffs and a strong dollar backed by gold. However, as fate would have it, and as noted earlier, Teddy the progressive took over, and in his final year as president, he pushed for a graduated income tax as part of his campaign against the evil, sinful rich. Naturally then, the Democrats tried again.

Their idea was that Republican opposition would reinforce their claim that the GOP was the party of the wealthy. Moreover, Teddy's seven-year-long campaign against the "evil" rich had all but assured that some substantial share of the public would welcome a "soak the rich" tax.

Aldrich was concerned that the Democrats might be right, so he and Taft came up with a plan. Taft would stop the legislative initiative in its tracks by arguing that it was unconstitutional and that a better approach would be a constitutional amendment that would make it legal by doing away with that document's uniformity requirement. Democrats were apoplectic. Such an amendment would first need a two-thirds vote in both houses on a proposal to send the amendment to the states for ratification, which then would require the approval of three-fourths of them. Aldrich was betting that it would not make it. The Democrats were convinced he was right. Rep. Cordell Hull, a democratic from Tennessee, put it this way:

> No person at all familiar with the present trend of national legislation will seriously insist that these same Republican leaders are over-anxious to see the country adopt an income tax. ... What powerful influence, what new light and deep-seated motive suddenly moves these political veterans to "about face" and to pretend to warmly embrace this doctrine which they have heretofore uniformly denounced? [9]

Hull need not have worried. You see, Teddy was on the scene to help push the measure through to victory. Teddy, you say? How could that be? Well, he was just winding up his yearlong safari in Africa with a swing through Europe where he had been feted by kings, queens, and other dignitaries, including Kaiser Wilhelm II, a dim-witted, intolerably pompous warmonger, who wrote on the back of picture of the two men "when we shake hands, we shake the world."[10]

During his time abroad, Teddy had become somewhat disenchanted with his friend "Big Bob." For starters, he was distressed at the way Taft had handled the tariff bill. More importantly, he was angry at Taft for firing the Chief of the US Forestry Service Gifford Pinoch, who had been Teddy's conservationist soul mate. According to Taft, Pinoch had been undermining the policies and reputation of his Secretary of the Interior, Richard Ballinger, a former mayor of Seattle who favored the development of the West's vast resources, up to and including the establishment of a syndicate, which Morgan had put together with the Guggenheims to open a copper mine in the Kennecott Glacier.

When Teddy arrived in New York City on June 18, 1910, his ego was fatter than a tick on a hound dog when the largest crowd in the city's history greeted him at the dock. Naturally, he loved being back on the stage. So, naturally, on August 23, he set out on a sixteen-state, three-week speaking tour spewing his hatred for "the rich," his disdain for the Constitution, and his strong support for a graduated income tax.

Thus, it came to pass that on July 12, 1909, the Senate approved the bill with a vote of 77–0 and the House approved it by a vote of 318–14. It took a while, of course, but on February 3, 1913, just four days before Taft left office, his attorney general Philander Knox quietly (and some insist, to this day, fraudulently, due to errors in the way several states had handled the approval) signed the Sixteenth Amendment into law.

As for the rich themselves? Well, they had recently set up "charitable foundations" designed and approved for the specific purpose of protecting their money from the tax collector, and the poor middle-class saps who wanted to soak the rich have been wet ever since.

With the notable exception of the Civil War, this would be the most egregious attack on the social fabric of the nation since its founding. Not only did it undermine virtually all the key characteristics of the American experiment in self-government, ranging from the inviolability of private property to equality under the law, but it set the stage for the great American political game of using the tax code to punish and reward various interest groups. This, in turn, assured that corruption would increase by leaps and bounds, and that class conflict, one of the most powerful weapons in the Left's arsenal, would emerge as a major factor in American society.

From the perspective of our concentration on the struggle between the Right and the Left, the interesting aspect of this affair is that neither Aldrich nor any other member of the Old Guard seems to have based their opposition to a graduated income tax on the Constitution's specific objection to such a thing. Nor is there is any record of these Old Guard Republicans having come to the defense of the Constitution when just three months into his presidency, Teddy had blithely asserted that the Constitution was out of date. In fact, not only was no one in the Republican Party interested in defending their political heritage, there was no one smart enough to understand that the best way to defend the industrialists was to protect the Constitution.

In any case, as the poet said, the best-laid schemes o' mice an' men Gang aft agley, as this one certainly did. We should add here, that this was in no small part to the efforts of good old Teddy. Nor, we should add, was this Teddy's last contribution to the dissolution of the Constitution. You see, during his voyage abroad, he had had the benefit of a new fount of wisdom in the form of a book by Herbert Croly entitled *The Promise of American Life*, which two of his friends had recommended to him. The first was Learned Hand and the other was Henry Cabot Lodge.

While this book seems little known today, it still stands today as one of the most important tomes in the history of Left in America, for it provided Teddy and his fellow Progressives with something they had never had, that being a unifying vision for Progressivism. Indeed, it is fair to say that while Croly came late to the progressive fold, he and he alone turned it from a gaggle of individual movements into a united, full-fledged ideology.

Croly was a forty-year-old journalist who wrote about architecture but was intensely interested in politics. His ideological inclinations were rooted in Comte's Positivism, with which his father had imbued him as a lad. Comte had been briefly popular in the United States, especially among the Unitarians and the transcendentalists, but by late in the eighteenth century, everyone in America believed in "progress" and everyone was an empiricist. So Comte became largely irrelevant.

However, Comte did have one intensely loyal devotee in America, and that was Croly's father David. He was an editor of the *New York World*, and according to Croly's biographer, Herbert Levy, he was such an enthusiastic devotee of Comte that he had his new-born son "christened" into the Comte's "Religion of Humanity." He also wrote a sixty-three-page book, which was published in 1871 and entitled *A Positivist Primer: Being a Series of Familiar Conversations on the Religion of Humanity*.[11]

Levy notes that the young Croly adored his father and fondly remembered many long walks in Central Park during which they discussed Comte's philosophy. Croly himself put it this way: "From my earliest years, it was his endeavor to teach me to understand and believe in the religion of Auguste Comte."[12]

Croly spent two years at Harvard, during which he carried on a regular correspondence with his father, who constantly warned his son against any and all the ideas that he encountered that conflicted with the wisdom of Comte. According to Croly himself, he used to send his father "packets of thirty or forty pages every other day," which David would answer "with marvelous regularity and unfailing kindness."[13]

Croly left Harvard in 1888 to care for his father who was ill, and to help him write and publish a specialty newspaper he owned that covered New York real estate business. During the next seventeen years, he wrote for an architectural magazine, returned briefly to Harvard, and had a nervous breakdown. In 1905, he cut back on his work at the magazine and spent the next four years working on *The Promise of American Life*, which was published in 1909. Levy described the impetus for this move as follows:

> Stimulated by the growing awareness of economic injustices and political corruption,

focused to some degree by the frenetic leadership of President Theodore Roosevelt, the nation
was rapidly moving toward a concerted effort at
social reform. It seemed obvious to Croly, however, that the infant movement lacked direction
and purpose. To be effective progressive instincts
needed to be guided by rigorous thought.[14]

So what exactly did Croly bring to the nation's fledgling and
tentative interest in progressive socialism in his groundbreaking
book? Well, for starters, he brought Comte's unique perspective on
the notion of history. Like Marx, Croly believed that history pro-
gressed toward a predetermined end. Unlike Marx, however, Croly
did not believe that the driving force behind history was economic,
that is, class struggle, or that it was leading inexorably toward some
sort of workers' paradise. He believed, with Comte, that scientific
advancement was behind the march of history and, given that, that
the course of history could be altered by understanding the nature of
this science and directing it accordingly.

Here we come to the crux of one of Croly's major contributions
to American socialism. Whereas Marx looked to the violent overthrow of capitalistic governments, Croly looked to the government
as the principal tool with which to manage the inevitable problems
and conflicts that were natural to this new, highly specialized age of
science. These problems were manifold and required governmental
controls based on the Comte's understanding of the scientific nature
of progress as well as a willingness to cast out the old outmoded ideas
that he believed were impediments to progress. Hence, one of the
centerpieces of his book was an aggressive, frontal attack on the US
Constitution. To wit:

> At the present time there is a strong, almost
> a dominant, tendency to regard the existing
> Constitution with superstitious awe, and to
> shrink with horror from modifying it even in
> the smallest detail; and it is this superstitious fear

of changing the most trivial parts of the fundamental legal fabric which brings to pass the great
bondage of the American spirit. If such an abject
worship of legal precedent for its own sake should
continue, the American idea will have to be fitted
to the rigid and narrow lines of a few legal formu-
las; and the ruler of the American spirit, like the
ruler of the Jewish spirit of old, will become the
lawyer.[15]

The book turned Croly into one of the nation's leading experts
on government and society. In fact, the progressive intellectuals of the
day hailed his thoughts as nothing short of biblical. Walter Lippmann
described Croly's book as "the political classic which announced the
end of the Age of Innocence with its romantic faith in American destiny and inaugurated the process of self-examination." His friend, the
radial lawyer and someday Supreme Court Justice Felix Frankfurter
said this: "To omit Croly's *Promise* from any list of half a dozen books
on American politics since 1900 would be grotesque." In fact, he
claimed that it "became a reservoir for all political writing after its
publication."[16]

Virginia Postrel said this about the book in the December 1997
issue of *Reason* magazine:

Croly's central message was that the government's job is to solve social problems and
to actively shape the future, not to be a neutral referee. ... Croly's ideas influenced, among
other contemporaries, Theodore Roosevelt and
Woodrow Wilson, political rivals who in retrospect had more fundamental agreements than
differences ... Crolyism overturned the ideal of
limited government in favor of a combination
of elite power—commissions to regulate and
plan—and mass democracy. It was this prag-
matic progressivism, not socialist utopianism,

that extinguished classical liberalism as the general philosophy of American government.

Frustrated with constitutional limits, Croly wrote, "The security of private property and personal liberty, and a proper distribution of activity between the local and the central governments, demanded [at the time of the Constitution's framing], and within limits still demand, adequate legal guarantees. It remains none the less true, however, that every popular government should in the end, and after a necessarily prolonged deliberation, possess the power of taking any action, which, in the opinion of a decisive majority of the people, is demanded by the public welfare." This statement, while extreme, pretty much sums up today's governing philosophy.[17]

To which, we will add a few truncated quotes on the nature of the changes Croly recommends from Levy's biography.

- More power must be granted to the central government.
- The national government must recognize the corporation and instead of breaking them to pieces allow them to grow freely ... but when the activities of a corporation ran directly counter to the interests of the country ... public ownership might prove necessary.
- Americans needed to understand that they now possessed legitimate and far-flung interests in the world and ... that Washington's Farewell Address and the Monroe Doctrine had ceased to be totally adequate guides to the problems of war and peace, commerce and colonization.
- Labor unions deserve to be favored because they are the most effective machine ...for the amelioration of the laboring class.
- The central government had to assert ... its responsibility for a more equitable division of wealth ... meet its obliga-

tion by progressive taxation, particularly by boldly moving to tax corporate profits and inherited wealth.

- Men must stop their relentless devotion to the ideal of making money and somehow transfer that energy to the pursuit of less selfish but more fruitful goals that had to be national in scope and democratic in practice.
- The final goal was a society based on "the religion of human brotherhood" … men must come to know "the loving kindness which individuals feel toward their fellowmen and particularly toward their fellow countrymen."[18]

Levy notes that the years between 1909 and 1914 were "thrilling" for Croly. He was famous, and his views were in demand by presidents of nations and great universities. It was during this period that he founded *The New Republic*, which was the nation's quintessential progressive magazine.

Funding for the magazine came from Willard Straight, a senior employee at J. P. Morgan, and his wife, Dorothy. She was a New York socialite and daughter of the wealthy industrialist William C. Whitney and his equally wealthy wife, Flora Payne, who was the daughter and heir of Oliver H. Payne, who was one of the richest men in the United States. The Straights also bankrolled the New School for Social Research in Greenwich Village, another of Croly's projects, which became the principle soapbox upon which many of the most famous of New York City's vibrant Progressive Movement advertised their wares.

One of these individuals was Columbia philosophy professor John Dewey, who was cofounder of the School and is widely regarded today as one of America's most important philosophers and advocates of what became known as "progressive education." He was neither a self-described Marxist nor a socialist, although one could argue that his work in the field of educational reform and his Marxist-like views on social theory did more to advance the leftist agenda in twentieth-century America than virtually any of the period's most ardent leftists, including those of his close friend and most aggressive promoter, Sidney Hook, who recognized that Dewey's philosophy was an easier sell to American leftists than classical Marxism.

Among other things, Dewey was an early advocate of "secular humanism," which Supreme Court Justice Hugo Black once included in a list of "religions ... which do not teach what would generally be considered a belief in the existence of God."[19] Its tenets can be found in a document called the Humanist Manifesto, which Dewey and numerous other leading leftists signed in 1933. Russell Kirk summarized its creed as follows:

> [It] declares that the universe is self-existing, not created; that science shows the unreality of supernatural sanctions for human values; that this earthly existence is the be-all and end-all; that religious emotions are best expressed in heightened personality and in efforts to advance social well-being; that man himself is maker and active power, unmoved by transcendent forces.[20]

Dewey himself said this of it:

> Here are all the elements for a religious faith that shall not be confined to sect, class, or race. Such a faith has always been implicitly the common faith of mankind. It remains to make it explicit and militant.[21]

As regard his contribution to educational theory, he denigrated the traditional practice of focusing on teaching such subjects as reading, writing, mathematics, and history, and promoted the teaching of social and "thinking" skills instead. His involvement in education began in 1897 with an essay entitled "My Pedagogic Creed," which contained such notions as the following:

> I believe that the school is primarily a social institution. ... I believe that much of present

education fails because it neglects this fundamental principle of the school as a form of community life. It conceives the school as a place where certain information is to be given, where certain lessons are to be learned, or where certain habits are to be formed. The value of these is conceived as lying largely in the remote future; the child must do these things for the sake of something else he is to do; they are mere preparation. As a result they do not become a part of the life experience of the child and so are not truly educative ... I believe that the teacher is not in the school to impose certain ideas or to form certain habits in the child, but is there as a member of the community to select the influences which shall affect the child and to assist him in properly responding to these influences. ... I believe that all questions of the grading of the child and his promotion should be determined by reference to the same standard. Examinations are of use only so far as they test the child's fitness for social life and reveal the place in which he can be of most service and where he can receive the most help ... I believe that much of the time and attention now given to the preparation and presentation of lessons might be more wisely and profitably expended in training the child's power of imagery and in seeing to it that he was continually forming definite, vivid, and growing images of the various subjects with which he comes in contact in his experience ... I believe it is the business of every one interested in education to insist upon the school as the primary and most effective instrument of social progress and reform in order that society may be awakened to realize what the school stands for, and aroused to the

necessity of endowing the educator with sufficient equipment properly to perform his task.[22]

In 1916, he published a book entitled *Democracy and Education*,
which was listed by the conservative newspaper *Human Events* as the
fifth most harmful book of the nineteenth and twentieth century.[23]

It was during this period that Croly wrote his second book,
this one called *Progressive Democracy*, which was published in 1915.
Among other things, it urged Americans to abandon both the
Constitution and Christianity in favor of progressivism. In this way,
he said they could fulfill the dreams contained in his first book by
opposing the "old formulations that pretended to eternal truth ...
that blinded men to the unique problems of an every-changing environment ... [and that] excused men from the hard thought required
to meet new situations."[24]

Of course, the attack on the Constitution was not new to progressives. But Croly went beyond Teddy's claim that this was justified by the fact that changing economic and social conditions since
the founding had rendered the document obsolete. He argued,
instead, that progressivism had rendered the constitution unnecessary. Moreover, this devotee of Comte said that the "very essence
of Christianity" requires "the emancipation of humanity from constrained obedience to the law or a code." That indeed St. Paul himself
said as much. Croly put it this way:

> "Before the faith came," says St. Paul in his
> Epistle to the Galatians, "we were kept under the
> Law, shut up into the faith, which should after-
> wards be revealed. Wherefore the Law was our
> schoolmaster to bring us into Christ, that we
> might be justified by faith. But after that faith has
> come, we are no longer under a school master."[25]

As to the substitution of progressivism for law, he said that one
had to have faith in the American people.

The assurance which American progressivism is gradually acquiring, and of whose necessity it is finally becoming conscious, is merely an expression of faith—faith in the peculiar value and possible reality of its own enterprise, faith in the power of faith … Faith in things unseen and unknowable is as indispensible to a progressive democracy as it is to an individual Christian.[26]

Finally, borrowing Rousseau's charge against the "defeatism" of the concept of original sin, he argued that it is demeaning to rely on a constitution. To wit:

Of course, if human nature is so essentially erring that it will certainly go astray unless it continues to be personally conducted along the highroad to civilization, then the Law and the schoolmaster constitute our only hope of salvation; but in that case the less said about the character of the American people the better. A political system based upon such a conception of human nature would imply an essential and permanent lack of character on the part of its beneficiaries.[27]

It is hard to say whether Teddy created Croly or Croly created Teddy, but either way, together they helped to clear the path for the destruction of the Constitution, the subsequent dominance of leftist thought in the United States, and, most importantly, the transformation from progressivism to liberalism, a process that would be deftly engineered by Taft's Democratic successor Woodrow Wilson.

You see, while the progressives had a spiritual side, and in the case of Teddy a strong Tartuffian bent, they, like the Fabians, concentrated their efforts almost exclusively on social and economic problems that were, theoretically at least, within the power of humans to solve or mitigate. The liberals would seek to solve problems that are beyond mankind's control, such as war, poverty, inequality, and even mankind's unattractive and unfit representatives.

On August 31, 1910, Teddy gave the above-mentioned appeal for the progressive tax in his famous speech in Osawatomie, Kansas, which was right out Croly's book. Historians generally refer to it as the New Nationalism speech. However, it was, in fact, not about nationalism. It was about pure, unadulterated socialism.

> The citizens of the United States must effectively control the mighty commercial forces which they have called into being ... It has become entirely clear that we must have government supervision of the capitalization, not only of public-service corporations, including, particularly, railways, but of all corporations doing an interstate business ... It is my personal belief that the same kind and degree of control and supervision which should be exercised over public-service corporations should be extended also to combinations which control necessaries of life, such as meat, oil, or coal, or which deal in them on an important scale. I have no doubt that the ordinary man who has control of them is much like ourselves. I have no doubt he would like to do well, but I want to have enough supervision to help him realize that desire to do well.
>
> Combinations in industry are the result of an imperative economic law which cannot be repealed by political legislation. The effort at prohibiting all combination has substantially failed. The way out lies, not in attempting to prevent such combinations, but in completely controlling them in the interest of the public welfare. For that purpose the Federal Bureau of Corporations is an agency of first importance. Its powers, and, therefore, its efficiency, as well as

that of the Interstate Commerce Commission, should be largely increased. We have a right to expect from the Bureau of Corporations and from the Interstate Commerce Commission a very high grade of public service. We should be as sure of the proper conduct of the interstate railways and the proper management of interstate business as we are now sure of the conduct and management of the national banks, and we should have as effective supervision in one case as in the other.

The absence of effective State, and, especially, national, restraint upon *unfair money-getting* has tended to create a small class of enormously wealthy and economically powerful men, whose chief object is to hold and increase their power. The prime need is to change the conditions which enable these men to accumulate power which it is not for the general welfare that they should hold or exercise. ... We grudge no man a fortune in civil life if it is honorably obtained and *well used*. It is not even enough that it should have been gained without doing damage to the community. *We should permit it to be gained* only so long as the gaining represents benefit to the community. This, I know, implies a policy of a far more active governmental interference with social and economic conditions in this country than we have yet had, but I think we have got to face the fact that such an increase in governmental control is now necessary. [Emphasis added]

No man should receive a dollar unless that dollar has been fairly earned. Every dollar received should represent a dollar's worth of service rendered—not gambling in stocks, but service rendered. The really big fortune, the swollen fortune, by the mere fact of its size, acquires qualities which differentiate it in kind as well as in degree from what is possessed by men of relatively small means. Therefore, I believe in a graduated income tax on big fortunes, and in another tax which is far more easily collected and far more effective—a graduated inheritance tax on big fortunes, properly safeguarded against evasion, and increasing rapidly in amount with the size of the estate.[28]

In the meantime, Taft had begun to file myriad antitrust suits relying on his aggressive attorney general George Wickersham for guidance rather than on Herbert Knox Smith's Bureau of Corporations, which had been highly friendly to the industrialists under Roosevelt. Smith, by the way, had run interference for Teddy when, shortly after the Panic of 1907, Congress began asking for documents relating to his decision in the Tennessee Coal acquisition.

Not surprisingly, Taft's support among the progressives was slipping badly due to the tariff reform debacle, as was his standing with the business community due to the filing of his many antitrust suits. Naturally then, Teddy's traveling tent show began building a groundswell for another run at the White House.

Initially, Teddy did not encourage this effort. In fact, he publicly supported Taft and worked hard at trying to patch up relations between the progressives and the Old Guard. Then, on October 27, 1911, the tension between the two men broke into open warfare when Taft's Justice Department filed an antitrust suit against US Steel that alleged that the company had obtained its monopoly by, among other things, duping Teddy into approving the Tennessee Coal purchase.

Teddy had been defending his role in the acquisition for four years, and, in fact, just a few months earlier had had to appear before a Congressional committee to discuss it. Adding insult to injury, Taft filed another highly political antitrust suit in April against International Harvester, while at the same time releasing documents outlining the previously mentioned collaboration on this deal between Roosevelt, Perkins, and the Bureau of Corporations.[29]

Of course, Teddy fired back, charging that Taft's policy toward the trusts had been foolhardy. Adding to Taft's woes, and encouraging Teddy's ambitions, the Democrats won control of the House in the midterm elections, picking up fifty-eight seats. This meant that James Beauchamp "Champ" Clark from Missouri would replace Uncle Joe Cannon as majority leader. Moreover, the Democrats would gain twelve seats in the Senate and win more than half the gubernatorial races, one of which went to Woodrow Wilson, which made him one of two leading contenders for the Democratic nomination for the presidency in 1914, the other being "Champ" Clark.

This humiliating defeat for the Republicans set the stage for a classic political battle between two men who had once been friends. It was clear that Taft would win a second term if Teddy stayed out of the race. It was not clear what would happen if Teddy challenged him. Many observers thought it would assure that a Democratic would be the next president. In any case, everyone agreed that the battle would be a bully of a contest. Teddy, however, was reluctant. For one thing, a challenge would be expensive. Who would finance it? And why?

Well, funny you should ask. Unbeknown to the public, there were powerful forces at work behind the scenes that were about to make history.

To understand this, we need to go back in time to the Panic of 1907, which historians agree had greatly elevated the public concern over the nation's dependence on Morgan and had thus piqued public interest in banking reform. We agree with this, but we would argue that the better way to put it would be that the Panic had convinced Morgan that the time had come for him to take advantage of this public concern and strengthen his increasingly beneficial partnership with the federal government by formalizing the role of the large banks in maintaining orderly financial markets.

The first step in the process occurred in May 1908 when Aldrich established and assumed the chairmanship of something called the National Monetary Commission, which was vested with the authority to do a study of the banking system and make recommendations as to its reform. We should also point out that one of Aldrich's senior advisors on the Commission would be Henry P. Davison, who had been at Morgan's side throughout the Panic of 1907.

The members of this august group then set off for Europe to study the various banking systems there. On their return home, they held a series of hearings on the subject and issued a remarkable number of reports. A return to prosperity temporarily took the urgency out of the matter, but then, in March 1909, Taft became president, and Aldrich had to turn his attention to sabotaging "Big Bill's" plan to lower tariffs. When Aldrich finally returned to the task of banking reform, he discovered that despite the tour of Europe, the hearings, and the studies, neither he nor any of its members could come up with a plan that would satisfy both the bankers and the public.

One man, however, had stayed involved in the issue throughout this period. His name was Paul Moritz Warburg. He was an extremely wealthy and influential scion of the internationally powerful M. M. Warburg bank in Hamburg, Germany, which had been founded by his grandfather Moses Warburg and had very close ties to the powerful Rothschild financial empire.

Along with his brother Felix, he had immigrated in 1902 to the United States where he married Nina Loeb, the daughter of Solomon Loeb, and became a partner in his father-in-law's firm, Kuhn, Loeb & Co. Felix married Frieda Schiff, the daughter of Jacob Schiff, who was married to Solomon Loeb's other daughter, Therese.

Schiff was a German banker who had come to America shortly after the Civil War to run Kuhn, Loeb & Co, whose two founders, Solomon and Abraham Kuhn, had made their money in the textile business and thus had no experience in banking. He was one of the most extraordinary and powerful of the so-called Titans. Indeed, it is fair to say that by the turn of the century, Kuhn, Loeb, under his leadership, had become second only to the house of Morgan in money and influence. Among other things, Schiff had extensive contacts to the Rothschild interests in Europe as well as to the British royal family through his close friendship with Sir Earnest Edward Cassell, a

German-born British merchant banker who was close friends with King Edward VII and one of the world's richest men.

Paul Warburg was an expert on the European models of central banking, and he was appalled at the backwardness of the American banking system. In fact, in an article entitled "Defects and Needs of Our Banking System," which the *New York Times* published in January 1907, he said the following: "The United States is in fact at about the same point that had been reached by Europe at the time of the Medicis, and by Asia, in all likelihood, at the time of Hammurabi."[30]

After the Panic of 1907, he followed that article up with several revisions and gave numerous well-received speeches to leading economic groups around the country. Thus, in late 1910, when Aldrich finally turned his attention back to the issue of banking reform, he discovered that Warburg had done what his commission had failed to do.

Thus, late on the night of November 22, 1910, he, Warburg, and four other leading figures in the banking community boarded Aldrich's private railway car in Hoboken, New Jersey, bound for a secret meeting at a private resort owned by J. P. Morgan on Jekyll Island off the coast of Georgia. Their goal was to establish a central bank in America. The other four men were Frank A. Vanderlip, president of William Rockefeller's National City Bank of New York; the aforementioned Henry P. Davison, a senior partner in the investment bank J. P. Morgan Company; Abram Piatt Andrew Jr., assistant secretary of the US Treasury; and Benjamin Strong, son-in-law and protégé of Edmund Converse, the president of J. P. Morgan's Bankers Trust, protégé of Davidson, and Morgan's personal auditor during the Panic of 1907. Estimates vary, but estimates are that the collective wealth of these men represented the interests of about one-fourth of the total wealth of entire world.[31]

Secrecy was paramount. The public anger over the Panic of 1907 was still high, and the notion that the nation's bankers were meeting in private to establish a central bank under their control would have caused a firestorm of opposition that probably would have smothered the idea in its crib. Among the many cautionary means taken by the men to hide their activities was calling each other by their first names only so that no one on the staff at the resort could guess who they were. Ostensibly, they were there to hunt ducks.

Of course, the secrecy surrounding this meeting, the power of the characters involved, and the subsequent twisted path to the establishment of the Federal Reserve Board fostered a plethora of vast and elaborate conspiracies, many of which are still in full bloom today. Depending upon whose axe the teller of the tale happens to be grinding, these theories involve a boiling and bubbling mixture of secret meetings of the elusive Illuminati, nefarious Jews in the pay of the European Rothschild dynasty, Russian Bolsheviks, ruthless American industrialists and their greedy bankers—all engaged in a dastardly plan to control the world. Moreover, there are still myriad disagreements among historians about the role that certain individuals played in the drama. All of which makes it difficult one hundred years later to be certain who to believe about what. However, we will do the best to get the gist of the story.

It took them ten days to agree upon a plan. Warburg is largely credited with having been the intellectual driver behind its outline. On January 9, 1911, Aldrich introduced the reform bill into the Senate claiming that it was the work of the National Monetary Commission. It immediately ran into furious opposition, which continued throughout the year. Not only did this hostility come from the entire Democratic establishment but also from some leading Republican Progressives led by La Follette in the Senate and Minnesota congressman Charles Lindbergh Sr. in the House. Lindbergh summed up the opposition's position as follows in testimony December 1911:

> The Aldrich Plan is the Wall Street Plan. It is a broad challenge to the Government by the champion of the Money Trust. It means another panic, if necessary, to intimidate the people. Aldrich, paid by the Government to represent the people, proposes a plan for the trusts instead.[32]

Making matters worse, Taft went along with the Lindbergh and La Follette crowd, announcing that he would only support a reform bill if it did not give control to bankers. Thus, by January 1912, it had become obvious to Aldrich and the bankers that if they wanted a central bank of the kind envisioned by the men from Jekyll Island, they would have to convince the public of the need for banking reform and replace Taft with someone better suited to the task ahead.

Warburg took on the job of selling the reform idea to the public by arranging financing for the establishment of the National Citizens League for the Promotion of a Sound Banking System. This group was made up exclusively of Midwestern businessmen whose mission was to "show that Main Street was just as enthusiastic as Wall Street about banking reform." Warburg explained, "It would have been fatal to launch such an enterprise from New York."[33]

J. Laurence Laughlin led the effort. He was an economics professor at the University of Chicago, which was friendly territory to the bankers, having been financed in part by a $50 million grant from Rockefeller. Laughlin was also close friends with a former graduate student of his, H. Parker Willis, who had taken a job as administrative assistant to Democratic congressman Carter Glass of Virginia, the ranking member of the House Banking Committee. Glass had just been given the chairmanship of one of two subcommittees set up to address the issue of banking reform. His job was to study the issue itself. The other, chaired by Louisiana Democrat Arsene Pujo, was to investigate the need for reform.

Perkins took on the task of defeating Taft. He enlisted the support of his friend and business associate Frank Munsey, who was an extremely wealthy and highly influential newspaper and magazine publisher who had made his initial fortune when Perkins cut him in on the fruits of the International Harvester deal.

Their first step was to convince Teddy to challenge Taft for the Republican nomination. As noted above, Teddy had been reluctant to take up the challenge, partly because it would require substantial political and financial backing. Perkins and Munsey assured him that they would finance and run the entire operation. Hence, on January 16, 1912, Teddy wrote a letter to Munsey saying that he would "serve if the country demanded him and needed him but that he was not seeking the nomination and would not do so." He sent a copy of the letter to Root, who wrote him back, questioning whether Teddy, "because of your temperament," would be able to stick to this decision, which, Root said he supported because he believed that neither he nor Taft could beat the Democratic candidate if they fought each other for the nomination.[34]

Two days later, Teddy wrote a letter to three state governors asking them to round up a few other governors who would join them in asking him, Teddy, if he would "respond to public demand" and seek the nomination. Not surprisingly, he said in his letter that he was "honestly desirous of considering the matter solely from the standpoint of the public interest."[35]

On February 9, he wrote Root again thanking him for his advice, but telling him that he no longer believed that it is "possible for me to refrain from speaking publicly." After all, he said that nine state governors had just asked him to run and that he could not treat their request "as I have treated mere private requests."[36] The race for the Republican nomination was on.

Root was conflicted. He had been a friend of Teddy's for years, but he was also working closely with Taft at the time. Teddy made the decision for him on February 21, when he spoke to the Ohio State Constitutional Convention and complained bitterly about judges that stood in the way of "justice." As to the cure, he expressed his support for not only removing those judges who overrule the "popular will," based on their personal opinions that something is unconstitutional, but to permit voters to recall any judicial decision that they feel is in defiance of justice. He put it this way:

> If the Constitution is successfully invoked to nullify the effort to remedy injustice, it is proof positive either that the Constitution needs immediate amendment or else that it is being wrongfully and improperly contrasted. ...
> Our aim is to get the type of judge that I have described, to keep him on the bench as long

> as possible, and to keep off the bench, and, if
> necessary, take off the bench, the wrong type of
> judge. ... Therefore, the question of applying the
> recall in any shape is one of expediency merely.
> Each community has a right to try the experi-
> ment for itself in whatever shape it pleases.[37]

According to the journalist and historian Henry L. Stoddard, the speech caused an "explosion" in the media. He described it as "the most sensational campaign utterance since Burchard's 'Rum, Romanism and Rebellion' speech that led to James G. Blain's loss to Cleveland in 1884."[38] It was, after all, an egregious attack on the Constitution, which revealed an astonishing ignorance of the scholarship and wisdom behind the founding fathers' efforts to construct a society free from the ill effects of faction, or, shall we say, mob rule. Philosophically speaking, Teddy was advocating the application of Rousseau's concept of the "general will," which, as we previously noted, assumes that people are good by the very nature, and, this being the case, assumes that these inherently good people could and should act collectively as the "sovereign," answerable to no one but themselves.

The Founders described this form of government as direct democracy and agreed with Plato that it was undesirable. In fact, they assumed that one result of direct democracy would be the appearance of "factions," which would contend against each other and sow social discontent. To be more specific, they feared it would spark the appearance of a radical yet charismatic blowhard such as Teddy, who would deliberately court the favor of one faction of citizens and lead it into battle against another. Once again, we turn to Madison and Federalist #10.

> The effect of the first difference [between
> direct democracy and a republic] is, on the one
> hand, to refine and enlarge the public views, by
> passing them through the medium of a chosen
> body of citizens, whose wisdom may best dis-

cern the true interest of their country, and whose patriotism and love of justice will be least likely to sacrifice it to temporary or partial considerations. Under such a regulation, it may well happen that the public voice, pronounced by the representatives of the people, will be more consonant to the public good than if pronounced by the people themselves, convened for the purpose. On the other hand, the effect may be inverted. Men of factious tempers, of local prejudices, or of sinister designs, may, by intrigue, by corruption, or by other means, first obtain the suffrages, and then betray the interests, of the people. The question resulting is, whether small or extensive republics are more favorable to the election of proper guardians of the public weal; and it is clearly decided in favor of the latter by two obvious considerations.[39]

It would be hard to exaggerate the negative effect that Teddy's speech had on his relationship with some of his closest friends and political allies. Root for one threw in the towel. In a letter dated March 9, he tried to excuse Teddy's actions to a friend by saying that "he [Teddy] is essentially a fighter and when he gets into a fight he is completely dominated by the desire to destroy his adversary ... I have no doubt he thinks he believes what he says, but he doesn't."[40]

Nevertheless, Root would support Taft in the upcoming contest, as would the esteemed senator from Massachusetts, Henry Cabot Lodge; Teddy's son-in-law and congressman from Ohio, Nicholas Longworth; Teddy's postmaster general when he was president and was at the time Taft's Secretary of the Navy, George Meyer; the man who had been Teddy's choice for New York governor and was at the time Taft's Secretary of War, Henry Stimson; and Lodge's son-in-law and congressman from Massachusetts, Augustus Gardner.[41]

Teddy lost the fight, of course, largely because Root used his authority as chairman of the convention so aggressively that one participant famously charged that the "steam roller is exceeding the speed limit."[42] At this point, Perkins and Munsey talked Teddy into running on a third-party ticket and agreed to arrange financing for the venture, which would virtually assure that a Democrat would win the White House.[43]

In the meantime, the public was getting an earful on banking reform. Laughlin's group was engaging in a soft sell, while Pujo had opened eight months of hearings into the dangers of the concentration of wealth among a handful of individuals. He blistered the wealthy, and in doing so made banking reform a popular issue, which Laughlin and his board could never have done by themselves. In fact, Pujo was so successful that some historians have argued that the hearings were a setup, part of the bankers' plan. The historian Gabriel Kolko put it this way:

> Five banking firms, the elaborate tables of the committee showed, held 341 directorships in 112 corporations with an aggregate capitalization of $22 billion. The evidence seemed conclusive, and the nation was suitably frightened into realizing that reform of the banking system was urgent—presumably to bring Wall Street under control. ...
>
> The orgy of Wall Street was resurrected by the newspapers, who quietly ignored the fact that the biggest advocates of banking reform were the bankers themselves, bankers with a somewhat different view of the problem. ... Yet it was largely the Pujo hearings that made the topic of banking reform a serious one."[44]

The final step in the plan was to find a suitable Democrat. Fortunately, for the bankers, Morgan's friend George Harvey, the highly influential and esteemed editor of *Harper's Weekly*, which Morgan had once bailed out of bankruptcy, had someone in mind whom he, Harvey, had helped to become the governor of New Jersey.

That person was, course, Woodrow Wilson, a progressive with a markedly conservative bent who had, as Ferdinand Lundberg put it in his classic *America's 60 Families*, "moved in the shadow of Wall Street" for more than twenty years.

Besides being indebted to Harvey for gaining him the governorship of New Jersey, he was close friends with two former classmates of his at Princeton who had become very wealthy and, as members of the board at Princeton, had helped Wilson to obtain a job teaching economics there and a few years later to obtain the presidency of the College. Moreover, when Wilson found the pay at Princeton too low to meet his needs, these men had established a fund to provide a subsidy. Their names were Cleveland Dodge and Cyrus McCormick. Both were also on the board of Rockefeller's National City Bank, along with such wealthy industrialists as the younger J. P. Morgan, William Rockefeller, Frick, Schiff, and Vanderlip.[45]

Naturally, Wilson won.

Let's let the poets in on the fun.

Excerpt from *Paradise Lost*:

> For Man will hearken to his glozing lies,
> And easily transgress the sole Command,
> Sole pledge of his obedience: So will fall
> Hee and his faithless Progeny: whose fault?
> Whose but his own? ingrate, he had of mee
> All he could have; I made him just and right,
> Sufficient to have stood, though free to fall ...
> They trespass, Authors to themselves in all
> Both what they judge and what they choose; for so
> I form'd them free, and free they must remain ...
> John Milton, 1671

Chapter 18

Wilson: The Third Way

> *To avoid, therefore, the evils of inconstancy
> and versatility, ten thousand times worse than those
> of obstinacy and the blindest prejudice, we have
> consecrated the state, that no man should approach
> to look into its defects or corruptions but with due
> caution; that he should never dream of beginning
> its reformation by its subversion; that he should
> approach to the faults of the state as to the wounds
> of a father, with pious awe and trembling solicitude.
> Society is indeed a contract. But it is not a part-
> nership in things subservient only to the gross ani-
> mal existence of a temporary and perishable nature.*
> (Edmund Burke, *Reflections on the Revolution in
> France*, 1790)

The year 1998 was the year of the "third way." Left-wing politicians the world over were trumpeting this "new" middle ground
between capitalism and socialism. In fact, President Clinton opened
his State of the Union speech that year with the dramatic announcement that "we have moved past the sterile debate between those who
say government is the enemy and those who say government is the
answer. We have found a third way."[1]

British Prime Minister Tony Blair quickly came on board, and in September of that year, he and Clinton held a conference in New York to officially launch their new ideology. On the opening day of that meeting, Blair published Fabian Pamphlet 588 in which he said that "the 'Third Way' is, to my mind, the best label for the *new* politics which the progressive centre-left is forging in Britain and beyond."[2] And wouldn't you know it, Professor Anthony Giddens from the London School of Economics wrote a book that same year entitled *The Third Way and Its Critics*, which was widely hailed among the leftist as a guideline for the future.

This was all nonsense, of course. There was nothing new about the concept of a middle ground between capitalism and socialism. Indeed, it had been the primary topic of discussion within the world of the Left ever since it became apparent in the nineteenth century that Marxism simply would not work in the real world. As noted previously, Lassalle was one of the first to figure this out. Then, of course, there was Bernstein, Maurras, Sorel, Mussolini, and Hitler.

Woodrow Wilson was the first US president to join this long line of individuals who were determined to attempt to put lipstick on this pig. Teddy deserves a mention here, but as we noted, he was just a foolish man, not an ideologue. Wilson was a confirmed socialist who pursued his belief in the necessity for vast governmental controls over large segments of society with a religious fervor.

Unlike Teddy, who came from the secular, political/reformist branch of the progressive movement, Wilson's roots were firmly set in the Social Gospel. He was a devout Calvinist, the son, and grandson of Presbyterian ministers, and a former student of Richard Ely. He believed that God had personally selected him to lead the nation to its predetermined destiny and that government was the tool that he was to use. You see, Wilson was mad as a hatter. If there had been reports of a white whale swimming up the Potomac, he would have been out chucking harpoons at it like Captain Ahab, who coined the slogan for the Wilson presidency, "All my means are sane, my motive and my object mad."

How can we say this? Well, from a purely medical standpoint, we could be wrong. Yet speaking generally, people who believe they have been "chosen" by God for a particular role in life and act accordingly are not wrapped too tight. Wilson fervently believed this. William Frank McCombs, chairman of the Democratic National Committee and the man who was largely responsible for Wilson's victory in his first presidential race, relates the following conversation with him immediately after the election.

> At last the President-elect deigned to recognize me. He imperiously beckoned me into his library. When we reached there, I said: "Governor, I came over to offer you my sincerest congratulations upon your election and to express my hope that you will have a happy and successful administration."
>
> The president-elect took my hand in a frigid, mechanical way. His stenographer started to leave the room. He said to the stenographer: "You need not leave, I shall continue my dictation". Surprised, I inquired: "What does this mean, Governor"? The governor fidgeted a bit and jerked out: "It means that every word that passes here is to be recorded in black and white."
>
> Then I became provoked and insisted upon an explanation of the affront which I believed had been deliberately offered me. When I protested, the President-elect, with a heartlessness of which up to this time I was ignorant, turned upon me and in measured tone said: "Before we proceed, I wish it clearly understood that I owe you nothing". I modestly suggested that I might be given credit for doing a little toward his nomination and election.
>
> Haughtily, Governor Wilson retorted: "Whether you did little or much, remember that God ordained that I should be the next President

of the United States. Neither you nor any mortal or mortals could have prevented that"![3]

Lest you believe that McCombs was exaggerating, we offer the following from Wilson's July 1919 address in which he asked the Senate to ratify America's participation in the League of Nations: "The stage is set, the destiny disclosed. It has come about *by no plan of our conceiving, but by the hand of God*. We cannot turn back. The light streams on the path ahead, and nowhere else."[4]

When considering the presumptuousness, not to mention the heretical nature, of Wilson's contention that God had selected him as an agent of His will, compare it to the following response by President Lincoln during the Civil War to someone who asked him if he believed that God was on the side of the North:

> I am not at all concerned about that, for I know the Lord is always on the side of the right. But it is my constant anxiety and prayer that I and this nation should be on the Lord's side.[5]

As noted in the previous chapter, Teddy had routinely claimed the moral high ground, as had other presidents before him. However, Teddy's moralizing, as well as that of all former presidents, always took the form of support for some sort of policy action.[6] Wilson's, on the other hand, harkened back to the Puritan belief that he was, in the words of historian Daniel Boorstin, conducting a "noble experiment in applied theology."[7] And should anyone doubt this, he made it clear in his first inaugural address.

> The Nation has been deeply stirred, stirred by a solemn passion, stirred by the knowledge of wrong, of ideals lost, of government too often debauched and made an instrument of evil. The feelings with which we face this new age of right and opportunity sweep across our heartstrings like some air out of God's own presence, where

justice and mercy are reconciled and the judge and the brother are one. We know our task to be no mere task of politics but a task which shall search us through and through, whether we be able to understand our time and the need of our people, whether we be indeed their spokesmen and interpreters, whether we have the pure heart to comprehend and the rectified will to choose our high course of action.[8]

This was, of course, straight out of the Social Gospel movement's adaptation of Hegel's theory of historical progress. You see, like Marx, Wilson firmly believed that history had both meaning and direction and that it would culminate in a final, rational form of society. Richard J. Bishirjian, Professor of Government at Yorktown University, outlined Wilson's version of this Hegelian-based millenarianism as follows in an article entitled "Croly, Wilson, and the American Civil Religion" in the Winter 1979 issue of *Modern Age*:

History, Wilson believed, moves according to a plan in which America plays a major role. His view of history is one of a progressive development, moving slowly but inexorably to a condition of reconstituted reality.

In an address in Pittsburgh, Pennsylvania at a Y.M.C.A. celebration on October 24, 1914, he said: " ... no man can look at the past of the history of this world without seeing a vision of the future of the history of this world; and when you think of the accumulated moral forces that have made one age better than another age in the progress of mankind, then you can open your eyes to the vision. You can see that age by age, though with a blind struggle in the dust of the road, though often mistaking the path and losing its way in the mire, mankind is yet—sometimes with bloody hands and battered knees—nevertheless struggling step after step up the slow stages to the day when he shall live in the full light which shines upon the uplands, where all the light that illumines mankind shines direct from the face of God."

The role of America in this plan of history, Wilson was persuaded, was shaped and directed by God from the beginning ... Wilson's view of history in which America and mankind were moving to a world immanent transfiguration of the human condition was an integral aspect of his attitude towards life and the skills required if political life was to be governed rightly. Politics, for Wilson, required "vision," and vision for Wilson meant knowledge of God's purpose in history. In his First Inaugural, Wilson was speaking of his own visionary politics when he described his task as "no mere task of politics." The politics of Wilson were not "mere politics," they were a special capacity to announce the immanence of a new age certified by the political leader who experienced a special revelation.[9]

Of course, the practical result of Wilson's intense insistence that he and God were partners in cleaning up America was entirely predictable. You see, it is not humanly possible to play convincingly the part of God's alter ego for very long, especially if the god you choose to replicate is the Christian god of absolute love and charity. So Wilson did as the many other pretenders to celestial guidance had done, he redefined God's will to be more in line with his own ideas of virtue while continuing to insist that they were divinely inspired.

Quite naturally, those who were invested in Wilson agreed to this fix, which came easily to the progressives, who were not all that happy anyway with the way God's plan had worked out so far. And lo, progressivism began to evolve from a loosely defined, left-wing, social activist undertaking to a quasi-religious political ideology that would come to be called liberalism.

One of the key differences between the two was that, unlike the progressives, who served their God by engaging in practical activities on behalf of individuals who were in need of their love and hands-on assistance, Wilson and his fellow proto-liberals drew their feelings of self-worth from lofty pretenses. Catholic university professor Claes Ryn describes this phenomenon as follows in his classic *The New Jacobinism: Can America Survive?*

> [Liberalism] lets individuals claim moral worth who show no particular signs of moral character in their actual conduct and who may, by traditional moral standards, actually be personally odious ... their virtue is that they entertain benevolent sentiments for various abstract entities, such as "the people," "mankind," "the proletariat," "the poor," "the downtrodden," "the staving third world," or the like—categories that are all comfortably distant from the emoting person and which therefore impose no concrete and personally demanding obligations on the individual. Still, this sentimental posture of caring contains a pleasant ingredient of self-applause. It is, as it were, morality made easy. It presupposes no difficult improvement of self in actual human relationships.[10]

At this point it is important to note that, lacking any sort of transcendent or religious foundation, the leftist catechism varies from country to country based on a variety of factors including customs and established beliefs, the personal prejudices and ambitions of its leaders, the strength of the opposition, the preexisting form of government, and most importantly, the nature of the utopian vision shared by its followers, which is invariably influenced by the social circumstances that the leftists find most offensive and discomforting.

In continental Europe, where society was highly class conscious, the Left's principal culprit was capitalism and the "unfair" power and wealth disparities it created. In contrast, as noted previously, the English Fabians were not as interested in transferring power and wealth to the lower classes as they were in eliminating them. They viewed themselves and their social class as the glorious culmination of civilization's Darwinian-like, natural advancement toward a higher social order, and delighted in the possibility of speeding up the global ascendency of their fraternity of enlightened intellectuals by eliminating undesirable humans via a program of selective breeding. Yet as also noted, they did not succeed in converting their ideas into law.

American progressives and proto-liberals agreed with the Fabians. Unfortunately for the nation's underclasses, they were significantly more successful in their plans to eliminate those whom they found to be "offensive." The result was a veritable flood of legal restraints and physical assaults on thousands of Americans who were judged to be "paupers," "imbeciles," "insane," "feeble-minded," "epileptic," "morally weak," or any of a host of other highly subjective, "undesirable" characteristics.

Indeed, none other than the great Social Gospel leader Richard Ely became a pioneer in this undertaking with the publication in 1903 of his book *Studies in the Evolution of Industrial Society*, in which he waxed optimistic about the positive effects that could be achieved by the ongoing efforts in the various states to limit the ability of objectionable people to breed.[11] Edwin Black described the widespread popularity of eugenics this way in his book *War against the Weak, Eugenics and America's Campaign to Create a Master Race.*

> Mandatory sterilization laws were enacted in some twenty-seven states to prevent targeted individuals from reproducing more of their kind. Marriage prohibition laws proliferated throughout the country to stop race mixing ... The goal was to immediately sterilize fourteen million people in the United States and millions more worldwide ... ultimately some 60,000 Americans

were coercively sterilized and the total is probably much higher. ... The victims of eugenics were
poor urban dwellers and rural "while trash" from
New England to California, immigrants from
across Europe, Blacks, Jews, Mexicans, Native
Americans, epileptics, alcoholics, petty criminals,
the mentally ill and anyone else who did not
resemble the blond and blue-eyed Nordic ideal
the eugenics movement glorified.[12]

The leader and putative founder of the American eugenics
movement was the Harvard zoologist Charles Davenport. A follower
and fan of Galton, Davenport was a fanatical racist who believed,
in the words of Black, that "most of the non-Nordic types ... swam
at the bottom of the hereditary pool, each featuring its own distinct
and indelible adverse genetic features. Italians were predisposed to
personal violence. The Irish had 'considerable mental defectiveness,'
while Germans were "thrifty, intelligent, and honest.'"[13] Not surprisingly, the very notion of America being a melting pot sickened him.

Davenport's formal campaign to "improve the race" began in
1904 when the Carnegie Institution funded his plan to establish
the Station for Experimental Evolution at the Cold Spring Harbor
Laboratory in New York to study heredity and evolution through
breeding experiments with plants and animals, which the state would
use to promote the "improvement of the human race."

In addition to gaining the support of the Carnegie Institute,
Davenport became a favorite of the progressives. In fact, Teddy was so
enamored with the project of improving mankind that he established
a federal eugenics advisory group called the Heredity Commission in
1906 and placed Davenport on the board. The Commission's purpose was to encourage "the increase of families of good blood and
discouraging the vicious elements in the cross-bred American civilization" and to discover whether "a new species of human being may
be consciously evolved."[14] Nor did Teddy's enthusiasm wane with
time. Indeed, seven years later, a few days before Wilson took office,
Teddy wrote a letter to Davenport saying the following:

I agree with you ... that society has no business to permit degenerates to reproduce their kind. It is really extraordinary that our people refuse to apply to human beings such elementary knowledge as every successful farmer is obliged to apply to his own stock breeding ... Some day, we will realize that the prime duty, the inescapable duty, of the good citizen of the right type, is to leave his or her blood behind him in the world; and that we have no business to permit the perpetuation of citizens of the wrong type."[15]

However, Teddy's support was tepid when compared to Wilson's. In fact, when this icon of American proto-liberalism was governor of New Jersey, he signed one of the nation's first and most Draconian state eugenics laws, which, as noted by Black, was drafted by none other than Dr. Katzen-Ellenbogen, who would later turn against his fellow Jewish prisoners and become a notorious killer doctor in Hitler's Buchenwald concentration camp.[16] Among other things, Wilson's law created a special three-man "Board of Examiners of Feebleminded, Epileptics, and Other Defectives," which Black describes as follows:

The Board would systematically identify when "procreation is advisable" for prisoners and children residing in poor houses and other charitable institutions. The law included not only the "feebleminded, epileptics [and] certain criminals," but also a class ambiguously referred to as "other defectives."[17]

The irony here is that as a child, Wilson "did not appear at first to be very bright." He "was slow in learning to read," "had not learned his letters until he was nine," and "did not read comfortably until he was twelve."[18] Today it is assumed by many that he suffered from dyslexia. Yet if a poor child in New Jersey had had a similar handicap when Wilson was governor of that state, it is highly likely that he would have lost his testicles.

Black's explanation of how this so-called Christian nation could come to embrace such evil laws begins with the statement that "America was ready for eugenic breeding precisely because the most established echelons of American society were frightened by the demographic chaos sweeping the nation." For starters, he says, "eighteen million refugees and opportunity-seeking immigrants arrived between 1890 and 1920. German Lutherans, Irish Catholics, Russian Jews, Slavic Orthodox—one huddled mass surged in after another. But they did not mix or melt; for the most part, they remained insoluble."

Thus, he says, the "romantic 'melting pot' notion was a myth." That, in fact, the country during this period of heavy immigration was actually a "cauldron of undissolvable minorities, ethnicities, indigenous people and other tight-knit groups—all constantly boiling over," that race and group hatred crisscrossed the continent, involving not just the millions of immigrants from Europe, but millions of Native American who were being dislocated, Mexicans who had lost their ownership of much of West and Southwest, and emancipated African slaves who were subjected to a network of state and local Jim Crow laws and a plethora of lynchings.[19]

Sociologically, Black's explanation makes sense. Man is, after all, a tribal, territorial, combative, and acquisitive animal who is capable of great cruelty when he believes his extended family or even his personal comfort is threatened. Indeed, as noted in a previous chapter, Nietzsche was highly critical of Christianity for attempting to suppress these natural human characteristics. Our response to Nietzsche's concern is that at least as far as the self-described Christian members of the progressive movement were concerned, he need not have worried. Their cruelty made Torquemada look like a bleeding heart.

Nevertheless, one cannot help but be surprised by how little opposition to eugenics there was in Christendom. In fact, the eugenics movement had advocates throughout Europe who shared "scientific" advances and propaganda efforts with their American counterparts. Germany was one of the hotbeds of European eugenics, so much so that by the mid-1930s, Joseph DeJarnette, the superintendent of Virginia's Western State Hospital, famously described the Germans as "beating us at our own game." DeJarnette's particular "game" was to save millions of dollars for the state by sterilizing the "clans" in the remote regions of the Appalachians "who have no right to be born" and who lay "incalculable burdens" on the state budget.[20]

For what it's worth, the great English poet, philosopher, dramatist, journalist, orator, literary and art critic, biographer, and Christian apologist G. K. Chesterton was one of the few notable individuals who opposed eugenics. In his classic essay, *Eugenics and Other Evils*, written in 1913, he argued that the state had no right to "dragoon and enslave one's fellow citizens as a kind of chemical experiment; in a state of reverent agnosticism about what would come of it." Then, as to the notion that poverty had something to do with breeding, he said the following:

> [It is] a strange new disposition to regard the poor as a race; as if they were a colony of Japs or Chinese coolies ... The poor are not a race or even a type. It is senseless to talk about breeding them; for they are not a breed. They are, in cold fact, what Dickens describes: "a dustbin of individual accidents," of damaged dignity, and often of damaged gentility. The class very largely consists of perfectly promising children lost like Oliver Twist, or crippled like Tiny Tim." ... The Eugenists for all I know would regard Tiny Tim as a sufficient reason for massacring the whole family of Cratchit.[21]

The Catholic Church opposed eugenics from its inception, but it did not make a formal challenge until 1930 when Pope Pius XI issued an encyclical entitled *Casti connubii* largely in response to the Anglican Church's efforts to legalize involuntary sterilization. Regarding sterilization specifically, Pius XI cited St. Thomas: "No one who is guiltless may be punished by a human tribunal either by flogging to death, or mutilation, or by beating." On a broader note, he said the following about those who wished to restrict marriage between people who are "naturally fit for marriage."

> Those who act in this way are at fault in losing sight of the fact that the family is more sacred than the State and that *men are begotten not for the earth and for time, but for Heaven and eternity.* Although often these individuals are to be dissuaded from entering into matrimony, certainly it is wrong to brand men with the stigma of crime because they contract marriage, on the ground that, despite the fact that they are in every respect capable of matrimony, they will give birth only to defective children, even though they use all care and diligence.[22]

British Labor joined the Church's opposition, arguing, understandably, that the eugenics movement targeted the poor. And they won. In the United States, neither the Catholic Church nor organized labor was powerful enough even to slow the movement down. In fact, in May 1927, none other than Supreme Court Justice Oliver Wendell Holmes ruled in the famous case of Buck v. Bell that involuntary sterilization was entirely in keeping with the Constitutional right of the many victims to life, liberty, and the pursuit of happiness. He put it this way:

> We have seen more than once that the public welfare may call upon the best citizens for their lives. It would be strange if it could not call upon those who already sap the strength of the State for these lesser sacrifices, often not felt to be such by those concerned, to prevent our being swamped with incompetence. It is better for all the world, if instead of waiting to execute degenerate offspring for crime, or to let them starve for their imbecility, society can prevent

those who are manifestly unfit from continuing their kind. The principle that sustains compulsory vaccination is broad enough to cover cutting the Fallopian tubes. Three generations of imbeciles are enough.[23]

The Buck, in this case, was Carrie. It was 1924, and she was eighteen years old, the daughter of a mother of three who had come upon hard times and was thusly deemed to be unfit and was committed to the Virginia Colony for Epileptics and Feeble-Minded. Carrie was adopted at the age of three by the Dobbs family, attended school for five years, reached the sixth grade, spent her time helping Mrs. Dobbs with housework, and was subsequently raped by her foster parents' nephew and became pregnant. At this point, the family had her committed to the Virginia colony where her mother was, claiming that she was "subject to some hallucinations and some outbreaks of temper," although they agreed that "she had never been subject to epilepsy, headaches, nervousness, fits or convulsions," and had not had "fits or spasms of any kind." Upon arriving there, the doctor who examined her found no evidence of psychosis, noting that she could read and write and "keeps herself in tidy condition."[24]

Nevertheless, the superintendent of the Colony called her a genetic threat to society and had her sterilized. They released her soon after the operation. She married Charlie Detamore and stayed married to him until her death in 1983. The state also sterilized her sister, without her knowledge, during an appendectomy. Not surprisingly, Carrie's child Vivian was perfectly normal. She died at the age of eight from a childhood illness. Davenport's long-time collaborator Harry Laughlin, the son of minister and holder of a doctorate from Princeton, said all that needs to be said about the "science" behind this and thousands of other similarly disgraceful actions: "These people belong to the shiftless, ignorant and worthless class of anti-social whites of the South."[25]

Now the American Left would like us all to forget this chapter in their history. Barring that, they would have us regard it as a brief period of folly brought on by unusual circumstances that were unrelated to the progressive agenda. However, the fact is that the eugenics movement bears study because it was, like the onset of a fever, the first sign that a deadly disease had pierced through the veneer of Christianity, which theretofore had protected the American political system from the evils of leftist utopianism. Here we find American Christians—not atheistic radicals, not leftist labor leaders, not a group of angry immigrants manning the barricades—but self-described Christians abandoning the fundamental Christian belief that each and every person is a product of God's love and equally valuable in God's eyes in favor of a fantasy goal of improving on God's work.

As noted above, we would not even attempt to explain how self-described Christians could enthusiastically support such an atrocity. We would simply say that it is evidence, as once demonstrated by Robespierre, of the overwhelming power of evil when dressed up in the "respectable" clothing of humanitarianism. Perhaps a better explanation would be C. P. Snow's famous observation that "there is not much between us and the horrors underneath. Just about a coat of varnish."[26]

However, it wasn't only the pesky nuances of the Constitution and orthodox Christianity that stood in Wilson's way of achieving his utopian goals. In his opinion, "the people" themselves were a problem. He first made this point publicly shortly after completing his doctoral studies at Johns Hopkins at the tender age of thirty-one in an article entitled "The Study of Administration," which earned him the dubious distinction of being the "father of public administration." Briefly stated, he began the piece by stating that it "is the object of administrative study to discover, first, what government can properly and successfully do, and, secondly, how it can do these proper things with the utmost possible efficiency and at the least possible cost either of money or of energy." Then, he noted the difficulty that he and other reformers faced when charged with the task of accomplishing this purpose. To wit:

> In government, as in virtue, the hardest of things is to make progress. Formerly the reason for this was that the single person who was sover-

eign was generally either selfish, ignorant, timid, or a fool, -albeit there was now and again one who was wise. Nowadays the reason is that the many, the people, who are sovereign have no single ear which one can approach, and are selfish, ignorant, timid, stubborn, or foolish with the selfishness, the ignorances, the stubbornnesses, the timidities, or the follies of several thousand persons, -albeit there are hundreds who are wise.

Once the advantage of the reformer was that the sovereign's mind had a definite locality, that it was contained in one man's head, and that consequently it could be gotten at; though it was his disadvantage that the mind learned only reluctantly or only in small quantities, or was under the influence of some one who let it learn only the wrong things. Now, on the contrary, the reformer is bewildered by the fact that the sovereign's mind has no definite locality, but is contained in a voting majority of several million heads; and embarrassed by the fact that the mind of this sovereign also is under the influence of favorites, who are none the less favorites in a good old-fashioned sense of the word because they are not persons by preconceived opinions; *i.e.*, prejudices which are not to be reasoned with because they are not the children of reason.[27]

Twenty-five years later, he expanded on this theory in his book *The New Freedom*, arguing that Jefferson's contention that the best government consisted in as little government as possible was no longer valid, that without the "assistance" of government, the stupid little human would be left helpless. To wit:

But I feel confident that if Jefferson were living in our day he would see what we see: that the individual is caught in a great confused nexus of all sorts of complicated circumstances, and that to let him alone is to leave him helpless as against the obstacles with which he has to contend; and that, therefore, law in our day must come to the assistance of the individual. It must come to his assistance to see that he gets fair play; that is all, but that is much. Without the watchful interference, the resolute interference, of the government, there can be no fair play between individuals and such powerful institutions as the trusts. Freedom to-day is something more than being let alone. The program of a government of freedom must in these days be positive, not negative merely.[28]

Of course, the idea that "the people" are not equipped to rule themselves was by no means a new one. Plato had said essentially the very same thing, only better. Indeed, this may have been one of the few points of agreement between Wilson and one of the most brilliant of his contemporary critics, the previously mentioned Harvard professor, Irving Babbitt, who famously argued that the "notion that wisdom resides in a popular majority at any particular moment should be the most completely exploded of all fallacies." To which he added, "If the plain people at Jerusalem had registered their will with the aid of the most improved type of ballot box, there is no evidence that they would have preferred Christ to Barabbas."[29]

However, what Wilson refused to recognize was that the founding fathers understood this problem better than he did, which is why they chose to reject the notion of a plebiscitary democracy in favor of a Republic in which numerous Constitutional provisions place checks on the numerical majority. James Madison described the system as follows in Federalist #51:

But the great security against a gradual concentration of the several powers in the same department, consists in giving to those who administer each department the necessary constitutional means and personal motives to resist encroachments of the others. The provision for defense must in this, as in all other cases, be made commensurate to the danger of attack. Ambition must be made to counteract ambition. The interest of the man must be connected with the constitutional rights of the place. It may be a reflection on human nature, that such devices should be necessary to control the abuses of government. But what is government itself, but the greatest of all reflections on human nature? If men were angels, no government would be necessary. If angels were to govern men, neither external nor internal controls on government would be necessary. In framing a government which is to be administered by men over men, the great difficulty lies in this: you must first enable the government to control the governed; and in the next place oblige it to control itself. A dependence on the people is, no doubt, the primary control on the government; but experience has taught mankind the necessity of auxiliary precautions.[30]

Of course, Wilson was God's emissary, and no "auxiliary precautions" established by mere mortals would hinder his divine mission. The Constitution had to go. Ronald J. Pestritto describes Wilson's attitude toward this document that he had pledged to "preserve, protect and defend," as follows in *Woodrow Wilson and the Roots of Modern Liberalism*:

> For Wilson, the separation of powers, and all of the other institutional remedies that the founders employed against the danger of faction,

stood in the way of government's exercising its power in accord with the dictates of progress.

Wilson, therefore, sought a reinterpretation of the founding—a reinterpretation grounded in historical contingency. To the founding's ahistorical notion of human nature, Wilson posed the historical argument that the ends, scope, and role of just government must be defined by the different principles of different epochs, and that therefore it is impossible to speak of a single form of just government for all ages ... In a 1911 address Wilson remarked that "the rhetorical introduction of the Declaration of Independence is the least part of it ... If you want to understand the real Declaration of Independence, do not repeat the preface."[31]

For the record, that preface begins:

> We hold these truths to be self-evident, that all men are created equal, that they are endowed by their Creator with certain unalienable Rights, that among these are Life, Liberty and the pursuit of Happiness.

According to Pestritto, Wilson

> looked instead to what he believed to be the democratic spirit of the founding—one that launched national government as a work-in-progress, a government that would require continual adjustment to historical circumstances as it tried to fulfill the broad democratic vision of the founders. But this interpretation of the founding ran up against the founders' own self-understanding, as Wilson well knew. This is why much

of his scholarship is devoted to a reinterpretation and critique of both the political theory of the founding, and of the implementation of that theory in the institutional design of the national government. In other words, both the Declaration of Independence and the Constitution had to be understood anew through a progressive lens.[32]

Now, as we have noted previously, the nation's founders knew that unscrupulous, ambitious, prideful, and unbalanced men would fret over the Constitutional barriers that prevented them from accumulating dictatorial powers and would attempt to tear them down. Burke, with whom the founders were all familiar, had described such men perfectly in *Reflections*:

> They have no respect for the wisdom of others; but they pay it off by a very full measure of confidence in their own. With them it is a sufficient motive to destroy an old scheme of things, because it is an old one. As to the new, they are in no sort of fear with regard to the duration of a building run up in haste; because duration is no object to those who think little or nothing has been done before their time, and who place all their hopes in discovery. They conceive, very systematically, that all things which give perpetuity are mischievous, and therefore they are at inexpiable war with all establishments. They think that government may vary like modes of dress, and with as little ill effect: that there needs no principle of attachment, except a sense of present conveniency, to any constitution of the state. They always speak as if they were of opinion that there is a singular species of compact between them and their magistrates, which binds the magistrate, but which has nothing reciprocal in it,

but that the majesty of the people has a right to dissolve it without any reason, but its will. Their attachment to their country itself is only so far as it agrees with some of their fleeting projects; it begins and ends with that scheme of polity which falls in with their momentary opinion.[33]

Washington, who was certainly familiar with Burke, had also specifically warned against such men thusly in his Farewell Address, which, as we noted above, Croly said had ceased to be a totally adequate guide to the problems of war and peace, commerce, and colonization.

Towards the preservation of your government, and the permanency of your present happy state, it is requisite, not only that you steadily discountenance irregular oppositions to its acknowledged authority, *but also that you resist with care the spirit of innovation upon its principles, however specious the pretexts. One method of assault may be to effect, in the forms of the Constitution, alterations which will impair the energy of the system, and thus to undermine what cannot be directly overthrown.* In all the changes to which you may be invited, remember that time and habit are at least as necessary to fix the true character of governments as of other human institutions; that experience is the surest standard by which to test the real tendency of the existing constitution of a country; that facility in changes, upon the credit of mere hypothesis and opinion, exposes to perpetual change, from the endless variety of hypothesis and opinion; and remember, especially, that for the efficient management of your common interests, in a country so extensive as ours, a government of as much vigor as is consistent with the perfect security of liberty is indispensable. Liberty itself will find in such a government, *with powers properly distributed and adjusted*, its surest guardian. [Emphasis added] [34]

Yet, Wilson was undeterred. The "old formulations," as Croly had called them, had to go. Moreover, Wilson had the tools to make it happen. One of these was the Seventeenth Amendment to the Constitution, which his fellow progressives had handed to him as a gift one month after he took office. Consisting of just three paragraphs, it established the direct election of senators by popular vote, rather than by the state legislatures. To wit:

The Senate of the United States shall be composed of two Senators from each State, elected by the people thereof, for six years; and each Senator shall have one vote. The electors in each State shall have the qualifications requisite for electors of the most numerous branch of the State legislatures.

When vacancies happen in the representation of any State in the Senate, the executive authority of such State shall issue writs of election to fill such vacancies: Provided, That the legislature of any State may empower the executive thereof to make temporary appointments until the people fill the vacancies by election as the legislature may direct.

This amendment shall not be so construed as to affect the election or term of any Senator chosen before it becomes valid as part of the Constitution.[35]

The ostensible purpose of this amendment was to promote the election of more honest senators, the argument being that the state legislatures were hotbeds of corruption and that this led to the selection of crooks and lackeys of the state machines. The idea had been around since before the civil war, but it picked up steam in 1906 during Teddy's administration with the publication, mentioned in a previous chapter, of David Graham Phillips's article "The Treason of the Senate."

Naturally, opposition came from the Senate's senior members, who did indeed represent the special interests in their states, just as the founding fathers had expected them to do. And yes, some were crooks. However, they were in good company in Washington during this Gilded Age, and there was no reason to expect that "the people" themselves would elect cleaner advocates in Washington. Nevertheless, Teddy, Taft, Wilson, Bryant, and the entire progressive cast of characters supported the measure because it would vest more power in the hands of the People's House, which was their source of strength.

It seemed like a minor alteration at the time, but the fact is that it radically changed the entire nature of the American public's relationship with the federal government by stripping the individual states of their most important constitutional guarantee of protection from the collective will of the entire polity. As previously mentioned, the British liberals had accomplished the same thing by drastically limiting the power of the House of Lords with the Reform Act of 1832. The National Center for Constitutional Studies explains the Seventeenth Amendment as follows:

> For more than a century, senators were elected by state legislators rather than by popular vote. The founders said they had organized Congress in such a way that "the people will be represented in one house, the state legislatures in the other." Thus the states were an integral part of the federal government and had a strong voice in the formation of federal policy. As James Madison put it, "No law or resolution can now be passed without the concurrence, first, of a

majority of the people, and then of a majority of the states."

According to George Mason of Virginia, the object of this design was to arm the state legislatures with "some means of defending themselves against encroachments of the national government ... And what better means can we provide than [to give] them some share in, or rather to make them a constituent part of, the national establishment?"

Madison explained that the House of Representatives was always regarded as a "national" institution because its members were elected directly by the people, but "the Senate, on the other hand, will derive its powers from the states. [and in this respect] the government is federal, not national." In other words, the government in Washington is a "federal" government only if it incorporates the states into its very structure.

The founders even cautioned us about the dangers of altering this arrangement. For example, Fisher Ames of Massachusetts declared in 1788: "The state governments are essential parts of the system ... The senators represent the sovereignty of the states; ... they are in the quality of ambassadors of the states ... [But suppose] that they [were] to be chosen by the people at large ... Whom, in that case, would they represent? Not the legislatures of the states, but the people. *This would totally obliterate the federal features of the Constitution.* [Emphasis added.] What would become of the state governments, and on whom would devolve the duty of defending them against the encroachments of the federal government?"[36]

On whom indeed?

However, the Seventeenth Amendment was by no means the only highly powerful new tool that Wilson's progressive predecessors had handed him. Thanks to Teddy and Taft, a greatly strengthened Interstate Commerce Commission gave him myriad new powers over the states, and the Sixteenth Amendment provided him with an entirely new source of money with which to pursue the goal of strengthening the federal government.

This brings us to one of the most damaging of all of the attacks on the Constitution that Wilson pursued during his time at the White House, that being the creation of the Federal Reserve System. As noted in a previous chapter, the so-called "moneyed interests" had placed Wilson in the White House specifically to create a central bank. Needless to say, they had made a good choice, for Wilson loved the idea of putting "experts" in charge of this difficult problem, even, we might add, if the "experts" happened to be the bankers themselves.

The problem was to convince the public and a few skeptical democrats in Congress that this was not a sellout to the bankers and to explain to them the dire need for a central bank. The first step in this process was to discard the Aldrich bill and take up a "Democratic" bill that Glass's administrative assistant Willis and his pal Laughlin had written. The bill differed very little from Aldrich's plan, but it was sponsored by good, solid Democrats; Glass in the House and Robert L. Owen of Oklahoma in the Senate. This, coupled with the support of Bryan, which he happily provided in exchange for the post of secretary of state, assured its passage.

Among other things, the new bill called for the creation of twelve regional banks and a Federal Reserve Board, made up of members appointed by the president and approved by the Senate. Advocates said these changes would guard against the power of the bankers, but, of course, that was nonsense. Indeed, when the dust settled, it was obvious that the bankers were and had been in control all along. In fact, in no time at all, J. P. Morgan's man Benjamin Strong was in charge of the New York Fed, which quickly became the dominate player and remains so today.

Wilson praised the new plan as being independent of special interests, claiming that the elected government would control the new system "so that the banks may be instruments, not the masters, of business and of individual enterprise and initiative."[37] At long last, then, the nation's bankers had a central bank that could create an endless supply of fiat currency that would, in the words of Wilson's son-in-law and Secretary of the Treasury William McAdoo, "so alter and strengthen our banking system so that the enlarged credit resources demanded by the needs of business and agricultural enterprise will come *almost automatically into existence*, and at rates of interest low enough to stimulate, protect, and prosper all kinds of legitimate business and to bring about ultimately a greater equality in interest rates throughout the country."[38] Ah, yes, *almost automatically*.

Of course, not everyone believed that this was a benevolent and useful gesture on the part of the bankers. New York senator Elihu Root, for one, gave one of the most impressive and insightful speeches on the subject of fiat currency and inflation ever given, one that every conservative should read, understand, and take with him or her into the battle with the Left. To wit:

> What is an elastic currency? We all agree that it is a currency which expands when more money is needed and contracts when less money is needed. It is important not merely that the currency shall expand when money is needed, but that it shall contract when money is not needed, for to an industrial and commercial country a redundant currency is the source of manifold evils, some of which I shall presently point out. At present I observe that this is in no sense a provision for an elastic currency. It does not provide an elastic currency. It provides an expansive currency, but not an elastic one. It provides a currency which may be increased, always increased but not a currency for which the bill contains any provision compelling reduction. ...

The universal experience, sir, is that the tendency of mankind is to keep on increasing the issue of currency. Unless there is some very positive and distinct influence tending toward the process of reduction, that tendency always has, in all the great commercial nations of the world, produced its natural results, and we may expect it to produce its natural result here, of continual, progressive increase. The psychology of inflation is interesting and it is well understood. No phenomenon exhibited by human nature has been the subject of more thorough, careful, and earnest study than that presented by the great multitude of individuals making up the business world in any country in the process of gradual inflation. It is as constant as the fundamental qualities of humanity. ...

It is manifest that when banks issue currency there is a certain limitation involved in the nature of things, because their credit is not unlimited ... But we are proposing to furnish everybody who can draw and sign a bill currency that has behind it the credit of the American people—the Government of the United States. What limit is there to that credit now? What limit up to this time? There may be a limit owing to the working of this bill, but there is none yet. ...

So as to the sale of Government securities. Ah, yes; now, behind the system under which we are working, and under which we have grown so great and strong, stands always the Government of the United States, with its credit unimpaired, with its solvency undoubted, always ready to come to the rescue by the sale of its securities to bring gold. This bill proposes, however, to put in pawn the credit of the United States; and when your time of need comes, it is the United States that is discredited by the inflation of its demand obligations which it cannot pay.

Mr. President, my colleague has observed that power is given to the central reserve board to regulate the issue of currency. That is true; but I observed at the time that we have our duty to perform, and that we cannot discharge it by transferring it to anybody else. Always up to this time the American Congress has attempted to perform its own duty in regard to the vital matter of currency. Always the American Congress, when it did not want inflation, has undertaken so to frame its legislation that its injunctions and requirements would prevent inflation. Now it is proposed that we shall make it possible that an appointive officer, or a body of appointive officers, shall bring upon the country the result of inflation; and we are to appease our own consciences by assuming that that board will perform the duties that we ought to perform.[39]

In the end, Root voted for the bill, as noted by Kolko, in hope of "making the best of it."[40] Wilson signed it on December 23, 1913, and the Fed opened for business on November 16, 1914, and promptly set the nation on the path to the economic and social debauchery that is the constant handmaiden of a fiat currency.

In the meantime, a war involving all the major nations in Europe had started on July 28, 1914, pitting the "Allies" or the "Triple Entente," consisting of the Russian Empire, the French Third Republic, and the United Kingdom of Great Britain and Ireland, against the "Central Powers," consisting of Germany and Austria-Hungary. The spark was lit when a Serbian national named Gavrilo Princip, angry at Austria's de facto control over Serbia, assassinated the Archduke Franz Ferdinand, heir to the Austro-Hungarian throne. Austria responded by declaring war on Serbia, after getting assurance from Germany that it would help if the Serbians received help from their Slavic friends in Russia. When Russia said that it would help Serbia, Germany declared war on Russia. The Germans then warned France to stay out of it. The French said they would not, that they would support the Russians, with whom they had signed a defense pact as insurance against German aggression. Germany declared war on France. They then invaded Belgium on their way to France, which prompted the British, who had an agreement with Belgium, to declare war on Germany. The Japanese then took advantage of the melee by seizing control of Germany's Micronesian colonies, which led to a declaration of war between Japan and both Germany and Austro-Hungary.

Geopolitically, the diplomat George Kennan described it this way. It began as a simple struggle between Russia and the Austro-Hungarian Empire for succession to the declining power of Turkey in the Balkans. Then, when the Russian and Austro-Hungarian empires became so beaten down by the war that they no longer cared much about their original points of difference, the Allies began to portray it as a fight over Germany's position in postwar Europe and the role of its navy in the global trade routes. At this point, the war began to be viewed as a struggle between autocracy and democracy, which, Kennan notes, was unconvincing since Germany, at its worst, was closer to the Western ideas of justice and parliamentarianism than was Tsarist Russia, whose collaboration the Western allies were so happy to accept in the early days of the war. "The truth is," Kennan concluded, that "the war was being waged against Germany, not because of the ideology of her government but because of her national aspirations."[41]

Initially, Wilson wanted no part of this war. In fact, he made staying out of it *the* paramount issue of his reelection campaign in 1916 against Charles Evans Hughes. The election was held on November 7, 1916. Wilson took his oath of office on March 5, 1917. And on April 2, he asked Congress to declare war on Germany. Naturally, this sudden change of plans promoted a debate among historians about his motives. We agree with William Appleman Williams's assertion that Wilson had sincerely "hoped to remain a nonbelligerent until a stalemate developed and then step in as the arbiter of the settlement and as the architect of a world organization to establish and maintain peace."[42] After all, as a Christian, he was naturally wary of war and delighted at the prospect of being the arbiter of peace.

On the other hand, his decision to stay out of the war had always been predicated on the comforting belief that the allies would win. In fact, a year earlier he had been involved in a secret scheme, cooked up in cooperation with the British, to force Germany to the peace table by proposing a settlement plan and threatening that the United States would to go to war against whichever side opposed it. The idea was that Germany would oppose it, and the United States could then enter the war not for selfish reasons but as a paladin of peace. Wilson's chief political advisor and diplomat during the war, Edward M. (Colonel) House, described the idea as follows:

> If the Allies understood our purpose, we could be as severe in our language concerning them as we were with the Central Powers. The Allies, after some hesitation, could accept our offer or demand and, if the Central Powers accepted, we would then have accomplished a master-stroke of diplomacy. If the Central Powers refused to acquiesce, we could then push our insistence to a point where diplomatic relations would first be broken off, and later the whole force of our Government—and perhaps the force of every neutral—might be brought against them.[43]

The allies rejected the plan. House explained their action this way:

> [They, the Allies] looked forward to utilizing their prospective victory as a means to extensive annexations and crushing indemnities. They were doubtless perfectly sincere in their protestations of a desire for justice and a stable peace,

but they interpreted "justice" so as to conform with the particular interests of their own nation and the stability of peace as meaning the political destruction of the enemy.[44]

Everything changed on February 1, 1917, when Germany resumed its unrestricted submarine warfare, which caused serious people to conclude that Germany would win the war. And this led Wilson to conclude that his hope of stalemate moderated by the United States was not going to happen and that he had little choice but to enter the war on the side of the Allies. Opinions differ as to why he had little choice. Ferdinand Lundberg posited one of the most interesting of these in his previously mentioned book, *America's 60 Families*. To wit:

> Early in 1917 the Allied governments, which now owed the American bankers and their clients nearly $1,500,000,000, had been brought virtually to their knees by the German armies, and it was believed that the limit of Allied credit had been reached. In March 1917, the Czar's government, which had also been fighting to make the world safe for democracy, collapsed, threatening to release the German army of the East for duty in France. On March 5, 1917, Walter Hines Page, American Ambassador to England, sent to President Wilson a long dispatch which Page summarized as follows: "I think that the pressure of this approaching crisis has gone beyond the ability of the Morgan Financial Agency for the British and French Governments. The need is becoming too great and urgent for any private agency to meet, for every such agency has to encounter jealousies of rivals and of sections." Page said that the outlook was "alarming" to America's industrial and financial prospects, but

pointed out frankly, "If we should go to war with Germany, the greatest help we could give the Allies would be such a credit. In that case our Government could, if it would, make a large investment in a Franco-British loan or might guarantee such a loan. ... Unless we go to war with Germany our Government, of course, cannot make such a direct grant of credit ..." The alternative to war, Page warned, was domestic collapse. Within four weeks President Wilson asked Congress for a declaration of war, ostensibly because submarine warfare against shipping had been renewed. ...

American participation in the war made it possible for the government to place the credit of the whole American people behind the Allies, whose fortunes were, early in 1917, at such a low ebb that the American holders of nearly $1,500,000,000 of English and French paper stood to suffer a disastrous loss. The declaration of war by the United States, in addition to extricating the wealthiest American families from a dangerous situation, also opened new vistas of profits.[45]

Williams does not dispute this explanation, but he argues that Wilson's immediate concern was access to foreign markets. He notes that the American economy was heavily dependent on exports, and that the Entente and their colonies had purchased 77 percent of these exports in 1913. To make matters even more urgent, he points out that the American economy was already in deep trouble, that "business throughout the country was depressed, farm prices were deflated, unemployment was serious, the heavy industries were working far below capacity, bank clearances were off." Moreover, he continues, Germany "was from the beginning considered a dangerous economic rival and *an enemy of Progressive Values*" (Emphasis added). In fact,

Williams quotes Robert Lansing, Wilson's secretary of state, as saying that a German victory would "mean the overthrow of democracy in the world ... and the turning back of the hands of human progress two centuries."[46] Williams summed it up this way:

> In restoring America's foreign trade by tying it to England and France (and by expanding old connections with such nations as Russia), rather than by insisting upon economic neutrality, Wilson and American businessmen tied themselves to a prosperity based on the Allied war program. Wilson developed no other plan to end the depression, and hence this way of dealing with the problem exerted a subtle but persuasive influence on later decisions.[47]

Now concern over free access to foreign markets had been a centerpiece of American policy since the McKinley initiated the "Open Door" policy. Williams describes this policy as having been "derived from the proposition that America's overwhelming economic power could cast the economy and the politics of the poorer, weaker, underdeveloped countries in a pro-American mold." He further notes that this policy was "hard-headed and practical, [and] in some respects ... the most impressive intellectual achievement in the area of public policy since the generation of the Founding Fathers." Indeed, he attributes its "ultimate failures" to the "failures generated by its success in guiding Americans in the creation of an empire."[48]

Wilson had been a big supporter of this concept from the very beginning. In fact, in one of his earliest political speeches, given at Columbia University in 1907, while he was president of Princeton and desiring to be governor of New Jersey, he spoke rather candidly about the use of force in the pursuit of both national security and economic prosperity. To wit:

> Since trade ignores national boundaries and the manufacturer insists on having the world as

a market, the flag of his nation must follow him, and the doors of the nations which are closed against him must be *battered down.* [Emphasis added] Concessions obtained by financiers must be safeguarded by ministers of state, even if the sovereignty of unwilling nations be outraged in the process. Colonies must be obtained or planted, in order that no useful corner of the world may be overlooked or left unused.[49]

Then in his first campaign for the White House in 1912, he said the following:

Our industries have expanded to such a point that they will burst their jackets if they cannot find a free outlet to the markets of the world ... Our domestic markets no longer suffice. We need foreign markets ... We have reached, in short, a critical point in the process of our prosperity. It has now become a question with us whether it shall continue or shall not continue ... our domestic market is too small.[50]

Teddy too had been a supporter. But Teddy being Teddy, he turned what had been an economic issue into a quasi-moral one. Williams explains as follows:

[Teddy's] concern for economic expansion was complemented by an urge to extend Anglo-Saxon ideas, practices, and virtues throughout the world. Just as his Square Deal program centered on the idea of responsible leaders using the national government to regulate and moderate industrial society at home, so did his international outlook revolve around the idea of American supremacy being used to define and promote the interests of "collective civilization." ... In his mind, at any rate, it was America's "duty toward the people living in barbarism to see that they are freed from their chains" ... thus, he concluded, "peace cannot be had until the civilized nations have expanded in some shape over the barbarous nations."[51]

Of course, this view was remarkably close to Wilson's own. Here's Williams again.

Wilson's imperialism of the spirit was well defined by his attitude toward the Philippines. The United States should grant independence to the Filipinos just as soon as American leadership had instructed them in the proper standards of national life, instilled in them the proper character, and established for them a stable and constitutional government. Such noble objectives justified—even demanded—the use of force. "When men take up arms to set other men free," he declared, "there is something sacred and holy in the warfare. I will not cry 'peace' as long as there is sin and wrong in the world."[52]

Naturally then, when it came time to declaring war, Wilson refrained from telling the American people the very real and practical considerations for joining the Allies. Instead, in words reminiscent of Robespierre's flowery promises of the "peaceful enjoyment of liberty and equality" and "the reign of that eternal justice," Wilson said that the war would elevate America to a theretofore unseen force in world history, turning it into a noble champion of global peace, ready to sacrifice its men to rid the world of an evil nation that had abandoned "all scruples of humanity." He put it this way in his "War Message to Congress" on April 2, 1917.

The world must be made safe for democracy. Its peace must be planted upon the tested foundations of political liberty. We have no selfish ends to serve. We desire no conquest, no dominion. We seek no indemnities for ourselves, no material compensation for the sacrifices we shall freely make. We are but one of the champions of the rights of mankind. We shall be satisfied when those rights have been made as secure as the faith and the freedom of nations can make them ... Our motive will not be revenge or the victorious assertion of the physical might of the nation, but only the vindication of right, of human right, of which we are only a single champion. But the right is more precious than peace, and we shall fight for the things which we have always carried nearest our hearts—for democracy, for the right of those who submit to authority to have a voice in their own governments, for the rights and liberties of small nations, for a universal dominion of right by such a concert of free peoples as shall bring peace and safety to all nations and make the world itself at last free. To such a task we can dedicate our lives and our fortunes, everything that we are and everything that we have, with the pride of those who know that the day has come when America is privileged to spend her blood and her might for the principles that gave her birth and happiness and the peace which she has treasured. God helping her, she can do no other.[53]

So it was that Wilson relegated Washington's sage warning against involving the nation in the quarrels of others to the same dustbin in which he wished to place Constitution, and in doing so began the process that T. S. Eliot would later describe as "destroying our ancient edifices to make ready the ground upon which the barbarian nomads of the future will encamp in their mechanized caravans."[54]

Let's let the poets in on the fun.

> Rendezvous
> I have a rendezvous with Death
> At some disputed barricade,
> When Spring comes back with rustling shade
> And apple-blossoms fill the air—
> I have a rendezvous with Death
> When Spring brings back blue days and fair.
> It may be he shall take my hand
> And lead me into his dark land
> And close my eyes and quench my breath—
> It may be I shall pass him still.
> I have a rendezvous with Death
> On some scarred slope of battered hill,
> When Spring comes round again this year
> And the first meadow-flowers appear.
> God knows 'twere better to be deep
> Pillowed in silk and scented down,
> Where love throbs out in blissful sleep,
> Pulse nigh to pulse, and breath to breath,
> Where hushed awakenings are dear ...
> But I've a rendezvous with Death
> At midnight in some flaming town,
> When Spring trips north again this year,
> And I to my pledged word am true,
> I shall not fail that rendezvous.
> Alan Seeger, 1915

A Sneak Peek at Volume II

The philosopher Eric Veogelin put it this way: "Measures taken which are intended to establish peace increase the disturbances that will lead to war."

"All the horrors of all the ages were brought together, and not only armies but whole populations were thrust into the midst of them. The mighty educated States involved conceived—not without reasons—that their very existence was at stake. Neither peoples nor rulers drew the line at any deed which they thought could help them to win."

This brings us to another of Schmitt's most disquieting observation, namely that the wars of the future would not be over property, political hegemony, or the definable, practical interests of the nations involved, but over "values."

"In 1917 European history, in the old sense, came to an end. World history began. It was the year of Lenin and Woodrow Wilson, both of whom repudiated the traditional standards of political behavior. Both preached Utopia, Heaven on Earth. It was the moment of birth for our contemporary world; the dramatic moment of modern man's existence."

Yes, death, famine, and war had been loosed upon the land. But here's the rub. *The war had also dealt a blow to Marxism in Europe.*

Enter Wilson and Lenin, both of whom were in need of a new vision, a new "look," a new image, a new promise. You see, aside from "human nature," the leftists had another problem, that being that they had been in the retail business throughout the 19th century. They had marketed their product to society's poorest, weakest, and most disgruntled individuals, for use as a weapon in their war against the richest and most powerful members of society.

We will begin our discussion of the birth of National Socialism on the same day and in the same place that we began our discussion of the birth of Marxism sixteen chapters ago. That would be in 1770 in a small house on a quiet street in Königsberg, Prussia, where a kindly, well-meaning, forty-six-year-old professor of philosophy named Immanuel Kant is building the intellectual scaffolding upon which the God of Abraham would be executed.

The cold hard fact is that Mussolini's Fascism and Hitler's National-Socialist German Workers' Party were just two more in a long line of attempts by leftist ideologues to fashion a workable model out of Marx's mishmash of economic and social nonsense . . . In short, despite their publicly expressed antagonism toward Marxism, Mussolini and Hitler were, like Marx, products of Rousseau's utopianism, Kant's skepticism, Fichte's atheism, and Hegel's historicism.

Franklin Roosevelt seems to have understood that Hitler was evil. But he could never come to grips with the fact that Stalin was equally so, and, moreover, that he, Franklin Roosevelt, was marching the United States down the path to the same satanic iniquity."

Our interest is focused on two men who would develop a final new iteration of leftist dogma that would come to be called Cultural Marxism, which, when fully implemented, would create a crisis in Western Civilization unlike anything it had experienced since 732 when Charles Martel rescued Christendom from the Arab conquest of Europe.

Franklin Roosevelt's presidency was an unmitigated disaster for the country and for the world. Of course, he didn't plan it that way. That is, he had no evil intention .... Unfortunately, he was also intellectually, educationally, and emotionally far over his head in the role of president at that particular time. His worldview was naïve and sophomoric during a period when the world was awash with genuinely evil men who had detailed plans to destroy the foundations of Western Civilization. And to make matters worse, he was incapable of recognizing evil, even when resident among some of his closest friends and advisers.

Roosevelt described Stalin as having "something else in him besides this revolutionist Bolshevist thing." The President thought it had something to do with his training for the "priesthood ... I think that something entered into this nature of the way in which a Christian gentleman should behave."

For the undisputable fact is that there were quite literally hundreds of Russian spies scattered throughout the Roosevelt administration, some at the very highest levels, and many, many more individuals who were sympathetic to their existence."

While the dimwits at the FBI were finally beginning to understand that Hiss might be a Russian spy, Truman welcomed the birth of the United Nations, which had been designed and organized under the loving direction of none other than Hiss.

The Left, as outlined in the preceding pages of this book, disappeared into the dustbin of history during the second half of twentieth century. You see, the Left was a child of the Enlightenment. Its sole purpose was to create a moral system based on science and reason to replace the Judeo-Christian framework, which was based on faith in a loving god. Marxism became the prototype for this project, but it was hopelessly sophomoric both practically and philosophically. In a sane world, this would have led to its disappearance along with countless other nonsensical notions akin to the belief in a flat earth. Instead, myriad political activists, murderous madmen, and philosophers attempted to "revise" it.

The philosophical odyssey from Marxism produced a particularly noxious mixture of the thoughts, dreams, and speculations of Marx, the philosopher Martin Heidegger, the psychiatrist Sigmund Freud, the mass murder Chairman Mao, and the Lord only knows who else. The result was that somewhere in this process, they lost sight of creating a heaven on earth, and decided to concentrate instead on destroying the existing society.

By 1935, nihilism had taken a tremendous toll on Christianity in Europe, the dogs of war were straining at their leashes, and Nietzsche's Übermensch, in the person of Hitler and Stalin, each armed with a hammer, had put an end to Europe's flirtation with the notion of a Leftist utopia and introduced a rough version of the prototype that threatened the future of all of Western Civilization.

Notes

Part I—Premise and Purpose

Chapter 1—The Bloody Birth of the Left

1. George Orwell, *A Collection of Essays* (Boston: Houghton Mifflin Harcourt, 1970), 104.

2. *The Stanford Encyclopedia of Philosophy*, http://plato.stanford.edu/entries/kant/.

3. Immanuel Kant, *The Critique of Pure Reason* (Henry G. Bohn, 1855), xix.

4. Crane Brinton, *English Political Thought in the Nineteenth Century* (Harvard Press, 1949), 6.

5. Isaac Newton, *Principia,* First American Edition, Book III (Daniel Adee, 1846), 504–505.

6. Émilie du Châtelet, *Selected Philosophical and Scientific Writings,* "Examination of the Books of the New Testament" (University of Chicago Press, 2009), 201–250.

7. Will and Ariel Durant, *The Age of Voltaire* (Simon & Schuster, 1965) 715.

8. Hanna Arendt, *The Life of the Mind* (Harcourt Inc., 1971), 7.

9. Leo and Joseph Cropsey, *History of Political Philosophy,* Third Edition (University of Chicago Press, 1987), 425–438.

10. Georges Sorel, *The Illusions of Progress* (University of California Press, 1969), 17.

11. Marvin Richard O'Connell, *Blaise Pascal: Reasons of the Heart* (Wm. B. Eerdmans Publishing, 1997), pp. xi, 185.

12. Gottfried Wilhelm Freiherr Leibniz, *The Monadology and Other Philosophical Writings* (Oxford University Press, H. Milford, 1898), 66.

13. Voltaire, *Candide* (Easton Press, 1977), 123.

14. *Encyclopedia Britannica*, Ninth Edition, Volume IX (Werner Company, 1893), 74.

15. Lord Acton, *Lectures on the French Revolution* (Liberty Fund, 1965), 4–5.

16. Thomas Babington Macaulay, *Life of Frederick the Great* (American Book Exchange, 1879), 143–144.

17. Hippolyte Taine, *The Ancient Regime* (Henry Holt & Co., 1888), 266–267.

18. Sorel, op. cit., 68.

19. Heinrich Heine, *Heinrich Heine, Selected Works* (Vintage Books, 1973), 333.

20. *The Cambridge Dictionary of Philosophy*, Second Edition (Cambridge University Press, 1999), 398–403.

21. Will Durant, *The Story of Philosophy* (Simon and Schuster, 1961), 176.

22. Malcolm Muggeridge, *Things Past* (Morrow, 1979), 220.

23. Michael Burleigh, *Earthly Powers* (HarperCollins, 2005), 42–43.

24. Roberto Calasso, *The Ruin of Kasch* (Belknap Press of Harvard University, 1994), 100.

25. *Letters of Voltaire and Frederick the Great* (Brentano's, 1927), 285.

26. Germaine de Staël, *Considerations on the Principal Events of the French Revolution* (Liberty Fund, 2008), 42.

27. Ibid., 43.

28. Plato, *Plato: The Complete Dialogues,* Laws, Book X (Princeton University Press, 1961), 1440–1465.

29. Sophocles, *The Oedipus Tyrannus of Sophocles*, edited with introduction and notes by Sir Richard Jebb (Cambridge University Press, 1887).

30. Edward Gibbon, *The History of the Decline and Fall of the Roman Empire*, Volume I (Harper & Brothers, 1837), 20.

31. Ibid., 18.

32. Niccolò Machiavelli, *Discourses on the First Decade of Titus Livy* (Penguin Books, 1970), 139–142.

33. Edmund Burke, *Reflections on the Revolution in France* (Penguin Books, 1968), 187–188.

34. Jakob Herman Huizinga, *Rousseau: The Self-Made Saint* (Grossman Publishers, 1976), 165–167.

35. Lord Acton, op. cit., 14.

36. Thomas Carlyle, *On Heroes, Hero-Worship, and the Heroic in History* (Chapman and Hall, 1869), 221.

37. Karl Löwith, *From Hegel to Nietzsche* (Columbia University Press, 1964), 260.

38. Jean-Jacques Rousseau, *Emile* (Barron's Educational Series, 1964), 55.

39. W. H. Auden, *The Complete Works of W. H. Auden: Prose 1939–1948* (Princeton University Press, 2002), 94.

40. Paul Johnson, *The Intellectuals* (Weidenfeld and Nicolson, 1988), 4.

41. Jean-Jacques Rousseau, *The Social Contract: & Discourses* (J. M. Dent & Sons, Limited, 1920), 207.

42. Peter Kropotkin, *The Great French Revolution* (G. P. Putnam's Sons, 1909), 1.

43. Alexis de Tocqueville, *The Old Regime and the Revolution* (University of Chicago Press, 1998), 197–198.

44. Thomas Carlyle, *The French Revolution*, Volume I (Colonial Press, 1899), 151.

45. Hyppolyte Taine, *The French Revolution* (H. Holt, 1897), 40–41.

46. John Milton, *Paradise Lost, Book 1* (Easton Press, 1976), 3.

47. Carlyle, op. cit., 163 and 167.

Chapter 2—The Left's First Mass Murder

1. Elisabeth Luther Cary, "John Adams and Mary Wollstonecraft," *The Lamp*, Volume XXVI (Charles Scribner's Sons, 1903).

2. Hippolyte Taine, *The French Revolution, Volume I* (Liberty Fund, 2002), 253, 247–249, 261–262.

3. Hippolyte Taine, *The French Revolution*, Volume II (Liberty Fund, 2002), 413.

4. Ibid., 441–442.

5. Crane Brinton, *The Jacobins* (Transaction Publishers, 2012), xix–xxiv.

6. Jean-Jacques Rousseau, *The Social Contract: & Discourses* (J. M. Dent & Sons, 1920), 90.

7. Ibid., 121.

8. François-René de Chateaubriand, *Mémoires d'Outre-tomb, Book IX*, chapter 4.

9. François Mignet, *History of the French Revolution from 1789 to 1814* (G. Bell and Sons, 1891), 240.

10. *The Holy Bible*, John 5:43.

11. Tocqueville, op. cit., 12–13.

12. Mignet, op. cit., 247.

13. William Doyle, *The Oxford History of the French Revolution* (Oxford University Press, 1989), 16.

14. Stephen R. C. Hicks, *Explaining Post-Modernism, Skepticism and Socialism from Rousseau to Foucault* (Scholargy Publishing, 2004), 101.

15. *Proceedings of the British Academy, Volume 117: 2001 Lectures* (Oxford University Press, 2002), 320.

16. John Boyer, *University of Chicago Readings in Western Civilization, Volume 7* (University of Chicago Press, 1987), 370.

17. Edmund Burke, *The Works of the Right Honourable Edmund Burke*, Volume 2 (John West, 75, Cornhill, and O. C. Greenleaf, 3, Court Street, 1807), 98.

18. Louis Madelin, *The French Revolution: Crowned by the French Academy Gobert Prize* (G. P. Putnam's Sons, 1916), 491.

19. Edmund Wilson, *To the Finland Station* (Noonday Press, 1972), 83.

20. Philippe Buonarroti, *History of Babeuf's Conspiracy for Equality* (H. Hetherington, 1836), viii.

21. Buonarroti, op. cit., 315–316.

22. James Billington, *Fire in the Minds of Men* (Basic Books, 1980), 73.

23. Rose. R. R., *Gracchus Babeuf* (Stanford University Press, 1978), 209–214.

24. Albert Fried and Ronald Sanders, *Socialist Thought: A Documentary History* (Columbia University Press, 1992), 66–67.

25. Carlyle, op. cit., volume 2, 370.

26. Burke, op. cit., 342.

Chapter 3—Burke: The Birth of the Right

1. Lord Acton, *Lectures on the French Revolution* (Liberty Fund, 1965), v.

2. Russell Kirk, *The Conservative Mind*, seventh revised edition (Regnery Gateway, 1993), 7–9.

3. *The Oxford Dictionary of National Biography*, http://www.oxforddnb.com/public/dnb/14918.html.

4. Samuel Johnson, *Johnson Miscellanies*, Volume I (Barnes and Noble, 1966), 290.

5. Francis Wrigley Hirst, *Adam Smith* (Macmillan & Co., 1904), 161.

6. Jim McCue, *Edmund Burke and Our Present Discontents* (Claridge Press, 1997), 16.

7. Russell Kirk, *Edmund Burk: A Genius Reconsidered* (ISI Books, 1997), 6.

8. Edmund Burke, "Speech on Conciliation with the Colonies" (Longmans, Green & Co., 1896), 20–21, 28–29, 78–79.

9. Thomas Babington Macaulay, *Critical and Historical Essays*, Third Volume (Longman, Brown, Green, and Longmans, 1846), 449–451.

10. Burke, *Reflections*, op. cit. (Penguin Books, 1986), 80.

11. Burke, *The Writings and Speeches of Edmund Burke*, Volume 2 (Cosimo, 2008), 228.
12. Brinton, *Political Thought*, op. cit., 13.
13. Alexander M. Bickel, *The Morality of Consent* (Yale University Press, 1977), 13.
14. Burke, op. cit., 218.
15. Ibid.
16. Burke, *Reflections*, op. cit., 93–94.
17. Edmund Burke, *Further Reflections on the Revolution in France* (Liberty Fund, 1992), 25.
18. A. N. Whitehead, *Process and Reality* (Free Press, 1979), 39.
19. Burke, *Reflections*, op. cit., 89–91.
20. Peter J. Stanlis, *Edmund Burke: The Enlightenment and the Revolution* (Transaction Publishers, 1993), xiii.
21. Ibid., 208.
22. Burke, *Reflections*, op. cit., 183.
23. Ibid., 284.
24. Burke, *Further Reflections*, op. cit., 69.
25. Burke, Reflections, op. cit., 149.
26. Burke, *Further Reflections*, op. cit., 47.
27. Charles Kegan Paul, *William Godwin: His Friends and Contemporaries*, Volume 1 (Roberts Brothers, 1876), 80.
28. *Encyclopedia Britannica*, Ninth Edition, Volume X, 717.
29. Ibid., 718.
30. *Encyclopedia Britannica*, Eleventh Edition, Volume I, 915.
31. William Godwin, *Adventures of Caleb Williams*, Volume 1 (Harper, 1831), 19.
32. William Godwin, *An Enquiry Concerning Political Justice*, Volume I (G. G. J. and J. Robinson, 1793), 31.
33. Burke, *Further Reflections*, op. cit., 196.

Chapter 4—Communism and Utopian Socialism

1. Durant, *Philosophy*, op. cit., 227.
2. Billington, op. cit. (Basic Books, 1980), 173.

3. Karl Marx and Friedrich Engels, *The Holy Family* (Рипол Классик, 1975), 161.

4. Billington, op. cit., 87 and 173.

5. Buonarroti, op. cit., 102.

6. Billington, op. cit., 174.

7. Georges Lefebvre, *The Directory* (Vintage Books, 1967), 37.

8. John Belushi, *Animal House*, 1978.

9. Tristram Hunt, *Marx's General: The Revolutionary Life of Friedrich Engels* (Macmillan, 2010), 132.

10. Frederick Engels, "Progress of Social Reform on the Continent," November 1843.

11. Plato, *The Republic* (Easton Press, 1980), 277.

12. Frank and Fritzie Manuel, *Utopian Thought in the Western World* (Harvard University Press, 2009), 583–584.

13. Frederick Engels, "The Peasant War in Germany," Summer 1850.

14. Frederick Engels, "Anti-Dühring," 1877.

15. F. A. Hayek, *Studies on the Abuse and Decline of Reason: Text and Document* (Routledge, 2013), 187.

16. Ibid., 189–190.

17. Ibid, 191.

18. Manuels, op. cit., 592–593.

19. Manuels, op., cit., 599.

20. Ibid.

21. Wilson, op. cit., 86.

22. Hayek, op., cit., 215–216.

23. Heine, op. cit., 306.

24. Frederick Engels, *Socialism: Utopian and Scientific* (1880).

25. Alasdair MacIntyre, *Marxism: An Interpretation* (SCM Press, 1953), 10.

26. Maneuls, op. cit., 641.

27. Jonathan Beecher and Richard Bienvenu, *The Utopian Vision of Charles Fourier* (Beacon Press, 1971), 63.

28. Manuels, op. cit., 649.

29. Bienvenu Beecher, op. cit., 93.

30. Manuels, op. cit., 643.

31. Bienvenu Beecher, op. cit., 98.

32. Manuels, op. cit., 665–666.

33. Bienvenu Beecher, op. cit., 45 and 52–53.

34. Manuels, op. cit., 645.

35. Frederick Engels, *Socialism: Utopian and Scientific* (1880).

36. Morris Hillquit, *History of Socialism in the United States* (Funk and Wagnalls, 1903), 81.

37. Engels, op. cit., *Socialism*.

38. Brinton, *Political Thought*, op. cit., 43.

39. Robert Owen, *The Life of Robert Owen*, Volume 1 (Wilson, 1858), 132–133.

40. Hal Draper, *Socialism from Below* (Humanities Press, 1992), 8.

41. Engels, op. cit., *Socialism*.

42. Crane Brinton, *The Political Ideas of the English Romanticists* (Oxford University Press, H. Milford, 1926), 177–193.

43. Percy Bysshe Shelley, *Shelley's Poetical Works* (James B. Smith Co., c1860), 111.

44. Ibid., 109.

45. Lewis Piaget Shanks, *Anatole France* (Open Court Publishing Company, 1919), 112.

Chapter 5—Kant, Hegel, Marx, Marxism

1. Manfred Kuehn, *Kant: A Biography* (Cambridge University Press, 2001), 179.

2. Immanuel Kant, *Kant's Critical Philosophy for English Readers* (Longmans, Green, 1872), 8.

3. Immanuel Kant, *The Philosophy of Kant: As Contained in Extracts from His Own Writings* (J. Maclehose & Sons, 1888), 296.

4. Heine, op. cit., 379.

5. Ibid.

6. Ibid., 368.

7. William Wallace, *Kant* (William Blackwood & Sons, 1882), 82.

8. David H. DeGrood, *Dialectics and Revolution,* Volume 2 (John Benjamins Publishing, 1979), 75.

9. Heine, op. cit., 375.

10. Ibid., 381.

11. Johann Gottlieb Fichte, *Introductions to the Wissenschaftslehre and Other Writings, 1797–1800* (Hackett Publishing, 1994), 160.

12. Heine, op. cit., 385.

13. Michael Allen Gillespie, *Nihilism before Nietzsche* (University of Chicago Press, 1996), 66.

14. Arthur Schopenhauer, *The World as Will and Representation,* Volume II (Digireads.com Publishing), 22.

15. *Cambridge Dictionary,* op. cit., 366.

16. *Oxford Companion to Philosophy* (Oxford University Press, 1995), 339.

17. Karl R. Popper, *The Open Society and Its Enemies, Volume II* (Princeton University Press, 1966), 62.

18. Alasdair MacIntyre, *Marxism and Christianity* (University of Notre Dame Press, 1968), 7.

19. Hicks, op. cit., 48.

20. MacIntyre, op. cit., 8–14.

21. Georg Wilhelm Friedrich Hegel, *The Philosophy of History* (Colonial Press, 1900), 15.

22. Karl Löwith, *Meaning in History* (University of Chicago Press, 1949), 54.

23. *Routledge Handbook of Public Diplomacy,* edited by Nancy Snow and Philip M. Taylor (Routledge, 2008), 38.

24. MacIntyre, op. cit., 15.

25. Karl Marx, *Das Kapital* (Charles H. Kerr & Company, 1912), 14–15.

26. John Milton, *Paradise Lost,* Book 1 (Easton Press, 1976), 10–11.

27. Karl Marx and Frederick Engels, *Collected Works, Volume 2* (International Publishers, 1976), 334.

28. Karl Marx and Frederick Engels, *Collected Works, Volume 3* (International Publishers, 1975), 404.

29. Wilson, op. cit., 136.
30. Wilson, op. cit., 193.
31. Paul Johnson, op. cit., 80.
32. Francis Wheen, *Karl Marx: A Life* (W. W. Norton & Co., 2001), 37.
33. Ibid., 32.
34. MacIntyre, op. cit., xxxx.
35. James Huneker, *Egoists* (C. Scribner's Sons 1909), 363.
36. Marx and Engels, *Volume 2*, op. cit., 336, 339, 346.
37. Löwith, *Hegel to Nietzsche*, op. cit., 317.
38. Huneker, op. cit., dust cover of Libertarian Book Club edition (1963).
39. Sidney Hook, *From Hegel to Marx* (Columbia University Press, 1994), 166.
40. Max Stirner, *The Ego and His Own* (A. C. Field, 1913), 268.
41. Marx and Engels, *Volume 3*, op. cit., 404.
42. Michael Goldfarb, *Emancipation: How Liberating Europe's Jews from the Ghetto Led to Revolution and Renaissance* (Simon and Schuster, 2009), 212.
43. Ibid., 215.
44. Wheen, op. cit., 104.
45. Karl Marx, *The Letters of Karl Marx*, edited by Saul Kussiel Padover (Prentice-Hall, 1979), 160.
46. Paul Johnson, op. cit., 73.
47. Wheen, op. cit., 65.
48. Francis Fukuyama, *The End of History and the Last Man* (Simon and Schuster, 2006), 65.
49. Eric Voegelin, *The New Science of Politics* (University of Chicago Press, Paperback Edition, 1987), 127.
50. Karl Marx, *The German Ideology* (Prometheus Books, 1998), 53.
51. Leo Strauss and Leo Cropsey, op. cit., 813.
52. Hanna Arendt, *On Violence* (Harcourt, 1970), 10.
53. Karl Marx, *Neue Rheinische Zeitung*, No. 136, November 1848.

54. Tristram Hunt, *Marx's General: The Revolutionary Life of Friedrich Engels* (Macmillan, 2010), 72.

55. Löwith, op. cit., 95.

56. *A Dictionary of Marxist Thought*, Second Edition (Blackwell, 1991), 437.

57. Marx, *German Ideology*, 569.

58. http://www.marxists.org/archive/marx/works/1848/communist-manifesto.

59. Wilson, op. cit., 338.

60. Karl Marx, *Capital: A Critique of Political Economy—the Process of Capitalist Production* (Cosimo, 2007), 83.

61. Marx, *Letters*, op. cit., 282.

62. Karl Löwith, *Max Weber and Karl Marx* (Routledge, 1993), 15.

63. Voegelin, op. cit., 120–124.

64. Carlyle, op. cit.

65. Herbert Spencer, *The Study of Sociology* (D. Appleton, 1873),

66. Friedrich Nietzsche, *The Gay Science* (Courier Corp., 2012),

Chapter 6—Anarchy and the First Whiff of Fascism

1. Pierre-Joseph Proudhon, *What Is Property?* (1840).

2. Robert Heilbroner, *The Worldly Philosophers* (Simon and Schuster, 1999), 153.

3. Pierre-Joseph Proudhon, *The Philosophy of Poverty* (1847).

4. Pierre-Joseph Proudhon, *General Idea of a Revolution in the 19th Century* (Courier Dover Publications, 2013), 294.

5. J. Salwyn Schapiro, *Liberalism and the Challenge of Fascism* (McGraw-Hill Book Company, 1949), 339.

6. Ibid., 344.

7. Mark Leier, *Bakunin: The Creative Passion—a Biography* (Seven Stories Press, 2011), 105.

8. Daniel H. Foster, *Wagner's Ring Cycle and the Greeks* (Cambridge University Press, 2010), 164.

9. Frederick Copleston, *Philosophy in Russia: From Herzen to Lenin and Berdyaev* (Bloomsbury Publishing, 2010), 82.
10. Max Nomad, *Apostles of Revolution* (Little, Brown & Co., 1939), 224.
11. James Guillaume, *Bakunin on Anarchy* (Vintage Books, 1971), 30.
12. Richard Suskind, *By Bullet, Bomb and Dagger* (Macmillian, 1971), 31.
13. Guillaume, op. cit., 34.
14. Paul Thomas, *Karl Marx and the Anarchists* (Psychology Press, 1980), 283.
15. Guillaume, op. cit., 26.
16. http://www.marxists.org/reference/archive/bakunin/works/mf-state/ch03.htm.
17. Peter Kropotkin, *Memoirs of a Revolutionist* (Dover Publications, 1971), 344.
18. Suskind, op. cit., 36–37.

Part II—The Early Years in Europe

1. Alfred D. Chandller Jr., *The Visible Hand* (Harvard University Presss, 1993).

Chapter 7—Germany: Bismarck, Lassalle, and Schmoller

1. Marx, *The Letters of Marx*, op cit., 411.
2. Ibid., 480.
3. David Footman, *Ferdinand Lassalle, Romantic Revolutionary* (Yale University Press, 1947), 175.
4. Gildea, op. cit., 202.
5. Emile Ludwig, *Bismarck: The Story of a Fighter* (Blue Ribbon Books, 1931), 237.
6. Élie Halévy, *The Era of Tyrannies* (Anchor Books, 1965), 273.
7. Moritz Busch, *Our Chancellor: Sketches for a Historical Picture*, Volume II (Scribner's Sons, 1884), 265.

8. Ludwig, op. cit., 383.
9. Ludwig, op. cit., 548 and 549.
10. Gildea, op. cit., 357.
11. Ludwig von Mises, *Socialism: An Economic and Sociological Analysis* (Ludwig von Mises Institute, 2009), 567.
12. Gildea, op. cit., 357.
13. Ludwig, op cit., 571–576.
14. Heilbroner, op. cit., 84.
15. Ludwig von Mises, *Theory and History* (Ludwig von Mises Institute, 1985), 255.
16. Carl Menger, *Investigations into the Method of the Social Sciences with Special Reference to Economics* (New York University Press, 1985).
17. Arno Mong Daastøl, *Interpretation and Generalization— and Empiricism, Rationalism as Traditions in Economic Methodology*, thesis on social economy, University of Oslo, Summer 1992.
18. Jürg Niehans, *A History of Economic Theory* (John Hopkins University Press, 1990), 525.

Chapter 8—England: The Fabians and the Bloomsburies

1. Brinton, op. cit., 13.
2. Brinton, op. cit., 295.
3. *Oxford Companion*, op. cit., 890.
4. Ibid., 85.
5. Brinton, op. cit., 15.
6. Brinton, op. cit., 19.
7. Benjamin Disraeli, *Whigs and Whiggism: Political Writings* (Macmillan, 1914), 118.
8. *The Cambridge Dictionary of Philosophy,* op. cit., 568.
9. Tony Davies, *Humanism* (Routledge, 2006), 29.
10. John Stuart Mill, *The Positive Philosophy of Auguste Comte* (Henry Holt & Co., 1873), 139.
11. Hayek, op. cit., 275.

12. *The Methodist Review*, Volume 90 (J. Soule and T. Mason., 1908), 113.

13. Padover, op. cit., 213.

14. Alasdair MacIntyre, *Marxism: An Interpretation* (SCM Press, 1953), 10.

15. Hayek, op. cit., 278.

16. John Stuart Mill, *On Liberty* (J. W. Parker and Son, 1859), 13.

17. Kirk, *Conservative Mind*, op. cit., 301.

18. Charles Darwin, *The Origin of Species by Means of Natural Selection* (G. Richards, 1904), 4.

19. T. S. Eliot, *The Use of Poetry and the Use of Criticism* (Harvard University Press, 1986), 106.

20. Emile Faguet, *On Reading Nietzsche* (Moffat, Yard, 1918), 71.

21. Thomas Nagel, *Secular Philosophy and the Religious Temperament* (Oxford University Press, 2009), 37.

22. Thomas Malthus, *An Essay on the Principle of Population*, chapter 9 (1798).

23. Richard Steele and Joseph Addison, *The Lucubrations of Isaac Bickerstaff Esquire*, Volume 2 (Bathurst, 1723), 159–160.

24. Robert J. Mayhew, *Malthus* (Harvard University Press, 2014), 129–130.

25. Charles Dickens, *A Christmas Carol* (Bradbury & Evans, 1858), 9.

26. Charles Darwin, *The Autobiography of Charles Darwin* (Collins Clear Type Press, 1958), 120.

27. Herbert Spencer, *A Theory of Population, Deduced from the General Law of Animal Fertility* (Herbert Spencer, 1852), 33.

28. Stephen Jay Gould, *Ever Since Darwin: Reflections in Natural History* (Norton, 1977), 13.

29. Spencer, op. cit., 34.

30. Marc Stears, *Progressives, Pluralists, and the Problems of the State* (Oxford University Press, 2002), 38.

31. Alasdair MacIntyre, *Three Rival Versions of Moral Enquiry* (University of Notre Dame Press, 1990), 21.

32. Thomas Hill Green, *Works of Thomas Hill Green*, Volume 3 (Longmans, Green, & Co, 1891), 367.

33. Irving Babbitt, *Democracy and Leadership* (Houghton Mifflin, 1924), 267.

34. Durant, *Philosophy*, op. cit., 284.

35. Friedrich Hayek, "The Intellectuals and Socialism," *The University of Chicago Law Review* (Spring 1949): 417–433, 421–423.

36. George Bernard Shaw, *The Fabian Society: Its Early History*, Issue 41 (Fabian Society, 1906).

37. George Bernard Shaw, *The Fabian Society: Its Early History*, Issue 41 (Fabian Society, 1906).

38. Sidney Webb, *The Basis and Policy of Socialism*, Fabian Socialists Series, No. 4 (A. C. Fifield, 1908), 3.

39. Joseph Schumpeter, *Capitalism, Socialism, and Democracy* (Routledge, 1994), 322–325.

40. Sidney Webb, "The Decline of the Birth Rate," Fabian Tract 131 (1907).

41. Karl Pearson, *The Life, Letters and Labours of Francis Galton*, Volume 3 (Cambridge at the University Press, 1933), 355.

42. Alberto Spektorowski and Liza Ireni-Saban, *The Politics of Eugenics* (Routledge, 2013), 43.Top of Form

43. Bottom of Form

44. Richard Milton, *Best of Enemies* (Icon Books, 2007), 128.

45. Matthew Yde, *Bernard Shaw and Totalitarianism: Longing for Utopia* (Palgrave Macmillan, 2013), 32.

46. *The Living Age*, Volume 250 (E. Littell & Company, 1906), 84.

47. Sidney Webb, "The Difficulties of Individualism," Fabian Tract 69 (1896).

48. H. L. Mencken, *Diary of H. L. Mencken*, chapter 4 (Random House, 2012).

49. Paul Holland, *Political Pilgrims: Western Intellectuals in Search of the Good Society* (Transaction Publishers, 1981), 121.

50. Ronald Hingley, *Joseph Stalin: Man and Legend* (Smithmark Pub, 1994), 225.

51. Jamie Glazov, *United in Hate: The Left's Romance with Tyranny and Terror* (WND Books, 2009), 31.

52. Ian Hunter, *Malcolm Muggeridge: A Life* (Regent College Publishing, 2003), 86.

53. Malcolm Muggeridge, *Things Past* (Morrow, 1979), 33.

54. Paul Johnson, *Modern Times* (HarperCollins, 1991), 275.

55. Babbitt, op. cit., 314.

56. Eric Hoffer, *The True Believer* (Harper and Bros., 1951) 14.

57. Johnson, *The Intellectuals*, op. cit., 191.

58. *The Harper Dictionary of Modern Thought* (Harper & Row, 1977), 305.

59. Christine Froula, *Virginia Woolf and the Bloomsbury Avant-Garde: War, Civilization, Modernity* (Columbia University Press, 2013), 19–20.

60. http://spectator.org/articles/40805/dark-horse.

61. Alasdair MacIntyre, *After Virtue*, Second Edition (University of Notre Dame Press, 1984), 11.

62. Ibid., 18.

63. John Maynard Keynes, *Two Memoirs: Dr. Melchior, a Defeated Enemy, and My Early Beliefs* (A. M. Kelley, 1949), 81, 82, 99.

64. Draper, op. cit., 3.

65. Wyndham Lewis, *The Revenge for Love* (Black Sparrow Press, 1991), 152.

Chapter 9—France: Dreyfus, Maurras, Sorel

1. Jean-Denis Breden, *The Affair: The Case of Alfred Dreyfus* (George Braziller, 1986), 18.

2. Ibid., 21.

3. Ibid., 241–242.

4. Ibid., 251.
5. Ibid., 250.
6. G. Whyte, *The Dreyfus Affair: A Chronological History* (Springer, 2005), 194.
7. Breden, op. cit., 338.
8. Ernst Nolte, *Three Faces of Fascism* (Holt, Rinehart and Winston, 1966), 65.
9. Eduard Bernstein, *Evolutionary Socialism*, introduction by Sidney Hook (Schoken Books, 1961), xii–xiv.
10. V. I. Lenin, *What Is to Be Done* (Peking: Foreign Language Press, 1973), 96–116.
11. Georg Wilhelm Friedrich Hegel, *Elements of the Philosophy of Right* (Cambridge University Press, 1991), 366.
12. Michael Sutton, *Nationalism, Positivism and Catholicism* (Cambridge University Press, 1982), 71.
13. Michael Curtis, *Three Against the Third Republic* (Transaction Publishers, 2010), 224.
14. Nolte, op. cit., 126 and 138.
15. Sutton, op. cit., 18.
16. Nolte, op. cit., 137–138.
17. Gene Edward Veith Jr., *Modern Fascism* (Concordia Publishing House, 1951), 47.
18. Charles Maurras, *The French Right*, edited by J. S. McClelland (Harper & Row Publishers, 1970), 250.
19. Nolte, op. cit., 128.
20. Sorel, *Reflections*, op. cit., 268.
21. Ibid., 216.
22. Zeev Sternhell, *The Birth of Fascist Ideology* (Princeton University Press, 1994), 37.
23. Sorel, op. cit., 267.
24. Sternhell, op. cit., 91.
25. Sorel, op. cit., 38.
26. Sternhell, op. cit., 53.
27. Sorel, op. cit., 45.
28. Ibid., 99.
29. Ibid., 90–91.

30. Ibid., 70.
31. Sorel, op. cit., *Progress*, 129.
32. Sorel, op. cit., *Reflections*, 152.
33. Ibid., 23–24.
34. Ibid., 22–26.
35. Plato, *Phaedrus* (Easton Press, 1979), 182.
36. Sorel, op. cit., *Reflections*, 26.
37. Sorel, *Reflections*, op. cit., 35.
38. Thomas Mann, *Doctor Faustus* (Modern Library, 1948), 366.

Part III—Capitalism, Socialism, Progress, Decay

Chapter 10—On Capitalism

1. Deirdre McCloskey, *The Bourgeois Virtues* (University of Chicago Press, 2010).
2. Jerry Z. Muller, *The Mind and the Market: Capitalism in Western Thought* (Random House, 2007), 9.
3. Heilbroner, op. cit., 26–27.
4. Ibid., 29–37.
5. John Locke, *Second Treatise on Government*, Chapter V, Sections 26–27.
6. Muller, op. cit., 7.
7. Thomas More, *Utopia* (1516).
8. Max Weber, *The Protestant Ethic and the Spirit of Capitalism* (Charles Scribner's Sons, 1958), 159.
9. Ibid., 80–81.
10. Ibid., 82.
11. John Calvin, *Institute of the Christian Religion* (Hendrickson Publishers, 2008), 470.
12. Weber, op. cit., 108–109.
13. E. Belfort Bax, *The Peasants War in Germany, 1525–1526* (S. Sonnenschein, 1899), 27.
14. Cicely Veronica Wedgwood, *The Thirty Years War* (Jonathan Cape, 1966), 511 and 513.

15.   Ibid., 525–526.

16.   John Fiske, *The Beginnings of New England or the Puritan Theocracy in Its Relations to Civil and Religious Liberty* (Houghton Mifflin, 1889), 36–37.

17.   Elie Wiesel, preface to a new translation of *Night* (Hill and Wang, 1958).

18.   James Hutchison Stirling, *Lectures on the Philosophy of Law* (Longmans, Green & Company, 1873), 27.

19.   Adam Smith, *The Theory of Moral Sentiments* (Liberty Fund, 1976), 180 (IV.1.4).

20.   Adam Smith, *An Inquiry into the Nature and Causes of the Wealth of Nations* (Liberty Fund, 1981), 455–6 (IV.ii, 9 and 10).

21.   David Hume, *Enquiry Concerning the Principles of Morals* (Clarendon Press, 1902), 154–155.

22.   Smith, *Theory*, op. cit. 163 (III.5.2).

Chapter 11—On Communism and Socialism

1.   Thomas Malthus, *An Essay on the Principle of Population* (Cambridge University Press, 1991), 101.

2.   Seymour Drescher, *Dilemmas of Democracy: Tocqueville and Modernization* (University of Pittsburgh Press, 1968), 109.

3.   Alexis de Tocqueville, *Memoir on Pauperism* (Civitas London, 1968), 30–37.

4.   Evelyn Beatrice Hall, *The Friends of Voltaire* (Putnam's, 1906), 87.

5.   Heilbroner, op. cit., 179.

6.   Frederic Bastiat, "Justice and Fraternity," *Journal des economists* (1848).

7.   Pope Pius IX, Qui Pluribus (On Faith and Religion) (1846).

8.   Oron J. Hale, *The Great Illusion* (Harper and Rowe, 1971), 83.

9.   Herbert Spencer, *The Man versus the State: A Collection of Essays* (M. Kennerley, 1916), 36–15, 248–249, 284.

10. http://www.newadvent.org/cathen/12783a.htm.

11. Pope Leo XIII, Rerum Novarum (On Capital and Labor), http://www.papalencyclicals.net/Leo13/l13rerum.htm.

12. Friedrich Nietzsche, *Human, All Too Human: A Book for Free Spirits* (Cambridge University Press, 1996), 173–174.

13. Georges Sorel, *Reflections on Violence* (B. W. Huebsch, 1912), 129.

14. Ibid., 138.

15. Ibid., 179.

16. Ibid., 182.

17. Ibid., 185.

18. Ibid., 25.

19. Ibid., 53–54.

20. Ibid., 81.

21. Bertrand de Jouvenel, *The Ethics of Redistribution* (Liberty Press, 1990), xii.

22. Ibid., 30.

23. Ibid., 72–77.

24. John Gray, Introduction to *The Ethics of Redistribution* (Liberty Press, 1990), xiii, xv, xvi.

25. Alexis de Tocqueville, *Democracy in America* (Cambridge: Sever and Francis, 1863), 391.

26. George Orwell, *Nineteen Eighty-Four* (Houghton Mifflin Harcourt, 1949), 577.

27. George Orwell, *Orwell's Nineteen Eighty-Four: Text, Sources, Criticism* (Harcourt Brace Jovanovich, 1982), 373.

28. Hanna Arendt, *The Origins of Totalitariansim* (Harcourt Brace & Co., 1973), 6.

29. George Orwell, "Britain's Struggle for Survival," *Commentary Magazine*, January 1, 1948.

30. Arendt, op. cit., xxxiv and 306.

Chapter 12—On Decay

1. Appianus (of Alexandria), *Appian's Roman Hisory* (W. Heinemann, 1912), 637.

2. Polybius, *The General History of the Wars of the Romans* (J. Davis, 1812).

3. Plutarch, *Plutarch's Lives* (W. Heinemann, 1921), 166–167.

4. Procopius, *History of the Wars: The Vandalic Wars, Books 3–4* (Cosimo, 2007), 17.

5. Edward Gibbon, *The History of the Decline and Fall of the Roman Empire: Volume III* (Phillips, Sampson, 1851), 129.

6. Livy, *The Early History of Rome* (Penguin UK, 2005), 30.

7. Rudyard Kipling, *The Mother Hive: The Writings in Prose and Verse of Rudyard Kipling*, Volume 24 (C. Scribner's Sons, 1911), 113.

8. Gustave Le Bon, *The Crowd* (Transaction Publishers, 1994), 37–38.

9. Patrick Devlin, *The Enforcement of Morals* (Oford University Press, 1965), 10.

10. Glyn-Jones, op. cit., dust jacket.

11. Ibid., 8.

12. Pitirim Aleksandrovič Sorokin, *Social and Cultural Dynamics* (Transaction Publishers, 1962), 35–36.

13. Orestes Augustus Brownson, *The Works of Orestes A. Brownson* (T. Nourse, 1885), 349.

14. George Washington, *Washington's Farewell Address: Delivered September 17th, 1796* (D. Appleton and Company, 1861), 16.

15. Russell Kirk, *Eliot and His Age* (Sherwood Sugden & Co., 1984), 140.

Chapter 13—On Progress

1. Henri Frankfort, *The Birth of Civilization in the Near East* (Indiana University Press, 1951), 20.

2. John Mansley Robinson, *An Introduction to Early Greek Philosophy* (Houghton Mifflin, 1968), 89 and 91.

3. Karl Popper, *The Open Society and Its Enemies* (Princeton University Press, 1971), 12.

4. Ibid., 13.

5. Aristotle, *Problemata,* Book XVII (Aeterna Press, 2015), 4.

6. Robert Nisbet, *History of the Idea of Progress* (Basic Books, 1980), 64.

7. Peter Bernstein, *Against the Gods: The Remarkable Story of Risk* (John Wiley & Sons, 1998), 17.

8. Löwith, op. cit., 13.

9. Nisbet, op. cit., 103.

10. Ibid., 106.

11. Jacques Amyot, preface to *Plutarch's Lives of the Noble Grecians and Romans*, Volume 1, The Tudor Translations, 10–111.

12. Leibniz, op. cit., 350–351.

13. Michael Mooney, *Vico in the Tradition of Rhetoric* (Lawrence Erlbaum Associates, 1995), 4.

14. Giambattsta Vico, *The Autobiography of Giambattista Vico* (Cornell University Press, 1944), 38.

15. Löwith, *Meaning in History*, op. cit. 116.

16. Eric Voegelin, *The Collected Works of Eric Voegelin*, Volume 13 (University of Missouri Press, 2001), 180.

17. Vico, op. cit., 52.

18. Quentin Lauer, *Hegel's Idea of Philosophy* (Fordham University Press, 1983), 133.

19. Löwith, *From Hegel to Nietzsche*, op. cit., 216.

20. William Wallace, *Life of Arthur Schopenhauer* (W. Scott, 1890), 19.

21. Friedrich Nietzsche, *Untimely Meditations* (Cambridge University Press, 1997), 148.

22. Löwith, op. cit., 224.

23. Charles Baudelaire, *Baudelaire: His Prose and Poetry* (Boni and Liveright, 1919), 221, 228, 243.

24. Löwith, *Meaning in History*, op. cit., 21, 25.

Part IV—The Left in America

1. Eric Foner and John A. Garraty, *The Reader's Companion to American History* (Houghton Mifflin Company, 1991), 467.

2. John Howard Smith, *The First Great Awakening: Redefining Religion in British America, 1725–1775* (Rowman & Littlefield, 2014), 2.

3. William Dudley and **Terry** O'Neill, *Puritanism* (Greenhaven Press, 1994), 191.

4. William Wainwright, "Jonathan Edwards," *The Stanford Encyclopedia of Philosophy*, edited by Edward N. Zalta (Winter 2012 edition).

5. James Paterson Gledstone, *The Life and Travels of George Whitefield, M. A.* (Longmans, Green, and Co., 1871), 489, 508.

6. Cotton Mather, *Magnalia Christi Americana* (S. Andrus & Son, 1853), 208.

Chapter 14—The European Left Comes to America

1. Carroll Quigley, *Tragedy and Hope* (Macmillian Company, 1966), 72.

2. http://query.nytimes.com/mem/archive-free/pdf?res=9803E3D91E3EEF33A25753C2A9619C94679F-D7CF.

3. Philip S. Foner, *History of the Labor Movement in the United States*, Volume II (International Publishers, 1955), 38.

4. Morris Hillquit, *History of Socialism in the United States* (Funk & Wagnalls, 1906), 236–237.

5. Barbara W. Tuchman, *The Proud Tower: A Portrait of the World Before the War, 1890–1914* (Random House LLC, 2011), 81.

6. Emma Godman, *Living My Life*, Volume 1 (Cosimo, 2008), 40.

7. Michael J. Schaack, *Anarchy and Anarchists* (F. J. Schulte, 1889), 291.

8. *Politics and Politicians of Chicago*, Cook County, and Illinois: Memorial Volume, 1787–1887 (Blakely Printing Company, 1886).

9. Suskind, op. cit., 6.

10. Alexander Berkman, *Life of an Anarchist: The Alexander Reader* (Seven Stories Press, 1992), 11.

11. https://archive.org/details/trialexecutionau00macd.

12. John A. Farrell, *Clarence Darrow: Attorney for the Damned* (Knopf Doubleday Publishing Group, 2012), 66.

Chapter 15—America's Homegrown Left

1. Draper, op. cit., 20.

2. Edward Bellamy, *Looking Backward* (Signet Classic, 1960), xxx.

3. Ibid., foreword by Erich Fromm, x.

4. Ibid., v–vii.

5. Draper, op. cit., 5.

6. Douglas W. Steeples and David O. Whitten, *Democracy in Desperation: The Depression of 1893* (Greenwood Publishing Group, 1998), 121.

7. Leslie Fishbein, *Rebels in Bohemia: The Radicals of the Masses, 1911–1917* (University of North Carolina Press, 1982), 15.

8. Jonathan Auerbach, *Male Call: Becoming Jack London* (Duke University Press, 1996), 121.

9. Fishbein, op. cit., 125.

10. Max Horn, *The Intercollegiate Socialist Society, 1905–192* (Westview Press, 1979), 41.

11. Anna Strunsky Walling, "Memoirs of Jack London," *The Masses* (July 1917).

12. John Bunyan, *The Pilgrim's Progress* (Harper & Brothers, 1837), 250–251.

13. Ida M. Tarbell, *The History of the Standard Oil Company: Briefer Version* (Courier Corp., 2012), 66.

14. Ibid, 44.

15. Fine, op. cit., 80.

16. Luigi Bradizza, *Richard T. Ely's Critique of Capitalism* (Palgrave, Macmillian, 2013), 11.

17. Bruce E. Kaufman, *The Global Evolution of Industrial Relations* (International Labour Organization, 2004), 60.

18. *The Johns Hopkins University Studies in Historical and Political Science*, Volume 2 (Johns Hopkins University Press, 1884), 202.

19. Fine, op. cit., 47, 52, 53.

20. B. E. Fernow, speech contained in the *Poceedings of the American Association for the Advancement of Science* (AAAS, 1896).

21. *The Encyclopaedia Britannica*, Ninth Edition, Volume 14 (Maxwell Sommerville, 1894), 301.

22. http://www.hawking.org.uk/does-god-play-dice.html.

23. Louis Menand, *The Metaphysical Club: A Story of Ideas in America* (Farrar, Straus and Giroux, 2001), 196.

24. Ibid., 183.

25. Ibid., 187.

26. Ibid., 188.

27. Ibid., 191.

28. Ibid., 193.

29. Ibid., 194

30. Henry Thomas Buckle, *History of Civilization in England*, Volume 2 (Parker, Son, and Bourn, 1861), 1.

31. *Current Literature*, Volume 43 (Current Literature Publishing Company, 1907), 50.

32. Nancy Cohen, *The Reconstruction of American Liberalism, 1865–1914* (University of North Carolina Press, 2002), 164–165.

33. William Graham Sumner, Testimony before a Congressional Committee of House investigating the Causes of the

General Depression in Labor and Business, August 22, 1878.

34. William Graham Sumner, *Essays* (Yale University Press, 1913), 230.

35. Cohen, op. cit., 176.

36. Menand, op. cit., 302.

Chapter 16—Teddy's Medicine Show

1. Carl Schmitt, *The Concept of the Political* (University of Chicago Press, 1996), 25.

2. Ron Chernow, *Titan: The Life of John D. Rockefeller Sr.* (Knopf Doubleday, 2007), 388.

3. Edmund Lester Pearson, *Theodore Roosevelt* (Macmillan Company, 1920), 76.

4. H. W. Brands, *T. R.: The Last Romantic* (Basic Books, 1998), 397.

5. Nathan Miller, *Theodore Roosevelt: A Life* (William Morrow, 1992), 352 and 356.

6. Lincoln Steffens, *The Autobiography of Lincoln Steffens*, abridged (Hardcourt, Brace, 1937), 347–348.

7. Ortega y Gasset, *The Revolt of the Masses* (W. W. Norton, 1932), 48.

8. T. R. Roosevelt, First Annual Message, December 3, 1901.

9. Jim Powell, *Bully Boy: The Truth about Theodore Roosevelt's Legacy* (Crown Publishing Group, 2006), 9.

10. Thomas Kessner, *Capital City: New York City and the Men Behind* (Simon and Schuster, 2004), 278–279.

11. Miller, op. cit., 367.

12. Jean Strouse, *Morgan: American Financier* (Random House, 1999), 440–441.

13. Andrew Sinclair, *Corsair: Life of J. Pierpont Morgan* (Littlehampton Book Services Ltd., 1981), 142.

14. Miller, op. cit., 369.

15. Ron Chernow, *The House of Morgan* (Grove Press, 2010), 78.

16. Vincent P. and Rose C. Carosso, *The Morgans: Private International Bankers, 1854–1913*, 434.

17. Jean Strouse, *Morgan: American Financier* (Random House, 2012), 436.

18. Philip Burch, *The Civil War to the New Deal* (Holmes & Meier, 1981), 196.

19. Ron Chernow, *The House of Morgan* (Grove Press, 2010), 110–111.

20. Gabriel Kolko, *Triumph of Conservatism* (Simon and Schuster, 2008), 69.

21. T. R. Roosevelt, Speech at Music Hall, Cincinnati, Ohio, September 20, 1902.

22. Sinclair, op, cit., 169.

23. Miller, op. cit., 380.

24. Kolko, op. cit., 72.

25. Miller, op. cit., 440.

26. Ibid., 452.

27. Peter Hartshorn, *I Have Seen the Future: A Life of Lincoln Steffens* (Counterpoint Press, 2011), 120.

28. T. R. Roosvelt, Fourth Annual Message, December 6, 1904.

29. Chernow, op. cit., 29.

30. T. R. Roosvelt, Address at Union League Club, January 30, 1905.

31. Fred S. McChesney, *The Causes and Consequences of Antitrust: The Public-Choice Perspective* (University of Chicago Press, 1995), 270.

32. Miller, op. cit., 455.

33. T. R. Roosevelt, Fifth Annual Message, December 5, 1905.

34. Miller, op. cit., 456–457.

35. David Graham Phillips, "The Treason of the Senate," *Cosmopolitan*, February 17, 1906.

36. Robert Penn Warren, *All the King's Men* (Modern Library, Random House, 1953), 22.

37. Thomas Carlyle, *On Heroes, Hero-Worship, and the Heroic in History* (John B. Alden, 1892), 100.

38. T. R. Roosevelt, address at the laying of the cornerstone of the office building of the House of Representatives, April 14, 1906.

39. Miller, op. cit., 459.

40. John Morton Blum, *The Republican Roosevelt* (Atheneum, 1965), 91.

41. Miller, op. cit., 462.

42. Luigi Bradizza, *Richard T. Ely's Critique of Capitalism* (Palgrave, Macmillan, 2013), 45–46.

43. T. R. Roosevelt, Address in Harrisonburg, Pa, at dedication of new capitol building on October 4, 1906.

44. Daniel Yergin, *The Prize: The Epic Quest for Oil, Money & Power* (Simon and Schuster, 2011), 92.

45. T. R. Roosevelt, Sixth Annual Message, December 3. 1906.

46. Jean Strouse, *Morgan: American Financier* (Random House, 1999), 574.

47. T. R. Roosevelt, Address in Provincetown, Massachusetts, August 20, 1907.

48. Miller, op. cit., 477–478.

49. T. R. Roosevelt, Special Message to the Two Houses of Congress, January 31, 1908.

Chapter 17—Taft: The Post Turtle

1. Paul F. Boller Jr., *Presidential Wives* (Oxford University Press, 1988), 207.

2. Philip C. Jessup, *Elihu Root*, Volume II (Dodd, Mead & Co., 1938), 125.

3. Edward L. Purcell, *Vice Presidents: A Biographical Dictionary* (Infobase Publishing, 2010), 256.

4. Henry F. Pringle, *The Life and Times of William Howard Taft*, Volume I (Farrar & Rinehart, 1939), 331.

5. H. Paul Jeffers, *An Honest President* (William Morrow, 2000), 201–201.

6. Allan Nevins, *Grover Cleveland: A Story in Courage* (Dodd, Mead, 1962), 586.

7. James Madison, *The Federalist*, Number X (Eaton Press, 1979), 57–58.

8. Pollock v. Farmers' Loan and Trust Company, Appeal from the Circuit Court of the United States for the Southern District of New York, 1895, http://www.law.cornell.edu/supct/html/historics/USSC_CR_0157_0429_ZX.html.

9. US Congress, House, Congressional Record, July 12, 1909, p. 4404.

10. Henry F. Pringle, *Theodore Roosevelt: A Biography* (Harcourt Brace, 1931), 518.

11. David W. Levy, *Herbert Croly of the New Republic* (Princeton University Press, 1985), 3 and 23.

12. Ibid., 28.

13. Ibid., 70.

14. Ibid., 94.

15. Herbert Croly, *The Promise of American Life* (Macmillan, 1911), 278.

16. Levy, op. cit., 135.

17. Virginia Postrel, "The Croly Ghost," *Reason Magazine* (December 1997).

18. Levy, op. cit., 113–117.

19. Paul Finkelman, *Encyclopedia of American Civil Liberties* (Routledge, 2013), 1619.

20. Russell Kirk, *Rights and Duties* (Spence Publishing Co., 1997), 183.

21. John Dewey, *A Common Faith* (Yale University Press, 1960), 87.

22. John Dewey, *My Pedagogic Creed* (John Dewey, 1897), 7–17.

23. *Human Events*, "Ten Most Harmful Books of the 19th and 20th Centuries," May 31, 2005.

24. Ibid., 177.

25. Herbert David Croly, *Progressive Democracy* (Macmillan, 1914), 168.

26. G. K. Chesterton, *Orthodoxy* (Doubleday, 1990), 15.

27. Croly, *Progressive*, op. cit., 170.

28. Theodore Roosevelt, New Nationalism Speech, August 31, 1910.

29. Kolko, op. cit., 191.

30. Paul Moritz Warburg, *Essays on Banking Reform in the United States* (Academy of Political Science, 1914), 391.

31. G. Edward Griffin, *The Creature from Jekyll Island*, Fifth Edition (American Media, 2007), 5.

32. Melvin Pugh, *Roman Rule: The Eternal Empire* (Author House, 2011), 32.

33. Roger Lowenstein, *America's Bank: The Epic Struggle to Create the Federal Reserve*, chapter 8 (Penguin Press, 2015).

34. Jessup, op. cit., 173.

35. Ibid., 176.

36. Ibid., 177.

37. T. R. Roosevelt, Address before the Ohio Constitutional Convention, February 21, 1912.

38. Henry L. Stoddard, *As I Knew Them: Presidents and Politics* (Harper and Brothers, 1927), 397.

39. Madison, op. cit., 60.

40. Jessup, op. cit., 180.

41. Patricia O'Toole, *When Trumpets Call: Theodore Roosevelt after the White House* (Simon and Schuster, 2005), 153.

42. Paul F. Boller, *Presidential Campaigns* (Oxford University Press, 2004), 192.

43. Stoddard, op. cit., 421.

44. Kolko, op. cit., 220.

45. Ferdinand Lundberg, *America's 60 Families* (Halcyon House, 1939), 114–115.

Chapter 18—Wilson: The Third Way

1. Bill Clinton, State of the Union Speech, January 27, 1998.

2. Norman Fairclough, *New Labour, New Language?* (Routledge, 2002), 4.

3. William Frank McCombs, *Making Woodrow Wilson President* (Fairview Publishing Company, 1921), 207–208.

4. Woodrow Wilson, Speech to US Senate, July 10, 1919.

5. Thomas Brackett Reed, *Modern Eloquence: Anecdotes, Indices* (D. Morris and Company, 1900), 79.

6. Colleen J. Shogun, *The Moral Rhetoric of American Presidents* (Texas A&M University Press, 2007), 27.

7. Daniel J. Boorstin, *The Colonial Experience.*

8. Woodrow Wilson, First Inaugural Address, March 4, 1913.

9. Richard J. Bishirjian, "Croly, Wilson, and the American Civil Religion," *Modern Age* (Winter 1979) (Intercollegiate Studies Institute).

10. Claes Ryn, *The New Jacobinism: Can Democracy Survive* (National Humanities Institute, 1991), 27.

11. Richard Ely, *Studies in the Evolution of Industrial Society* (Kennikat Press, 1903), 164–188.

12. Edwin Black, *War against the Weak: Eugenics and America's Campaign to Create a Master Race* (Four Walls Eight Windows, 2003), xv–xvi.

13. Ibid., 35.

14. Harry Bruinius, *Better for All the World: The Secret History of Forced Sterilization and America's Quest for Racial Purity* (Vintage Books, 2007), 160.

15. Ibid., 190.

16. Black, op. cit., 322.

17. Ibid., 68.

18. John Milton Cooper, *Woodrow Wilson: A Biography* (Vintage Books, 2011), 19.

19. Black, op. cit., 22.

20. Paul A. Lombardo, *Three Generations, No Imbeciles: Eugenics, the Supreme Court, and "Buck V. Bell"* (JHU Press, 2008), 209.

21. G. K. Chesterton, *Eugenics and Other Evils* (Inkling Books, 2000), 96–97.

22. Pope Pius XI, *Casti connubii* (On Christian Marriage), 1930.

23. Charles P. Nemeth, *Criminal Law*, Second Edition (CRC Press, 2011), 6.

24. Lombardo, op. cit., 103–105.
25. Stephen Jay Gould, *The Richness of Life: The Essential Stephen Jay Gould* (W. W. Norton, 2006), 570.
26. C. P. Snow, *A Coat of Varnish* (House of Stratus, 2000), 43.
27. Woodrow Wilson, "The Study of Administration," *Political Science Quarterly* 2, No. 2 (June 1887).
28. Woodrow Wilson, *The New Freedom* (Doubleday, Page, 1921), 284.
29. Babbitt, op. cit., 289–290.
30. James Madison, *The Federalist*, Number LI (Easton Press, 1979), 347–348.
31. Ronald J. Pestritto, *Woodrow Wilson and the Roots of Modern Liberalism* (Rowman & Littlefield Publishers, 2005), 6.
32. Ibid., 3.
33. Burke, *Reflections*, op. cit., 184.
34. George Washington, "Farewell Address," 1796, http://avalon.law.yale.edu/18th_century/washing.asp.
35. *Constitution* of the United States, Article 1, Section 3.
36. National Center for Constitutional Studies, http://www.nccs.net/2009–06-states-demand-return-to-federalism.php.
37. William Greider, *Secrets of the Temple: How the Federal Reserve Runs the Country* (Simon & Schuster, 1989), 277.
38. William McAdoo, Report of the Secretary of the Treasury on the State of the Finances (US Dept. of the Treasury, 1916), 12.
39. Elihu Root, "The Banking and Currency Bill," Speech of Hon. Elihu Root of New York (US Government Printing Office, 1913).
40. Kolko, op. cit., 250.
41. George Kennan, *Russia and the West under Lenin and Stalin* (Little, Brown & Co., 1960), 7.
42. William Appleman Williams, *The Tragedy of American Diplomacy* (W. W. Norton, 2009), 87.
43. CharlesSeymour, *The Intimate Papers of Colonel House* (Houghton Mifflin Co., 1926), 85.

44. Ibid., 86.
45. Lundberg, op. cit., 141.
46. William Appleman Williams, *The Contours of American History* (Verso Books, 2011), 421.
47. Williams, *Tragedy*, op. cit., 87.
48. Ibid., 57.
49. Ibid., 72.
50. Woodrow Wilson, "Crossroad of Freedom," speech, September 16, 1912, (United States Congressional serial set, issue 6179).
51. Williams, *Tragedy*, op. cit., 63.
52. Ibid., 69.
53. Woodrow Wilson, War Message to Congress, April 2, 1917.
54. T. S. Eliot, Notes toward the Definition of Culture (Faber and Faber, 1948), 108.

Index

Y

About the Authors

 **Mark Melcher** is the president and editor of *The Political Forum*, which is an "independent research provider" that delivers research and consulting services to the institutional investment community, with an emphasis on economic, social, political, and geopolitical events that are likely to have an impact on the financial markets in the United States and abroad.

He has followed global and domestic social and political trends from Washington for the financial community since 1973, when he joined the Washington Forum, a subsidiary of Drexel Burnham Lambert. He left Drexel in July 1983 to open a Washington research office for Prudential Securities. Mr. Melcher ran Prudential Securities' Washington Research Office for seventeen years, leaving in October 2000. During that time, his office won first place in the Washington Research category of *Institutional Investor* magazine's annual All-American Research Team in each of the eight years that the category was in existence. Shortly after leaving Prudential, Mark joined the Washington Research office of Lehman Brothers on a part-time basis. He left there in April 2002 to found *The Political Forum*.

 **Steve Soukup** is the vice president and publisher of *The Political Forum*. He has followed politics and federal regulatory policy for the financial community since coming to Washington in 1996, when he joined Mark Melcher at the award-winning Washington-research office of Prudential Securities. Mr. Soukup left Prudential with Mr. Melcher to join Lehman Brothers in the fall of 2000 and stayed there for two years, before leaving early in 2003 to become a partner at *The Political Forum*.

While at Lehman, Mr. Soukup authored macropolitical commentary and followed policy developments in the Natural Resources sector group, focusing on agriculture and energy policy. He also headed Lehman's industry-leading analysis of asbestos litigation reform efforts. At *The Political Forum*, Mr. Soukup was initially the editor and junior partner, but is now the senior commentator and publisher.

CPSIA information can be obtained
at www.ICGtesting.com
Printed in the USA
LVHW090844021218
598964LV00003B/20/P

9 781640 039902